J2EE™ Platform Web Services

RAY LAI

PRENTICE
HALL
PTR

PRENTICE HALL
Professional Technical Reference
Upper Saddle River, NJ 07458
http://authors.phptr.com/lai/

Sun Microsystems Press
A Prentice Hall Title

Library of Congress Cataloging-in-Publication
Lai, Ray.
    Java Web services / Ray Lai.—1st ed.
      p. cm.
     ISBN 0-13-101402-1
   1. Web services.   2. Application software—Development.   3. Business enterprise—Data processing. 4. JAVA (Computer program language) I. Title.
   TK5105.88813.L35 2003
     005.7'2—dc21   2003012524

© 2004 Sun Microsystems, Inc.—
Printed in the United States of America
4150 Network Circle, Santa Clara, CA
95054 U.S.A.

For information regarding corporate and government bulk discounts please contact: Corporate and Government Sales (800)382-3419 or corpsales@pearsontechgroup.com. Or write: Prentice Hall PTR. Corporate Sales Dept., One Lake Street, Upper Saddle River, NJ 07458.

Sun Microsystems Press Publisher: Myrna Rivera
Executive Editor: Greg Doench
Marketing Manager: Debby vanDijk
Manufacturing Manager: Alexis Heydt-Long
Cover Design Director: Jerry Votta
Cover Design: Anthony Gemmellaro
Compositor: Carlisle Publishers Services
Editorial/Production Supervision: Ann Imhof
Full-Service Production Manager: Anne Garcia

10 9 8 7 6 5 4 3 2 1
ISBN 0-13-101402-1

Sun Microsystems Press
A Prentice Hall Title

About Prentice Hall Professional Technical Reference

With origins reaching back to the industry's first computer science publishing program in the 1960s, and formally launched as its own imprint in 1986, Prentice Hall Professional Technical Reference (PH PTR) has developed into the leading provider of technical books in the world today. Our editors now publish over 200 books annually, authored by leaders in the fields of computing, engineering, and business.

Our roots are firmly planted in the soil that gave rise to the technical revolution. Our bookshelf contains many of the industry's computing and engineering classics: Kernighan and Ritchie's *C Programming Language*, Nemeth's *UNIX System Adminstration Handbook*, Horstmann's *Core Java*, and Johnson's *High-Speed Digital Design*.

PH PTR acknowledges its auspicious beginnings while it looks to the future for inspiration. We continue to evolve and break new ground in publishing by providing today's professionals with tomorrow's solutions.

PRENTICE
HALL
PTR

Contents

Acknowledgments

Many thanks to my God for His wisdom and blessings, my wife Angela for her sacrifice in relocating with me to the United States, and my son Johanan for his patience when waiting to play with me after nights and weekends spent on this book. Also, thanks to my senior management—Jonathan Schwartz, Cheryln Chin, Edward Schwarz (now GorillaLogic), Sharon Moore, and Dr. Glen Reece—for their support; the Prentice Hall team Greg Doench and Eileen Clark for this opportunity; reviewers Daniel Malks, Sridhar Reddy, and Casey Chan; editor Ralph Moore; the numerous research groups for their honest review and endorsement; the Sun support team May Goh, Alana Lee, and Patrick Spencer who made this book a reality; Weili Zhong (ex-Sun colleague) and Bob Morgan (Fortune 100 financial services company) for their personal advice and constructive comments; the production team (Ann Imhof, Nicole Schlutt, and Anne Garcia) and those heroes/heroines who have made this book project happen.

Foreword

This book is about big ideas and fine details—the possible and the practical. Amid the hype surrounding Web services, the central question is this: When will we get there?

The answer, as you'll see in the following pages, is that we're already there—and still have a long way to go.

By now, the vision is almost universal: Emerging standards will increase the Internet's ability to deliver exactly what we need, precisely when we need it.

Indeed, the conveniences are fun to imagine: Your car's navigation system checking your calendar to see where you want to go next and showing you the best way to get through traffic. Your flight delay triggering a change in your dinner reservation and an instant notification on your wireless phone or pager.

In this book, that vision of the future is at once tempered and validated with examples of present-day projects. In other words, nirvana may be a ways off, but companies are already deploying less complex Web services to eliminate steps and lower costs.

This is a book for true practitioners. By that I mean not the dilettantes but the doers. It's for those interested in designing and implementing Web services now—and preparing for new opportunities on the horizon.

At Sun Microsystems, we believe that Web services are only partly about technology. The real starting point is identifying existing resources and mapping them to the different communities you deal with day to day—customers, partners, suppliers, your own employees.

Once you know who needs access to what, you'll have a clear indication of the kinds of services you should offer—to boost employee productivity, streamline the supply chain, or personalize your marketing efforts. Then it's simply a matter of prioritizing: Which services have the most value to your constituents? Which offer you the best payback?

This book can help you turn your vision into a reality.

Jonathan Schwartz
Executive Vice President, Software
Sun Microsystems, Inc.

Chapter 1

JUMPSTART

1.1 What Are the Next Frontiers?

1.1.1 The Web Services Phenomenon

In June of 2003, there were more than 113 printed books on Web Services available at Amazon.com, compared to 2 printed books in September of 2001, 45 printed books in March of 2002, and 86 printed books in February of 2003. Do a search on the Web, and you will be faced with a huge collection of articles and Web sites devoted to Web Services. Additionally, there are a large number of printed books available to the Web Services audience about an almost identical subject: WSDL-UDDI-SOAP technology. With all of these resources available, how does one choose the best of the bunch?

Scanning through a few titles on the subject, readers may notice that while there are abundant printed materials on Web Services concepts and SOAP programming. There is a general lack of emphasis on the Quality of Services (or so-called "ilities" such as scalability and availability) and real-life, full-scale implementations of Web Services in the printed media. It is not easy to differentiate market hype from a reliable technology implementation, but this book intends to do so—differentiate real-life examples from the market hype technology, define the Quality of Services for successful Web Services implementation, and discuss how it is applied to legacy mainframe interoperability and Business-to-Business integration.

1.1.2   The Web Services Evolution

Web Services technology and associated vendor products have evolved greatly over the past few years, from SOAP 1.0 to SOAP 1.2. New related technologies emerge from time to time, such as the earlier releases of the Java Web Services Developer Pack™ (including JAX Pack) and Apache Axis. Java™ has become the de facto lingua franca of Web Services. Previously, developers needed to build their own application infrastructure tools to handle security, exceptions, and logging. They also needed to write programming routines to handle message acknowledgement and exception handling routines to ensure SOAP messages were reliably exchanged. Nowadays, new Web Services tools such as Java Web Services Developer Pack™ and Apache Axis provide many built-in Web Services security features, SOAP messaging capabilities, and SOAP server infrastructure tools. These technologies have almost completely changed the previous Web Services programming model and landscape.

As more developers become familiar with these new enabling Web Services technologies, they need to assemble different infrastructure and application components together in order to provide a complete Web Services solution. Most literature today addresses how to build SOAP programs or lab prototypes, but does not address how to implement a complete Web Services solution to interoperate with legacy mainframe applications or to integrate with a Business-to-Business application. There are also many design elements and considerations for the cross-platform interoperability (such as mainframe interoperability), integration experience (such as cross-enterprise integration), and best practices (for example, architecture patterns) that constitute the bigger picture of Web Services technology implementation. These elements are the extended frontiers of Web Services technology toward a total business solution. This book attempts to explore these frontiers by discussing a structured framework for mainframe interoperability, cross-enterprise integration, and some design best practices.

1.2   How This Book Is Different

Although there are a number of recent books on the topic of Web Services, much of the information currently available is purely marketing hype about what Web Services can do, with little practical information for developers and architects. To emphasize how this book differs from others, I have identified five distinctive features. I also expand on three key ideas, and finish this section by presenting an overview of its unique values.

1.2.1 Five Distinctive Features of This Book

In addition to the list of technical subjects covered in the table of contents, there are five distinctive features in this book. These features are designed to address different needs of the developer and architect audience. They also help differentiate this book from similar Web Services books.

The Frontiers of Web Services

The frontiers of Web Services technology that describe how to build a total business solution include mainframe and legacy systems interoperability and cross-enterprise integration (for example, SOAP-JMS binding). The book also introduces how to use some cool developer toolkits (such as the Java Web Services Developer Pack™ and Apache Axis) for building Web Services prototypes. This goes beyond a textbook on SOAP programming or a concept book on Web Services technology. These technology areas are helping to bring Web Services implementations closer to reality.

Real-Life Examples

Current, publicly available Web Services implementations are analyzed throughout the book. Real-life examples and business scenarios make the technology contextual and make it easier for developers and architects to reapply appropriate Web Services technology in their own business environment. They differentiate the book from others that focus primarily on the technology details. Different use cases or business scenarios applying Web Services, will be outlined to help establish a business case for implementing Web Services.

Design Patterns and Best Practices

Some Web Services design patterns and when-to-use architecture principles are discussed. The Web Services design patterns and best approaches address the different needs of infrastructure architects, J2EE developers, security architects, and integration architects. These best practices are accumulated and extracted from past customer engagement experience. The emphasis will be on building Quality of Services (the so-called "ilities") for reliable, available, and scalable Web Services. This can be the basis for customizing a Web Services development and deployment cookbook.

Web Services Technology Market Space

A sampler of major Web Services vendor architectures and products is supplied in Appendix B. It provides a quick overview and a handy guide to the Web Services technology market space. A list of URLs and other resources is also provided because these usually provide more up-to-date information on vendors and products. These resources can assist developers and architects who want to do a tool selection and vendor assessment.

Paper and Pencil Lab Exercise

Guided hands-on labs are offered to build complete examples incrementally. Developers and architects can start with basic skills in Web Services technologies such as SOAP, WSDL, and JAXM in earlier chapters, and then Web Services development tools and security add-on tools in later chapters. These exercises help build up the skills needed to develop a complete prototype in Chapter 8, Web Services in Action: Case Study.

1.2.2   Three Key Ideas

There are three key ideas conveyed in this book, and they are backed up by technical details of various Web Services technologies.

Technology With Business

Technology is an enabling tool to collaborate with business; it does not rule over business. What is the business case for Web Services? Web Services technology can tie business benefits and service level to a company's bottom-line goals. This book will provide ideas and examples on how to establish a business case for Web Services solutions. It helps developers and architects collaborate with business, ties the technology solutions to their business environment, and identifies the benefits to their bottom-line goals.

The Big Picture

SOAP and UDDI are only parts of the big picture of Web Services technology. Web Services applications do not begin and end with a SOAP program or a UDDI look-up. Web Services solutions using ebXML provide a richer set of messaging and workflow functionality for Business-to-Business integration (B2Bi), and they have become more visible in the industry recently. Quality of Services, or so-called "ilities" such as scalability and reliability, becomes a key challenge to developers and implementation managers. Thus, it is important to look at different components of Web Services technology solutions and at various aspects of designing and scaling the Web Services solutions. This book examines different aspects of Web Services technology. It intends to present a bigger picture of Web Services technology, instead of focusing on solely WSDL, UDDI, and SOAP.

What Makes Web Services a Killer Application

What makes a solution a killer application is dependent on whether it creates "stickiness" (good user experience), ease of use, and the flexibility to implement and integrate. There is much market hype about Web Services being killer applications. The underlying enabling technology of WSDL, UDDI, and SOAP is not new. Web Services applications may be relatively simple to implement and can address existing technology challenges. But there is a fine distinction between the Web Services phenomenon and the Web Services market hype. This book discusses business scenarios where Web Services solutions can become killer applications, and clarifies any market hype by exploring what can be done (the capabilities of Web Services technology based on its associated strengths) and cannot be done (the weaknesses of Web Services technology).

1.2.3 Inside the Big Ideas

This book is about what Web Services technology is and how different technology components can be assembled to build solutions. The following paragraphs summarize some key technology components and relate them to the big ideas in the book.

Web Services 101

The first few chapters provide a refresher course on Web Services technology basics, including WSDL, UDDI, SOAP, and ebXML technology. It also explains what makes the WSDL-UDDI-SOAP technology more popular than CORBA—it is easier to understand and implement. WSDL-UDDI-SOAP technology was heavily marketed by Microsoft in the early days (before it became open). Today, WSDL-UDDI-SOAP technology is not the only Web Services technology; ebXML is one alternative. C# and Java are not the only programming languages for Web Services; we also have Perl (for example, SOAP-Lite is a package on top of Perl to implement Web Services) and some others. The paper and pencil exercises at the end of the first few chapters provide building blocks to build simple synchronous and asynchronous Web Services clients using Java or SOAP-Lite. Chapter 8, Web Services in Action: Case Study, brings these building blocks together as a solution and reinforces the big picture of Web Services technology discussed in the previous sections.

The Big Picture

Many Web Services books discuss WSDL, UDDI, and SOAP technology. Nevertheless, they have limited coverage on implementing Web Services, especially about how Web Services handles end-to-end security, mainframe or legacy systems interoperability, and cross-enterprise integration. There are Quality of Services design patterns available for enhancing performance and scalability of Web Services. Chapter 2, The Web Services Phenomenon and Emerging Trends, provides examples and business scenarios about partnering technology and business to produce end-to-end solutions using Web Services technology. Chapter 3, Web Services Technology Overview, introduces different technology components such as SOAP and ebXML (the parts), and discusses how these components can be integrated and interoperated to become a solution (the big picture) in the subsequent chapters on Web Services architecture, mainframe interoperability, cross-enterprise integration, and security. This book emphasizes a vendor-independent architecture framework and reusable Web Services patterns, which can help create end-to-end solutions based on past experience and best practices easily.

Web Services Architecture

There are many published Web Services architectures available today. Yet most of them are vendor product architectures, rather than a generic Web Services reference architecture (such as W3C's Web Services architecture). It is important to differentiate vendor product architectures from a Web Services architecture framework and methodology. A generic Web Services architecture provides a repeatable and consistent way to design and deploy scalable, reliable Web Services, independent of the underlying vendor products. Chapter 4, Web Services Architecture and Best Practices, introduces a vendor-independent architecture framework to design Web Services and to bring different technology pieces together in a big, complete picture. It also discusses some best practices of delivering Web Services solutions with Quality of Services. Appendix B summarizes various Web Services architectures based on different vendor products, which can be good reference materials for the vendor-independent Web Services architecture framework depicted in Chapter 4.

Mainframe Interoperability

Many business functions or killer applications today are still provided by mainframe or legacy systems, which can be wrapped as a business service (using EJB or XML-RPC) for reuse by Open Systems (such as Java front-ends) and interoperability with other systems (such as Business-to-Business integration). This will require the use of some Java classes (such as CICS or VSAM connectivity jar files provided by Java Connector Architecture products) on the mainframe. This book introduces new underlying integration technology concepts using Web Services and discusses different alternatives on how to expose business functionality provided by mainframe or legacy systems. On an IBM z/OS mainframe, legacy systems running on an MVS or a VSE operating system can be invoked and interoperated from the Unix services of the same machine. It opens up new opportunities to integrate with legacy systems, as opposed to the traditional integration approach using proprietary middleware.

For customers who have less flexibility in maintaining legacy systems, legacy Cobol applications on MVS or VSE can be also cross-compiled as Java byte codes running under the Java Virtual Machine (JVM) of the same mainframe. EAI products can be used as the underlying adapter to interoperate with the mainframe as Web Services. This book also introduces other interoperability options, such as transcoding Cobol codes to Java components. It discusses the rationale and benefits of each interoperability option, as well as the constraints that are essential during the design stage.

Web Services technologies enable the reuse of business functionality provided by mainframes and legacy systems. They help protect past investments of business functionality developed on legacy and proprietary platforms and ease building killer applications based on existing customer and account data kept by these legacy systems. Killer applications create user stickiness by aggregating useful and timely customer and account information from different data sources that may run on legacy systems using Web Services as the technology enabler.

Web Services and EAI

EAI, B2Bi, and Web Services are technologies for integrating business corporations. EAI are traditional middleware products (for example, Message Oriented Middleware). B2Bi is specific for integrating business corporations with workflow. Some people generalize that Web Services technology is another EAI and can replace traditional EAI middleware. This is a misconception. There is a close synergy between Web Services and EAI technology. This book clarifies the relationship. It confirms that Web Services can be used for lightweight integration, but it cannot replace EAI. In addition, it discusses various patterns showing how Web Services technology is used for B2Bi, and how it would differentiate from EAI technology.

Web Services Security

Web Services security is probably the most fast-changing aspect in Web Services technology. There are a few challenges in this technology. Much of today's Web Services literature has covered SOAP message level security and the general security requirements addressed by SOAP security only. The infrastructure level security for a Web Services infrastructure or appliance is not well covered. Another challenge is that there is no cohesive coverage to bring the technology pieces of authentication (such as Liberty Alliance), authorization (such as SAML, XACML), traceability (such as tracking a SOAP message), data privacy/confidentiality/data integrity (such as XML encryption), availability (such as making SOAP server resilient), and non-repudiation (such as XKMS, digital signature) together under an end-to-end security framework.

This book clarifies the roles of different Web Services security technologies; HTTPS and digital signatures are the building blocks to providing authentication and non-repudiation. The recent WS-Security specification does not specify how network transport, infrastructural, or application security should be handled. The notion of XML Trust Service attempts to provide a broader perspective of different aspects of XML Web Services security, such as key registration and authentication (XKMS), entitlement and identity (SAML), and fine-grained data access rights (XACML).

This book also discusses the outlook of recent Web Services security initiatives led by major vendors, and their underlying technology. WS-Security used to be Microsoft-proprietary. IBM has recently partnered with Microsoft and VeriSign to support it under the "Web Services Security Roadmap" (*http://www-106.ibm.com/developerworks/webservices/library/ws-secmap/*). This initiative supersedes previous IBM and Microsoft XML Security specifications. Sun and many other vendors now also support WS-Security. Security continues to be a problem area for Microsoft platforms, despite their commitment to address it. Microsoft PASSPORT has been criticized by Microsoft opponents for its design objectives and implementation, which will lock in customers and intrude on their privacy.

Project Liberty (*http://www.projectliberty.org/*) is a market response to PASSPORT and provides a choice of network identity solutions. It provides a platform-independent architecture for Single Sign-on and network identity management to support authentication and authorization with SAML. There is a misconception that Liberty Alliance is competing with WS-Security. This book clarifies that misconception and discusses the role of Liberty in identity management, which complements the message-level and application-level security provided by the WS-Security specification.

Finally, this book proposes a security framework to design end-to-end Web Services security. It addresses security at different levels, from network level, infrastructure level, message level, to application level. It reinforces the idea of the big picture, bringing different security technologies together.

The Frontiers of Web Services Technology

Web Services technology initiatives are fast-changing. The frontiers of Web Services technology also extend to wireless Web Services (such as enabling the mobile device to support SOAP messaging via kSOAP and J2ME). There are generally one or more events every week. The challenge to many developers and architects is how to manage these fast-changing technologies. We have seen the convergence of Web Services Security from SOAP-SEC, WS-Security, and various security specifications, followed by the convergence of XLANG and WSFL into BPEL4WS (Business Process Execution Language for Web Services, or *http://www.106.ibm.com/developerworks/library/ws-bpel/*). We also see the recent Web Services Choreography Interface (or WSCI) specification, which defines business process orchestration for Web Services similar to BPEL4WS. This book suggests some strategies to manage these new emerging technologies by reviewing the forthcoming standards specification and partnering with technology thought leaders to reduce implementation risks.

There are "no new things under the sun." New technology and tools emerge from time to time. This book identifies and analyzes several factors that foster the fast-changing Web Services technologies. It is important to understand the basics, the limitations, and the future direction of Web Services to prepare for the next frontiers. Apache Axis is a next-generation SOAP engine. It is based on IBM's Web Services Toolkit and has included utilities to generate WSDL. It is a good penetration strategy for vendors to incorporate their technology into Open Sources. It is also a good tactic for developers and architects to keep track of some leading Open Source tools for Web Services because they may be embedded into commercial Web Services products soon.

The developer dictates the market. Web Services products that can win developer support and dominate the developer desktop may become the next dominant Web Services technologies. The success of Windows-based product has led the .NET marketing strategy. Sun's Java Web Services Developer Pack™ (JWSDP) is an all-in-one developer kit, a response to Web Services market. All-in-one will become a key element for future developer kits.

Apart from watching new products and tools, a list of forthcoming Web Services specifications (such as JSRs) are identified and may be the next frontiers of Web Services technology.

1.2.4 Values of the Book

This book focuses on Sun's Web Services technology (for example, JWSDP and JAX) with a Sun ONE architecture and J2EE flavor. The majority of Web Services books available today introduce WSDL-UDDI-SOAP programming exercises and concepts. This book introduces the frontiers of Web Services technology and the steps for designing the entire application with scalability and availability. Experience says that putting the technology to use in real-life examples can make learning more effective, so this book focuses on doing that.

It provides some program codes and small hands-on labs for illustration, but it does not replicate other beginner's Web Services books or SOAP programming-level books. Thus, it is a good accompaniment for other Web Services books. This book also includes extensive pointers to URLs and to other Web Services resources.

1.3 Bringing the Pieces Together

1.3.1 Service Requester–Service Provider Relationship

Web Services technology can be described in terms of a Service Requester–Service Provider relationship (refer to Figure 1–1). The Service Provider runs business services from their systems locally and remotely. Business services provided can be found in a Service Registry. In order to register and publish the business service in the Service Registry, the Service Provider defines (authors) service description and configuration information (such as configuration files or WSDL—Web Services Description Language) and then codes the implementation (Service Implementation). The Service Implementation may be from existing legacy system functionality via Remote Procedure Calls or new applications.

The Service Requester is a consumer of business services. This can be the end-user (as in Business-to-Consumer) or server (as in Business-to-Business scenario). The Service Requester finds the business services from the Service Registry via a Service Proxy (such as an Apache SOAP server). Upon a successful search, the Service Registry, which may be provided by the same Service Provider or by a public Service Registry node, fetches the appropriate service description (for example, WSDL) and returns the service end-points (that is where the business service is located) to the Service Requester. Then the Service Requester can "bind" the business service to the actual service end-point or location.

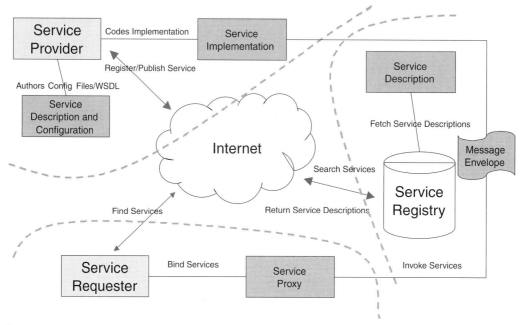

Figure 1–1   Web Services Consumer–Service Provider Relationship

In summary, the Service Provider uses WSDL to describe the business service and configuration to implement business services. Service descriptions (such as WSDL) are then published in the Service Registry (either UDDI or ebXML).

The Service Provider also uses SOAP technology (such as SOAP Proxy) to wrap existing legacy system functionality as reusable business services. The Service Requester discovers business services dynamically via a SOAP Proxy from the Service Registry, and binds the business services to the actual URI (Universal Resource Identifier) locally or remotely. The business services are encapsulated in XML messages using a SOAP message envelope. This enables easier data manipulation and processing using XML-based products and applications.

1.3.2   Software Tools

Table 1–1 provides a list of the software tools that you will need to work with the examples and labs throughout this book.

Table 1–1   List of Software Tools Used in This Book

Software Tools	Description	Where to Download
Java Web Services Developer Pack	Also known as JWSDP, this is an all-in-one development toolkit with Apache Tomcat 4.1.2, Apache SOAP 2.2, and JAX packs. This is the core component for this book.	*http://java.sun.com/webservices/ downloads/webservicespack.html*
Axis	New generation Apache SOAP engine. This is a good complementary product to JWSDP, and is essential to run many of the samples in this book.	*http://xml.apache.org/axis/index.html*
Trust Services Integration Kit	Also known as TSIK, this product provides XKMS and WS-security support. This component is essential to run the Case Study sample programs.	*http://www.xmltrustcenter.org/developer/ verisign/tsik/download.htm*
jSAML Toolkit	A pre-Liberty SAML-based toolkit for implementing Single Sign-on. You'll need to register to download this tool. Select download from the "Product Downloads" on the left hand column at this Web site.	*http://www.netegrity.com/products/ index.cfm?leveltwo=JSAML&levelthree =download*
SOAP-Lite	This product lets you access SOAP from a Perl client. Requires Perl version 5.0 or above. This is instrumental to illustrate that we do not require a Java client to invoke Web Services.	*http://www.soaplite.com/*

1.4 Tour of the Book

The map in Figure 1–2 shows the conceptual structure of the book, which is targeted for two different purposes: strategy, or management perspective, and technical orientation.

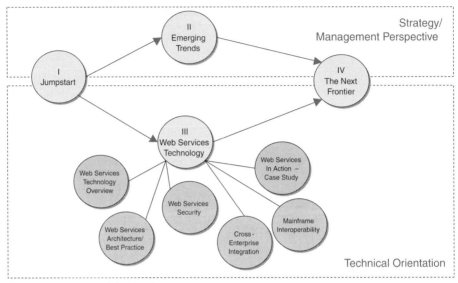

Figure 1–2   Tour of the Book

Chapter 2: The Web Services Phenomenon and Emerging Trends
This chapter provides an impact analysis of the major business drivers of
the changing economic landscape in banking, capital markets, and B2B
Exchanges. New intermediaries now challenge traditional business. Services have become more competitive with new mergers and consolidations. There is a growing awareness of the importance of a reliable and
scalable business and solution architecture. This chapter provides business
scenarios for implementing Web Services, illustrated by establishing a
business case for Web Services.

Chapter 3: Web Services Technology Overview This section gives a
refresher hands-on lab for various Web Services enabling technology (including UDDI, SOAP, and ebXML), technology stack, and the latest development tools. It outlines how to enable your applications for Web Services
in four steps. A sampler of the market space, existing Web Services vendors,
and guidelines for choosing appropriate tools are discussed.

Chapter 4: Web Services Architecture and Best Practices Several
vendors' Web Services architectures are discussed in this chapter. A discussion of what architecture framework is suitable to build different large-scale
business solutions is offered. A service-based reference architecture is depicted, followed by some architecture principles and design patterns for
best practices.

Chapter 5: Mainframe Integration and Interoperability This chapter introduces different ways for legacy mainframe COBOL applications to interoperate with open systems, compares the pros and cons of using Web Services, and discusses when to use Web Services. An overview of existing market products for enabling mainframe interoperability is also offered.

Chapter 6: Enterprise and Cross-Enterprise Integration XML Web Services has some competitive advantages in enterprise and cross-enterprise integration. Different e-Business enterprise and cross-enterprise integration design patterns are discussed. A comparison is made between Web Services–based and EAI-based integration, and when to use each.

Examples will be elaborated in Chapter 8, Web Services in Action: Case Study.

Chapter 7: Web Services Security End-to-end Web Services security is the key to securing financial transactions. Most solutions focus security in specific tiers and layers but do not put it in an end-to-end perspective. Web Services security is often viewed as insecure due to lack of understanding. This chapter discusses the key components of PKI-based and Web Services security infrastructure, buy versus build (for example, should we outsource digital certificate management to an external trust service provider?), what to use, and when to use. It will also suggest ways to enable leveraging existing security infrastructure as Web Services.

Several Web Services security initiatives are discussed in this chapter, such as XML security (XKMS, SAML, XACML, WS-Security) and Project Liberty.

Chapter 8: Web Services in Action: Case Study This chapter goes through a case study of how Web Services is designed and implemented with the real-life example of a Foreign Exchange service. It illustrates a small-scale Use Case requirements analysis and a SunTone architecture design. The demonstration program is based on JWSDP to illustrate synchronous and asynchronous Web Services with secure message services.

Chapter 9: The Next Frontiers This is an industry survey of different emerging technology variants and how they may impact different industries over the next few years.

Appendices

    Appendix A—Resources and References

    Appendix B—Some Web Services Vendors

    Appendix C—Demo Environment Set Up

1.5   Special Features

1.5.1   Building a Complete Example

Throughout the book, a Foreign Exchange trading Web application example will be built. To build a complete application (see Figure 1–3), you can follow the examples and concepts in the book to wrap an existing business service as Web Services (for example, using JWSDP's wsdeploy or Axis), publish it in a Service Registry (for example, using JAXR), expose the business service via a Message Provider (for example, using JAXM), and/or parse data from the business partners using JAXP and XSLT.

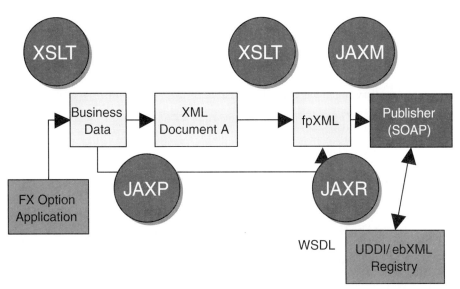

Figure 1–3   Building a Complete Example

1.5.2   Chapter Overview

The "Chapter Overview" highlights the main ideas of each chapter for both quick preview and recapitulation.

For Example:

- Web Services, units of business services and components, is positioned as the next IT strategy for enterprises. The enabling technologies are built on top of Java and XML. They are also referenced as "Java Web Services" or "XML Web Services."

- The Web Services technology stack includes the transport layer (such as SOAP), a service description language (such as WSDL), and transaction routing and service negotiation (such as BP).

- Web Services has many associations with CORBA. Some perceive Web Services technology is a reincarnation of Application Service Provider and CORBA.

- Microsoft's version of Web Services is .NET, with C# as one key development language. Sun, IBM, and other technology vendors are using Java as the key underlying technology.

1.5.3   Objectives

The "Objectives" section identifies the learning objectives of each chapter to help you appreciate why and how the technology is used.

For Example:

- To identify the root and derivation of Web Services technologies

- To have an appreciation of the underlying Web Services technologies, their benefits, and when to use them

- To establish some guidelines in choosing a Web Services developer tool and platform in the marketplace

- To illustrate four steps to enable a simple application for Web Services

- To illustrate what Web Services solutions are available on the market, along with their benefits and limitations

1.5.4   Best Practices and Pitfalls

The "Best Practices and Pitfalls" section suggests industry-best practices and pitfalls for the specific Web Services technology. You can use this section as a checklist for good design practice or pitfalls to avoid.

For Example:

Pitfalls

- Do not try to have too many dependencies or items that require longer lead time (for example, do not try to SOAP-enable a mainframe platform).

- Do not start implementation without senior management support.

- Do not start a pilot using a mission-critical functionality.

- Do not involve a big team in the pilot. Start with a small team.

1.5.5 Case Study

The "Case Study" section illustrates how the technology is used, its critical success factors, and its implementation pitfalls.

For Example:

Challenges

A medium-size listed financial institution in Hong Kong wants to reduce its operating costs associated with supporting legacy systems on a mainframe. The corporation has been innovative and reputable in providing securities trading, retail banking, and credit card services to the local market.

The CEO is concerned about implementing new technology for technology's sake and believes that not all legacy systems need to be migrated to UNIX, as they are fairly stable.

Is it relevant to introduce Web Services technology to meet its challenge?

1.5.6 Paper and Pencil

The "Paper and Pencil" section provides some study questions and simple hands-on exercises for practice.

For Example:

Hands-on Lab. Download the Web Services Developer Pack from *http://java.sun.com.* Install and configure it according to the Installation Guide. Based on the sample sniplet tradeOrder.xml in the text below (see Figure 1–4), write your first JAXM-SOAP program with your favorite editor or your favorite Integrated Developer Environment to send the following XML message:

```
    <trade>
  <tradeHeader>
    <partyTradeIdentifier>
      <partyReference href = "#XYZ"/>
    </partyTradeIdentifier>
    <partyTradeIdentifier>
      <partyReference href = "#ABC"/>
    </partyTradeIdentifier>
    <tradeDate>2002-01-15</tradeDate>
  </tradeHeader>
```

Figure 1–4 Trade Order in XML (tradeorder.xml)

```
<fxSimpleOption>
  <productType>Nondeliverable Option</productType>
  <buyerPartyReference href = "#XYZ"/>
  <sellerPartyReference href = "#ABC"/>
  <expiryDateTime>
     <expiryDate>2002-04-09</expiryDate>
     <hourMinuteTime>1000</hourMinuteTime>
     <businessCenter>USNY</businessCenter>
  </expiryDateTime>
  <exerciseStyle>European</exerciseStyle>
 </fxSimpleOption>
</trade>
```

Figure 1–4   Trade Order in XML (tradeorder.xml)—*continued.*

1.5.7   Resources and References

The "Resources and References" section lists useful and relevant articles, magazines, books, and URLs for further reading. URLs provide a frequently updated link to major Web Services resources where books may become outdated.

For Example:

Web Services Resource Web Sites

http://www.webservices.org

http://www.theserverside.com/home/index.jsp

Web Services Overview

John Hagel III and John Seely Brown. *"Your Next IT Strategy."* Harvard Business Review, October 2001.

IBM Web Services Overview Team. *"Web Services Architecture Overview."* IBM, September 2000. *http://www-106.ibm.com/developerworks/library/w-ovr/*

Lawrence Wilkes. *"Web Services—Right Here, Right Now."* IBM, 2002. *http://www.3.ibm.com/software/solutions/webservices/pdf/cbdi.pdf*

THE WEB SERVICES PHENOMENON AND EMERGING TRENDS

2.1 Chapter Overview

- The term *Web Services* has quickly becomes a buzzword in the market. There are true successes and also much hype about Web Services technology solutions. Much of the market hype focuses on what it can do, rather than integration. Some generalize that Web Services technology can address all types of business problems. Web Services technologies are a good technology enabler for legacy system integration and cross-platform interoperability, but may not necessarily be the perfect solution to all types of business problems.

- Such Web Services interest has coincided with the proliferation of XML and Java technology and Business-to-Business (B2B) commerce. The key attraction of Web Services comes from the business drivers of cost reduction and B2B integration.

- There are many aspects of the changing economic landscape and emerging trends that support the potential use of Web Services, especially in the financial services and B2B commerce areas.
- Three major business scenarios are illustrated, using good candidates for Web Services. The key benefits are the system interoperability among a number of trading partners and the reusability of existing business functionality and infrastructure.
- To establish a business case for Web Services, we highlight the business benefits of the interoperability, ease of integration, and reusability. Quantitative figures, if available, would be useful to support Return On Investment justification.

2.2   Chapter Objectives

- To identify emerging trends that favor utilizing and deploying Web Services as the next IT strategy
- To identify early success in implementing Web Services
- To outline sample scenarios that may build a business case for using Web Services

2.3   Changing Economic Landscape

The business landscape has been changing drastically during the last five years. New business models have brought surprises to traditional business corporations and financial institutions. For example:

- Could a courier company provide trade financing (Letter of Credit service) to traders? Yes, UPS Capital, not a pure-play courier company today, has emerged as a financial intermediary for different trade financing services to major buyers.
- What is the largest financial institution in the United States? Is it Citigroup? Nope, it is General Motors. It finances every car it sells to consumers.

The Internet and its associated technology have also played a significant influencing role as well. We have seen megamergers or acquisitions, competing Web delivery channels, and new emerging financial intermediaries. These forces have helped the industry evolve, as in the transformation of traditional financial institutions in a changing marketplace, changing their focus from product-centric to customer-centric, and providing more customer-initiated services, convergence of different banking and securities services, emergence of mobile commerce, and integration.

2.3.1   Business Challenges

Achieving a lower operating cost, or Total Cost of Ownership (TCO), is probably the key business challenge for today's business. This is particularly important in a slow economy. To become more competitive, many traditional institutions (so-called bricks and mortars) have transformed themselves into responsive service organizations. The fundamental business models may need to adapt or change completely in order to survive. Moving from product-centric to customer-centric models, Customer Relationship Management (CRM) has become inevitable in many firms.

"White labeling" of services is another growing trend. Traditional businesses, which do not want to invest in expensive infrastructure in order to deliver a new business within a short period of time, now turn to established service providers to share their infrastructure, while keeping their branding intact. Some firms may give up their existing delivery channels and white label other infrastructures for a lower operating cost. For instance, JPM Chase white labels TradeCard for their Business-to-Business (B2B) payment service, Amazon online store white labels Target, Toys "R" Us, and Borders.

Business process automation and service integration are driven by reducing costs, improving accuracy, and aggregating and matching customer information against transactions from multiple sources. However, dynamic business changes often result in building one-time services and components in silos to meet time-to-market requirements. Integrating these silos with legacy systems, for example, will unavoidably incur more cost. Thus, what integration technology should architects and managers choose in order to develop a solution that can bear minimal cost, while providing a time-to-market solution that improves accuracy and aggregates customer information from legacy systems and silo applications?

The current business model often dictates ever-increasing integration with preferred partner sites. A strong business branding requires tighter B2B integration, but cross-enterprise integration is extremely complex and time-consuming. This often involves business process re-engineering, compromising certain system functionality in order to accommodate single sign-on and automated order processing. But, a shallow business integration model may simply require, for instance, URL hot-links (that is, URL rewriting) on both Web sites.

Large corporations and new mergers often have multiple services and business units that are not integrated. In other words, these business units have many stand-alone systems in silos, and these systems do not share information between applications. Customer account information is often stored in duplicate, or not synchronized across different accounts (such as different addresses) even if under the same customer name. Integrating different newly acquired companies is complex and time-consuming, especially when you must customize to accommodate proprietary systems and interfaces. For instance, a customized interface with a private Foreign Exchange marketplace may take from six to nine months.

There is an increasing demand for a high level of Quality of Service. The general awareness of and expectations for scalability, performance, and availability are higher, as people realize the pitfalls of the many Internet commerce and online stores that have struggled in the past few years.

2.3.2 Technology Challenges

Nowadays, most customers expect customer and financial information to be readily available and aggregated at real time. This requires interoperability across heterogeneous platforms (such as integrating legacy mainframe, Unix, and Windows systems) and with business partners' systems. If using multiple product solutions, the expertise and service support skills needed to provide such functionality are also demanding.

In a cost-reduction environment, there is a stronger motive to optimize existing system capabilities and leverage the existing legacy system functionality. From the IT management perspective, reusability and maintainability are top priorities. A classic example is the mobile commerce services in Japan, which need to be cloned and customized for each of the local telecommunications service providers (NTT DoCoMo, J-Phone, and KDDI EzWeb). A reusable device-sensitive XML-based mobile commerce would be attractive.

Most integration deals with complex legacy back-end systems. Unfortunately, these legacy systems are often undocumented, and the interfaces work like a black box. The original developers may not be with the company any more. Thus, partners dealing with business integration need to evolve their technology independently on a trial-and-error basis.

2.3.3 The Web Services Alternative

Many of the challenges depicted above can be addressed by re-engineering business processes, introducing new and innovative product technology, upgrading to new versions for better performance, deploying EAI products for cross-platform integration, exploiting tactical and point-to-point interfaces such as screen scraping, or customizing proprietary APIs to meet the customer requirements. In some cases, these are expensive and time-consuming options.

On the other hand, XML Web Services technology already addresses these challenges and is a good alternative with the use of open standards to interoperate between legacy systems and vendor-dependent middleware/EAI. It overcomes some of the technical shortcomings of existing technologies (such as EJB/RMI over firewall), provides time-to-market with easier integration, and allows reusable components (for example, for partner integration and lower operating cost).

Web Services technology provides a single, common framework for many business services and many partners. It enables "loose coupling" with stable interfaces and a common code base. Besides, Web Services technology is integration-ready. In other words, it can be designed to support a high Quality of Service infrastructure. It also has the framework to support federated identity solutions.

For example, People's Insurance Company of China, a large national insurance company in China, uses Web Services technology to update and share customer information among call center applications, the enterprise portal, and back-office systems (an IDC case study is available at *www.sun.com/service/about/success/recent/picc.html*). Legacy systems functionality can be wrapped as Web Services and accessed via a SOAP service call, the enterprise portal, or the call center. It allows large enterprises to better manage their customer relationships with timely account information and reuse existing infrastructure at a lower cost of ownership. Without it, architects may need to rewrite the back-office systems or spend enormous resources in building one-time interfaces between the call centers and the back-office systems.

Another example is the use of Web Services technology in providing white label services by wrapping existing business services, publishing in Web Services calls, and enabling customers to subscribe to them. i-Deal (*http://www.i-deal.com/* and *http://ws.demo.i-deal.com*) is a financial services company that provides an online intelligent engine for capital raising using the Application Service Provider (ASP) model. It uses Web Services technology to handle deal calendars, indication of interests from proprietary systems, synchronizing client data between systems, and so forth. Customers can subscribe to the capital raising service with white labelbranding. This solution addresses the total cost of ownership issue by reusing existing infrastructure and interoperating with legacy systems.

There is more industry-wide support seen in application server and middleware vendors, including Sun, IBM, Microsoft, and BEA. As Web Services become more pervasive, partners will be able to implement B2B integration more easily and quickly.

2.3.4   The Web Services Phenomenon

John Hagel III and John Brown, in the *Harvard Business Review* (October 2001), describe Web Services as the next IT strategy. They emphasize that Web Services technology is a solution that addresses data silos or restrictive ERP-based enterprise architectures and is a cost-effective approach to addressing integration with external processes and institutions. It is also a risk mitigation to obsolete technology, making it easier to adopt outsourced or managed services using standardized and plug-and-play Web Services.

Business Perspective. Web Services technology enables aggregation and re-branding of heterogeneous services across the enterprise and white labeling of business services that can meet time-to-market requirements speedily. It also allows faster partner integration, providing better integration tools and a better framework for legacy systems and mainframe integration.

Technology Perspective. XML becomes a common business data language and interface standard between systems. Java technology, XML, SOAP, UDDI, WSDL, and ebXML are building blocks for implementing Web Services. ebXML also offers message services and business process elements that are designed to address bigger problems such as security, reliable messaging, business processing, and Quality of Services for transaction processing.

2.4 Emerging Trends

2.4.1 New Business Trends

New Intermediaries

There are a few new business models that have emerged over the last few years, primarily related to brokers or intermediaries for large corporations and many service providers. Many of these corporations are highly successful. Still, some models are sound, but cannot survive the Internet bubble, as in the case of Digilogistics. This may be due to a combination of different factors, such as management and implementation issues. The following examples show a few business models, both successful and closed:

- **eBay Model**—This model acts as an intermediary with an escrow-like function for reverse auction marketplace (for example, eBay and Amazon).

- **Amazon Model**—Amazon extends its business line from an online bookstore to an online specialty store, providing Application Server Provider services for Target and Toys "R" Us.

- **New Banking Intermediaries**—For example, UPS Capital, a UPS subsidiary, provides Letter of Credit and financing services; Standard Chartered Bank's eXonomy provides B2B banking services for a niche market.

- **New Logistics Intermediaries**—Information brokers supply logistics services, (for example, Bolero or Digilogistics [already closed]).

Like the white label service discussed previously, Web Services technology is a good technology enabler to provide subscription services (white labeling), and aggregate services from different service providers.

Death of Dot-com

Many dot-com arms or spin-offs are reabsorbed into the traditional delivery channels (for example, CitiCommerce). Some weaker dot-coms or intermediaries cannot survive the economic landscape changes, and have filed Chapter Eleven for bankruptcy protection. Dot-com becomes a taboo to many firms.

Economy Slowdown

Since the Internet bubble burst, many business managers are interested in immediate cost savings, not long-term cost reduction. The implication for IT solution development is that business users have very different expectations for services, and they are very cost-sensitive. Web Services technology is considered as a cost-reduction technology favorable to the slow economic environment. Workforce layoffs have also led to skill readaptation for many engineers and developers. Many IT personnel turn to online training or e-learning for skill adaptation. Security, J2EE, and Web Services technology are examples of hot technologies that interest developers.

Multisourcing

More large corporations outsource operations and IT development to developing countries, such as India, to lower operating costs. This opens up opportunities for ASP models to reincarnate using Web Services technology; for example, i-Deal provides an online capital raising service using an ASP model.

Real-Time Information and More Automation

The acceleration of online securities trading and cross-border trade has helped push the securities industry to implement straight-through processing (or automated trade processing and next-day settlement) by 2005. With the proliferation of such wireless capability as 3G phones and broadband service for homes, many people expect information to be pervasive (anytime, anywhere) and available in real-time.

Web Services technology can be used to create a virtual layer that can collect, aggregate, and disseminate business information in real-time and in an automated manner. An example is Blue Titan Network Director (*http://www.bluetitan.com/ products/overview.htm*).

Less Cost for Research and Development

Customers are expecting technology that can help them reduce costs immediately, especially where cross-platform integration and customization can be done more economically. Web Services emerges as the right fit, because it can address costly cross-platform integration and customization using Open Standards technology, without rewriting the legacy systems.

2.4.2   New Technology Trends

New Generation 64-bit High-Speed Computing Platform

The arrival of 64-bit processors running at 4 GB MHz blurs the line between home computing and business computing. Developers are using low-end 64-bit machines for small office servers, Internet appliances (such as Sun Cobalt and Sun LX50 Server), and development platform. These appliances are attractive because of their high computing capability and entry-level server features. HP also has manufactured machines that have the flexibility to use 64-bit Intel-based or RISC chips to run Unix.

Grid computing is a new technology area that makes use of available, low-cost, and high-speed computing resources to process business application requests and transactions. Together with Web Services, developers can make use of a low-cost 64-bit computing platform to perform computing-intensive tasks such as risk management and data mining in a distributed network environment. Each host is installed with a grid computing agent that can discover other Web Services or invoke Web Services calls (*http://www.gridforum.org/ogsi-wg/drafts/draft-ggf-ogsi-grid-service-23_2003-02-17.pdf*). This will provide a cost-effective distributed computing environment without a dedicated high-end hardware platform. Recently, grid computing with Web Services has gained some momentum in the securities industry (*http://www.simc-inc.org/ archive0203/Grid/index.htm*).

Proliferation of Open Standards

More companies are willing to exploit Linux for small office servers, small-scale Web servers, and peer-to-peer publishing services. NetCraft (*http://www.netcraft.com*), a Web site survey company that polls Internet-connected computers, reports on the growing market share (56.38 percent in April of 2002) of those using the Apache HTTP Web Server platform for Web sites on the Internet. There are more Open Source products, such as Netbeans (Sun ONE Studio codes donated by Sun), Eclipse (WebSphere™ source codes donated by IBM) and Apache SOAP, used for implementing solutions.

XML has become a de facto standard for many commercial off-the-shelf products, from application servers (such as Websphere Application Server™) and infrastructural products (such as Sun ONE Directory Server) to office desktop products (such as Microsoft Office™). Web Services technology is also one of the key Open Standards under OASIS (*http://www.oasis-open.org/*) and W3C (*http://www.w3.org/2000/xp/Group/*).

Broadband Internet and Wireless Technology

3G mobile phones have been deployed in Asia and Europe, and some areas of the United States. Utilizing WAP over the CDMA protocol, the GSM technology enables digital phones—even non-GSM phones—to access WML services. iMode, a simplified version of WML, caught on with a huge critical mass very quickly in Japan. There are a few killer applications (such as Hello Kitty) running on iMode-enabled mobile phones in Japan.

Broadband Internet has heavily penetrated major cities in Asia Pacific, Europe, and many North American cities now. It has also created new business models for home office, Virtual Private Network (VPN), and consumer computing. Among other services, multimedia applications and e-learning, both of which require heavy bandwidth infrastructure, have become viable using broadband Internet, whereas just a few years ago these were merely challenging ideas. In terms of Web Services, a classic example would be a multimedia-based e-learning solution that can be best exploited as a Web Service on a pay-per-use basis.

Bluetooth™, another wireless technology, has become pervasive with electronic appliances such as digital camcorders, notebook PCs, and refrigerators. A few years ago, Gartner Group Research identified Bluetooth™ as one of the key technologies of the future. However, it currently runs on a GSM network only.

With various wireless technologies ranging from WAP phone, SMS short messages, and email, the notion of Unified Messaging becomes inevitable. Information captured from one channel (or touch point) can be accessible via another channel. Customer and account information at different touch points can then be integrated and managed seamlessly, without the need of duplicate data entry.

Broadband and wireless technologies have made multichannel support a key service element and an early adopter for Web Services. Zefer and Sun collaborated to define the first Smart Web Services architecture for wireless clients accessing remote Web Services. (Refer to the technical notes at *http://sunonedev.sun.com/building/tech_articles/webserv_refarch.html*).

Wireless Web Services

The proliferation of mobile devices such as Personal Digital Assistants (PDAs) and Pocket PCs has made pervasive computing with Wireless Web Services attractive. Nowadays, developers can deploy Web Service clients on those mobile devices (see Figure 2–1) that can support Mobile Information Device Profile or MIDP™ (that is,

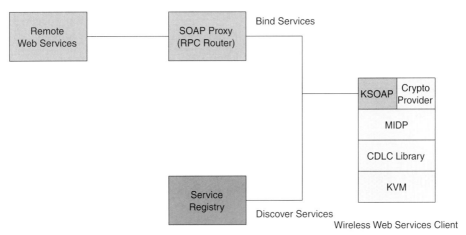

Figure 2–1   Wireless Web Services Client Stack

J2ME™ clients) with kSOAP jar files. kSOAP (*http://www.ksoap.org/*) provides light-weight SOAP capability to these MIDP-compliant devices, just as a rich SOAP client. It runs on top of MIDP and Connected, Limited Device Configuration (CDLC) library with the Java™ virtual machine KVM. Java 2 Platform Micro Edition or J2ME™ with cryptographic provider (such as the Bouncy cryptography provider) will also provide good secure data transport to support WS-Security.

Core Banking

As a result of banking deregulation rules in many countries, many banks have begun to provide customized product pricing for different customer segments. For instance, retail banks price deposit account interest rates differently by location and customer segments. Thus, the capability to segment and profile customers based on consolidating customer transactions and behavior here is key. Web Services is one option to provide such dynamic customer data consolidation from heterogeneous sources.

Home banking has begun to pick up some momentum recently, probably because it provides lower cost of banking services and more timely account information. Interestingly, it has not been that popular in small cities where a variety of banking channels, such as ATM or IVRS-based phone banking, are convenient.

Peer-to-peer banking, such as Yahoo!-HSBC peer-to-peer banking service, is emerging where traditional retail banking does not provide such flexibility and low-cost (free!) interbank fund transfers. There is also increasing interest in such peer-to-peer computing technology as JXTA and a potential marriage of Web Services and peer-to-peer computing.

Many core banking solution vendors now support the J2EE platform, and some of them (such as Eontec) also provide Web Services support for remote interface and system interoperability. This enables banking services to be easily accessible by and integrated with different technology platforms.

Branch Consolidation

With increasing mergers and consolidations in many countries, such as at the Misuho Bank in Japan and the Bank of China in China, Web Services technology becomes more attractive for aggregating services from different units and system functionality without rewriting both back-end systems.

Credit Card

Credit cards still represent a high wallet-share business for banks. Bonus points and membership-reward marketing continue to be the key components for customer-loyalty programs. The capability for providing a self-service facility for redeeming member rewards is a good example of a Web Services real-life application.

Nevertheless, credit card payments and card issuance remain high-risk areas. Fraud protection and prevention with good security mechanisms is essential. Network Identity with digital signatures for online shopping using credit cards becomes critical. Web Services security standards play a significant role in realizing this.

Relationship Banking

Customer Relationship Banking, previously known as Database Marketing, involves sophisticated customer segmentation and behavioral scoring based on historic account activities. Web Services technology eases the capture and aggregation of customer information and account activities from multiple touch points. Traditional data warehouse technology can be supplemented by Web Services-based data capture and extraction for easier interoperability and lower cost integration.

In parallel with integrating different touch points, many banks are also interested in supporting multiple delivery channels. This means delivery of customer and account activities via multiple devices such as a Web browser, PDAs, mobile phones, and pagers. With XML technology, data can be presented differently to different client devices using XML style sheets without writing twice. This enables higher reusability of banking services.

Wholesale Banking

Electronic Banking is entering the second generation. The dot-com wave has pushed many traditional banks to Web-enable their legacy Electronic Banking systems. Compared to rich clients, thin-client browser deployment is cheaper and faster to market. Some banks also take this chance to revamp their legacy architecture and migrate to Open Systems.

Online trade finance is a good example. Multinational banks such as HSBC and Standard Chartered Bank have deployed Web-based international trade services (Letter of Credit) using SureComp's NetIMEX. On the other hand, JPM Chase has chosen to private label Tradecard for their B2B trade services.

Many cash management solutions now support the J2EE platform. Some of these vendors (such as Bottomline Technologies) also support Web Services technology as a means to integrate with legacy systems and external corporate customers.

B2B Financial Exchanges

Many large banks spin off a separate business unit to become an e-marketplace or financial exchange (with a marketplace partner usually), Citi-Commerce (Citibank) for example. These exchanges act as an intermediary for buyers and sellers, who may come from the existing customer base of the financial institution. This will not only grow the customer base, but also increase the banking services. However, after the death of dot-coms, the financial exchange or e-marketplace is often reabsorbed into the banking group. (Standard Chartered Bank's eXonomy may be an exception—it launched production in November of 2002. The URL is *http://www.scb2bex.com.*)

Escrow is another new intermediary that provides escrow-based payment services for marketplaces; escrow.com is a good example.

New business models such as new intermediaries, require an appropriate IT technology model, especially integration between trading partners in the value chain. Web Services technology has a lot to offer in this space.

Capital Markets

Straight-through Processing (STP) or T+1(next day) settlement is the goal in the capital markets. Having a flexible integration framework and messaging infrastructure can help extract and reuse trade order information to achieve the next-day settlement goal.

In the last few years, more and more investment banks have merged or consolidated. We saw large conglomerates develop, such as JPM Chase (JP Morgan and Chase), CSFB (Credit Swiss First Boston and DLJ), Morgan Stanley Dean Witter, and Citi-group (Citibank and Salomon Smith Barney). This presents the challenge of consolidating silos architecture within a short period.

With the fast growth of equities trading business and mergers, many silo processes in the middle office can be consolidated to improve efficiency, and to reduce cost. This may require refactoring business services, application and server consolidation, as well as aggregating contents from different applications.

Wealth management, a variant theme of Customer Relationship Management, is another fast-growing area in Capital Markets. It can generate new revenue sources from consolidating investment profiles and banking services from private banking customers and cross-sell for other related short-term or long-term banking services.

We have seen many areas in capital markets share similar infrastructure and integration needs. Web Services can play a key role as an enabling technology for application consolidation, contents aggregation, and STP. Wall Street and Technology (*http://www.wallstreetandtech.com/story/WST20021007S0006*) has identified some pilots and early implementations of Web Services solutions in the capital market area, for instance, data distribution (Accenture), financial reporting (Nasdaq Stock Market, Microsoft, and IBM PricewaterhouseCoopers), stock charting (Streetline), and corporate applications (Aspelle).

B2B Commerce

Many small and medium-size buyers and suppliers want to automate their supply chain management, but cannot afford to buy expensive ERP systems. Hosted (ASP-based) supply chain management service has become more attractive to them, as they do not need to build an infrastructure. Such automation is also driven by the demand for low-cost international trade. Suppliers can collaborate and share manufacturing and order information with buyers without purchasing expensive ERP systems.

B2B marketplaces, or e-marketplaces, are good vehicles to create critical mass for buyers and suppliers. The B2B market has orientated toward a private marketplace model. In the last few years, Ariba and Commerce One are two major competing B2B marketplace models while many small and medium-size marketplaces have shut down since the global economy slowed down. Nevertheless, e-marketplaces continue to be a key driver for B2B integration.

Just-In-Time delivery requires all suppliers to be linked online to the commerce sites. Trade orders taken from the commerce sites can be piped to ERP systems to process order fulfillment and logistics tracking. Shipment information tracking is an important element in Just-In-Time delivery. There are emerging information broker intermediaries for multiple shipping and logistics service providers. Digilogistics (though out of business now) is an example.

B2B commerce requires sophisticated many-to-many partner integration. Smaller suppliers either turn to a low-cost ASP-based supply chain management service (for which Web Services technology is the key enabler) or an ERP-based product implementation (for which XML connector and Web Services are likely to be used for integration).

Private UDDI service registry will be seen as necessary to manage private trading communities. It is intended to be a service registry for vendors and suppliers, much like the Yellow or White Pages. For instance, Sun has implemented a private UDDI service registry for Business-to-Business processes under an internal project called "XWS." In a B2B commerce scenario, suppliers can be preregistered in a private UDDI within a private community. The e-marketplace can use this private UDDI as a control mechanism for service providers and business services.

2.5   Case Studies

2.5.1   Overview

This section introduces a few case studies of current Web Services implementations. They cover examples from the service industry (Trans-Canada Pipeline, Dollar Rent-A-Car) and healthcare management (Hewitt Associates).

Apart from these case studies, there are also some early success stories from the financial services industry. Merrill Lynch (U.S.) aggregates customer account information and risk profile in real-time from multiple systems and countries for wealth management. CIBC (Canada) develops SOAP calls to wrap payment messages and banking services for their Tandem and IBM mainframe legacy systems. At the Sun-Gard User Conference 2001, OM and SunGard shared experiences in interoperating two software products using Web Services.

Other success stories include ASU Solutions (an electronic solution to expensive hand-done property tax payment), Jarna (integrating applications with people and handheld devices), Adobe Systems (single server interface for image services), Comvia (data exchange across desktop applications through a central server), and POSC (data and application access standards for the petroleum industry).

2.5.2   TCPL Case Study

Trans-Canada Pipeline (TCPL) has a large-scale IT infrastructure full of silos applications. Sun has introduced a service-oriented architecture based on Sun ONE called SPINE, which leverages an existing infrastructure with enabling technology such as SOAP and UDDI. A Web Services framework (SPINE) is now being deployed. Sun and HP also leverage on the SPINE Web Services framework for service provider infrastructure management. Recently, TCPL has implemented a messaging infrastructure using Sun ONE Message Queue, Java Message Service, and JAXM under the project code CORTEX. This infrastructure addresses the reliability issues of SOAP messaging by binding SOAP messages to JMS.

By engaging Sun, TCPL is able to define and transform the existing applications and utilities into reusable services.

Further details can be found at: *http://www.infoworld.com/articles/hn/xml/02/03/18/020318hnspine.xml* and *http://www.sun.com/software/sunone/wp-cortex.pdf*

2.5.3   Dollar Rent-A-Car Case Study

Business travel often involves a series of related services from airlines and car rental companies. Unfortunately, they are not automated and integrated. Dollar adapts Web Services to provide an online booking system, with direct integration with the Southwest Airlines reservation system. This involves cross-platform interoperability between legacy systems—Dollar's booking system runs on Solaris OE™ and Southwest on OpenVMS™.

Such B2B integration using Web Services enables the unit processing cost to be reduced from $5 to $1.

2.5.4   Hewitt Associates Case Study

Hewitt Associates is a global Human Resources (HR) consultancy firm and provides HR services such as 401(k). The majority of HR operations are done on legacy mainframe systems. To integrate with 2,000 corporate customers (who may have thousands of employees), Hewitt Associates needs to use a reusable framework with Open Standards. Time-to-market and easy implementation are two major business drivers. Hewitt Associates has implemented the solution using Apache SOAP server and CICS Transaction Gateway™ on z/OS™.

By adapting Web Services with SOAP and UDDI, integration with legacy HR systems has become easier and faster. Hewitt Associates only spent three to four months and two staff members to implement the Web Services architecture. It helps meet customer expectations, system responses, and service levels.

2.6   Establishing a Business Case

2.6.1   Overview

This section depicts two scenarios where Web Services technology may be a good fit. The first scenario is a membership award program, which is a common customer loyalty program, and provides a seamless integration between a credit-card bonus point system and business partners for redemption, account balance, activity tracking, and cross-selling. The second scenario is a single payment gateway that enables corporate banking customers to utilize payment services from multiple banks.

To establish a business case for Web Services implementation, some common characteristics and prerequisites of the candidates are discussed, followed by the selection criteria of a pilot project, business benefits, and some risk analysis. Typically, many corporations would start a pilot program (or Proof of Concept) to justify the business case and to mitigate the technology risks. A sample Return On Investment (ROI) model, based on the pilot scenario, is provided in the business case.

2.6.2   Candidate Characteristics

The target candidate for Web Services implementation is one where we might de-compose existing monolithic services into more atomic business services. By exposing these atomic business services, we should then aggregate business information from various sources with a business process engine into meaningful business information and customer-oriented services. Ideally, the target candidate should have the follow-ing characteristics:

Trading Partners. There may be more than one external trading partner involved. There is also a need to interoperate with back-end legacy systems and heterogeneous platforms. Otherwise, the low complexity does not jus-tify using Web Services technology.

Reusability. The reusability of business services and customer information should be high. If the solution is very unique and cannot be reusable any-where, then there is no business case.

Branding. Some people believe integrating two different services may lose the original branding, as either or both parties may need to compromise in some areas to accommodate technical constraints. While keeping a consis-tent branding, we need to provide flexibility (such as providing personalized or customized services for managed services), especially for white labeling services. The integration technology used must be flexible enough to ac-commodate the different constraints of the back-end services.

Technology Constraints. Back-end business services or application func-tionality are unlikely to be re-engineered. Thus, the technology used should coexist and leverage existing back-end services and should not require a rewrite or significant modification.

Limited Delivery Time Window. There should be a short and limited time window to deliver the system. Thus, the technology used must be easy and quick to deploy. The integration framework needs to support different protocols and message formats, including a variety of industry standards and platforms.

2.6.3   Membership Award Example

Membership award is a common customer loyalty program widely used in credit-card services. Customers who register with the credit card company Web site can redeem bonus points in exchange for gifts from the membership award site. The ob-jective is to provide a seamless integration for bonus point redemption and partner services. Today, there is no integration among the bonus point system, the credit card company's call center, or the trading partners' system. Membership award redemption requests are usually done via fax, and the award details are often re-entered into the back-end system. Membership award information is often re-entered into the service provider's back-end system and the credit card company's call center system. Some service providers may have electronic file transfer between the credit card company and their back-end system. However, there are also integration and inter-operability issues with the service providers' ERP and legacy systems, because each system requires specific data formats and different protocols for data exchange. If there are numerous service providers, the integration effort for the bonus point system would have to be substantial in order to handle multiple data formats and protocols.

In Figure 2–2, the point of sales (POS) terminal residing in the merchant's store connects to a credit card gateway, which will dial up to the Processor (such as the ac-quirer bank that offers merchant accounts) to request authorization and debit pro-cessing. Upon successful authentication and authorization, the Processor will process the card payment via the payment gateway with the credit card company. The current business processes do not allow any Point of Sales information (such as bonus points gained from the sales) to be captured automatically for the bonus point system. In other words, Customer Service Agents or Operations personnel from the credit card company need to re-enter the payment transaction details into their bonus point sys-tem in order to process the reward redemption requests. Nor can the Business Intel-ligence applications retrieve the membership award activities for the purpose of data mining or direct marketing.

Web Services technology can be used here to wrap the Point of Sales payment functionality as a reusable business service. This enables the POS or merchandise in-

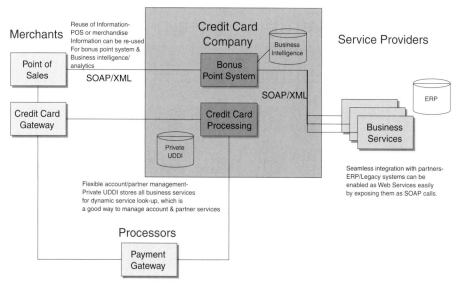

Figure 2–2   Membership Award Example

formation (such as payment transactions) to be captured in SOAP messages and reused by the bonus point system. The credit card company can also make available partial contents of the customer transactions with other business service providers who need them to process the award redemption request. This not only reduces paper work, it can also expedite the processing time of the reward redemption.

The bonus point system can also make use of Web Services technology to integrate seamlessly with back-end ERP or legacy systems or to exchange membership award information with service providers via SOAP messages. This allows a flexible and low-cost means of Business-to-Business integration, without creating proprietary and dedicated interfaces.

In addition, with the use of a private UDDI service registry, the credit card company can store the service information of different service providers to enable dynamic service look-up of various membership award services. Customer and business information will then become timely, and thus the award redemption service becomes a good user experience. Besides, consumers, merchants, or service providers participating in the membership award service (or affinity program) need to preregister first in the private UDDI service registry with the credit card company. They are authenticated each time before they can use the membership award service. This registration process can facilitate better account and partner management with security and foster the growth of the user community.

Figure 2-3 depicts five business scenarios or use cases for the membership award processes. Before a credit card holder can enjoy his membership award services, he needs to register with the credit card company's call center (or Web site.) He also needs to administer his membership details.

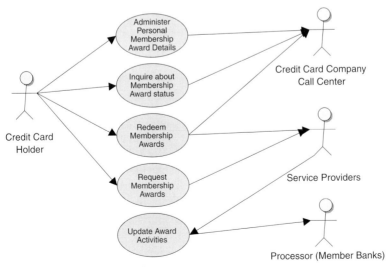

Figure 2–3   Membership Award Use Cases

Upon successful membership registration, the credit card holder, who has just made a POS purchase using his credit card, can go to the credit card company's Web site to inquire about his membership award status. If he has enough bonus points to redeem some merchandise, he would like to make a redemption request with a service provider. Service providers will then process the redemption requests, arrange merchandise delivery to the credit card holder, and return membership award status to the credit card company's call center (or the Processor, if they share the same affinity program) so that they can update their bonus point system.

Figure 2-4 shows similar process details in the form of a sequence diagram. The credit card holder self-registers for the membership award program with the credit card company's call center. This is a typical online service, or a self-registration service exposed as a Web Service from the call center system.

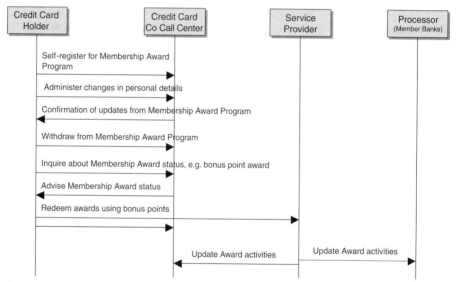

Figure 2–4   Membership Award Sequence Diagram

Upon successful registration, the credit card holder can administer changes to his personal details, such as address changes. The call center system confirms the update with the credit card holder. Similarly, the credit card holder can withdraw from the membership award program online. The membership administration or update can be a typical online functionality from the call center system, or Web Services provided by the call center system (if the call center system is provided by an Application Service Provider).

If the credit card holder inquires about the current status of membership awards (such as the bonus point balance), the call center system can generate an inquiry request in a SOAP message, where the call center system can aggregate membership award information in real-time from different service providers using Web Services.

Similarly, if the credit card holder wants to redeem an award with his bonus points, the call center system can generate a redeem award request and send it to the relevant service provider for award redemption. Upon completion of the award redemption, service providers can send SOAP messages to the call center system and/or the Processor to update the membership award activities. The benefit of using Web Services technology here is the ease of integration and interoperability with multiple service providers.

The benefit of using XML Web Services is to enable interoperability and integration among Processors (in this case, banks), trading partners, and credit card company with reusable data over the existing infrastructure. It also reuses the existing Point of Sales (POS) and merchandise information (thus no duplicate re-entry) for bonus point processing, business intelligence, and award redemption. There is seamless integration with trading partners' legacy and ERP systems. It also enables flexible account and partner service management.

2.6.4   Payment Services Example

Today, buyers have many Electronic Banking systems, but they cannot use one single front-end to settle payments with multiple banks. These Electronic Banking systems also support cross-border payment. Besides, there is no agreeable data format for B2B Exchanges, buyers, suppliers, banks, or credit card companies to share and reuse.

The objective is to provide a single payment gateway to settle cross-border payments with multiple banks. XML Web Services technology enables multiple banks and credit card companies to reuse the same purchase order contents. It also enables interoperability and integration between banks and credit card companies with reusable data over existing infrastructure.

Today, most Business-to-Business transactions are exchanged in physical documents. A payment (or Documentary Credit) can be issued only if there is a physical purchase order document that is backed up by other shipping documents (showing the physical delivery and order fulfillment). Nowadays, Business-to-Business payment can be handled by credit card services such as TradeCard and Visa Commerce. Payment can be released after there is a physical delivery of goods and services. However, it is labor intensive, error prone, and may impose a time delay. In addition, if there is any exception that impacts the shipment delivery or payment, there is no proactive measure such as alerts to notify the buyer, the supplier, or the bank. Some buyers or suppliers may use proprietary electronic media to exchange trade and shipping documents, but each party may have a different data format or protocol that makes the integration and interoperability difficult. Some buyers or suppliers use

Electronic Data Interchange (EDI) to exchange trading documents as well. But the operating cost is fairly high, and it requires both ends to use the same EDI standards and version numbers.

Figure 2–5 depicts a complex business scenario for Business-to-Business payment services. An international buyer has a supply chain management system hosted in a data center managed by an outsourcing (or out-tasked) service provider. The buyer is making online purchases via Trading Exchange A and Trading Exchange B with suppliers from different parts of the world. Each Trading Exchange has many service providers (or suppliers) and uses different banks to settle payment upon delivery of goods to the buyers. If credit cards (in this case, B2B corporate cards, not consumer credit cards) are used to purchase merchandise, the buyer's bank (either Bank A or Bank B) will clear payment of the merchandise with the credit card company.

Web Services technology can play a key role in facilitating B2B payment services. In this business scenario, the Trading Exchange may have a UDDI or ebXML service registry that stores service provider information, their merchandise, and their corresponding business services. Buyers can browse the merchandise from the service registry, and make a purchase by invoking an online order request service. This allows a SOAP call to the remote order management system to confirm a trade order or to decline the order if it is out of stock. Upon completion of order execution, the service provider's system may return an order acknowledgement or order delivery in a SOAP message to the buyer's procurement system.

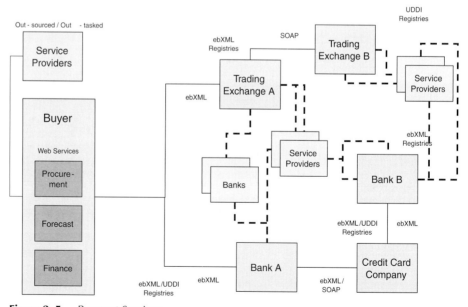

Figure 2–5   Payment Services

Upon delivery of merchandise, the buyer's back office system (finance module) can settle the payment using a B2B credit card service. It will also generate a payment instruction in a SOAP message to the credit card issuer bank, which will then clear the payment with the credit card company. As service providers may be using different messaging protocols and data formats, they may use SOAP or ebXML messaging to exchange trading documents or payment instructions. The benefit of using SOAP or ebXML messaging is that they are able to integrate with the buyer's or service providers' back-end systems. Trading documents encapsulated in XML structure within a SOAP message can be easily transcoded into a format that can be understood by the back-end ERP or legacy systems. Thus, the integration effort can be lower and reusable for other Trading Exchanges. It does not require all service providers to use the same vendor solution or to adopt a proprietary data format.

Figure 2–6 depicts five business scenarios or use cases for the payment services. Upon browsing the service registry (aka online catalog), the buyer can select the merchandise and issue an online purchase order. In this example, the buyer uses a B2B payment service from the credit card company to place an online purchase order. Upon delivery of merchandise, the buyer can issue payment instructions to the buyer's bank (Bank A). The buyer's bank will then authorize the payment and advise the supplier's bank (Bank B). Bank B will then notify the supplier about the payment instructions. Finally, the credit card company will act as a clearing agent for Bank A and Bank B.

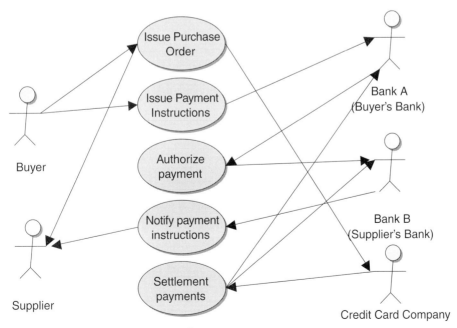

Figure 2–6   Payment Services Use Cases

Figure 2–7 shows similar process details in the form of a sequence diagram. The buyer issues an electronic purchase order to the supplier in a SOAP message and also copies the purchase order to the buyer's bank for reference. Upon successful delivery of merchandise, the buyer would like to make payment by issuing payment instructions to the buyer's bank. The buyer's bank in turn relays the payment instructions to the supplier's bank in a SOAP message. Upon receipt of the payment instructions, the buyer's bank will authorize payment with the credit card company, because the buyer is using B2B payment service from the credit card company. The supplier's bank will also notify the supplier about the receipt of payment instructions from the buyer.

Then the buyer's bank will initiate clearing the payment with the credit card company and the supplier's bank. Upon completion of clearing the payment, both banks will update the payment status and notify their corresponding banking customers (the buyer and the supplier, respectively). The notification may be in the form of alerts sent to their email addresses or mobile devices in SOAP messages.

The benefit of using Web Services is to enable high-value cross-border payment using a credit card. As a result, banks can enjoy seamless integration with buyers and suppliers' back office systems using reusable system components over the existing infrastructure.

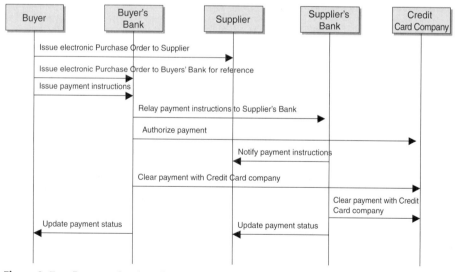

Figure 2–7 Payment Services Sequence Diagram

2.6.5   Business Case Prerequisites

To establish a business case for Web Services implementation, there must be a clearly defined business problem. A Web Services initiative is usually driven by addressing specific business problems or pain points, such as cost reduction or integration issues. Typically, a business case will include a pilot or a small Proof of Concept to illustrate the cost-benefits and to mitigate technology risks. The pilot project can also act as a "lessons learned" experiment before Web Services becomes a technology strategy.

Executive sponsorship is mandatory, even though this is a small Proof of Concept. Besides, the Web Services candidate should be scoped with a target delivery time frame of not more than six months. There should be a ready-to-go task force. The internal project team should be equipped with Web Services technology training, awareness of the implementation process, or case studies.

2.6.6   Selection Criteria of a Pilot Project

The above two scenarios are examples of potential pilot projects that may be selected for the business case. There are five key factors when determining whether the business scenario is suitable as a pilot project:

Business Value. The target pilot project needs to have considerable (nontrivial) business value or have a positive impact to the company's bottom-line cost or revenue. Some pain points can be chosen as the basis for a pilot project if Web Services technology can address them in short-to-medium-term. For instance, a company is currently receiving customer information from business partners via backup tapes or file transfer. This may be labor intensive and costly, especially when there are large numbers of partners. By replacing the tape media or file transfer with Web Services technology, the company can improve timeliness and reliability of data, which can be translated into quantifiable business value, such as cost saving.

Thought Leadership. The vendor (or architects within the company) should demonstrate thought leadership in Web Services areas. The architects or resources from the vendor (or within the company) should also exhibit some working knowledge or perhaps subject matter expertise in the vertical solution (for example, financial services).

Choice of Solution Options. From an IT investment perspective, it is too risky to bet on a single vendor product. The software vendor solution set should interoperate with other Web Services products.

Process. A Web Services architecture framework, methodology, or development tool should be available and adapted, supplemented by a sensitive development methodology. Implementation is often made successful with appropriate, though not excessive, processes.

Service Support. Service support from the vendor should be available locally. For example, Asian companies find that U.S.-centric vendors lack local service support, and they often need to pay expensive overseas trips for expertise.

2.6.7   Business Case Risk Analysis

Business Risks. Implementing a business service with Web Services in a narrow time window (for example, six weeks) may be too risky if the company does not have prior experience in Web Services. For the first time pilot, it is more pragmatic to implement Web Services for a longer time window (for example, at least four months).

If Web Services technology is used to implement new business models, the business risk is increased two-fold or more. In case of failure, it is difficult to tell if the business model or the technology implementation work. Thus, it is useful to address one area at a time (for example, use a proven business model with Web Services).

Technology Risks. Web Services standards are changing, and it may be too risky to bet on an early release, especially when the company is large and slow to implement technology changes. For example, Apache SOAP evolved from 2.0 to Apache Axis within a year. It is evolving so fast that customers with a slow implementation schedule may begin with Apache SOAP 1.1 implementation for a year, but by the time the system is deployed, the market is ready for Apache Axis.

To mitigate the risk, customers may partner with a Web Services thought leader vendor who can assure backward compatibility and agility for new upgrades.

Implementation Risks. Human resources with a good understanding of Web Services technology and large-scale integration experience are hard to find. One of the best alternatives is for the customer project team to collaborate with Web Services consultants so that they can be mentored.

Risk Mitigation. Common technology implementation risks are point-to-point or proprietary interfaces (for example, EAI integration is proprietary and often point-to-point), inconsistent Quality of Services (for example, scalability, support, and maintainability for screen-scraping-based solutions), and the security risks associated with tactical screen-scraping or point-to-point interfaces.

To mitigate these implementation risks, Web Services (using asynchronous messaging) provide reusable interfaces using open standards, not point-to-point. Web Services solutions can be easily scalable and available (refer to Web Services design patterns in Chapter 4 Web Services Architecture and Best Practices). Besides, Web

Services-enabled legacy systems and mainframes are maintained "as-is" (run-time bindings for XML-RPC), and no system infrastructure needs to be changed. There is also an established security framework to address different levels of security threats.

2.6.8   Benefits of Using Web Services

There are three major benefits of implementing Web Services technology:

Interoperability. Web Services technology is a low-cost technology tool to meet time-to-market requirements. It provides better integration and interoperability for cross-platform systems and legacy back office applications. In contrast, EAI is usually proprietary, and does not easily interoperate with another EAI if they are from different vendors.

Reusability and Maintainability. Business services can be exposed as Web Services. These become highly reusable, and are platform- and vendor-independent. The service calls and interfaces are also easy to maintain. In contrast, EAI products and screen-scraping technology are usually platform- and vendor-dependent.

ROI. Web Services technology can be deployed within weeks or months, with lower cost of integration and maintenance. Return on immediate cost savings can be measured.

2.6.9   Return on Investment Model

There are a few approaches to measure the ROI of adopting and implementing Web Services:

Sunk Cost. Implementing new technology may incur sunk cost, which may not generate ROI. You may like to treat such investment as part of your infrastructure cost. In such a case, this includes investment cost for training and technology skill transfer. With appropriate senior management support, the sunk cost does not expect any ROI or cost savings. However, this approach may be difficult in the current economic atmosphere.

Soft ROI. This denotes a nonquantitative analysis of different investment options, and compares the business benefits. Management needs to be convinced of the vision and its associated long-term benefits.

Product ROI. Based on a specific scenario, you may want to identify the manual processing cost, internal implementation cost, legacy system marginal/upgrade cost, and Web Services implementation cost. In such a scenario, management may expect you to compare this with other alternatives such as using screen scraping or EAI technology for integration.

Soft ROI Example

Assumptions. Table 2–1 depicts a comparison of implementing the Membership Award scenario using Web Services, a proprietary screen scraping, and EAI technology. There are certain assumptions made for each technology option in the table.

Table 2–1   List of Assumptions While Comparing the Return on Investment Using Web Services, Screen Scraping, and EAI

	Web Services	Proprietary Screen Scraping	EAI
Fixed cost (for example, base software tool cost)	US$50,000	US$100,000	US$300,000
Number of screens/functional units	1 Web Services call	200 screens	5 adapters are needed
Unit cost for screen scraping a screen	US$80,000	US$56.25/day	US$24,000
Reusability for other similar services	Yes	No Need customization	Yes Need customization
Subtotal (development cost per partner per site)	US$130,000	US$111,250	US$420,000
Cost for two partners/sites	US$130,000	US$222,500	US$550,000

Figure 2–8 illustrates the development/implementation cost and deployment time frame for each technology option. Web Services technology is relatively more scalable and less costly (development/implementation cost), and has a shorter deployment time window (deployment time frame).

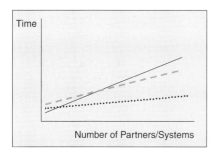 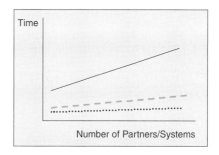

Development/Implementation Cost   Deployment Time Frame

Legend: .... Web Services
                _____ Proprietary screen scraping
                − − EAI

EXAMPLE

Figure 2–8   Soft ROI

Product ROI Example

Scenario. This sample scenario assumes we are implementing the Membership Award program using Web Services technology. We are comparing using Web Services technology, home-grown proprietary API, and EAI approaches.

Assumptions. There is no major architecture change if using Web Services (for example, there is no need to install an additional hardware component or upgrade legacy systems). Some basic training or a technology awareness workshop of Web Services is conducted. Two developers and one project manager are the available resources. Additional software licenses for EAI need to be purchased for the EAI option. The data center cost is about 12 percent of the hardware and software cost per year plus service staff cost.

Implication. The total cost will multiply if more partners are involved and the integration framework must be cloned or replicated. Web Services will have a higher reusability and lower deployment cost.

Table 2–2 shows an example of the case. In this Membership Award example, different implementation cost components using Web Services, proprietary API, and EAI technologies are estimated and compared. The Web Services solution approach has a lower total cost. It has a lower development cost because the integration effort is smaller using open standards, and the reusability of existing infrastructure and functionality is high.

Table 2–2   Comparing Implementation Cost by Web Services, Screen Scraping, and EAI

	Web Services	Proprietary API	EAI
Baseline cost. Manual Processing Cost if no enhancement with these technology options	US$1,000,000 p.a. (service running cost)	US$1,000,000 p.a.	US$1,000,000 p.a.
Infrastructural cost (for example, hardware and software upgrade)	US$50,000	US$50,000	US$300,000 (EAI licenses)
Internal development cost	US$80,000 (4 man-months)	US$160,000 (8 man-months)	US$120,000 (6 man-months)
Internal implementation cost	US$40,000	US$80,000	US$40,000
Professional services, such as mentoring or consultancy services	US$40,000 (3 man-weeks)	N/A	US$27,000 (2 man-weeks)
Managed services, such as service support cost, outsourced cost, and data center processing cost (if not hosted in-house)	US$240,000 p.a. (support staff) US$100,000 p.a. (data center/support services)	US$240,000 p.a. (support staff) US$200,000 p.a. (data center/ support services)	US$240,000 p.a. (support staff) US$500,000 p.a. (data center/support services)
Other costs, such as training	US$100,000 training	N/A	US$100,000 training
Subtotal (first year)	US$350,000	US$530,000	US$817,000

2.7   Perspectives

2.7.1   Highlights

- Reduction of total cost of ownership and easier integration with partners and legacy systems are the key business drivers for Web Services.
- Web Services is gaining more momentum in industry implementation and has wider vendor support.

- There are early success stories of Web Services implementation.
- There are a few ways to present a business case to implement Web Services, but they must be put in the context of the future (long-term benefits, non-quantitative benefits) and reusability, not one-off development costs.

2.7.2 Best Practices and Pitfalls

The following are some ideas regarding establishing a business case for Web Services implementation.

Best Practices

- When presenting a Web Services business case, always present both the short-term and long-term benefits.
- Compare alternatives with risk mitigation.
- Cite scenarios showing how your company can make use of Web Services. Remember to bring Use Case Studies as part of your story.

Pitfalls

- Do not quantify ROI for the business case—it is too early to see the result. Using hard figures too early will not win the confidence of your business audience.
- Do not start the business case with Web Services technology details. Business audiences do not like a business case for technology's sake.

2.7.3 Paper and Pencil

Objective

Invoking Web Services can be very easy. The objective of this exercise is to learn how to invoke a public Web Service (with a Web Services Description Language) using a rich client (non-Java) and a Java client, respectively.

Exercise

The following site: *http://www.xmethods.net/sd/2001/CurrencyExchangeService.wsdl* contains a service definition for a currency exchange service provided by xmethods.net. Write a rich client to invoke the remote Web Service. You may develop a Java™ client or a SOAP-Lite client. A Java™ sample program is available from *http://www.xmethods.net/download/servicefiles/CurrencyClient.java*. You can download SOAP-Lite from *http://www.soaplite.com*.

Procedures for Java™ Client

You need to install and configure your J2SE™ SDK with CLASSPATH and PATH set. Refer to Appendix C in this book for details. Download the CurrencyClient.java and save a local copy. Execute the following commands to compile and execute the client program (see Figure 2–9):

```
D:\Dev\mydemo>javac CurrencyClient.java
D:\Dev\mydemo>java CurrencyClient
34.19
```

Figure 2–9   Invoking a public Web Service with Java™ client

The CurrencyClient.java program will invoke the currency exchange service at *http://services.xmethods.com:80/soap*. It specifies the sell/buy cross-currency pair United States to Taiwan, which returns the spot rate US$1 = 34.19 Taiwan yen.

Procedures for SOAP-Lite Client

You need to install and configure SOAP-Lite with Perl 5.0 or higher with PATH pointing to the Perl 5.x distribution. Refer to Appendix C for details.

The sample SOAP-Lite client is shown in Figure 2–10. You only need to specify the "service" with the WSDL, and the operation name (that is, getRate) with the input parameters. The result is shown in Figure 2–11.

```
#!perl -w
#!d:\perl\bin\perl.exe

BEGIN { warn "Invoking a public FX Web Services...\n" }

# import interface. All methods from loaded service
are imported by default
use SOAP::Lite
    service =>
'http://www.xmethods.net/sd/2001/CurrencyExchangeService.
wsdl',
;

warn "Loaded...\n";
print getRate('us', 'taiwan'), "\n";
```

Figure 2–10   Sample SOAP-Lite Client Code

Execute the SOAP-Lite program just like any Perl script. This should render the same result as the Java™ client for the sell/buy currency pair United States to Taiwan.

```
D:\Dev\mydemo>perl myCurrencyRate.pl
Invoking a public FX Web Services...
Loaded...
34.19
```

Figure 2–11   Invoking a Public Web Service with SOAP-Lite Client

2.7.4   References

Web Services Trends

John Hagel III and John Seely Brown. *"Your Next IT Strategy."* Harvard Business Review, October 2001.

Web Services Case Studies

David Chappell and Tyler Jewell. Java Web Services. (California: O'Reilly, 2002).

Anton Fricko. *"Tasting SOAP—Project Experience with Web Services."* IBM developerWorks Live! Conference 2002.

Tim Hilgenberg and John A. Hansen. *"Building a Highly Robust, Secure Web Services Conference Architecture to Process 4 Million Transactions per Day."* IBM developerWorks Live! Conference 2002

IDC. "People's Insurance Company of China: eBusiness Portal Attracts New Customers and Reduces Costs." *http://www.sun.com/service/about/success/recent/picc.html*

Chris Nelson. *"Web Services Real Enterprise Usage."* IBM developerWorks Live! Conference 2002.

Trans-Canada (TCPL). *http://www.infoworld.com/articles/hn/xml/02/03/18/020318hnspine.xml*

Kevin Yin. *"A Reference Architecture for Smart Web Service."* August 17, 2001. *http://dcb.sun.com/practices/devnotebook/webserv_refarch.jsp*

Ezra Zask, ed. *The e-Finance Report.* New York: Wiley, 2001.

Grid Computing and Web Services

Global Grid Forum. *http://www.gridforum.org/ogsi-wg/drafts/draft-ggf-ogsi-gridservice-23_2003-02-17.pdf*

The Globus Project. *http://www.globus.org/research/papers.html#Overview Papers*

The Securities Industry Middleware Council. *"The Future of Middleware: Grid Computing and Web Services."* November 19, 2002, General Meeting. *http://www.simc-inc.org/archive0203/Grid/agenda19nov2002.htm*

Tom Sullivan. *"Sun Combines Grid Computing, Web Services."* *http://www.infoworld.com/article/02/02/15/020215hnsunonegrid_1.html*

Liang-Jie Zhang, Jen-Yao Chung, and Qun Zhou. *"Developing Grid computing applications, Part 1."* *http://www-106.ibm.com/developerworks/webservices/library/ws-grid1/*

Liang-Jie Zhang, Jen-Yao Chung, and Qun Zhou. *"Developing Grid computing applications, Part 2."* *http://www-106.ibm.com/developerworks/webservices/library/ws-grid2/*

Other References

White label service using Web Services (i-Deal). *http://www.lighthouse-partners.com/wallstreettng/presentations/Frank%20LaQuinta.ppt*

Chapter 3

WEB SERVICES TECHNOLOGY OVERVIEW

3.1 Chapter Overview

- Web Services, which are units of business services and components, are positioned as the next IT strategy for enterprises. The enabling technologies are built on top of XML. They are also referenced as *"XML Web Services."*

- The Web Services technology stack includes the transport layer (for example, SOAP over HTTP), a service description language (for example, WSDL), transaction routing (for example, ebXML Message Service), and service negotiation (for example, ebXML Business Process).

- Web Services have many similarities and associations with CORBA. Some see Web Services technology as a reincarnation of Application Service Provider and CORBA.
- Microsoft's version of Web Services is .NET, with C# as one key development language. Sun, IBM, and other technology vendors are using Java™ as the service enabler for Web Services.
- To enable your applications to be Web Services, you do not need to rewrite them in Java™ or C#. There are four simple steps to transform your existing applications into Web Service.
- Web Services solutions are still in the "technology-hype" stage.
- There are, however, at least three public UDDI nodes and numerous Web Services directories that enlist pilot Web Services applications.
- Many technology and solution vendors have already shipped their Web Services-enabled products. Consumers may not even know Web Services are already in action.

3.2   Chapter Objectives

- To identify the root and derivation of the Web Services technologies
- To establish an appreciation of the underlying Web Services technology, its benefits, and when to use it
- To establish some guidelines in choosing a Web Services developer tool and platform in the marketplace
- To illustrate four steps to Web Services-enable a simple application
- To illustrate what Web Services solutions are available on the market, the benefits, and the limitations

3.3   Web Services—The Evolution

3.3.1   What Is Web Service?

The term *Web Services* has become a buzzword in the industry recently. With the change in the economic landscape, there is an increasing interest in pursuing cost-effective solution development and implementation by Application Service Provider (ASP), out-sourcing, or out-tasking.

On the other hand, Business-to-Business integration (B2Bi) has always been a hot subject with the emergence of more e-Marketplace and Exchanges. Traditional point-to-point interfaces and proprietary message structures become difficult to manage as the number explodes exponentially. There is a need for an open standards-based, yet flexible solution for wide and speedy deployment.

These two driving forces have been crystallizing with the development of Web Services. Web Services are units of business services, applications, or system functionality that can be accessible over the Web (either Internet, extranet, or intranet). Web Services can enable legacy system functionality to be exposed as a reusable business service (for example, publish a legacy function as an API), without rewriting it. The technology can be used as a cross-system or cross-enterprise integration. This is particularly useful for outsourced or managed services interoperating with in-house applications.

What Is NOT Web Service?

It is usually easier to understand what a Web Service is by understanding what it is not:

- Yet another Enterprise Application Interface package
- A rebranding of CORBA technology
- A new technology that can develop and deploy applications with a few keystrokes using a wizard
- A common and agreed-upon standard for all application servers, database servers, or software products to interoperate with each other, without changing any piece of codes or customization

3.3.2   Web Services Features

Business services provided by existing system functionality are exposed to external systems as Web Services. This enables a legacy system to become a service-based or component-based architecture. However, the use of XML does not necessarily mean that the application is Web Services-enabled. SOAP is one of the key technologies for Web Services, but it is not the only technology (ebXML is another).

Applications and business services developed and deployed using Web Services technology have the following characteristics:

Loosely-Coupled Components.   They are loosely-coupled (for example, messages are decoupled from the data transport) and are easy to integrate with other platforms and open standards technology. In other words, changing the implementation of one component does not require changing the rest of the services, which makes configuration and deployment easier to manage. They are also highly reusable.

Self-Describing and Adapting.   Using XML technology for data contents and information exchange enables transactions and information to be self-describing and adaptive, without requiring a prior knowledge of the applications or the interfaces. Web Services technology uses the Web Services Description Language (WSDL) in the XML structure to define the interfaces, network connection, and service end-points. Only the business-level interfaces, rather than the fine-grained, low-level interfaces, need to be exposed. As a result, data is decoupled from process logic, which makes integration easier and cleaner.

Distributed and Location-Independent.   The use of ebXML and UDDI registries enables business services to be location-independent and highly distributed. This also enables noncore (and even core) business services to be out-tasked to a specialized service provider, even in remote areas, at a lower total cost ownership, while maintaining control of ownership and integrating with the core back office systems. The "contracted" functions of the Web Services make use of publicly available standard description languages (such as WSDL). This enables business services to be discovered and bound/unbound from the Web Services registries (for example, ebXML registries).

Dynamic and Extensible.   As information and transactions are encapsulated in XML, they can be dynamically aggregated, transformed, and processed at real-time. Thus, the business services become more dynamic and easily extensible without rewriting the back-end systems.

Open Standards-Based.   The architecture framework of Web Services is based on open standards technology such as J2EE™, XML, SOAP, and UDDI, instead of proprietary or vendor-specific technology. This enables a wider choice of vendor solutions and easier integration between components, as well as easy migration to newer technologies later.

3.3.3   Web Services History

Web Services technology standards are often demarcated by the contributors (mainly technology vendors). They changed rapidly between 2000 and 2002. Table 3–1 traces the history of Web Services technology.

Table 3–1   Web Services Technology History

Web Services Standard	Version	Release Date	Status
Web Services Description Language (WSDL)	1.1	Mar. 15, 2001	W3C Note submitted by IBM, Microsoft, Ariba. Refer to *http://www.w3.org/Submission/*.

Table 3–1   Web Services Technology History—*continued.*

Web Services Standard	Version	Release Date	Status
	1.2	Jan. 24, 2003	Currently as W3C Working Draft. There is a new WSDL bindings (using WSDL with SOAP 1.2, HTTP/1.1/GET/POST and MIME) working draft. Refer to *http://www.w3.org/TR/2003/WD-wsdl12-20030124/* and *http://www.w3.org/TR/2003/WD-wsdl12-bindings-20030124/.*
Universal Discovery, Discovery, and Integration (UDDI)			
	1.0	1999	Proposed by Microsoft and UDDI.org.
	2.0	2001	Managed by UDDI.org.
	3.0	July 19, 2002	Currently managed under OASIS. Refer to *http://www.oasis-open.org/committees/uddi-spec/* and *http://uddi.org/pubs/uddi_v3_features.htm.*
Simple Object Access Protocol (SOAP)			
	1.1	May 8, 2000	Proposed by Microsoft, IBM, UserLand, Developmentor. Refer to *http://www.w3.org/Submission/.*
	1.1 with Attachment	Dec. 11, 2000	Proposed by HP and Microsoft.
	1.2	Dec. 19, 2002	Currently as W3C Candidate Recommendation. Refer to *http://www.w3.org/TR/2002/CR-soap12-part0-20021219/,* *http://www.w3.org/TR/2002/CR-soap12-part1-20021219/* and *http://www.w3.org/TR/2002/CR-soap12-part2-20021219/.*

Table 3–1   Web Services Technology History—*continued.*

Web Services Standard	Version	Release Date	Status
ebXML Message Specification			
	1.0	May 11, 2001	Managed by OASIS. Use SOAP 1.1 with Attachment as transport and routing.
	2.0	Apr. 1, 2002	Managed by OASIS. The standard is approved on Sept. 5, 2002.
ebXML Service Registry			
	1.0	May 8, 2001	Managed by OASIS. Refer to *http://www.ebxml.org/specs/index.htm.*
	2.0	Dec. 18, 2001	Managed by OASIS. The standard is approved in Dec. 2001.
	2.1	June 2002	Addressed typo and minor errors in version 2.0. Refer to *https://www.oasis-open.org/committees/regrep/documents/2.1/specs/ebrim_v2.1.pdf* and *https://www.oasis-open.org/committees/regrep/documents/2.0/specs/ebrs.pdf.*

Implication

There are two major variants of Web Services standards (WSDL-UDDI-SOAP and ebXML) evolving in the Web Services space. WSDL-UDDI-SOAP technology has been gaining momentum with many vendor implementations in the past two years. ebXML uses SOAP 1.1 with Attachment as the transport and routing. It provides added values to Web Services with guaranteed messaging and workflow functionality. With JAX Pack, developers can use both variants of Web Services technology seamlessly.

It is important to understand the different value propositions, and when to use them. There are also trends toward the convergence and interoperability of two technology standards in the messaging and security areas.

3.3.4   Web Services Technology Stack

Figure 3–1 depicts different layers of the Web Services stack. It is followed by a short description of each layer.

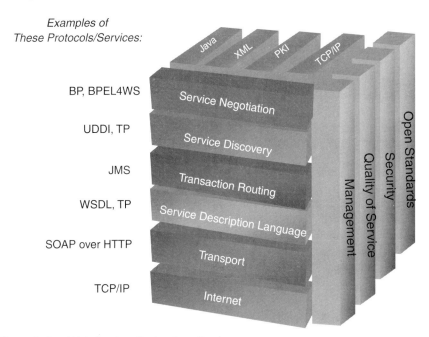

Figure 3–1   Web Services Technology Stack

Structural Framework

Internet. The underlying network for services is the public Internet over TCP/IP

Transport. The underlying transport layer may be HTTP, SMTP, SOAP over HTTP, and so forth

Service Description Language. The business service is described in a common language that depicts the service type and functionality (for example, URI, ports, end-points)

Transaction Routing. Transaction routing of the data contents and transactions to the next business service node, using the lower transport layer with guaranteed (or without guaranteed) message delivery

Service Discovery. Search and locate a business service from Service Registry nodes

Service Negotiation. Agreement on what can be exchanged and is interoperable between the service requester and the service provider

Service Dimension

Management. Provisioning of services and monitoring and administration of services

Quality of Service. Different aspects of "ilities," such as availability and scalability

Security. Message and transport layer security to support authentication, entitlement, and nonrepudiation

Open Standards. For example, XML

Judith M. Myerson, in her paper "Web Services Architectures" (Tect, 2002), summarized 10 different Web Services Architectures: WebServices.org, The Stencil Group, IBM, W3C, Microsoft, Sun, Oracle, HP, BEA, and Borland. Myerson maintains that there is no single Web Services architecture, and each vendor or organization has its own Web Services architecture (this book refers to these Web Services architectures as "vendor product architectures.") She explains that this is because the "number and complexity of layers for the stack" vary by organization. In other words, Myerson does not think there is a single Web Services stack or architecture that is unique to every organization. She summarizes different Web Services architectures from various vendors and categorizes them in a complexity scale (refer to Figure 3–2). Some organizations may require a simple architecture, and some require a complex one.

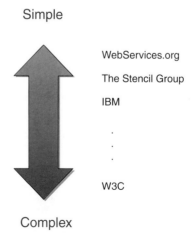

Figure 3–2   Web Services Stack Complexity Scale

There will be more coverage of the Web Services Technology Stack in Chapter 4, Web Services Architecture and Best Practices.

3.3.5 Logical Components

Web Services typically consist of several key players, including Service Requester, Service Provider, and Service Broker, as overviewed in Table 3–2. Service Registry is used by Service Requester to look up relevant business services.

Table 3–2 Web Services Logical Components

Logical Components	Description
Service Requester	The consumer (such as the buyers, buying agents, or suppliers) who requests a particular business service, upon searching (discovering) a service registry.For example, a buyer who is browsing a catalog is a service requester for sourcing/purchasing.
	Typically, a service requester will use a standard protocol to discover the services from a service registry (for example, ebXML or UDDI). Once a service is found, the service requester will bind the service via a SOAP Proxy.
Service Broker	Intermediary or broker that negotiates, aggregates, and provides business services of a particular request on behalf of the service requester (for example, a buying agent is a middleman/service broker for buyers). Typically, they are like portals for information and services, or trading exchanges. The business services typically reside in standards-based repositories such as ebXML or UDDI.
	A service provider can be the Service Broker itself.
Service Provider	The service provider creates and supplies the business services or system functionality (as a producer role—for example, a supplier is a service provider for retail services to buyers).
	Business services are published in standard description languages such as WSDL. The service requester produces the services with interfaces and descriptions that are available by standard protocols (of course, with appropriate security).
Service Registry	A Yellow or White Page that hosts all business services, and the associated service providers. It may be an ebXML or UDDI service registry.

Figure 3–3 depicts a typical scenario for using Web Services. The Service Requesters (in this case, Supplier and Buyer) are consumers of the business services. The Supplier is a client of the Service Provider. The Buyer is a client of the Service Broker. The Service Broker acts as an intermediary for different business services provided by the Service Provider. The Service Broker publishes their business services in a private Service Registry (both ebXML and UDDI Registries). The Service Provider also publishes their business services (using, for example, WSDL) in a private ebXML Service Registry and to the Service Broker.

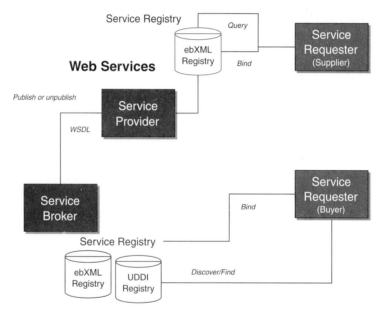

Figure 3–3   Web Services Logical Components

The Buyer is interested in finding a specific business product from the Service Broker. The Service Broker also stores the business services provided by the Service Provider. During service discovery, the Buyer finds an appropriate business service from the Supplier via the Service Broker's ebXML Service Registry. Then the Buyer binds and invokes the business service.

Actions in a typical Web Services scenario may include:

Discover/Find. Searching for a particular business service, usually by a standard reference (for example, UN/SPSC number)

Query. Inquiring about the service, using a predefined set of parameters (such as URI or end-point)

Bind. Run-time binding of the service name, the end-point, and the actual URL; this is like connecting the phone line after the actual phone number is dialed

Publish. Publishing the business service to the Service Registry using a standard interface specification (such as WSDL)

Unpublish. Unpublishing the business service to the Service Registry using a standard interface specification (such as WSDL)

Service Registry Contents

WSDL is the standard interface definition depicting the business service provided (such as the port or URI that can access the business service). The standard interface also describes the message content (such as message name and data type), operation name (such as what method or action can be operated on the message content), and binding name (what data transport is used, such as SOAP over HTTP using Remote Procedure Call). This provides all information necessary for browsing business services (from a user perspective) and developing system interfaces (from a developer or system perspective).

Web Services Use Case

Figures 3–4 and 3–5 are in UML notation that describes the use case and the associated sequence diagram. Figure 3–4 describes five business scenarios or use cases about how Web Services are used. A Service Requester wants to browse through a Service Registry and inquire (or query) about different business services that interest her. Once she discovers the appropriate business services that she would like to use (or invoke), the Service Registry will bind the services with the remote Service Provider.

Service Brokers and Service Providers need to preregister with the Service Registry owner first. Upon successful registration, they can publish or unpublish their business services, which are usually published to the Service Registry.

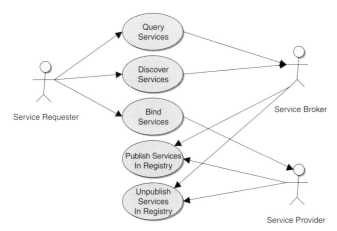

Figure 3–4 Web Services Use Case

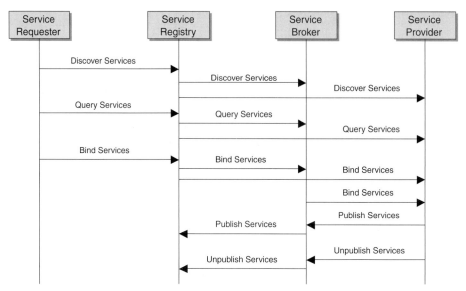

Figure 3–5   Web Services Sequence Diagram

In Figure 3–5, the Service Requester browses through a Service Registry, which contains different taxonomies of Service Brokers' or Service Providers' business organizations and their business services. Browsing through and looking up different taxonomies will initiate API calls such as find_business and find_service UDDI API calls (for UDDI Service Registry), or OrganizationQuery or ServiceQuery ebXML registry calls (for ebXML Service Registry). This is the process of discovering services.

Once the Service Requester has selected a specific business organization (either Service Broker or Service Provider), the Service Registry client will issue a query API to the Service Registry. If this is a UDDI Service Registry, it will be a `get_businessDetail` or `get_serviceDetail UDDI API`. If this is an ebXML Service Registry, the previous `OrganizationQuery` or `ServiceQuery` would have returned the business or service details in the registry query result already. The Service Registry will then return the organization information (such as business name, address, and contact person) or business service details.

If the Service Requester wants to use (or invoke) the business service immediately, the Service Registry client can issue a `find_binding` service call to locate the URI (Universal Resource Identifier, or the service end-point URL describing the Service Provider's service) specific to the business organization or service. Once the URI (or WSDL document) is retrieved, the Service Requester can initiate a SOAP call, based on the port type, the operation names, and the service end-point URL or URI. The service end-point URL refers to the business services that are denoted by URLs (such as *http://mydemo.nextfrontiers.com:8080/soap/rpc*), and are hosted by the Service Brokers or the Service Providers.

If Service Providers or Service Brokers need to publish a new business service to the Service Registry, or to update an existing business service, they need to use several APIs to publish the business organization, business service details, and the service end-point URL. For UDDI Service Registry, there are a few APIs available, such as save_business, save_service, and save_binding (refer to details at *http://uddi.org/ pubs/uddi-v3.00-published-20020719.htm*). For ebXML Service Registry, the Service Registry needs to specify the business organization and service details in the SubmitObject requests (refer to details at *http://www.ebxml.org/specs/ebrs2.pdf*). Similarly, if Service Providers or Service Brokers want to unpublish (remove business information) from the Service Registry, they can use the same set of APIs.

3.3.6   Web Services Architecture

There are a few Web Services architectures published by leading technology vendors. Among them, there are three significant ones put forth by Sun, IBM, and Microsoft.

Sun ONE™ Architecture Framework

The Sun ONE™ architecture framework consists of the following components:

Platform. The underlying hardware and storage platform

Identity. The security components (for example, authentication) and unified user management

Service Container. The Web and EJB container that provides the application services

Service Delivery. The delivery channels and the presentation tier

Web Services. The core business services deployable as reusable components

Service Integration. The integration between business services and legacy systems/resources

Service Creation and Assembly. Creation of contents and program codes

Implication

Sun ONE™ is evolving. It begins with a marketing flavor ("Service on Demand") to promote open standards. Sun hardware, storage, and Sun ONE™ solutions are the key underlying components. Figure 3–6 illustrates the Sun ONE™ framework. It now encompasses an architecture framework *(http://wwws.sun.com/software/sunone/ docs/arch/index.html),* a solution platform *(http://wwws.sun.com/software/sunone/ overview/platform/index.html),* and support by a number of software products *(http://wwws.sun.com/software/sunone/).* Zefer is a good reference example *(http:// sunonedev.sun.com/building/tech_articles/webserv_refarch.html)* where the Sun ONE™ architecture framework is used to implement online portal services with wireless clients.

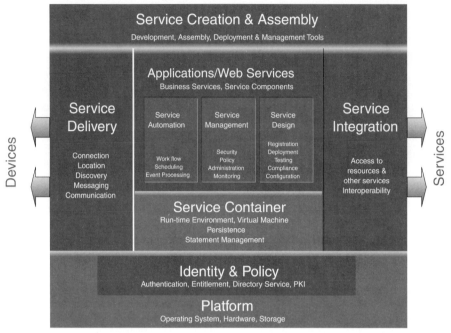

Figure 3–6 Sun ONE™ Framework

IBM Web Services Architecture

IBM's Web Services Architecture can be depicted by three models. It is primarily based on the existing WebSphere Application Server and WebSphere Studio (developer IDE tool) product architecture. Developers use WebSphere Studio to program Java objects and codes (programming model), and deploy in a J2EE run-time environment (run-time model).

Programming Model. Base Parts, Composite Parts, and processes (such as WSDL and XML Schema). Examples of Base Parts are Java Beans™, stored procedures, the database XML Extender, and the Java Script scripting language.

Run-time Model. This provides the "back plane" servicing the host and providing management, security, trace, and workload management for the run-time components (for example, service bus, application server, UI components).

Development Tool Model. This is based on the WebSphere Studio software set. WebSphere Studio is a software branding that includes an HTML home page builder (WebSphere Studio Homepage Builder), Web site builder (WebSphere Studio Site Developer), J2EE application developer workbench (WebSphere Studio Application Developer/Enterprise Developer), J2ME development tools (WebSphere Studio Device Developer), and analyzer tools (WebSphere Studio Asset Analyzer).

There are two models for deploying Web Services:

Shallow Model. This model deploys business services under a Servlet Container (such as Tomcat) with Web Service support and pluggable Service Providers, which map services to URLs and HTTP. Thus, programmers only need to configure to publish services through WSDL and SOAP.

Uniform Model. This model extends the Shallow Model by encapsulating the Base Parts with a Java Bean™ adapter.

Figure 3–7 depicts IBM's Web Services architecture, which consists of a servlet container for the run-time environment of SOAP messages (run-time model). The servlet container also provides pluggable SOAP Service Providers, including SOAP WSDL servlets, SOAP providers (shallow model), and SOAP EJB providers (uniform model). These providers help to map SOAP messages to database objects using XML extender and stored procedures, as well as other servlets, portlets, and EJBs via middleware or data transport protocols such as RMI/IIOP, JMS, and MQ (programming model).

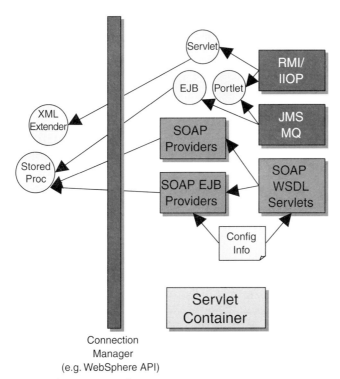

Figure 3–7   IBM Web Services Architecture

Implication

This architecture provides a structural framework to describe what Web Services components are available in the WebSphere Application Server and WebSphere Studio platform and how they support Web Services. More details can be found at *http://www.redbooks.ibm.com/redpieces/pdfs/sg246891.pdf.*

In IBM's Web Services architecture, the centerpiece is the servlet container with different IBM-specific SOAP providers. These providers are tightly coupled with WebSphere-specific products and are unlikely to be reusable on other vendor platforms. The servlet container, which now supports Apache AXIS using WebSphere SDK for Web Services version 5.0, allows developers to use simple servlets (shallow model) or EJBs (uniform model) to invoke remote business services. IBM brands these application design options under the term "eBusiness patterns." There are good code samples available in IBM Redbooks, such as Peter Kovari and colleagues' "Patterns: Building Message-based and Transactional Applications" (February 2003) at *http://www.redbooks.ibm.com/redpieces/pdfs/sg246875.pdf.*

Microsoft Global XML Web Services Architecture

Microsoft sees XML Web Services as the enabling technology in business ecosystems for integration and interoperability for (1) Enterprise Application Integration; (2) interoperability with key partners; and (3) interoperability across multiple companies. There are four design principles for Microsoft Global XML Web Services:

- **Modular/Building Block Style**

- **General Purpose** (for example, applied for B2B, EAI, P2P, and B2C independent of the application domains)

- **Federated/Decentralized**

- **Standards-based** (for example, SOAP, WSDL and UDDI)

Figure 3–8 depicts the Microsoft Global XML Web Services architecture. It is a high-level functional component, rather than a physical architecture. There are three key logical components. The first one is the "discovery" module, which consists of Microsoft UDDI registry server and provides the functionality of directory, inspection, and business service description. The second component consists of SOAP modules, which relate to the WS-Security roadmap published by Microsoft, IBM, and VeriSign. This provides the rules about SOAP message handling and business process orchestration. The last component is the infrastructure protocols, which provide reliable data transport and messaging.

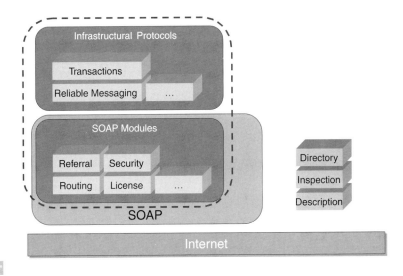

Figure 3–8   Microsoft Global XML Web Services Architecture

Implication

There is a considerable number of developers who are using the Microsoft developer platform today. Understanding Microsoft Global XML Web Services architecture, its roadmap, and the proprietary Web Services extension is helpful in building interoperability between Java and .NET clients.

Although Microsoft claims to follow standards, there are many new and proprietary features of the implementation (or proprietary Web Services extension), such as:

MSXML (versus XML). Microsoft's implementation of XML is MSXML and has some proprietary extension. It is adhered to Internet Explorer browser only.

WS-Security. Microsoft's implementation of WS-Security supports XML Signature and XML Encryption and is provided by Microsoft's CAPICOM developer toolkit.

Please note that after IBM and Microsoft jointly published the new WS-Security roadmap, Microsoft's Global XML Web Services architecture changed because the security components were superseded by the new specifications WS-Security, WS-Policy, WS-Trust, WS-Privacy, WS-SecureConversation, WS-Federation, and WS-Authorization.

Comparing Different Architectures

Table 3–3 shows a simple summary of the three previous architectures.

Table 3–3 Comparing Different Web Services Architecture

	Microsoft	Sun	IBM
Web Services standards support (SOAP 1.2, WSDL, UDDI)	Yes	Yes	Yes
Web Services architecture/framework	.NET	Sun ONE™	IBM Web Services
Comprehensive development environment and tools	.NET server .NET studio	Sun ONE™ Apps Server Sun ONE™ Integration Server Sun ONE™ Studio	WebSphere Application Server WebSphere Application Developer Studio
Expose EJB as Web Services	No (But can interoperate with other Web Services by exposing COM/COM+ objects through .NET interoperability.)	Yes	Yes
Synchronous (Sync) and Asynchronous (Async) message support	Sync—DCOM	Sync—JAXM, SAAJ Async—JAX-RPC	Sync—SAAJ Async—JAX-RPC
Methodology to design Web Services architecture	No	Yes—SunTone™, J2EE Patterns™	Partial—eBusiness patterns
When to Use	Wintel PC platform only PASSPORT/Active Directory already in use	Open platform and interoperability	WebSphere platform with proprietary extension

References

SunTone Architecture Methodology™ can be referred to at Sun Professional Services, *Dot-com and Beyond: Breakthrough Internet-based Architectures and Methodologies*, Prentice Hall, 2001.

J2EE Patterns™ can be referred to at Alur Deepak, John Crupi, and Dan Malks, *Core J2EE Patterns*, Prentice Hall, 2001.

3.3.7   Benefits

Web Services technology enables easier interoperability between systems to aggregate information. It is a technology enabler for consolidating services (for example, UDDI Service Registry) and customer information (such as wealth management/eCRM). It is designed to enable developers to develop and deploy services quicker, compared with traditional technology tools. Besides, business services can be exposed to be easily deployable, reusable, and independent of the underlying platform.

Web Services technology is also an alternative to integrating with legacy systems without rewriting them. It resolves the firewall-unfriendly interoperability of RPC-based applications (for example, tight firewall policies often block RMI and RPC-based internal applications from external Internet access). Use of XML data transformation and message exchanges allows a simpler architecture (for example, consolidating interfaces and services), which may result in lower operating cost.

3.4   Enabling Technology

3.4.1   XML

eXtensible Markup Language (XML) is a tag language, derived from the Standard Generalized Markup Language (SGML) and endorsed by W3C, to describe business data in human-eligible format and is intended to facilitate machine-to-machine or system-to-system communication over the Internet.

The XML data construct can be defined and validated (with XML parsers) by either:

*   XML 1.0 syntax (for example, Document Type Definitions [DTDs])
*   XML Namespaces
*   XML Schemas

Reference

http://www.w3c.org/TR/2000/REC-xml-20001006

Components of an XML Document

Figure 3–9 shows a Foreign Exchange Option trade sold by ABC Buyer Bank with a trade date Jan. 15, 2002. It illustrates the three key components of an XML document (based on FX trading XML standard fpML): Prolog, Body, and Epilog.

```
<?XML version="1.0" " encoding = "UTF-8"?>
<!DOCTYPE trade PUBLIC "-//FpML//DTD 3-0//EN" "" ->
[
 <!- DTD declarations omitted ->
]>
<trade>
  <tradeHeader>
    <partyTradeIdentifier>
      <partyReference href = "#XYZ"/>
    </partyTradeIdentifier>
    <partyTradeIdentifier>
      <partyReference href = "#ABC"/>
    </partyTradeIdentifier>
    <tradeDate>2002-01-15</tradeDate>
  </tradeHeader>
  <fxSimpleOption>
      <productType>Nondeliverable Option</productType>
      <buyerPartyReference href = "#XYZ"/>
      <sellerPartyReference href = "#ABC"/>
      <expiryDateTime>
          <expiryDate>2002-04-09</expiryDate>
          <hourMinuteTime>1000</hourMinuteTime>
          <businessCenter>USNY</businessCenter>
      </expiryDateTime>
      <exerciseStyle>European</exerciseStyle>
  </fxSimpleOption>
  <party id = "XYZ">
      <partyId>CHASUS33</partyId>
      <partyName>XYZ BUYER BANK</partyName>
  </party>
  <party id = "ABCN">
      <partyId>ABCANL2A</partyId>
      <partyName>ABC Seller Bank</partyName>
  </party>
</trade>
<!- end of DTDs ->
```

Figure 3–9   Sample XML Document

Document Type Definitions (DTDs)

DTDs specify rules about the tag names, data structure (for example, string), and permissible elements (for example, repeatable elements). DTDs can be stand-alone or incorporated in an XML document.

DTDs include:

- <!ENTITY>
- <!ELEMENT>
- <!ATTLIST>

DTDs came from SGML and the text/documentation-processing scenario. Today, XML applications have expanded into business applications, and DTDs are fairly limited in providing a data-typing mechanism. For example, DTDs cannot tell us if the data type is an integer or a range of values. This data-typing requirement is particularly important in data validation for business transactions. Hence, W3C has come up with a newer standard to address these issues in "XML Schema" (refer to the next section).

When to Use

It is recommended to exchange DTDs with trading partners before exchanging XML documents (if the DTDs are relatively static). Besides, developers are recommended to include DTDs to validate the syntax of the XML document, particularly when there are different versions.

Outlook

DTDs are not easily readable. XML Schema is widely used in XML Web Services due to its flexibility. W3C declares that XML Schema will be used in lieu of DTDs.

Example—DTD

```
<!ELEMENT partyTradeIdentifier (partyReference)>
<!ELEMENT partyReference EMPTY>
<!ATTLIST partyReference
    href CDATA #REQUIRED
>
```

XML Namespace

The XML Namespace is a collection/group of names—aka prefix added to XML element to differentiate elements with the same name (such as name, customer:name, or buyer:name). Using a unique element, this addresses conflicting names while exchanging XML documents with partners. It is identified by a URI reference, qualified names/elements, and attribute names within an XML document (such as buyer:tradeHeader).

The syntax is:

xmlns:<Namespace prefix>=<URI>

What Is Not an XML Namespace

- Network namespace (or programming-level namespace)
- Directly related to XML Schema

Example—XML Namespace

```
<trade xmlns:buyer="urn:fpML:www.nextfrontiers.com/fxOptions">
   <buyer:tradeHeader>
      <buyer:partyTradeIdentifier />
         ...
   </buyer:tradeHeader>
</trade>
```

XML Schema

An XML Schema is a more general and flexible way to describe the data structure of an XML document (for example, data type or attributes). Although not required, SOAP uses XML Schema instead of DTD to represent data in the SOAP requests and responses. SOAP can use XML Schema to serialize/deserialize data from parameters to method calls and returned values.

The syntax is as follows:

```
Element
<xsd:element name="xxx" />
Simple Types
<simpleElement attribute1="name" attribute2="address" />
Complex Types
<xsd:complexType name = "Address">
   <xsd:sequence>
     <xsd:element name="address1">
     <xsd:element names="city">
   </xsd:sequence>
</xsd:complexType>
Attribute Declaration
<attribute name = "USA"  use="required" />
```

Example—XML Schema

```
<?xml version = "1.0" encoding = "UTF-8" ?>
<!-- This XML schema definition conforms to W3C
http://www.w3.org/2001/XMLSchema -->
```

```
<xsd:schema xmlns:xsd = "http://www.w3.org/2001/XMLSchema"
            targetNamespace = ""
            xmlns:tc = "" >
   <xsd:annotation>
      <xsd:documentation>
         This schema example illustrates a FX option.
         XYZ bought a FX option from ABC dated Jan 15 2002.
      </xsd:documentation>
   </xsd:annotation>

   <xsd:element name = "trade">
      <xsd:complexType>
         <xsd:sequence>
            <xsd:element ref = "tradeHeader"
                         minOccurs = "0" maxOccurs =
                         "unbounded" />
            <xsd:element ref = "fxSimpleOption"
                         minOccurs = "1" maxOccurs = "1" />
            <xsd:element ref = "party"
                         minOccurs = "2" maxOccurs =
                         "unbounded" />
         </xsd:sequence>
      </xsd:complexType>
   </xsd:element>

   <xsd:element name = "tradeHeader">
     <xsd:complexType>
         <xsd:sequence>
            <xsd:element ref = "partyTradeIdentifier"
                         minOccurs = "0" maxOccurs =
                         "unbounded" />
            <xsd:element ref = "tradeDate"
                         type = "xsd:date" />
         </xsd:sequence>
      </xsd:complexType>
   </xsd:element>

   <xsd:element name = "partyTradeIdentifier">
     <xsd:complexType>
         <xsd:sequence>
            <xsd:element ref = "partyReference"
                         minOccurs = "1" maxOccurs =
                         "unbounded" />
         </xsd:sequence>
```

```
        </xsd:complexType>
</xsd:element>

<xsd:element name = "partyReference">
  <xsd:complexType>
    <xsd:attribute name = "href" type = "xsd:string" />
  </xsd:complexType>
</xsd:element>

<xsd:element name = "fxSimpleOption">
  <xsd:complexType>
     <xsd:sequence>
        <xsd:element ref = "productType"
                     minOccurs = "1" maxOccurs =
                     "unbounded" />
        <xsd:element ref = "buyerPartyReference"
                     minOccurs = "0" maxOccurs = "1" />
        <xsd:element ref = "sellerPartyReference"
                     minOccurs = "0" maxOccurs = "1" />
        <xsd:element ref = "expiryDateTime"
                     minOccurs = "1" maxOccurs = "1" />
        <xsd:element ref = "exerciseStyle"
                     minOccurs = "1" maxOccurs = "1" />
     </xsd:sequence>
   </xsd:complexType>
</xsd:element>

<xsd:element name = "expiryDateTime">
  <xsd:complexType>
     <xsd:sequence>
        <xsd:element ref = "expiryDate"
                     minOccurs = "1" maxOccurs = "1"
                     type ="xsd:date" />
        <xsd:element ref = "hourMinuteTime"
                     minOccurs = "1" maxOccurs = "1"
                     type = "xsd:int" />
        <xsd:element ref = "businessCenter"
                     minOccurs = "0" maxOccurs = "1"
                     type ="xsd:string" />
     </xsd:sequence>
   </xsd:complexType>
</xsd:element>
```

```
<xsd:element name = "party">
   <xsd:complexType>
      <xsd:attribute name = "id" type = "xsd:string" />
      <xsd:sequence>
         <xsd:element ref = "partyID"
                          minOccurs = "1" maxOccurs = "1"
                          type ="xsd:string" />
         <xsd:element ref = "partyName"
                          minOccurs = "1" maxOccurs = "1"
                          type = "xsd:string" />
      </xsd:sequence>
   </xsd:complexType>
</xsd:element>

</xsd:schema>
```

XML Parsers

XML documents are usually validated by XML parsers for their well-formedness. There are three major types of parsers:

- Document Object Model
- Simple API for XML
- JDOM

When to Use XML Parsers

DOM (Document Object Model). Frequently retrieves an XML node from the DOM in memory throughout the session

SAX (Simple APIs for XML). One-off retrieval or parsing of the XML data structure

JDOM (Java for Document Object Model). Requires lightweight but high performance and speed for parsing XML (note: JDOM relies on a SAX/DOM parser)

Some XML Parser Implementations

Apache Xerces. Mainly contributed by IBM; claims the best performance

Apache Crimon. Donated by Sun; now incorporated in JWSDP

MSXML. Microsoft-specific XML parser

What XML Can Do

- **Lightweight Parser**–More efficient than EDI translator
- **All-purpose Data Representation**–Decoupling presentation and business logic; easy for multichannel support (for example, XSL, Cocoon)
- **Platform-Neutral Interface**–Self-described data good for system-to-system interfaces, especially when used as a JCA adapter
- **Easy to Integrate and Implement**–Flexibility to extend and to scale up

What XML Is Not Good At

- **Memory Overhead**–If DOM tree is heavily used
- **Parsing between Proprietary Formats (Without XML)**–Memory and I/O overhead
- **Bulky Binary Data**–Such as image or voice (note: denoted by <![CDATA[...]]>)
- **Data Encryption**–CPU-bound
- **Storing and Retrieving XML Data in Uncompressed Format in a RDBMS**–Overhead in XML Extender-like technology

3.4.2   Java™ and Java API

Why Java™?

Java™ is platform independent. It has a "sandbox" architecture that has inherent application security. Besides, it is easier to write. On the enterprise level, Java 2 Enterprise Edition™ (J2EE™) is the building block for components and integration points.

Both Java and .NET have similar programming strengths. Java™ is more popular with cross-platform deployment consideration, yet .NET is also now available on Linux.

What Is JAX Pack?

The Java™ XML Pack (JAX Pack) is an all-in-one download of Java technologies for XML. Java™ XML Pack brings together several of the key industry standards for XML—such as SAX, DOM, XSLT, SOAP, UDDI, ebXML, and WSDL—into one convenient download, thereby giving developers the technologies needed to get started with Web applications and services.

JAX Pack is a bag of Java-based APIs for developing and managing XML, SOAP, and UDDI:

- **JAXP**—Java API for Parsers
- **JAXM**—Java API for Messaging

- **JAXB**—Java API for Binding
- **JAXR**—Java API for Registries
- **JAX-RPC**—Java API for RPC

JAX Pack (*http://java.sun.com/xml/downloads/javaxmlpack.html*) is a reference implementation for JAX, and is now part of Sun's Java Web Services Developer Pack (*http://java.sun.com/webservices/webservicespack.html*).

JAXP

JAXP (*http://java.sun.com/xml/jaxp/index.html*) is a lightweight Java API library for parsing and transforming XML documents. It is a high-level wrapper for different parsers; it can use Xerces or Crimson as the underlying parser. It allows parsing of an XML document using:

- Event-driven (SAX 2.0)
- Tree-based (DOM Level 2)
- XML documents transformation
- XML to XML/other data format using XSL/XSLT
- Rendering to PDF or graphics using Cocoon

Figure 3–10 depicts the components of JAXP. JAXP provides an interface layer to XML parsers. The reference parser is Apache Crimon, but developers can use other parsers such as Apache Xerces. The reference parser supports both event-driven (SAX) and tree-based XML parsing (DOM).

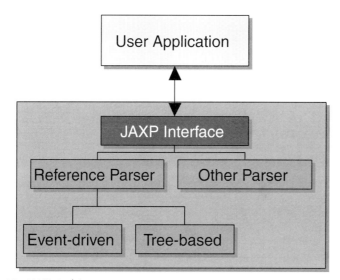

Figure 3–10 JAXP Architecture

SAX

SAX performs well-formedness validation of XML documents. It can be used for reading specific elements. SAX is based on a specific event and enables sequential read access only (that is, one-time access).

The strength of SAX is that documents do not have to be entirely in memory, thus it is fast and efficient. However, it cannot modify elements of the XML document.

Figure 3–11 depicts the SAX parser architecture. To parse an XML document, developers simply define a Java class that extends the DefaultHandler, which will create a new instance of SAXParserFactory. The SAXParserFactory provides handlers such as startElement, endElement, and characters to process different events during the parsing.

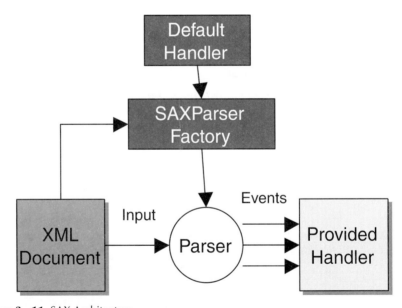

Figure 3–11 SAX Architecture

Example—SAX Parser

```
import java.io.*;
import org.xml.sax.*;
import org.xml.sax.helpers.DefaultHandler;

import javax.xml.parsers.SAXParserFactory;
import javax.xml.parsers.ParserConfigurationException;
import javax.xml.parsers.SAXParser;
```

```java
public class saxParse extends DefaultHandler
{
    public static void main(String argv[])
    {
        if (argv.length != 1) {
            System.err.println("Usage: saxParse xml-
            file");
            System.exit(1);
        }
// create new instance of SAXParserFactory
        DefaultHandler handler = new saxParse();
        SAXParserFactory factory =
        SAXParserFactory.newInstance();
        try {
            out = new OutputStreamWriter(System.out,
            "UTF8");
// call SAX Parser
            SAXParser saxParser = factory.newSAXParser();
            saxParser.parse( new File(argv[0]), handler);

        } catch (Throwable err) {
            err.printStackTrace();
        }
        System.exit(0);
    }
static private Writer out;

    public void startDocument()
       throws SAXException
    {
        display("<?xml version='1.0' encoding='UTF-8'?>");
        nl();
    }

    public void endDocument()
       throws SAXException
    {
        try {
            nl();
            out.flush();
        } catch (IOException ioExceptions) {
            throw new SAXException("I/O error",
ioExceptions);
        }
    }
```

```java
public void startElement(String namespaceURI,
                             String elementName,
                             String qualifiedName,
                             Attributes attributes)
    throws SAXException
    {
        String anyName = elementName;
        if ("".equals(anyName)) anyName = qualifiedName;
        display("<" + anyName);
        if (attributes != null) {
            for (int i = 0; i < attributes.getLength();
            i++) {
                String aName = attributes.getLocalName(i);
                if ("".equals(aName)) aName =
                attributes.getQName(i);
                display(" ");
                display(aName + "=\"" +
                attributes.getValue(i) + "\"");
            }
        }
        display(">");
    }

    public void endElement(String namespaceURI,
                             String simpleName,
                             String qualifiedName
                             )
    throws SAXException
    {
        display("</" + simpleName + ">");
    }
public void characters(char buffer[], int offset, int len)
        throws SAXException
    {
        String something = new String(buffer, offset, len);
        display(something);
    }

    private void display(String something)
        throws SAXException
    {
        try {
            out.write(something);
            out.flush();
        } catch (IOException err) {
```

```
              throw new SAXException("I/O error", err);
        }
    }

    private void nl()
        throws SAXException
    {
        String endOfLine =
System.getProperty("line.separator");
        try {
            out.write(endOfLine);
        } catch (IOException err) {
            throw new SAXException("I/O error", err);
        }
    }
}
```

DOM

The Document Object Model (DOM) is an API for processing XML documents. It defines the logical structure of documents and a way to access and manipulate it.

The strengths of DOM are that DOM can build documents, navigate their structure while in memory, and DOM can add, modify, or delete elements or content of the XML document. However, the in-memory processing is resource-hungry.

Figure 3–12 depicts the DOM architecture. To parse an XML document, developers need to define a Java class to create an instance of DocumentBuilderFactory, which will create a new object DocumentBuilder. The DocumentBuilder will then create nodes (objects in the DOM) for different XML elements and tags.

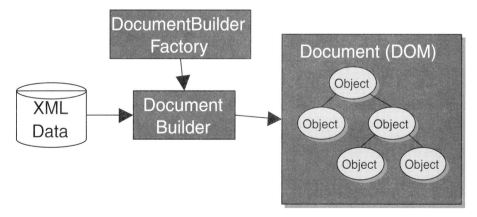

Figure 3–12   DOM Architecture

Example—DOM Parser

```
import javax.xml.parsers.DocumentBuilder;
import javax.xml.parsers.DocumentBuilderFactory;
import javax.xml.parsers.FactoryConfigurationError;
import javax.xml.parsers.ParserConfigurationException;

import org.xml.sax.SAXException;
import org.xml.sax.SAXParseException;

import org.w3c.dom.Document;
import org.w3c.dom.DOMException;

public class DomParse{
    static Document doc;

    public static void main(String argv[])
    {
// Command syntax
        if (argv.length != 1) {
            System.err.println("Usage: java DomParse xml-
            file");
            System.exit(1);
        }

import java.io.*;
// Create new instance, and call DOM to parse
        DocumentBuilderFactory factory =
            DocumentBuilderFactory.newInstance();

        try {
            DocumentBuilder builder =
factory.newDocumentBuilder();
            doc = builder.parse( new File(argv[0]) );
 // Standard exceptions handling
        } catch (SAXException saxException) {
            Exception  somethingWrong = saxException;
            if (saxException.getException() != null)
                somethingWrong =
saxException.getException();
            somethingWrong.printStackTrace();

        } catch (ParserConfigurationException parserError)
        {
```

```
            parserError.printStackTrace();

        } catch (IOException ioExceptions) {
            ioExceptions.printStackTrace();
        }
    }
}
```

JAXM

JAXM *(http://java.sun.com/xml/jaxm/index.html)* refers to the Java technology support for sending and receiving SOAP messages, which is based on the SOAP 1.1 and the SOAP with Attachment specifications. It supports higher level and application-specific protocols built on top of SOAP, including multiple transports such as HTTP, SMTP, and so forth. Besides, it supports both synchronous (request–reply) and asynchronous (one-way) mode. JAXM is preferable to JAX-RPC because of its support for asynchronous messaging, multiparty message routing, and reliable messaging (that is, guaranteed delivery).

Figure 3–13 depicts the JAXM architecture. JAXM is a pluggable provider class for the SOAP server. The provider class supports different data transports, such as HTTP, SMTP, and JMS. If Company X sends a SOAP message using a SOAP provider over HTTP to Company Y, the JAXM provider will create a connection to the specified URL end-point with Company A's SOAP provider, create a SOAP message instance, and get the SOAP envelope and body. With JAXM, developers can make SOAP messaging reliable with message acknowledgement and guaranteed message delivery using JMS.

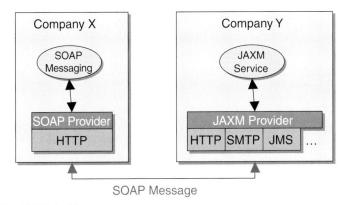

SOAP Message

Figure 3–13   JAXM Architecture

Example—Sending an FX Option Message Via JAXM

```java
import java.io.*;

import javax.xml.soap.*;
import javax.xml.messaging.*;
import java.net.URL;

import javax.mail.internet.*;

import javax.xml.transform.*;
import javax.xml.transform.stream.*;

import org.dom4j.*;

public class fxPost {

    static final String SIMPLE_SAMPLE_URI =
"http://localhost:8080/jaxm-simple/receiver" ;

    public static void main(String args[]) {

        try {
            URLEndpoint endpoint = null;
//          if( args.length > 0 )
//              endpoint=new URLEndpoint( args[0] );
//          else
//              endpoint=new
URLEndpoint(SIMPLE_SAMPLE_URI);
            endpoint = new
URLEndpoint(SIMPLE_SAMPLE_URI);

        SOAPConnectionFactory miniMe =
SOAPConnectionFactory.newInstance();
            SOAPConnection hookUp = miniMe.create
Connection();

            MessageFactory potatoJack = MessageFactory.
newInstance();

            SOAPMessage hotPotato = potatoJack.create
Message();
```

```
            SOAPPart soapPart=hotPotato.getSOAPPart();
            SOAPEnvelope envelope = soapPart.get
Envelope();

            if( args.length > 1 ) {
                StreamSource hotStream = new StreamSource(
                new FileInputStream(
            args[1] ));
                soapPart.setContent( hotStream );
            } else {
                // create fxOption message here
                SOAPBody body = envelope.getBody();

                Name bodyName =
                envelope.createName("trade" , "fx",
"http://www.nextfrontiers.com/fxOption/");
                SOAPBodyElement trade =
body.addBodyElement(bodyName);
                // create tradeHeader
                Name childName =
envelope.createName("tradeHeader");
                SOAPElement tradeHeader =
trade.addChildElement(childName);

                childName = envelope.
createName("partyTradeIdentifier");
                SOAPElement partyTradeIdentifier =
tradeHeader.addChildElement(childName);

                childName = envelope.
createName("partyReference");
                SOAPElement partyReference =
partyTradeIdentifier.addChildElement(childName);
                childName = envelope.createName("href");
                partyReference.addAttribute(childName,
"#XYZ");

                Name childName2 = envelope.
createName("partyTradeIdentifier");
                SOAPElement partyTradeIdentifier2 =
tradeHeader.addChildElement(childName2);
```

```
                   childName2 = envelope. createName
("partyReference");
                   SOAPElement partyReference2 =
partyTradeIdentifier2.addChildElement(childName2);
                   childName2 = envelope.createName("href");
                   partyReference2.addAttribute(childName2,
"#ABC");

                   // create fxSimpleOption
                   Name childName3 = envelope.
createName("fxSimpleOption");
                   SOAPElement fxSimpleOption =
trade.addChildElement(childName3);

                   childName3 =
envelope.createName("productType");
                   SOAPElement productType =
fxSimpleOption.addChildElement(childName3);
                   productType.addTextNode("Nondeliveable
options");

                   childName3 = envelope.
createName("buyerPartyReference");
                   SOAPElement buyerPartyReference =
fxSimpleOption.addChildElement(childName3);
                   childName3 = envelope.createName("href");
                   buyerPartyReference.addAttribute(childName3,
"#XYZ");

                   childName3 = envelope.
createName("sellerPartyReference");
                   SOAPElement sellerPartyReference =
fxSimpleOption.addChildElement(childName3);
                   childName3 = envelope.createName("href");
                   sellerPartyReference.
addAttribute(childName3, "#ABC");

                   childName3 = envelope.
createName("expiryDateTime");
                   SOAPElement expiryDateTime =
fxSimpleOption.addChildElement(childName3);
                   childName3 = envelope.
createName("expiryDate");
```

```
                SOAPElement expiryDate = expiryDateTime.
addChildElement(childName3);
                expiryDate.addTextNode("2002-04-09");
                childName3 = envelope.
createName("hourMinuteTime");
                SOAPElement hourMinuteTime =
expiryDateTime.addChildElement(childName3);
                hourMinuteTime.addTextNode("1000");
                childName3 = envelope.
createName("businessCenter");
                SOAPElement businessCenter =
expiryDateTime.addChildElement(childName3);
                businessCenter.addTextNode("USNY");

                childName3 = envelope.
createName("exerciseStyle");
                SOAPElement exerciseStyle =
fxSimpleOption.addChildElement(childName3);
                exerciseStyle.addTextNode("European");

                // create party information
                Name childName4 = envelope.
createName("party");
                SOAPElement party =
trade.addChildElement(childName4);
                childName4 = envelope.createName("id");
                party.addAttribute(childName4, "XYZ");

                childName4 = envelope.
createName("partyId");
                SOAPElement partyId = party.
addChildElement(childName4);
                partyId.addTextNode("CHASUS33");

                childName4 = envelope.
createName("partyName");
                SOAPElement partyName = party.
addChildElement(childName4);
                partyName.addTextNode("XYZ BUYER BANK");

                Name childName5 = envelope.
createName("party");
                SOAPElement party2 = trade.
addChildElement(childName5);
```

```
            childName5 = envelope.createName("id");
            party2.addAttribute(childName5, "ABCN");

            childName5 = envelope.
createName("partyId");
            SOAPElement partyId2 = party2.
addChildElement(childName5);
            partyId2.addTextNode("ABCANL2A");

            childName5 = envelope.
createName("partyName");
            SOAPElement partyName2 = party2.
addChildElement(childName5);
            partyName2.addTextNode("ABC Seller Bank");

        }

        hotPotato.saveChanges();


        System.err.println("Sending message to URL: "+
endpoint.getURL());

        SOAPMessage reply = hookUp.call(hotPotato,
endpoint);

        System.err.println("Sent message is logged in
\"logfile.txt\"");

        FileOutputStream logFile = new
FileOutputStream("logfile.txt");
        hotPotato.writeTo(logFile);
        logFile.close();

        System.out.println("Received reply from:
"+endpoint);

        // Display reply message
        boolean displayResult=true;
        if( displayResult ) {
            // Document source, do a transform.
            System.out.println("Result:");
            TransformerFactory
tFact=TransformerFactory.newInstance();
```

```
            Transformer transformer =
tFact.newTransformer();
            Source src=reply.getSOAPPart().getContent();
            StreamResult result=new StreamResult(
System.out );
            transformer.transform(src, result);
            System.out.println();
        }

        hookUp.close();

    } catch(Throwable e) {
        e.printStackTrace();
    }
    }
}
```

Remarks

Due to some changes in the Java Specification Request 067, SOAP messaging is now supported by both SAAJ (SOAP with Attachments APIs for Java) and JAXM. The package javax.xml.soap was removed from JAXM to become SAAJ.

Currently, JAXM APIs do not implement the full functionality of the ebXML Message Service. However, current JAXM reference implementations provide an additional class EbXMLMessageImpl to support ebXML Message Service. There are several vendor products such as Sun, TIBCO, and Sybase that are ebXML Message Service-compliant (refer to the vendor list at *http://www.ebusinessready.org/ebxmlms_3Q02UCCFinalReport.pdf*).

JAXB

JAXB *(http://java.sun.com/xml/jaxb/index.html)* denotes Java Architecture for XML Binding. JAXB creates an XML-to-Java binding schema (XJS), which maps XML elements to Java objects, and stores it in XJS files (.xjs extension). You can compile them with a schema compiler called xjc and output the source code to a set of Java classes for marshalling and unmarshalling.

What is an XML-to-Schema Compiler (xjc)? It is a Unix shell script that invokes com.sun.tools.xjc.Main, which reads in a DTD and a XJS binding schema, and generates a set of Java source files. An XJS binding schema file defines the mapping, for example:

```
<?xml version="1.0" encoding="ISO-8859-1" ?>
<xml-java-binding-schema version="1.0-ea">
  <element name="tradeDate" type="class" root="true"/>
```

```
  . . .
</xml-java-binding-schema>
```

Figure 3–14 depicts the JAXB architecture. The utility xjc creates Java source files to bind a DTD or XML Schema to Java data objects. Developers can then add additional program code if necessary and compile the Java source files into Java classes for execution. This can potentially reduce some coding effort and processing time to transcode XML elements in an XML document using JAXP.

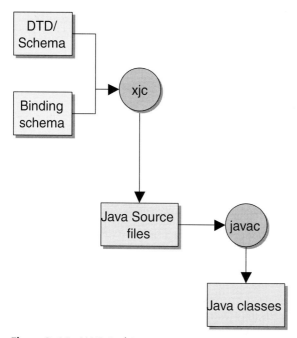

Figure 3–14 JAXB Architecture

Example—Sample Screen Output for xjc Compiler

Assuming there are a DTD "checkbook.dtd" and an XJS "checkbook.xjs" and all relevant jar files are placed under D:\Dev\WSPack\Common\Lib, executing the xjc compiler (com.sun.tools.xjc.Main) will render several Java source files in the following output (Figure 3–15):

```
D:\Dev\Test\xjc>xjc checkbook.dtd checkbook.xjs

D:\Dev\Test\xjc>java -classpath
d:\dev\wspack\common\lib\jaxb-xjc-1.0-
ea.jar;d:\dev\wspack\common\lib\jaxb-rt-1.0-ea.jar
com.sun.tools.xjc.Main checkbook.dtd checkbook.xjs
.\Check.java
.\CheckCategory.java
.\Checkbook.java
.\Cleared.java
.\DepCategory.java
.\Deposit.java
.\Entry.java
.\Pending.java
.\Transactions.java
.\Void.java
.\Withdrawal.java
```

Figure 3–15   Sample xjc Output

JAXB version 1.0 now supports both DTD and XML Schema. Developers can use the same xjc compiler to generate Java binding files for an XML Schema by using "-p <output package file name>" as a parameter, such as "`xjc checkbook.xsd -p checkbook.xjs`" under Windows or "`$JAXB_HOME/bin/xjc.sh checkbook.xsd -p checkbook.xjs`" under Unix. Please refer to the user documentation (*http://java.sun.com/ xml/jaxb/users-guide/jaxb-using.html#about_manual*).

Prior to version 1.0, early access versions of JAXB could only support DTD. Using JAXB to bind an XML Schema to the Java data structure, developers can probably write less program code using an XML parser (such as DOM or SAX) to transform XML content into Java data objects. This is a considerable benefit to the productivity.

JAXR

JAXR (*http://java.sun.com/xml/jaxr/index.html*) is a standard Java API for accessing diverse and heterogeneous Business Service Registries. It is a unified information model for describing business registry content. It provides multi-layered

API abstractions for simple, high-level, business API, and flexible, low-level, generic API. It is the enabling technology for Web Services and peer-to-peer computing in the J2EE™.

Figure 3–16 depicts the JAXR architecture. A JAXR client is basically a registry client (RC) that is connected to the registry service (RS) via a JAXR pluggable provider. The JAXR provider is able to use any capability-specific interfaces such as ebXML provider or UDDI provider that is specific to a particular Service Registry platform. Developers can also write their own JAXR provider class to accommodate any new Service Registry platform. In this way, the JAXR client only needs to use one single set of program code to access different service registries; it need not be rewritten and recompiled.

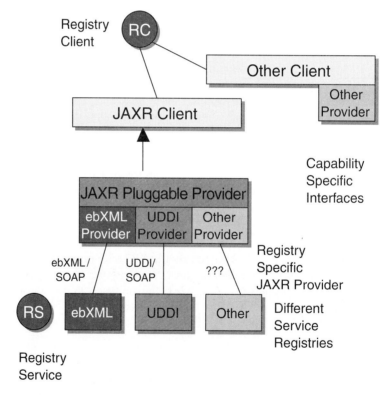

Figure 3–16 JAXR Architecture

JAX-RPC

JAX-RPC (*http://java.sun.com/xml/jaxrpc/index.html*) stands for Java API for XML-based Remote Procedure Calls (RPC). It enables Java technology developers to build Web applications and Web Services incorporating XML-based RPC functionality according to the SOAP 1.1 specification. JAX-RPC allows distributed client/server mode over the Web using the Standard Web Services technologies: SOAP, WSDL, and HTTP. Using the JAX-RPC API and the tools, it simplifies the creation of a Web Service for a Java programmer as it hides all the complexities of generating SOAP and WSDL, but provides tools to generate these using Java Interfaces and some additional configuration information.

All the code to map Java data type information to XML/SOAP is generated by the tools "wscompile" and "wsdeploy" from Java Web Services Developer Pack (JWSDP) 1.0.1 (which supersedes the tool "xrpcc" in JWSDP 1.0). The JAX-RPC runtime will take care of the transport. This is one of the key technologies in Web Services and will be incorporated into J2EE 1.4 and EJB 2.1.

Server-Side Operations

- Define service definition interfaces and implementation classes (for example, WSDL)
- Compile and generate configuration files
- Create stubs and ties
- Create deployment descriptor
- Package the service definition
- Deploy the service definition

Client-Side Operations

- Define the client codes
- Compile and generate client codes
- Invoke the client

Figure 3–17 depicts the JAX-RPC architecture. In order to invoke a remote business service, the client program needs to install a "stub," which enables it to communicate with the remote application service via the remote "ties." Both the client and the remote server (services) need to install JAX-RPC runtime, which enables both ends to exchange SOAP messages. This is a typical Remote Procedure Call model.

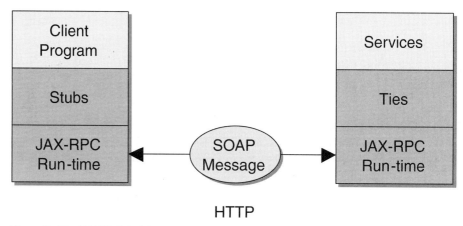

Figure 3–17   JAX-RPC Architecture

3.4.3   UDDI

Universal Description, Discovery, and Integration (UDDI) usually denotes a Service Registry like a business Yellow Page for an e-business service. It also denotes a standard specification for service discovery and description. There are at least three public operator nodes: Microsoft, IBM, and Ariba (said to be taken over by HP). SAP now provides a public UDDI node as well.

The business challenges for implementing UDDI come from several areas:

- Broader B2B (for example, a mid-size firm wants to establish an electronic trading relationship with 400 suppliers)
- Smarter search (for example, how to connect to hundreds of marketplaces in the world)
- Easier aggregation (for example, how to reuse trade data by integrating the entire supply chain seamlessly from sourcing and order management to order fulfillment)

Figure 3–18 depicts different roles and operations of the UDDI Service Registry.

Service Requester
- FINDS required services via the Service Broker
- BINDS to services via Service Provider

Service Registry
- Provides support for publishing and locating services
- Similar to the telephone Yellow Pages

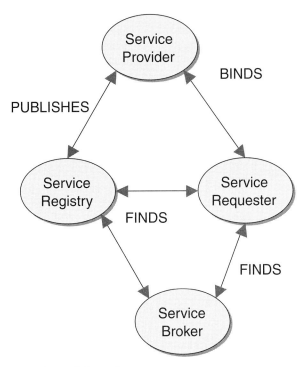

Figure 3–18 UDDI Roles and Operations

Service Provider
- Provides business services
- PUBLISHES availability of these services through a Service Registry

The UDDI registry enables businesses/corporations to register public information about themselves (such as service type, products, URL) and provides service categories or classifications using standards code such as NAICS (North American Industry Classification System, a product code classification system for trading used by the U.S. Census Bureau) and UN/SPSC (United Nation Standard Products and Services Classification, a product classification system developed by Dun & Bradstreet).

There are mainly three types of information: (1) White Pages—business names, description, contact information; (2) Yellow Pages—business categories using standard codes such as NAICS, UN/SPSC, and geographical taxonomy; and (3) Green Pages—information model to store implementation information of business processes, service descriptions, and binding information. The UDDI information model is a data model that encapsulates the business information of business organizations and service details. Figure 3–19 depicts how these pages are mapped to the UDDI information model.

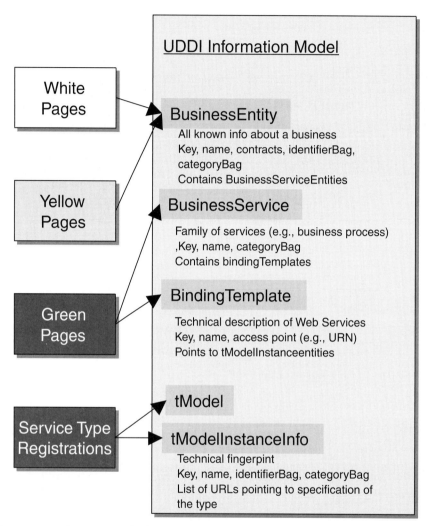

Figure 3–19 Three Types of Information in UDDI

Figure 3–20 further describes the relationship between UDDI entities and the WSDL document. In UDDI, a business entity contains the definition of business services (White Pages), and each business service contains a binding template (Yellow Pages) that shows the service end-points URL. The information in the binding template is also stored in the UDDI information model tModel and tModelInstance objects, which are accessed during the service discovery process.

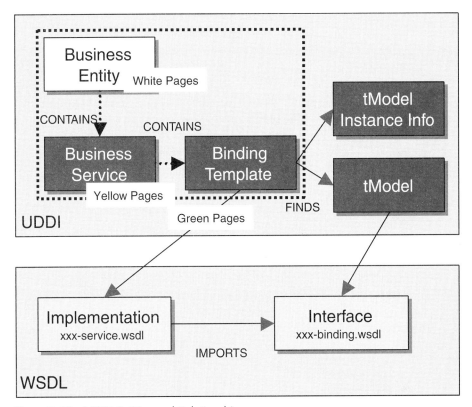

Figure 3–20   UDDI Entities and Relationship

The same information in the binding template is also referenced in the Implementation section of the WSDL document (Green Pages). The Implementation section is also referenced in the Interface section of the WSDL document. If developers want to store the WSDL document in the UDDI Service Registry, they can reference the Interface section in the tModel object.

IBM differentiates six types of UDDI:

- **UDDI operator node**–Publicly available UDDI
- **e-Marketplace UDDI**–For private shopping
- **Portal UDDI**–Portal to a company's services, usually private
- **Partner catalog UDDI**–For B2B exchange; private
- **Internal EAI UDDI**–For enterprise and internal integration
- **Test bed UDDI**–For system/unit testing

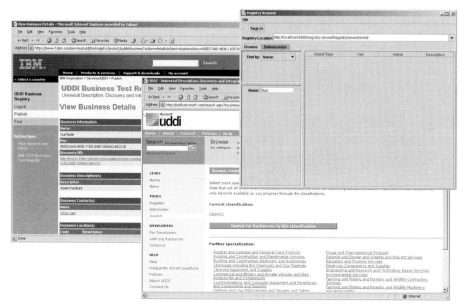

Figure 3–21   Examples of UDDI Implementation

Figure 3–21 shows some examples of UDDI implementation from IBM, Microsoft, and Sun. IBM and Microsoft have a public UDDI registry implementation for public testing. Sun has a free UDDI registry implementation for developer testing.

3.4.4   SOAP

SOAP stands for Simple Object Access Protocol. The original specification has three parts: extensible envelope (headers and body), simple type marshalling schema, and HTTP RPC protocol.

In SOAP 1.2, there are some small changes from SOAP 1.1:

- Does not permit elements after the body
- Different namespaces
- HTTP binding (for example, the SOAPAction header is not required)
- Few syntax changes, but several feature changes

Figures 3–22 and 3–23 depict the SOAP server components and how the client interacts with the server. Figure 3–22 elaborates on Figure 3–17 by expanding the logical components of the "stub" into the SOAP RPC layer. The SOAP RPC layer acts as a client proxy that initiates SOAP calls, creates SOAP envelope and message body, and exchanges with the SOAP server. The logical components of the "tier" are elaborated as the SOAP server. The SOAP server handles message routing, marshals, and unmarshals the SOAP messages via RPC router servlet and message router servlet (these are transport listeners). All SOAP messages are transported on top of HTTP or HTTPs, and can even be bound to JMS using customized pluggable providers.

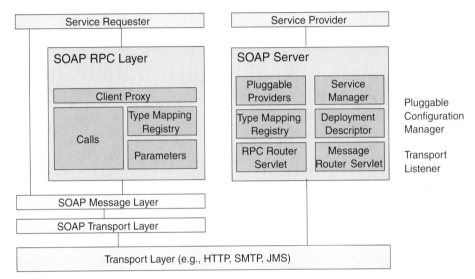

Figure 3–22 SOAP Server Components

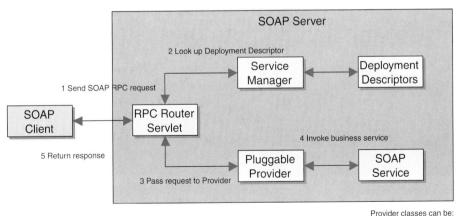

Figure 3–23 SOAP Client–server Interaction

Figure 3–23 describes the process of how a SOAP client communicates with a SOAP server. The SOAP client sends a SOAP RPC request to the RPC router servlet. The RPC router servlet looks up the Deployment Descriptor from the service manager. Upon successful retrieval, the RPC router servlet locates the configuration details and passes the request to appropriate pluggable provider. For instance, the pluggable provider is an EJB provider, and it invokes the remote business service via RMI/IIOP protocol.

3.4.5   WSDL

Web Services Description Language (WSDL) V1.1 uses XML to describe Web Services by:

- End-points operating on SOAP messages
- SOAP messages containing either document-oriented (for example, XML doc) or procedure-oriented (for example, XML-RPC) information
- Operations and messages
- Bindings of network protocol and message format to end-points

It also defines network accessible services functionality, such as protocol and deployment details. It is submitted to W3 as a basis for XMLP Web Service metadata definition (*http://www.w3.org/TR/wsdl.*).

Figure 3–24 shows the elements of a WSDL document. The service (service endpoint URL), operation name (the remote business service), message name (input or output), and the type (data type) are usually of interest to developers, as they are the key information to build a Web Services client.

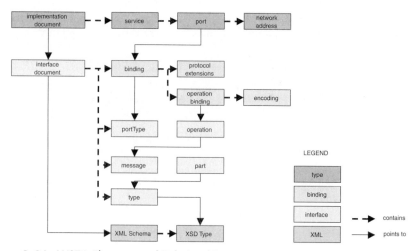

Figure 3–24   WSDL Elements and Relationship

WSDL documents can be stored in the UDDI registry. There is a close relationship between the UDDI information model and the WSDL documents. SOAP clients look up the UDDI registry for a specific business service and find the service key and the associated service end-points from the WSDL or the tModel. Then they can invoke the business service remotely. Figure 3–25 depicts the relationship between the WSDL document and the UDDI's tModel. In a WSDL document, the service name is mapped to the BusinessService attribute of a tModel, the port name to the BindingTemplate, and the service interface section to the tModel and tModelInstanceInfo attributes.

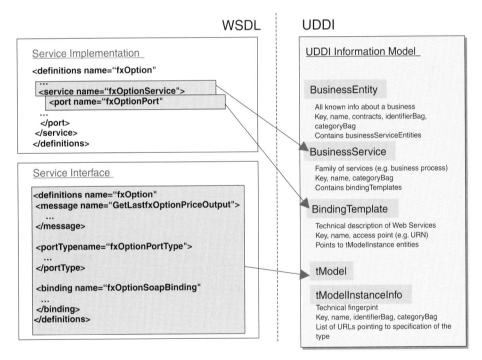

Figure 3–25 WSDL and UDDI Relationship

Example—WSDL for FX Option

```
<definitions name="fxOption"

targetNamespace="http://nextfrontiers.com/fxOption.wsdl"

xmlns:tns="http://nextfrontiers.com/fxOption.wsdl"

xmlns:xsd1="http://nextfrontiers.com/fxOption.xsd"
```

```
            xmlns:soap="http://schemas.xmlsoap.
org/wsdl/soap/"
            xmlns="http://schemas.xmlsoap.org/wsdl/"
>

   <types>
       <schema targetNamespace="http://
nextfrontiers.com/fxOption.xsd "
             xmlns="http://www.w3.org/1999/XMLSchema">
          <element name="fxOptionPriceRequest">
             <complexType>
                <all>
                   <element name="tickerSymbol"
type="string"/>
                </all>
             </complexType>
          </element>
          <element name="fxOptionPrice">
             <complexType>
                <all>
                   <element name="price" type="float"/>
                </all>
             </complexType>
          </element>
       </schema>
   </types>

<message name="GetLastfxOptionPriceInput">
       <part name="body" element="xsd1:fxOptionPrice"/>
</message>

<message name="GetLastfxOptionPriceOutput">
       <part name="body"
element="xsd1:fxOptionPriceResult"/>
</message>

<portType name="fxOptionPortType">
       <operation name="GetLastfxOptionPrice">
          <input
message="tns:GetLastfxOptionPriceInput"/>
          <output
message="tns:GetLastfxOptionPriceOutput"/>
       </operation>
</portType>
```

```
<binding name="fxOptionSoapBinding"
type="tns:fxOptionPortType">
        <soap:binding style="document"

transport="http://schemas.xmlsoap.org/soap/http"/>
        <operation name="GetLastfxOptionPrice">
           <soap:operation
soapAction="http://nextfrontiers.com/GetLastfxOptionPrice"
/>
           <input>
               <soap:body use="literal"
namespace="http://nextfrontiers.com/fxOption.xsd"

encodingStyle="http://schemas.xmlsoap.org/soap/encoding/"/
>
           </input>
           <output>
               <soap:body use="literal"
namespace="http://nextfrontiers.com/fxOption.xsd"

encodingStyle="http://schemas.xmlsoap.org/soap/encoding/"/
>
           </output>
        </operation>
</binding>

<service name="fxOptionService">
        <documentation>Your low cost online FX option
service</documentation>
        <port name="fxOptionPort"
binding="tns:fxOptionBinding">
           <soap:address
location="http://nextfrontiers.com/fxOption"/>
        </port>
</service>

</definitions>
```

3.4.6   ebXML

Electronic Business XML Markup Language (ebXML) is an international initiative to define a framework for finding, exchanging, developing, and implementing business services. It focuses on B2B and Small Medium Enterprise needs, and is backed up by standards bodies (such as OASIS, UN CE/FACT) and communities (such as the Open Applications Group or OAG *http://www.openapplications.org/downloads/whitepapers/ frameworks.htm*).

Figure 3–26 depicts the architecture components of ebXML. Two business applications want to exchange business documents in a reliable manner. Both ends need to establish a trading partner agreement (using CPP, CPA) prior to document exchange. The sender business application initiates a connection, sends the business documents in ebXML manifest (which is wrapped in a SOAP envelope using SOAP 1.1 with Attachment), and waits for message acknowledgement from the recipient business application. The ebXML architecture also allows business process collaboration using a business process specification shared between the business applications.

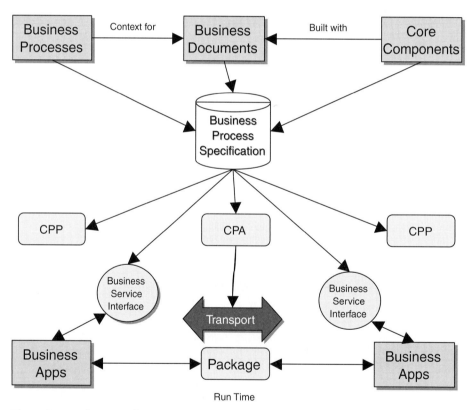

Figure 3–26   ebXML Architecture

Business Processes. Business models are defined in XML. These are now also known as ebXML Business Process. The associated specification includes Business Process Specification Schema.

Business Messages. Business information is exchanged in XML across trading partners and enterprises.

Trading Partner Agreement. Parameters specified for business to exchange data (interfaces). This includes Collaboration Protocol Profiles (CPPs) and Collaboration Protocol Agreement (CPAs). A CPP refers to the trading partner's technical capability to engage in electronic message interchange and collaboration. A CPA refers to the technical agreement between the trading partners in electronic message interchange and collaboration.

Business Service Interface. Implementation of Trading Partner Agreement.

Transport and Routing Layer. The underlying transport layer that delivers the XML messages. This is now known as ebXML Message Service. ebXML has used SOAP 1.1 with Attachments as the data transport and routing layer since March of 2001.

Service Registry/Repository. The "container" for process models, vocabularies, and partner profiles. This is now known as ebXML Service Registry. The associated registry specification includes ebXML Registry Information Model and ebXML Registry Service Specification.

A typical ebXML message makes use of the SOAP messaging as the transport and routing protocol. Figure 3–27 shows the message structure and a sample message. An ebXML message consists of a payload (usually called Manifest), which is wrapped by a SOAP envelope (including a SOAP envelope and SOAP body). ebXML encapsulates the SOAP envelope and the payload under a MIME MIME structure, and thus allows capturing either text or binary objects (such as a picture, or an EDI message) in the payload.

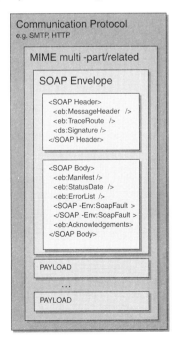

Figure 3–27 ebXML Envelope and Structure

Example—ebXML Message

```
<soap-env:Envelope
   xmlns:soap-
env="http://schemas.xmlsoap.org/soap/envelope/">
<soap-env:Header>

<eb:MessageHeader
xmlns:eb="http://www.ebxml.org/namespaces/messageHeader"
      eb:version="1.0" soap-env:mustUnderstand="1">
   <eb:From>
      <eb:PartyId
eb:type="URI">http://www.nextfrontiers.com/remote/sender
      </eb:PartyId>
   </eb:From>

   <eb:To>
      <eb:PartyId eb:type="URI">http://www.nextfrontiers.
com/remote/sender
      </eb:PartyId>
   </eb:To>

   <eb:CPAId>http://webservices.com/cpas/ourcpa.xml
   </eb:CPAId>

   <eb:ConversationId>20020509-242342-92343
   </eb:ConversationId>

   <eb:Service eb:type="">fxOptionProcessing
   </eb:Service>

   <eb:Action>NewOrder
   </eb:Action>
<eb:MessageId>7ac208cb-a1d4-6a71-9834-afb31c12ca32
      </eb:MessageId>

      <eb:RefToMessageId>20020510-242324-
92343@webservices.com
      </eb:RefToMessageId>

      <eb:Timestamp>1016592644013</eb:Timestamp>
   </eb:MessageData>
```

```
</eb:MessageHeader>

</soap-env:Header>
   <soap-env:Body>
   <eb:Manifest

xmlns:eb="http://www.ebxml.org/namespaces/messageHeader"
        eb:id="manifest" eb:version="1.0">
     <eb:Reference eb:id="bar01"
         xmlns:xlink="http://www.w3.org/1999/xlink"
         xlink:href="cid:bar01"
xlink:role="http://regrep.org/gci/fxoption">
           <eb:Schema
               eb:version="1.0"
eb:location="http://regrep.org/gci/fxoption.xsd"/>
     </eb:Reference>
   </eb:Manifest>
   </soap-env:Body>
</soap-env:Envelope>
```

Implication

ebXML is not an XML message standard like finXML, though XML messaging is used. Unlike SOAP and UDDI, which were designed for B2C, ebXML evolved from standards bodies and is designed for B2B business services. It has unique added values by providing guaranteed message delivery (ebXML Messaging Service), security (for example, ebXML's dependency of digital certificates, encryption, and digital signature to meet different security requirements), business processes (ebXML Business Process), and Quality of Services for transaction processing (for example, ebXML CPP/CPA). This entails areas and applications for which architects may use ebXML Web Services only. *http://www.ebxml.org/implementations/index.htm* shows a list of existing ebXML implementations and case studies.

The adoption of SOAP as the Transport and Routing Protocol (TRP) in March of 2001 marks the beginning of converging some common initiatives in the industry and reducing unnecessary competition between the two technologies. ebXML registry reference implementations are now available. ebXML registry also supports UDDI discovery. SOAP will evolve to cover more business-process and service-negotiation aspects as defined in the ebXML specification (for example, SOAP-JMS binding is one area that addresses the reliability of SOAP messaging across enterprises). The JAX Pack (specifically, JAXM for messaging service and JAXR for accessing Service Registries) has made it possible to implement both SOAP and ebXML Web Services using a single platform and enabling tool, instead of silo technology.

3.4.7   UDDI and ebXML Service Registries

Currently, Service Registry has two variants: UDDI and ebXML. OASIS now supports both variants. UDDI Service Registry (Version 2.0 is in production, and Version 3.0 specification is publicly available) has been on the market for some time. IBM, Microsoft, HP (taking over from Ariba), and SAP manage the public UDDI Service Registry nodes. Although they are intended to be a public Service Registry, most people use them for testing instead. There are also a few open-source implementations of UDDI Service Registries, including UDDI registry from Sun's Java Web Services Developer Pack. Most J2EE™ Application Server vendors also provide UDDI Service Registry.

Another variant is the ebXML Service Registry. This is a standards-based Service Registry. Its functionality is similar to UDDI. In addition, it supports service contracts (that is, CPA, CPP) and work-flow related entities (as per ebXML specifications). There is a reference implementation available at *http://ebxmlrr.sourceforge.net/*.

When to Use

Service Registry can be used in the following context:

Private Service Registry. For B2B transactions, business partners and consumers can be brought together in a closed private community (for example, stored value card, reward card). The private community environment also allows a more secure business environment for member services or credit card transactions. Customers and business partners need to be preregistered in the private community. The private community provides customized member services and benefits, and it can be a tool for increasing enterprise product usage and services.

Internal Service Directory. Service Registry can be implemented for Business-to-Employee use. Employees can look up different internal services, ranging from HR, staff travel, or home-grown applications. These internal services may be legacy mainframe systems or out-tasked services provided by Data Center services.

Developer Resources Directory. Utilities, common APIs, or libraries can be stored in the Service Registry, which functions as a "developer portal." Developer resources can be looked up and retrieved by WSDLs.

Selecting the Appropriate Service Registry

When selecting a specific Service Registry implementation, there are a few differentiators to consider:

Back-end Implementation. Some Service Registry implementations are very proprietary (for example, they require hard-coding or some proprietary design elements) and cannot port to other platforms. However, they are designed to optimize a specific database engine for faster performance. For example, IBM's UDDI Service Registry is designed to optimize database access performance but it cannot be ported to another database platform. There are some merits to implementing the UDDI Service Registry using Directory Server. Because the UDDI information model (tModel) is hierarchical, developers can leverage on Directory Server's replication features for easy master-slave replication and synchronization, as well as reuse the existing security and deployment policies. ebXML Service Registry implementation requires handling complex information models (for example, complex data type, object relationship) and can reside on different database platforms. However, hierarchical LDAP implementation may not be desirable for ebXML implementation.

Search Engine. Service Registry vendors implement the search engine differently with their home-grown search algorithm. Some of them just do an exact match of the service key entries, while others may be able to handle complex keyword search (for example, a partial keyword in one of the tModel elements) with a combination of logical operators (such as AND, OR). We would also recommend a benchmarking exercise to measure the look-up performance.

User Experience. Some Registry Browsers or Service Registry administration front-ends are much easier and intuitive to use. For example, some front-ends may require many data entry screens before administrators can complete a single business service record. This would not be a desirable experience for the user.

Registry Provider. Most Service Registries have different APIs (or servlets) to access their registry contents. If we use Java API for Registries (JAXR), we can use the same Java API with different registry properties (a property file stores the specific registry servlet or URIs).

Comparing the UDDI and ebXML Service Registries

Although these two variants of Service Registry provide similar functionality, there are considerable differences in what they provide. It is important to understand that these two Service Registries are not necessarily exclusive, as they have different value propositions for different business and technical requirements.

Information Model. UDDI focuses on publishing and discovering businesses (for example, NAICS codes), services, and technical specifications (such as WSDL). ebXML focuses on Organization and Registry Objects (such as service description, product catalogs, standards, XML Schema, WSDL documents, movies, and audios).

Relationship Support. A Service Registry allows the grouping of different business organizations under a specific classification taxonomy. In some classification taxonomies, two organizations can be grouped together under the same package or bundle of content, as in a parent–child relationship or holding company group subsidiary relationship. Currently, UDDI supports three classification taxonomies, but not all classification taxonomies support parent–child relationship. UDDI requires a change to the specification in order to add a new relationship. ebXML supports a general-purpose ability to define arbitrary relationships via UML modeling (for example, grouping Registry Object to one or multiple packages).

Classification Support. The UDDI Service Registry supports three classification taxonomies including NAICS, UN/SPSC, and ISO 3166 Geography (such as country codes). ebXML can download external classification taxonomies or create new classification taxonomies.

Query Support. The UDDI Service Registry provides querying the business organization, service name, or tModel by name, identity, and classification category. Boolean predicate or clause support (such as AND, OR) within the queries is not supported. The ebXML Service Registry provides a more sophisticated query capability with a general-purpose filter query and an advanced SQL query mechanism for ad hoc queries.

Registry Security. The UDDI Service Registry supports a user id and a password as credentials. It protects data confidentiality and integrity via HTTPS and local access control policy (depending on the back-end implementation, such as RDBMS). However, it does not support authenticity of contents (for example, it may not really be XXX who submits the contents even though the submitter declares its identity as XXX) or an audit trail. The ebXML Service Registry security is dependent on digital certificates, which address the requirements of authenticity of contents, data confidentiality, and integrity using encryption and a digital signature. An audit trail is implemented using AuditableEvent in the ebXML Service Registry.

Registry Interface. The UDDI Service Registry uses SOAP 1.1 over HTTP and HTTPs to access the registry contents. The ebXML Service Registry supports both ebXML Messaging Service (that is, SOAP 1.1 with Attachment over HTTP) and SOAP/HTTP binding. Now, the JAXR protocol provides a standardized interface to access both the UDDI and ebXML Service Registries.

Distributed Registry Support. The UDDI Service Registry supports a single global (centralized) Service Registry model and the replication capability is dependent on the back-end implementation (such as RDBMS, Directory Server). The ebXML Service Registry 2.0 and 3.0 support a federated registries (distributed) model. Farrukh Najmi has a good technical overview on ebXML Service Registry 3.0 and its federated registry capability at *http://www.oasis-open.org/committees/regrep/presentations/ ebxmlrrOverview/ siframes.html.*

3.4.8   XML Web Services Security

Most Web Services security has focused on SOAP message security. As the data contents in the SOAP message are decoupled from the data transport layer, the transport layer security is often overlooked. End-to-end Web Services security should support Authentication, Entitlement (authority and access control), Data and transaction integrity, Confidentiality, Auditing, and nonrepudiation.

A broader view of the Web Services security covers:

- SOAP message security (for example, DSIG, WS-security)
- Network/data transport security (for example, use of VPN)
- Transactional security (such as data encryption, authentication, and access control [SAML])
- Service Registry security (such as UDDI registry, WSDL in clear text)
- Client-side security (for example, a UDDI browser)
- Core security services and the integration with XML Web Services (for example, XML Key Management Specification [XKMS])

Figure 3–28 illustrates different areas of Web Services security, and they need to be considered during the design and implementation as a complete picture. Most of the security standards today tend to address one specific area, and the challenge of the architect is to put them into the right context. The scope of Web Services security covers message security (for example, WS-Security protects SOAP messages), data transport security (for example, HTTPs and data encryption secure the data transport layer), and platform security (for example, Solaris platform security hardening and intrusion detection system protect the platform). These are valid security mechanisms to support data integrity, data privacy, nonrepudiation, and traceability requirements. End-to-end Web Services security should also ensure that the identity of both the Service Requester and that the Service Provider is valid and trustable (authentication and authorization requirements). It may involve the use of Public Key Infrastructure, XKMS, Liberty, and SAML. This is particularly important if there is a requirement to perform a cross-domain single sign-on across multiple service providers. There will be more details in Chapter 7, "Web Services Security."

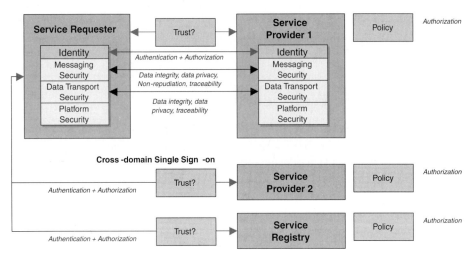

Figure 3–28   Broader Picture of Web Services Security

Examples of emerging security standards for Web Services include:

XML Key Management Specification (XKMS). XKMS is intended for requesting authentication of a specific user. It specifies different key storage and management tiers. These APIs defines XML messages that let applications register key pairs, locate keys for later use, and validate information associated with a key. VeriSign has built the first implementation of this Trust Web Service. Please refer to *http://developer.java.sun.com/developer/technicalArticles/Security/xkms/* for details.

SAML. This is initiated mainly by Netegrity and other vendors. The objective is to provide a vendor-neutral way to retrieve the access profile from a Policy Server. It is intended for Single Sign-on across enterprises.

WS-Security. This is a joint proposal from Microsoft, IBM, and VeriSign to converge different security token technologies (such as Kerberos, X.509v3 digital certificates) for Web Services security. It supersedes previous Web Services security standards proposed by Microsoft and IBM— namely, SOAP-SEC, WS-Security.

Implication

Industry collaboration among vendors to agree on common XML security standards is close and healthy. Each XML security standard tends to focus on a particular problem area and specifies interaction and protocols between two entities—-for example, SAML is designed to address the authentication request/reply between two servers, not from an enterprise/cross-enterprise perspective. There is a general lack of "a broader picture" to implement all these XML standards for enterprise applications using XML Web Services.

3.5   The Web Services Marketplace

3.5.1   Products

Vendor Product Categories

The vendor solutions in the Web Services marketplace can be described as follows:

Infrastructure

- Application server
- Middleware, such as JMS-enabled middleware
- Edge server, such as cache (using XML database)
- Registries, such as the UDDI or ebXML registry

Development Tools

- Developer workbench that can wrap apps logic into a SOAP proxy, and publish it to UDDI
- Automated testing tools, such as jTest

Web Services Tools

- JMS-SOAP bindings, such as the JMS bridge
- SDK, such as WSTK

Web Services Standards

- Java, such as JAX, Web Services Developer Pack
- C#
- XML standards, such as SOAP, SOAP-SEC, XAML, SAML

Specialized Market

- Porting .NET to Unix
- Porting Java to Windows platform

Web Services Management

- Metering Web Services calls performance and service level. This can also send alerts to administrators or system management tools based on user-defined business rules.

- Security appliance, such as XML firewall for SOAP messages; appliance for SOAP message encryption and decryption.

- Service versioning, such as mapping to different service end-point URLs based on the incoming SOAP request and user profile. This addresses many legacy systems or customized services that provide the same business functionality but exist in multiple versions and perhaps operate in different platforms.

Table 3–4 offers a sampler of the vendor products in the marketplace.

Table 3–4 A Sampler of Web Services Vendor Products

Category	Vendors	URIs
Application Servers	BEA	http://www.bea.com/products/index.shtml
	Sun ONE™	http://wwws.sun.com/software/products/appsrvr/home_appsrvr.html
	Novell	http://www.silverstream.com/Website/app/en_US/Products Landing
	IBM	http://www-3.ibm.com/software/info1/websphere/index.jsp?tab=highlights
	Microsoft	http://www.microsoft.com/net
IDE/ Develop-ment Environment	BEA	http://www.bea.com/products/index.shtml
	Sun ONE™	http://wwws.sun.com/software/products_categories/development_tools.html
	Novell	http://www.silverstream.com/Website/app/en_US/Products Landing
	IBM	http://www-3.ibm.com/software/info1/websphere/index.jsp?tab=highlights
	IONA	http://www.xmlbus.com/
	CapeClear	http://www.capeclear.com/products/index.shtml
	Bowstreet	http://www.bowstreet.com/products/businesswebfactory/index.html
	Avinon	http://www.avinon.com/products/overview.html
	Microsoft	http://www.microsoft.com/net

Table 3–4 A Sampler of Web Services Vendor Products—*continued.*

Category	Vendors	URIs
Service Registry	BEA	*http://www.bea.com/products/index.shtml*
	Sun ONE™	*http://wwws.sun.com/software/product_categories/directory_servers_identity_mgmt.html*
	Novell	*http://www.silverstream.com/Website/app/en_US/Products Landing*
	Systinet	*http://www.systinet.com/products/index.html*
	IBM	*http://www-3.ibm.com/software/info1/websphere/index.jsp?tab=highlights*
	The Mind Electric	*http://www.themindelectric.com*
	Microsoft	*http://www.microsoft.com/net*
Application Tools/Middleware	Sun ONE™	*http://wwws.sun.com/software/product_categories/development_tools/html*
	Bowstreet	*http://www.bowstreet.com/products/businesswebfactory/index.html*
	Systinet	*http://www.systinet.com/products/index.html*
	Novell	*http://www.silverstream.com/Website/app/en_US/Products Landing*
	XMLGlobal	*http://www.xmlglobal.com/prod/index.jsp*
	IBM	*http://www-3.ibm.com/software/info1/websphere/index.jsp?tab=highlights*
	Microsoft	*http://www.microsoft.com/net*
Process, Management, Methodology	Sun ONE™	*http://wwws.sun.com/sofstware/products/message_queue/home_message_queue.html*
	Bindsystems	*http://www.bindsystems.com/products.htm*
	Bowstreet	*http://www.bowstreet.com/products/businesswebfactory/index.html*
		http://www.silverstream.com/Website/app/en_US/Products Landing
	Novell	*http://www-3.ibm.com/software/info1/websphere/index.jsp?tab=highlights*
	IBM	
	Microsoft	*http://www.microsoft.com/net*

Table 3–4   A Sampler of Web Services Vendor Products—*continued.*

Category	Vendors	URIs
.NET to Java Porting	Halcyon Mono	*http://www.halcyonsoft.com* *http://www.go-mono.com/faq.html (Running .NET on Linux.* *This is still in the development stage. Currently, Mono* *provides a C# compiler on Linux, implements ADO.NET* *and ASP.NET. Please refer to the Mono status under* *http://www.go-mono.com/.*
Java to .NET Porting	Microsoft	*http://msdn.microsoft.com/visualj/jump/default.asp*
Web Services Management	Amberpoint	*http://www.amberpoint.com/*
	Flamenco Networks	*http://www.flamenconetwork.com/*
	Talking Blocks	*http://www.talkingblocks.com/*
	Westbridge Technology	*http://www.westbridgetech.com/*

Vendor Products by Development Life Cycle

Table 3–5 shows some examples of vendor solutions that are available to meet different needs of the development life cycle.

Table 3–5   Marketplace for Different Development Life Cycle Stages

Development Life Cycle	Types of Development Tools	Examples of Vendors
Discovery	UDDI ebXML	Sun ONE™, IBM, BEA, The Mind Electric, Systinet, Novell (Silverstream), MicrosoftSun ONE™, XMLGlobal
Creation	Developer Workbench (IDE)	Sun ONE™ Studio, IBM, IONA, CapeClear, Bowstreet, Avinon, Microsoft
Transforming	JAX, XML, SQL Mapping	Sun (JAX), IBM (Xerces), XMLGlobal, Microsoft
Building	SOAP, WSDL	OSF (Apache), Sun ONE™ Studio, IBM, CapeClear, Bindsystems, The Mind Electric, Killdara, Microsoft
Deploying	Deploying tools	OSF (Apache ANT)
Testing	Local/remote testing	Jtest
Publishing	Publish to registries	Sun (JAXR), IBM (UDDI4J)

Some Publicly Available Development/Productivity Tools

Here are some development or productivity tools that can be downloaded as a free trial:

XMLSpy. For developing XML Schema, DTD, and validating XML well-formedness. The new version 4.2 also provides SOAP debugging. See Figure 3–29.

Java Web Services Developer Pack. A freeware for developers to build Web Services using JAX. See Figure 3–30.

Editing DTD, XML Schema, XML files

Developer IDE workbench for debugging SOAP

Figure 3–29 XMLSpy 4.2

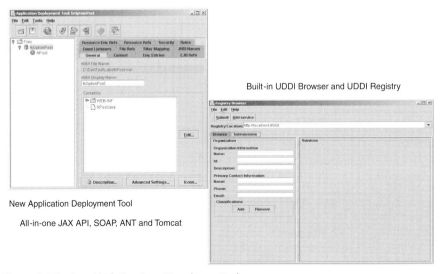

Built-in UDDI Browser and UDDI Registry

New Application Deployment Tool

All-in-one JAX API, SOAP, ANT and Tomcat

Figure 3–30 Java Web Services Developer Pack

The Java Web Services Developer Pack (JWSDP) from Sun Microsystems is a vendor-neutral Web Services Development Kit that avoids the need to purchase expensive Web Services packages. It provides basic tools but is not sufficient for serious or large-scale development. JWSDP provides:

- Tomcat engine with ANT deployment tool
- All-in-one JAR files—javamail, smtp, and so forth
- JAX pack—JAXP, JAXM, JAXR, JAXB
- UDDI browser and registry
- Application deployment tool
- Excellent tutorial book

How to Use JWSDP for Development

JWSDP can be used for proof of concept/prototyping, as a rudimentary development platform for road warriors, and for coding simple SOAP messages for integration testing. To best utilize JWSDP, you can run JWSDP on Linux, Solaris OE™, or Windows NT. You can run it with a SOAP server administration, or run it with Apache Cocoon for any-to-any delivery.

Something to Note. JWSDP has applied some special patches for JAR. There is also a version that is compatible with other stand-alone downloads of JAX Pack, Tomcat, or SOAP.

3.5.2   Selecting Your Web Services Tools

Selection Criteria

Here are some suggestions for selecting an appropriate Web Services tool for your IT shop:

General

- Total cost of ownership
- Reliability and support service of vendor (for example, financial stability, local support)
- Standards compliance (for example, J2EE™, EJB™ 1.2, SOAP 1.2, WSDL 1.1)
- Availability of technical documentation, such as examples, tutorial

Application Server Platform

- Clustering features benchmarking—failover recovery time, any manual intervention

- Logs—logging availability at different levels (for example, can it trace back different callers and intermediaries?)
- Automated testing and deployment platform
- Availability, of or integration with, other apps server analyzer tools (for example, thread performance analysis)

Web Services Development Platform
- Automatic WSDL generation from IDE
- IDE integration with other tools

Among these criteria, you may also look for:

- SOAP 1.1/1.2 support; SOAP 1.2 has some considerable changes
- Integration with J2EE™ application servers, and their positioning
- Compatibility with other Web Services products, such as JMS bridge
- Any proprietary features, such as Electric Server Page

3.5.3   Industry Development

There are three major Web Services development technologies in the industry:

ebXML. ebXML is a key technology supporting Web Services. It is backed by OASIS, CE/FACT, DISA, and many public communities. One motive driving these public communities is to use ebXML as an alternative for EDI-type transactions. ebXML uses SOAP 1.1 with Attachment as the transport and routing layer. It has much richer functionality and contents and is supported by business processes (such as BPSS) and better security.

SOAP. SOAP 1.0 used to be Microsoft NT-centric technology. IBM and other vendors have modified it to turn SOAP 1.1 into an open platform and submitted it to Apache Open Sources Foundation. SOAP 1.1 with Attachment is an extension to support object embedding with S/MIME, developed by HP and other vendors.

UDDI. UDDI is a business Service Registry that allows users to create, discover, and bind business services. IBM, Microsoft, and Ariba initially set up three different test UDDI sites. Recently, Ariba withdrew, but there is some discussion that HP will provide the UDDI test site on behalf of Ariba. SAP also now provides a public UDDI node.

Leading technology vendors such as IBM and Microsoft have large-scale initiatives in developing Web Services toolkits and White Papers. There are many Application Server and Middleware vendors developing components that support Web Services, including BEA Weblogic, webMethods, and TIBCO.

Many Web Services standard bodies have emerged since 2000. Among them, there are a few standard bodies (or related associations) that have large industry involvement:

OSF Apache. Open Source Foundation coordinates and distributes Web Services technology as public domain (*http://www.apache.org*)

UDDI.org. (now under OASIS) Standard body for promoting UDDI registry. It has recently transitioned to OASIS's management (*http://www.uddi.org* or *http://www.oasis.open.org*)

W3C. Worldwide Web Consortium that publishes and approves Internet-related standards (*http://w3c.org*)

Some examples of the supporting communities include:

OASIS. A community that supports ebXML standards and implementation (*http://www.oasis-open.org/*)

UN/CEFACT. Previously UN/EDIFACT, UN/CEFACT promotes EDI and also supports ebXML as the successor to EDI in collaboration with OASIS (*http://www.ebxml.org/*)

Open Application Group. A standards body that adopts the ebXML implementation (*http://www.openapplications.org/*)

DISA. A U.S. ANSI standard body that also adopts the ebXML implementation (*http://www.disa.org/*)

SOAP and ebXML

Web Services technology is intended to be platform- and vendor-neutral. It is expected that this technology be highly flexible for interoperability and integration. SOAP and ebXML standards are used for different reasons. This can be understood in the context of their underlying design principles and value proposition.

The initial design of SOAP does not cater to non-XML contents such as EDI transactions. SOAP 1.1 with Attachment is a major breakthrough; it uses MIME to embed binary objects. The original design principles behind SOAP also support non-HTTP transport, though it has not been implemented at all. The security design of SOAP is highly volatile and weak at this stage.

ebXML can be used to exchange XML contents (incorporating any XML document in the SOAP Body) and non-XML contents (embedding ANSI X12 transactions as attachments). The latter is the mechanism by which ebXML supports EDI documents. It now uses SOAP as the transport layer. ebXML differentiates from SOAP/UDDI by introducing business processes and JMS binding. It uses UML to model business processes. The business process and information models will help integrate with the business entities' back office applications. JMS binding provides a secure and reliable transport mechanism over HTTP.

Table 3–6 summarizes some facts about different Web Services technology thought leaders.

Table 3–6   Comparing Sun, Microsoft, and IBM Approaches

	Sun	Microsoft	IBM
Framework	Sun ONE™	.NET	IBM Web Services
Infrastructure	Open standards technology, e.g., J2EE™—Java™ and XML LDAP	.NET framework, including C#, VB, C++, VBScript, and JScript	WebSphere suite
Developer tools	Sun ONE™ Studio Sun ONE Integration Manager	Visual Studio.NET .NET framework SDK .NET enterprise servers	Web Services Toolkit Application Developer Studio Visual Age
Web Services dialects	Sun ONE™— Smart Web Services	Hailstorm (not available yet)	N/A
Discovery	UDDI ebXML	UDDI UpnP	UDDI
Security	WS-Security Liberty SAML	WS-Security	WS-Security
Business logic	J2EE™ ebXML WSCI	Biztalk BPEL4WS	J2EE™ ebXML BPEL4WS

References

Comparison of Web Services architecture

http://www.webservices.org/framework.php

Web Services Choreography Interface (WSCI)

http://wwws.sun.com/software/xml/developers/wsci/wsci-spec-10.pdf

Business Process Execution Language for Web Services (BPEL4WS)

http://www-106.ibm.com/developerworks/webservices/library/ws-bpel/

3.6   Web Services-Enabling Your Applications

3.6.1   Bringing the Technology Together

So far, we have reviewed different enabling technologies separately. But each of them is part of a much bigger picture. We need to bring the technology pieces together in order to build a workable Web Services solution.

Figure 3–31 illustrates some ideas on how to bring the technology pieces together.

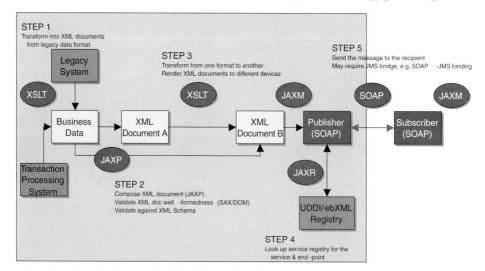

Figure 3–31   Bringing the Enabling Technology Together

Figure 3–31 depicts how business data in the existing transaction processing system or legacy system can be exchanged with trading partners using Java, XML and Web Services technologies. These enabling technologies will allow business data to be encapsulated in XML documents, transformed into a format that is easily understandable by the trading partners, and securely transmitted to the trading partners using SOAP messaging.

1.   Select a business service, which may be an existing Transaction Processing system or legacy system functionality. There are several approaches to XML-enable them, such as using an XML adapter or legacy system XML connector, writing JAXP codes, or using SOAP administration to map the data fields.

2.   Compose (or transform) XML documents, validate their well-formedness using SAX or DOM with XML Schema. Apply the example of JAXP in the earlier section entitled "Java™ and Java API."

3.   You may need to transform one format to another format or XML variant or render XML documents into different devices for multichannels. JAX and XSLT are likely to be the appropriate technologies.

4. The client looks up the UDDI/ebXML Service Registry for the business service, service key, and end-points using JAXR (see the earlier section, "Java™ and Java API").

5. Any transaction request or reply can be wrapped in a SOAP message to the service provider using JAXM (see the earlier section, "Java™ and Java API"). JAXM supports both SOAP and ebXML Messaging Services.

3.6.2 Four Steps to Web Services-Enable Your Applications

The steps outlined in Figure 3–32 follow:

Define Service Description

• Agree on the WSDL with your trading partners or adopt an industry-specific WSDL.

• Define service description, such as define WSDL—by hand or with a tool—generate WSDL using tools like WSTK or AXIS java2wsdl, and place your WSDL in your SOAP server and UDDI registry by deploying it.

Implement WSDL

• Determine your programming language (such as Java, C#) and the access method (XML document or XML-RPC).

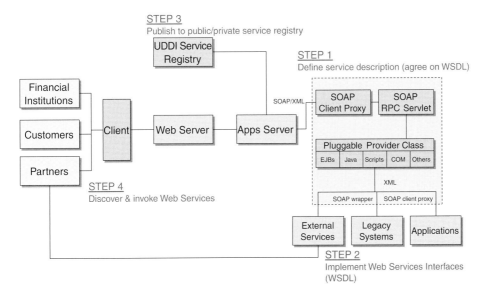

Figure 3–32   Four Steps to Web Services-Enable Your Applications

- Identify the end-point, access method, and binding method from the WSDL.

- Write your client by hand-coding with your favorite editor, using a developer workbench (IDE) environment, performing simple testing in testing environment, or with testing the SOAP server.

Publish to Registry

- Upon successful testing of the WSDL, the service, and client programs, publish the WSDL to the relevant UDDI/ebXML registry.

- Depending on the nature, the registry may be a public UDDI node or a private node.

- For the UDDI registry, exploit JAXR/UDDI4J to publish.

Invoke Web Services

- Discover/look up relevant services from the UDDI/ebXML Service Registry.

- Invoke the Web Services from a UDDI browser, a UDDI browser plug-in for Web browsers, host-to-host, or a rich client.

3.7   Web Services in Action

The *Harvard Business Review* describes Web Services as the next IT strategy. Web Services can be deployed as a solution that addresses "data silos" or restrictive ERP-based enterprise architectures. It is a cost-effective approach to addressing integration with external processes and institutions. It is also a risk mitigation to obsolete technology, making it easier to adopt outsourced or managed services using standardized and plug-and-play Web Services.

There are many Web Services conferences (including XML One and Web Services Conference), numerous articles, and a growing number of books (more than 86 books on SOAP, UDDI, and Web Services). There is also much hype about what Web Services can do and how quick and easy it is to deliver enterprise solutions. According to Gartner's Technology Hype Model, XML has passed the market-hype stage. We shall review some of the Web Services market and pilot solutions to assess readiness and maturity for mass implementation.

Many leading apps server and middleware vendors have already embedded SOAP into their products (for example, BEA Weblogic, Sun ONE™, IBM WebSphere, and Microsoft .NET).

Some vertical solutions have already been using XML for interfaces and export/import. They also expose their system functionality to SOAP, partly as a pilot in case the market is mature or as a response to customer requests (for example, CoRe Solutions and Bottomline Technologies).

Many large corporations and technology vendors presented their Web Services positioning and strategy at the W3C Web Services Conference 2001. Though they may not be visible to public, many large corporations, such as Visa International, CIBC, and UHG, have small pilot projects in XML Web Services (for example, many have SOAP-enabled some applications and have built a UDDI registry).

Finally, some public UDDI portals connect to some public Web Services applications (for example, *www.xmethods.org*).

3.7.1 Applying Web Services

The term Web Services has become a buzzword in the industry recently, as corporations explore solutions for service-based architecture and reusable components for internal as well as external systems. There are new standards coming out of the Web Services concept, including ebXML, SOAP, and UDDI. Leading technology vendors such as Sun, IBM, and Microsoft are gearing up their products to support Web Services.

One business driver for Web Services is the need for a service-based infrastructure that enables business applications to be deployed as reusable services and components, instead of silos and proprietary technology. In the short term, there may be cost savings as a result of better economy of scale and lower integration cost. More importantly, Web Services is positioned to be easier for development and deployment due to the nature of reusable components and Quality of Service.

Web Services can be also seen as continuing the exploitation of XML technology for business services. Different marketplaces and public bodies, such as UN/CEFACT and DISA, have been showing commitment to initiatives related to Web Services. We should anticipate that more Web Services will be adopted and implemented by marketplaces and portals in the near future.

There are also emerging trends for adopting Web Services. Customers are expecting quick return of the benefits, such as lower operating cost of integration, and faster development and deployment cycles. There are more vendor products embedding Web Services technology. Though there is market hype, that at least helps make the market more aware.

3.7.2 Web Services Solutions Sampler

Table 3–7 provides a sampler of public Web Services solutions that are published for public consumption or testing. They serve as good examples of what can be exposed as Web Services.

Table 3–7 Publicly Available Web Services Solutions Sampler

Category	Examples	WSDL
Supply Chain Management	Sporting goods finder (seanco.com)	*http://www.xmlme.com/WSSportingGoods. asmx?WSDLhttp://hosting.msugs.ch/aravindc/ BookPrice Comparison.asmx?wsdl*
	Product price comparison (araviindcorera)	*http://www.xmethods.net/sd/2001/ BNQuoteService.wsdl*
	Book price quote (xmethods.net)	
Logistics	Track shipment status (xmethods.net)	*http://www.xmethods.net/sd/2001/ FedExTrackerService.wsdl*
	Traffic condition (xmethods.net)	*http://www.xmethods.net/sd/2001/ CATrafficService.wsdl*
Syndicated News	Various headline news (sqldata.com)	*http://www.soapclient.com/xml/SQLDataSoap. WSDL*
	Weather forecast (unisysfsp.com)	*http://hosting001.vs.k2unisys.net/Weather/ PDCWebService/WeatherServices.asmx?WSDL*
Wireless	Instant messaging services (nims.nl)	*http://www.nims.nl/soap/oms.wsdl*
	Send SMS messages (lucin.com)	*http://www.soapengine.com/lucin/soapenginex/ smsx.asmx?wsdl*
Travel	Map service (dotnetmap.com)	*http://www.dotnetmap.com/webservices/ mapservice.asmx?wsdl*
Multimedia/ Entertainment	Video game finder (seanco.com)	*http://www.xmlme.com/WSVideoGames. asmx?WSDL*
Financial Services	Delayed stock quotes (cchenoweth/cdyne.com)	*http://ws.cdyne.com/delayedstockquote/ delayedstockquote.asmx?wsdl*
	Stock news (mybubble.com) NYSE/NASDAQ Stock quotes (durrios.com)	*http://www.mybubble.com:8080/ mybubbleEntServer/MyBubbleSoapServices. wsdlhttp://www.durrios.com/Finance.wsdl*
	Currency exchange rate (xmethods.net)	*http://www.xmethods.net/sd/2001/Currency ExchangeService.wsdl*
Payment Services	RichPayments.net— ePayment with card, checks (richsolutions.com)	*http://www.richsolutions.com/richpayments/ richpay.asmx?WSDL*

Table 3–7 Publicly Available Web Services Solutions Sampler—*continued.*

Category	Examples	WSDL
Utilities	UN/SPSC code search (CodeMechanisms.com)	*http://www.codemechanisms.co.uk/WebServices/UNSPSC.asmx?WSDL*
	Convert business data to/from CSV, EDI, xCBL, XML (dataconcert.com)	*http://transform.dataconcert.com/transform.wsdl*
Web Services Utilities	Business Services UDDI Finder (esynaps.com)	*http://www.esynaps.com/WebServices/BusinessList.asmx?WSDL*

3.7.3   Strengths of the Technology

- Ease of development and deployment (using SOAP wrapper concept), compared with traditional technology.
- Decoupling data layer (XML contents) from the transport layer (for example, SOAP and JMS-binding), which facilitates integration with heterogeneous platforms and different vendor technology.
- Open standards-based. Wider choice of vendor solutions. Easy to integrate with different vendor solutions.
- Tightly integrated with J2EE™ framework (for example, JAXM embeds ebXML and Web Services capability).
- Interoperability with UDDI and ebXML registries. There are cases where different business services are implemented in different types of registries.

3.7.4   Limitations

- Web Services technology is still evolving; the technology paradigm is vulnerable to changes by many vendor-specific extensions.
- Web Services security is rudimentary because many Web Services security standards only address some of the problem space but not the entire picture.
- WS-Security using DSIG is dependent on the deployment of digital certificates or Kerberos tickets, which may not be viable for some countries/companies.

- Difficult to measure scalability and performance improvement, as Web Services can be across different end-points.
- Messages between Web Services nodes (such as service providers) are not guaranteed using SOAP; need to be supplemented by technology such as asynchronous messaging with guaranteed message delivery.
- The workflow and process integration aspect is yet to be defined and enhanced; this is a good area for ebXML and SOAP convergence.
- Web Services is a lightweight approach for integration, and it cannot replace EAI.

3.7.5 Scenario

Figure 3–33 depicts a sample Web Services scenario. The Buyer is running Web Services internally for order management, production forecast, and finance applications. The finance applications are out-tasked to an external financial services service provider using Web Services. The Buyer places the Request for Quote and Purchase Orders with a Trading Exchange (in ebXML/Web Services), which in turn trades with another Trading Exchange (in SOAP/Web Services). The Buyer also uses B2B payment Web Services from Bank A and credit card/customer support Web Services from the Credit Card Company. Both of them use ebXML-based Web Services. The Credit Card Company also provides credit card Web Services to Bank A using ebXML.

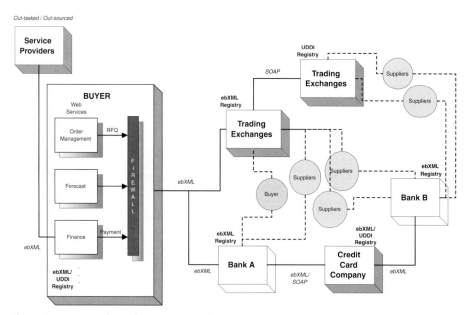

Figure 3–33 Sample Web Services Application Scenario

Objectives

To provide a single payment gateway in order to settle cross-border payments with multiple banks.

Problem Space

- Buyers have many Electronic Banking systems; cannot use one single front-end to settle payments with multiple banks.
- It cannot support cross-border payment.
- There is no agreeable data format for exchanges, buyers, suppliers, banks, or credit card companies to share and reuse.

Description

- XML Web Services technology enables multiple banks and credit card companies to reuse the same purchase order contents.
- It also enables interoperability and integration between banks and credit card companies with reusable data over the existing infrastructure.

Benefits

- Enables high-value cross-border payment using credit cards
- Seamless integration with buyers and suppliers' back office systems using reusable system components over existing infrastructure
- Better flexibility to their customers and trading partners
- Easier integration with multiple trading partners, trading exchanges, and business partners (for example, banks)
- Integration with out-sourced or out-tasked business services
- Platform-independent
- Support of open standards

In the sample business scenario, simple Web Services refer to simple synchronous Web Services calls (such as JAX-RPC) that invoke business functionality remotely. They do not require complex workflow or any additional dependency in order to complete the service call. Complex Web Services refer to sophisticated business functionality that requires additional steps or workflow, such as multilevel payment authorization, matching outstanding credit balance and payment amounts, and so forth. They are likely to be in asynchronous messages (or document-based Web Services) and require business process orchestration from multiple trading partners or systems.

In simple Web Services, the service requester will use XML, SOAP, WSDL, and UDDI to locate the Web Services via the Web. The client application will discover how to invoke the Web Services and then submit the request. The Web Services server will process the request and return the result to the requester.

In some complex Web Services, there will be multiparty and long-running transaction support, collaboration and business process management, transactional integrity, and transactional security (such as nonrepudiation and digital signature), as well as context sensitivity (ordering of steps and described conversations). Please refer to some detailed examples from *http://www.bea.com/products/weblogic/server/ paper_webservices4.shtml#Examples.*

3.7.1   Identifying and Selecting a Pilot

A pilot is highly recommended before adopting a Web Services strategy. Here are some suggestions to identify and select a pilot.

Business/Operational
- Processes that require intensive manual or semi-manual procedures or duplicate data entries
- Processes that take a long time (such as several days) because systems are not interconnected
- Meaningful and simple (reasonably sophisticated, not over-complicated) processes are required
- ROI or immediate benefits can be realized within a few months
- Management sponsorship for the pilot

Technology
- Applications that involve more than one external party
- Heterogeneous platform interoperability required
- Similar interfaces that can be refactored into reusable components
- Viability—achievable within two-three months; do not pick any system candidates that require heavy IT investment, or large infrastructural changes

3.7.2   Approach to Implementing Web Services

- Identify the business services for the Web Services candidate.
- Define the Web Services architecture for the candidate. Sun's ONE™ framework is the recommended Web Services architecture that supports open standards and easy interoperability.
- Integrate the Web Services with the business model and business processes.
- Integrate the Web Services with any back office systems, if necessary.

- Start a pilot.
- Interoperate with other Web Services and e-Marketplaces.

3.7.3 Critical Success Factors

Focused Business and Clear Vision. It is crucial to have a clear vision and a focused business. Noncore business services are good candidates for out-tasking as Web Services, which may result in better economy of scale.

Right Resources and Expertise. The right personnel, an appropriate combination of disciplined and creative staff, is critical to success. Subject matter experts related to e-Marketplaces and Web Services can be introduced from notable vendors such as Sun Professional Services.

Limited Scope. Do not be too aggressive in implementing too many business services at one time. Start small and grow.

Examples of applications are:

- **Credit card information for partners, merchants, third-party bill presenters, or aggregators**—This reduces individual customized integration efforts and provides timely reporting of card information.
- **Instant credit standings check**—A merchant or Service Provider submits a service request for credit checking to the bank's Web Services. A response is made from the bank's Web Services in real time to reduce business exposure to risks.
- **Customer support for new credit card applications**—The customer support center may be out-tasked to a third party. New customers can enter the Web Services to apply for a new credit card.
- **B2B payment services**—Purchase Orders and payment instructions can be exchanged between merchants or B2B exchanges and the banks.

3.8 Perspectives

3.8.1 Highlights

- Web Service is an emerging technology to address integration and proprietary technology silos.
- Java™, XML, SOAP, and UDDI are the typical technologies used.
- There is much market hype surrounding Web Services.

- Many technology vendors and vertical solutions have already embedded Web Services into their products and solutions.
- Web Services provides a service-based infrastructure with intelligent and reusable components.
- Web Services addresses technology issues of high implementation cost, legacy systems integration, and cross-platform interoperability.
- There are competitive advantages to implementing Web Services. Web Services technology provides a low-cost alternative to integrating with multiple trading partners using open standards. It is platform independent, and provides better flexibility to customers and trading partners, because it can accommodate local data formats, and can reuse existing infrastructure and business functionality from the legacy systems.

3.8.2   Best Practices and Pitfalls

Best Practices

Select a reasonably rich set of functionality that can be implemented within three to six months.

The candidate should be able to demonstrate the benefits immediately. A Total Cost of Ownership (TCO) model is required.

Involve leading Web Services vendors for technology skill transfer, for example:

- Customize a Web Services training workshop using the pilot requirements.
- Assess the Web Services solution architecture.

Pitfalls

Do not be too ambitious with too many dependencies or items that require longer lead time (for example, SOAP-enabling a mainframe platform).

Do not start implementation without support from senior management.

Do not start a pilot using a mission-critical functionality.

Do not involve a big team in the pilot. Start with a small team.

3.8.3   Challenge

A medium-size listed financial institution in Hong Kong wants to reduce its operating costs associated with supporting legacy systems on the mainframe. The corporation has been innovative and reputable in providing securities trading, retail banking, and credit card services to the local market.

The CEO is concerned about implementing new technology for technology's sake and believes that not all legacy systems need to be migrated to Unix, as they are fairly stable.

Is it relevant to introduce Web Service technology to meet its challenge?

3.8.4   Paper and Pencil

Study Questions

- What are the architectural differences between CORBA and XML Web Services in terms of exposing the services, method invocation, and security? What problems does each technology intend to resolve?

- What are the principles or guidelines to consider when choosing the Web Services developer tools and platform, say, for an IT shop with an established J2EE™ application platform?

- What are the prerequisites to Web Services-enable an application? For instance, can we expose a business service from a legacy mainframe application with only a CICS program name?

Lab Exercises

Exercise 1 XML to DTD

Your trading partner, XYZ investment bank, provides you with an XML document with real data. They support DTD, not an XML Schema, but they do not have a DTD.

The following XML document (an fpML example) describes an FX option bought by XYZ from ABC traded on January 15, 2002.

Exercise 1.1 Could you check whether this is a well-formed XML? You may use XMLSpy 4.3 Suite (evaluation copy) to validate it.

Note: What information (for example, attributes) do you need before you can validate a well-formed XML document?

Exercise 1.2 Could you reverse-engineer the XML into a DTD? If you generate a sample XML from the DTD, could you get the identical XML?

```
<?XML version="1.0" " encoding = "UTF-8"?>
<!DOCTYPE trade PUBLIC "-//FpML//DTD 3-0//EN" "" >
[
  <!- DTD declarations omitted -->
]>
<trade>
  <tradeHeader>
    <partyTradeIdentifier>
      <partyReference href = "#XYZ"/>
    </partyTradeIdentifier>
    <partyTradeIdentifier>
```

```
      <partyReference href = "#ABC"/>
  </partyTradeIdentifier>
  <tradeDate>2002-01-15</tradeDate>
 </tradeHeader>
 <fxSimpleOption>
    <productType>Nondeliverable Option</productType>
    <buyerPartyReference href = "#XYZ"/>
    <sellerPartyReference href = "#ABC"/>
    <expiryDateTime>
        <expiryDate>2002-04-09</expiryDate>
        <hourMinuteTime>1000</hourMinuteTime>
        <businessCenter>USNY</businessCenter>
    </expiryDateTime>
    <exerciseStyle>European</exerciseStyle>
 </fxSimpleOption>
 <party id = "XYZ">
    <partyId>CHASUS33</partyId>
    <partyName>XYZ BUYER BANK</partyName>
 </party>
 <party id = "ABCN">
    <partyId>ABCANL2A</partyId>
    <partyName>ABC Seller Bank</partyName>
 </party>
</trade>
<!- end of DTDs —>
```

To assist your understanding, the fxOption XML is depicted in Figure 3–34:

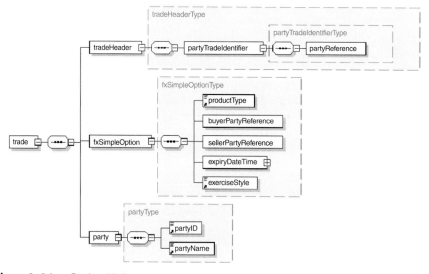

Figure 3–34 xOption XML

Answer Key

```
<!- Name:          'trade.dtd'              ->
<!- Description:    sample fpML FX option  ->



<!ELEMENT trade                (tradeHeader,
fxSimpleOption, party) >
<!ELEMENT tradeHeader          (partyTradeIdentifier)>
<!ELEMENT fxSimpleOption       (productType,
                                  buyerPartyReference,
                                  sellerPartyReference,
                                  expiryDateTime,
                                  exerciseStyle) >
<!ELEMENT party                (partyID, partyName) >


<!ELEMENT partyTradeIdentifier (partyReference) >


<!ELEMENT partyReference       EMPTY >
<!ATTLIST partyReference
                               href CDATA #REQUIRED >


<!ELEMENT productType          (#PCDATA) >
<!ELEMENT buyerPartyReference  EMPTY >
<!ATTLIST buyerPartyReference
                               href CDATA #REQUIRED >
<!ELEMENT sellerPartyReference EMPTY >
<!ATTLIST sellerPartyReference
                               href CDATA #REQUIRED >
<!ELEMENT expiryDateTime         (expiryDate,
                                  hourMinuteTime,
                                  businessCenter) >
<!ELEMENT expiryDate           (#PCDATA) >
<!ELEMENT hourMinuteTime       (#PCDATA) >
<!ELEMENT businessCenter       (#PCDATA) >
<!ELEMENT exerciseStyle        (#PCDATA) >

<!ELEMENT partyID              (#PCDATA) >
<!ELEMENT partyName            (#PCDATA) >
```

Figure 3–35 shows an example using XMLSPy to validate the DTD in this exercise.

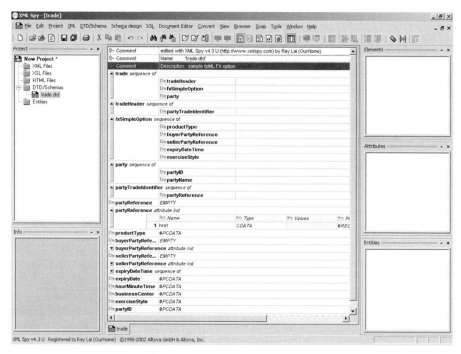

Figure 3–35   DTD Validated by XMLSpy

Exercise 2 Writing the First JAXM Program

You are going to install Java Web Services Developer Pack and write your first JAXM-SOAP program.

Exercise 2.1 Download the Java Web Services Developer Pack from *http://java.sun.com*. Install and configure it according to the Installation Guide.

Exercise 2.2 Based on the sample sniplet in the text, write your first JAXM-SOAP program to send the following XML message:

```
<?XML version="1.0" " encoding = "UTF-8"?>
<!DOCTYPE trade PUBLIC "-//FpML//DTD 3-0//EN" "" >
[
  <!- DTD declarations omitted -->
]>
<trade>
  <tradeHeader>
    <partyTradeIdentifier>
      <partyReference href = "#XYZ"/>
```

```
    </partyTradeIdentifier>
    <partyTradeIdentifier>
      <partyReference href = "#ABC"/>
    </partyTradeIdentifier>
    <tradeDate>2002-01-15</tradeDate>
  </tradeHeader>
  <fxSimpleOption>
     <productType>Nondeliverable Option</productType>
     <buyerPartyReference href = "#XYZ"/>
     <sellerPartyReference href = "#ABC"/>
     <expiryDateTime>
        <expiryDate>2002-04-09</expiryDate>
        <hourMinuteTime>1000</hourMinuteTime>
        <businessCenter>USNY</businessCenter>
     </expiryDateTime>
     <exerciseStyle>European</exerciseStyle>
  </fxSimpleOption>
  <party id = "XYZ">
     <partyId>CHASUS33</partyId>
     <partyName>XYZ BUYER BANK</partyName>
  </party>
  <party id = "ABCN">
     <partyId>ABCANL2A</partyId>
     <partyName>ABC Seller Bank</partyName>
  </party>
</trade>
<!- end of DTDs ->
```

Exercise 3 Creating a New Web Service With JWSDP

You are going to expose an existing Foreign Exchange currency rate conversion functionality as a Web Services call using JWSDP. The following sections show the procedures to define, implement, and deploy a new Web Services call using JWSDP. The procedures can be found in section "Four Steps to Web Services-Enable Your Applications" found previously in this chapter. The sample code in this exercise can be found on the CD-ROM accompanying this book under Chapter 3 labs. They are also reusable for Chapter 8 Web Services in Action: Case Study chapter.

Step 1: Define Service Description
Start with the business service you would like to expose. In this example, you are going to define a Web Services call to get a Foreign Exchange rate quote given the Sell and Buy currency codes. You need to define an interface file that defines the method and the parameters (refer to Figure 3–36). This interface file will be used to generate a service description (WSDL) file.

```
package myws;

import java.rmi.Remote;
import java.rmi.RemoteException;

public interface FXProviderIF extends Remote {
    public String getPrice(String sellCurrency, String
buyCurrency) throws RemoteException;
}
```

Figure 3–36 FXProviderIF.java Program

Step 2: Implement Web Services Description Language (WSDL)
A sample implementation of the business service is listed below in Figure
3–37. The getPrice method simply returns an exchange rate in String format,
when given a Sell/Buy currency pair (such as USD to HKD). Please note that
the "getPrice" method can be a remote Web Services call or functionality abstracted from any legacy backoffice system.

```
package myws;

import java.math.BigDecimal;
import java.util.*;

public class FXProviderImpl implements FXProviderIF {

//  FX conversion rate
    public String getPrice(String sellCurrency, String
buyCurrency) {

        if (sellCurrency.equalsIgnoreCase("HKD")) {
            if
(buyCurrency.equalsIgnoreCase("USD")) {
                return "0.128";
            } else
            if (buyCurrency.equalsIgnoreCase("EUR"))
{
```

Figure 3–37 FXProviderImpl.java Program

```
                         return "0.123";
              } else
              if (buyCurrency.equalsIgnoreCase("RMB")) {
                    return "1.25";
                 } else
                 if
(buyCurrency.equalsIgnoreCase("SGD")) {
                    return "0.22";
              } else
                 if
(buyCurrency.equalsIgnoreCase("MYR")) {
                    return "2.85";
                 } else return "0.00";
        } else
        if (sellCurrency.equalsIgnoreCase("USD")) {
                 if
(buyCurrency.equalsIgnoreCase("HKD")) {
                    return "7.78";
                 } else
              if (buyCurrency.equalsIgnoreCase("EUR"))
{
                       return "0.92";
                 } else
              if (buyCurrency.equalsIgnoreCase("RMB"))
{
                    return "8.20";
                 } else
                 if
(buyCurrency.equalsIgnoreCase("SGD")) {
                    return "2.5";
                 } else
                 if
(buyCurrency.equalsIgnoreCase("MYR")) {
                    return "3.45";
                 } else return "0.00";
           } else return "0.00";
           // end-if
    } // getPrice
} // class0
```

Figure 3–37 FXProviderImpl.java Program—*continued.*

There are a few files you need to customize in order to build a Web Services call—`build.xml`, `config.xml`, `web.xml`, `build.properties` and `jaxrpc-ri.xml`. A `build.xml` template can be used to customize your development environment. Typically, you need to modify the path names (file locations) in the `build.properties` file, which is used by `build.xml`. The files `build.properties` and `build.xml` reside in the same directory of your program source codes that your "ant" build tool or your favorite IDE developer tool will use to build your work files.

For `web.xml`, specify the display name of the Web Services and the session time-out parameters (in this case, 60 seconds). Refer to the excerpt in Figure 3–38:

```
<?xml version="1.0" encoding="UTF-8"?>
<!DOCTYPE web-app
    PUBLIC "-//Sun Microsystems, Inc.//DTD Web
Application 2.3//EN"
    "http://java.sun.com/j2ee/dtds/web-app_2_3.dtd">
<web-app>
  <display-name>FX Currency Exchange Service</display-
name>
  <description>FX Currency Exchange Rate
Service</description>
  <session-config>
    <session-timeout>60</session-timeout>
  </session-config>
</web-app>
```

Figure 3–38   web.xml Contents

The config.xml (Figure 3–39) simply defines the WSDL and the package name. JWSDP 1.01 has a new function to generate WSDL when adding a suffix "?WSDL" to the service end-point. Refer to the following program excerpt:

```
<?xml version="1.0" encoding="UTF-8"?>
<configuration
    xmlns="http://java.sun.com/xml/ns/jax-
rpc/ri/config">
  <wsdl
location="http://localhost:8080/myws/FXProvider?WSDL"
      packageName="myws"/>
</configuration>
```

Figure 3–39   config.xml Contents

For `jaxrpc-ri.xml` (refer to the following program excerpt), specify the interface file and the implementation file (that is, the class names `myws.FX-ProviderIF` and `myws.FXProviderImpl`) where JWSDP (`wscompile` and `wsdeploy` used in the `build.xml` script) will generate the stubs and WSDL files. Please note that `jaxrpc-ri.xml` (Figure 3–40) is a new configuration file introduced in JWSDP 1.01, and is not required in JWSDP 1.0 or Early Access releases. It is not a standard configuration file used in other Web Services tools.

```
<?xml version="1.0" encoding="UTF-8"?>
<webServices
    xmlns="http://java.sun.com/xml/ns/jax-rpc/ri/dd"
    version="1.0"
targetNamespaceBase="http://www.nextfrontiers.com/wsdl
"
typeNamespaceBase="http://www.nextfrontiers.com/types"
    urlPatternBase="/myws">
    <endpoint
        name="myws"
        displayName="FX Currency Exchange Service"
        description="FX Currency Exchange Service"
        interface="myws.FXProviderIF"
        implementation="myws.FXProviderImpl"/>
     <endpointMapping
        endpointName="myws"
        urlPattern="/FXProvider"/>
</webServices>
```

Figure 3–40 jaxrpc-ri.xml Contents

The `build.xml` script will compile all Java programs (in this case, FX-ProviderIF.java and FXProviderImpl.java), generate stubs, and get ready for deploying the Web Services.

The utility `wscompile` (from JWSDP) will generate the stubs using the `config.xml` that are necessary to build the client proxy. The WSDL file will be generated during the process, and it will be deleted afterward unless the -keep option is specified. The following excerpt in Figure 3–41 depicts how `wscompile` is used in the `build.xml` script:

```
<target name="generate-stubs" depends="set-ws-
scripts,prepare"
      description="Runs wscompile to generate the
client stub classes">
      <echo message="Running wscompile...."/>
    <exec executable="${wscompile}">
        <arg line="-gen:client"/>
        <arg line="-d ${build}/client"/>
        <arg line="-classpath ${build}/shared"/>
        <arg line="config.xml"/>
    </exec>
  </target>
```

Figure 3–41   Use of wscompile in build.xml

Next, you need to deploy the Web Services. You may like to execute the commands as follows:

```
D:\Dev\mydemo\myws>ant build
Buildfile: build.xml

clean:
   [delete] Deleting directory D:\Dev\mydemo\myws\build

clean-wars:
   [delete] Deleting: D:\Dev\mydemo\myws\dist\myws-
portable.war
   [delete] Deleting: D:\Dev\mydemo\myws\dist\myws.war

prepare:
     [echo] Creating the required directories....
    [mkdir] Created dir:
D:\Dev\mydemo\myws\build\client\myws
    [mkdir] Created dir:
D:\Dev\mydemo\myws\build\server\myws
    [mkdir] Created dir:
D:\Dev\mydemo\myws\build\shared\myws
    [mkdir] Created dir:
D:\Dev\mydemo\myws\build\wsdeploy-generated
    [mkdir] Created dir: D:\Dev\mydemo\myws\build\WEB-
INF\classes\myws

compile-server:
```

```
    [echo] Compiling the server-side source code....
   [javac] Compiling 2 source files to
D:\Dev\mydemo\myws\build\shared

setup-web-inf:
    [echo] Setting up build/WEB-INF....
  [delete] Deleting directory
D:\Dev\mydemo\myws\build\WEB-INF
    [copy] Copying 2 files to
D:\Dev\mydemo\myws\build\WEB-INF\classes\myws
    [copy] Copying 1 file to
D:\Dev\mydemo\myws\build\WEB-INF
    [copy] Copying 1 file to
D:\Dev\mydemo\myws\build\WEB-INF

package:
    [echo] Packaging the WAR....
     [jar] Building jar: D:\Dev\mydemo\myws\dist\myws-
portable.war

set-ws-scripts:

process-war:
    [echo] Running wsdeploy....
    [exec] info: created temporary directory:
D:\Dev\mydemo\myws\build\wsdeploy
-generated\jaxrpc-deploy-de5ada
    [exec] info: processing endpoint: myws
    [exec] Note: sun.tools.javac.Main has been
deprecated.
    [exec] 1 warning
    [exec] info: created output war file:
D:\Dev\mydemo\myws\dist\myws.war
    [exec] info: removed temporary directory:
D:\Dev\mydemo\myws\build\wsdeploy
-generated\jaxrpc-deploy-de5ada

build-service:

build:

BUILD SUCCESSFUL

Total time: 16 seconds
```

Next, you need to deploy the Web Services under the context "/myws." This enables any remote client to invoke the Web Services via RPC.

```
D:\Dev\mydemo\myws>ant deploy
Buildfile: build.xml

deploy:
    [deploy] OK - Installed application at context path
/myws
    [deploy]

BUILD SUCCESSFUL

Total time: 4 seconds
```

You may want to ensure that the context (in this example, myws) is not created before. Otherwise, you need to either use a new context name, or to undeploy the context (for example, ant undeploy).

Upon successful deployment of the Web Services call, you may like to verify the WSDL by entering the URL *http://localhost:8080/myws/FXProvider*, as in Figure 3–42:

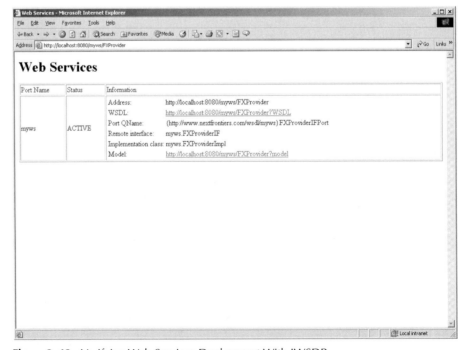

Figure 3–42   Verifying Web Services Deployment With JWSDP

You should be able to validate the WSDL by clicking from the WSDL URL (refer to Figure 3–43).

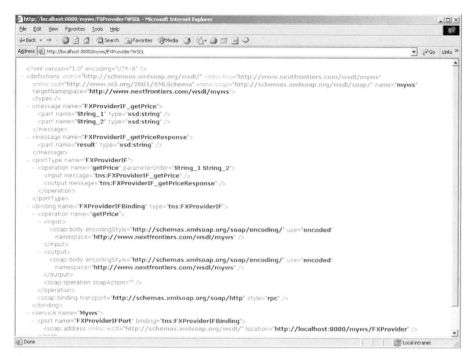

Figure 3–43 WSDL Generated From JWSDP

Step 3: Publish to Registry
This step is required if you want to publish to a Service Registry. In this example, we do not require the Web Services to publish to the UDDI Service Registry. Please refer to Chapter 8, Web Services in Action: Case Study, for an example of publishing to the UDDI Service Registry with JAXR.

Step 4: Invoke Web Services
SOAP-Lite is used here to illustrate that Web Services can be invoked from a non-Java client. A SOAP-Lite client reads in a Web Services service description (a URI pointing to the WSDL, which is *http://localhost:8080/myws/FXProvider?WSDL* in this case) and invokes the remote method "getPrice" via RPC. The script is written in Perl and can be executed from a Windows command prompt or a Unix terminal.

```perl
#!perl -w
#!d:\perl\bin\perl.exe


BEGIN { warn "SOAP-Lite is started...\n" }
```

```
# import interface. All methods from loaded service are
imported by default
use SOAP::Lite
    service =>
'http://localhost:8080/myws/FXProvider?WSDL',
    ;
warn "Invoking a remote Web Service...\n";
print 'The currency exchange for USD-to-HKD is ';
print getPrice('USD', 'HKD'), "\n";
```

Execute the SOAP-Lite script (in this example, myFX.pl) as follows:

```
D:\Dev\mydemo>perl myFX.pl
SOAP-Lite is started...
Invoking a remote Web Service...
The currency exchange for USD-to-HKD is 7.78
```

3.8.5   References

Some Web Services Resource Web Sites

http://www.webservices.org

http://www.theserverside.com/home/index.jsp

Web Services Overview

John Hagel III and John Seely Brown. "Your Next IT Strategy." *Harvard Business Review,* October 2001. IBM Web Services Overview Team. "Web Services Architecture Overview" IBM, September 2000. *http://www-106.ibm.com/developerworks/library/w-ovr/*

Lawrence Wilkes. "Web Services—Right Here, Right Now." IBM, 2002. *http://www-3.ibm.com/software/solutions/webservices/pdf/cbdi.pdf*

SOAP Interoperability Organization

SOAP Builders Interoperability Test Lab. *http://www.xmethods.net/ilab/*

White Mesa—for SOAP interoperability testing. *http://www.whitemesa.net/*

Web Services Standards

Business Process Execution Language for Web Services (BPEL4WS). *http://www-106.ibm.com/developerworks/webservices/library/ws-bpel/*

Web Services Choreography Interface (WSCI). *http://wwws.sun.com/software/xml/developers/wsci/wsci-spec-10.pdf*

Others

Alur Deepak, John Crupi, and Dan Malks. *Core J2EE Patterns.* Prentice Hall, 2001.

Judith M. Myerson. "Web Services Architecture." Tech, 2002.
http://www.webservicesarchitect.com/content/articles/webservicesarchitectures.pdf

Sun Professional Services. *Dot-com and Beyond: Breakthrough Internet-Based Architectures and Methodologies.* Prentice Hall, 2001.

Chapter 4

WEB SERVICES ARCHITECTURE AND BEST PRACTICES

4.1   Chapter Overview

- There are many interpretations of Web Services architecture, which range from product architecture to philosophical models.

- A good Web Services architecture provides a framework to systematically define components that can support different levels of Quality of Services ("ilities" based on individual requirements).

- A reference architecture for Securities Trading is used to illustrate how a deployment architecture is derived from a meta-architecture, with UDDI Service Registry and XML-RPC-based Web Services in the back-end.

- A comprehensive architecture framework also helps when selecting the appropriate tools to enhance productivity during the development and deployment life cycle (for example, Web Services load testing).

- Small code snippets (Web Services design patterns) can be added to the SOAP server side to provide caching, logging, and session control.

- There are different types of UDDI Service Registry. Usually the deployment architecture varies for public and private UDDI registries.

- General troubleshooting guidelines for XML-RPC-based Web Services are discussed, in conjunction with Web Services tools.

4.2   Chapter Objectives

- To introduce an architecture framework (of reusable components, principles, and design patterns) for building Web Services solutions.

- To identify some architectural constraints of SOAP, UDDI, and ebXML technology and some alternatives when designing large-scale Web Services solutions.

- To illustrate some Web Services design patterns that are essential to delivering Quality of Services.

4.3   Web Services Architecture

4.3.1   Need for an Architecture

Many systems are deployed today without a reliable, scalable architecture and thus suffer from capacity and performance issues. Some of them do not have reusable components. With an eye toward cost-reduction, there is a need to leverage application component framework and technical infrastructure investment by focusing on opportunities that can leverage reusable components.

Many Web Services initiatives today begin and end with SOAP-UDDI programming, yet lack a framework for reusable components, scalability, and performance management. One goal of Web Services technology is to better leverage limited component frameworks, distributed services, and platform and network engineering resources.

4.3.2   The Architecture Nirvana

The term *architecture* has been overloaded with different meanings. It can denote a system, product components, or an infrastructure. There are many architectures labeled under Web Services today. While they may offer good contributions to the field, some are primarily a rebranding of vendor product architecture.

A product architecture that lacks structure and guiding principles would not be useful for scalable and reliable Web Services. Both the previous chapter Web Services Technology Overview, and Appendix B provide a sampler of Web Services architectures. Which should a customer choose to implement? This chapter introduces a framework and reference architecture for building scalable and reliable Web Services.

4.3.3   Benefits of an Architecture

A structured Web Services architecture framework enables developers to build reusable components, distributed services, and sharable systems infrastructure (for example, server, storage, network, performance, and availability management). This can help improve programmer productivity (speed), compress development cycles (speed), reduce infrastructure and support costs (cost), mitigate risk through use of pretested components (quality), and enhance Quality of Services, such as scalability and availability (quality).

4.4   What Is a Reference Architecture?

In this book, a reference architecture has the following characteristics:

- **Underlying Architecture Framework**—This provides a structure (meta-architecture) that defines the logical and physical components that constitute the business services, and the processes used to develop it.

- **Architectural Principles**—These are rules and guidelines that help design and govern scalable, reliable architecture.

- **Design Patterns**—These are models that tell when and what technology to use.

- **Supporting Software Tools**—A reference architecture is not a laboratory product. It should have supporting commercial implementations and off-the-shelf vendor products. An overview of what product solution options are available.

Apart from the development methodology, the Vnified Process also provides a good approach to define and depict architecture, for instance, in terms of tiers and layers. This book will leverage on the architecture views and concepts to define reference architecture for Web Services technology.

4.4.1   Architecture Framework

A meta-architecture abstracts what the architecture components should have, so that the architecture can be easily extended or simplified based on the business needs. The meta-architecture is to the architecture as grammar is to a language. Nevertheless, it may sound too abstract or unnecessary for some practitioners.

A good meta-architecture should be product- and platform-neutral. Product architecture provides product-specific components. An application can derive the application architecture from a meta-architecture based on the business architecture (for example, data architecture and business object modeling) and technical architecture (for example, vendor products and physical infrastructure) components of the business system functionality.

Reference architecture can be defined for each domain based on a meta-architecture (for example, online securities trading) and used as a blueprint for designing and building applications. It provides a better context and vocabulary for developers and practitioners.

Sun ONE^{TM} is a good example of a meta-architecture. It defines a Web Services architecture with seven meta-components (for lack of a better word), with each having different architecture components to interact with one another. Figure 4–1 shows the first published example of a Sun ONE Web Services architecture—Zefer. Each meta-component (for example, identity and policy) consists of different components and services, (for example, directory services, privacy, and policy). Service Delivery

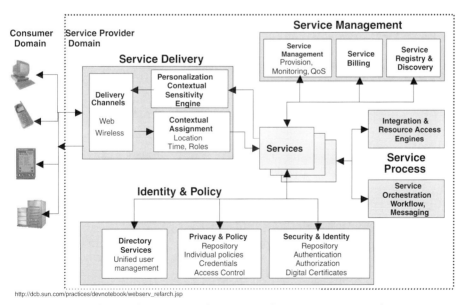

Figure 4–1   Zefer's Web Services Architecture With Sun ONE Framework

components (for example, delivery channels) may have multi-channel gateways (for example, Web wireless access and WAP). Services components (Web Services) may have an accounting system, such as a billing engine. Service Management components provide provisioning of business services (such as allocating an IP address to a wireless J2ME device), monitoring of the service level, and metering the business services for services billing. Service process components (for example, service orchestration) are the integration channels to the back-end systems or external trading partners.

Service Requesters (or consumers) may be accessing the business services from a variety of mobile devices or a browser. This belongs to the consumer domain. All other architecture components are part of the Service Provider domain. A client may use a phone to inquire about his account balance, where the relevant Web Services components will process the balance inquiry and perform transcoding for different client devices wherever necessary. A client may receive his account balance from his PDA, WAP phone, or another device based on his personalization profile.

Figure 4–2 depicts a detailed Web Services architecture Zefer has adopted. In the Service Delivery component, there is a controller servlet that can handle service requests from the Service Requester's mobile devices or browser. The Service Requester will initially look up the business service from a service directory (in this example, it is a UDDI registry) via the service directory proxy.

If this is a SOAP call, the controller servlet will pass control to the processor, which will then pass the SOAP service request to a service proxy (SOAP client proxy). The service proxy is a client stub and will communicate with the RPC router servlet (SOAP server). The RPC router servlet, which runs under a service container (such as J2EE

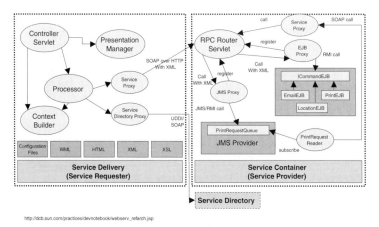

http://dcb.sun.com/practices/devnotebook/webserv_refarch.jsp

Figure 4–2 Zefer's Web Services Architecture

application server), will determine whether this is an RPC call (service proxy), RMI-IIOP call to EJBs (EJB proxy), or another asynchronous message provider (JMS proxy).

Any business data returned from the RPC router servlet will be captured by the service proxy in XML format. The presentation manager can reformat the data and transcode into HTML, or WML using XSL if applicable. This enables the Service Requester to view in a format that is displayable on any mobile device or browser.

4.4.2 Architecture Methodology and Development Life Cycle

Unified Process has a structured approach or methodology to define and analyze any architecture (including Web Services) by tiers, layers, or platform with different views. Rational Unified Process from IBM Rational is one of the commercial implementations commonly used in the IT industry. Large vendors usually have a customized version of Unified Process-based methodology (for example, Sun's SunTone Architecture Methodology). The Unified Process methodology defines different stages of IT development, ranging from the Inception phase (where requirements are defined), the Elaboration phase (where design or proof of concept is done), the Construction phase (where software is being built), the Transition phase (where software is being configured and deployed), the Production phase (where software enters into service), and the Retirement phase (where software reaches end-of-life). *http://www.enterpriseunifiedprocess.info* shows an example of the Unified Process methodology.

Architecture is usually defined during the Inception (for example, reference architecture, logical components) and Elaboration (for example, detailed application architecture design) phases of a development life cycle. It is important to trace back the architecture design from the functional requirements—that is, validate each architecture component from the functional requirements and service level. For instance, you would not have a component (say, personalization server) that is not supported by requirements.

The architecture methodology and development life cycle are generic to application development, including Web Services technology. The following diagram depicts an example of different activities of the architecture methodology with respect to the development life cycle.

Figure 4–3 shows an example of a Web Services development life cycle using the Unified Process development methodology. A Web Services project should be no different from any other IT project. A Web Services project usually starts with defining the business vision and strategy (Inception phase), then moves to crafting the architecture design (Elaboration phase), developing the integration and interoperability modules, integrating with the back-end systems and trading partners (Construction phase), testing, and finally deploying to production (Transition phase). Due to the nature of Web Services technology, there may be less development effort, but more integration effort and interoperability testing.

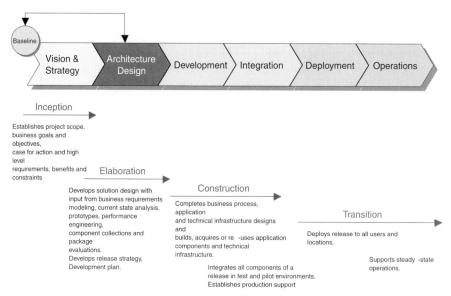

Figure 4–3   Web Services Development Life Cycle

4.4.3   Example—Securities Trading Reference Architecture

Figures 4–4 and 4–5 show an example of a reference architecture for securities trading, with the two diagrams showing servers and logical components respectively.

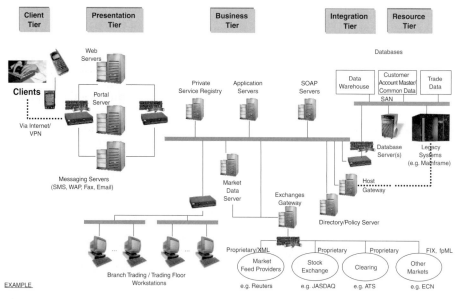

Figure 4–4   Securities Trading Reference Architecture—Server Level

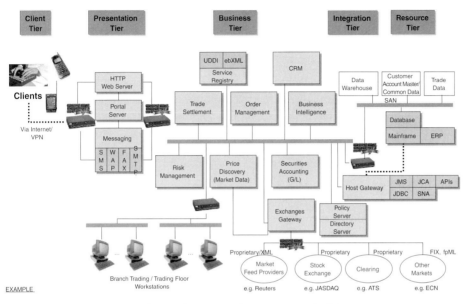

Figure 4–5 Securities Trading Reference Architecture—Logical Components

Figure 4–4 depicts a server-level architecture view of a securities trading (or brokerage) firm that adopts Web Services technology. The architecture components are categorized into five different tiers based on their functionality or role (these five tiers are depicted in SunTone Architecture Methodology under *http://www.sun.com/service/sunps/jdc/suntonearchmethod.html)*. Between the tiers, there are usually separate routers (thus creating different IP subnets) and firewalls that segregate the servers for security and network management reasons.

The Business Tier contains service components that provide the core business logic. Here, the core online securities trading applications run on clustered J2EE application servers. A private Service Registry (for dynamic service look-up), a set of SOAP servers (acting as a service proxy to back-end legacy systems or remote trading partners' systems), and a market data server (for publishing foreign exchange rates and latest stock prices) also reside in the same Business Tier.

The Integration Tier hosts the integration components (such as messaging bus), gateways (such as Host Gateway for legacy mainframe systems, and Exchanges gateway for Stock Exchanges), and security components (such as Directory Server and Policy Server). The Host Gateway provides a channel to invoke applications running on legacy mainframes. There is also an Exchanges gateway, which acts as a channel to execute trade orders with local exchanges (such as NASDAQ and JASDAQ) or other markets (such as Instinet, which is an Electronic Communication Network), subscribe market data from market data feeds providers (such as Reuters or Bloomberg), and clear trade orders with local clearing organizations (such as Hong Kong Exchange,

Deposit Trust, and Clearing Corporation). The Directory Server provides enterprise-level authentication. The Policy Server stores access rights and policies that govern the access level of each service component or system by users and by roles. These security components actually span different tiers.

The Resource Tier typically hosts all data stores (such as customer account master and trade data residing on a database server running a relational database), data warehouse, Enterprise Resource Planning (ERP) systems, and legacy mainframe applications. These resources may physically reside on a Storage Area Network (SAN) for better data availability and management.

On the client side, the Client Tier consists of any client front-end that accesses the online securities trading functionality. This includes browser, rich client (such as Java SWING client), and mobile devices (such as PDA and WAP phones).

The Presentation Tier handles HTTP requests from the client side, processes the presentation logic, and transforms it into some other messaging format. This includes the HTTP Web servers (handling static Web pages), a portal server (personalizing contents and aggregating information), and messaging servers (such as SMS server or WAP gateway).

The SOAP server and UDDI Service Registry are two key architecture components that characterize a Web Services architecture. In this example, Web Services technology is used for internal applications, not for public consumer use. The UDDI Service Registry is used as a private Service Registry and thus reduces the risk of external security attack. For similar reasons, both the SOAP servers and UDDI Service Registries reside in the Business Tier. If Web Services are provided to public consumers, then the UDDI Service Registry (public Service Registry) and SOAP server are likely to reside in the Presentation Tier. Segregating the SOAP server and UDDI Service Registry from the application server can lower the security risk of all servers being exploited.

The architecture components in Figure 4-4 are described as follows:

Web Servers. HTTP Web server farms that handle HTTP requests (such as Web pages navigation) from the browsers or mobile devices

Portal Server. Provides personalization of contents and channels to aggregate information contents and/or transactions

Messaging Servers. Delivery channels for emails (SMTP), pagers (SMS), WAP phones (WML), and faxes

Private Service Registry. UDDI or ebXML business Service Registry where users can look up any Service Providers by names, product codes, or industry categories

Application Servers. Servlets or EJB containers to support the complete life cycle of application services and data

SOAP Server. Servlet that handles SOAP messaging

Market Data Server. Market data feeds handler and administration to receive and broadcast multiple market data feeds

Databases. Back-end databases that provide data store for common data and codes, customer account master, trade data, and data mart/warehouses

Host Gateway. Gateway that connects and provides access to the back-end hosts or legacy systems

Directory/Policy Server. Directory server that stores user credentials and access rights; policy server stores access rights and security policies

Exchanges Gateway. Gateway that connects to and accesses external parties and exchanges

Figure 4–5 elaborates on the previous architecture diagram in Figure 4–4 by depicting the logical components in each server. Using the unified process methodology, this logical view is usually defined in the Inception phase, and it acts as a starting point to design the Quality of Services, such as reliability, availability, and scalability, for each component. The following describes the functionality of the logical components in the Business Tier, which may reside in one or multiple application servers.

- **Price Discovery.** This includes a quote server that provides the latest stock price quotes or foreign exchange rates based on the market data and a market data server that hosts all market data from market data feeds Service Providers.
- **Order Management.** An application that helps brokers handle trade orders from customers. This includes getting a quote, placing a trade order, acknowledging a trade order, confirming a trade order, routing a trade order, and executing a trade order.
- **Trade Settlement.** An application that performs matching between trade orders and executed trade orders and prepares for trade settlement with local clearing organizations.
- **Securities Accounting.** A back-office system that manages the accounting of trade orders, clearing, and settlement.
- **Business Intelligence.** This provides analytics (operations reporting), data mining (for cross-selling and marketing), and customer reporting (for compliance purposes).
- **Customer Relationship Management.** This makes use of different delivery channels or touch points to manage the life cycle of customers by cross-selling, up-selling, and call center services.

In a securities trading business, the logical components (such as order management and price discovery) resemble multiple business services, which can be exposed as Web Services. This logical view can help identify new service components that can be shared and reused. In this example, Web Services technology can help aggregate customer and account information that is captured in a trade order (order management), past credit history (risk management), and past trading history (securities accounting) to support cross-selling and customer sales analytics (CRM) in real-time. Without Web Services, architects may need to build interfaces to extract the customer information into a data warehouse. These interfaces may not be real-time, and may not be reusable for other systems.

Tiers Versus Platform Layers

Categorizing the architecture components in tiers helps architects segment the components, showing how each component operates and interacts with other components in different levels. Architects can also scale up the architecture components by exposing and distributing the business services into multiple machine instances (horizontal scaling) or by allocating workload to different instances by business functionality (for example, instance A performs equities trade orders for retail customers and instance B performs equities trade orders for private customers and options). These are different options showing how architects can improve the Quality of Service of the business services using Web Services technology. Thus, architects can scale up (or down) the workload easily without rewriting the application.

Analyzing the technology stacks by platform layers also helps improve the Quality of Services. The book *Dot-Com and Beyond: Breakthrough Internet-based Architectures and Methodologies (2001)* discusses what the tiers and platform layers are, and how to define the Quality of Services by comparing the tiers and platform layers (also see Tables 4–1 and 4–2). The platform layer categorization refers to the technology stack, from hardware to the application. The Application Platform Layer denotes the applications (such as risk management system) running on a host with the business logic. The Virtual Platform Layer denotes the middleware or protocol that communicates with the operating system, application server, or other external components, such as SOAP protocol, J2EE RMI/IIOP. The Upper Platform Layer is typically the application server, which consists of the Web container (such as a Web server) and the EJB container (such as a J2EE application server). This provides the application infrastructure for the applications with the business logic. The Lower Platform Layer is usually the operating system, such as Solaris OE. The Hardware Platform Layer refers to the underlying hardware, including the Sparc machine and the associated storage solutions.

Analyzing the architecture components by platform layers can help identify areas where Quality of Services measures (such as vertical scaling and high availability) can be applied. For instance, architects can use hardware and database clustering technology to improve the service level of availability for the UDDI service registries. The tiers versus platform layers analysis (as in Table 4–1) identifies the service components that need to be scaled or made reliable. Then a Quality of Services analysis (as in Table 4–2) can be applied to each tier or platform layer, so that reliability, availability, and scalability options are identified prior to the Web Services implementation.

Table 4–1 shows an example of categorizing the logical components by tiers and platform layers. Please note that some components may span tiers. This is the first step in determining what business services are available, where the service components are, and which ones can be made reliable, available, and scalable. For instance, Service Requesters around the world need to browse through a UDDI Service Registry for different products and services and to look up and invoke appropriate remote business services, such as placing a trade order. Therefore, it is crucial that the Service Registry be able to operate around the clock (7 days × 24 hours). Because the Service Registry resides in the Integration Tier and in the Application Platform Layer, architects may review options within this tier or layer to scale up the Application Platform Layer, and to make it highly available.

Table 4–1   Tiers Versus Platform Layer Architecture Analysis

Tiers/ Platform Layer	Client Tier	Presentation Tier	Business Tier	Integration Tier	Resource Tier
Application Platform Layer			Order management Trade settlement Risk management Price discovery Securities accounting CRM Business Intelligence	Service Registry	ERP systems Policy Server Directory Server
Virtual Platform Layer		J2EE		SOAP ebXML	Policy Server Directory Server
Upper Platform Layer	Client Browser	Messaging Servers Web Server Portal Server	Application Server		Database Server Policy Server Directory Server
Lower Platform Layer	PDA WAP phone	Solaris OE	Solaris OE	Solaris OE	Policy Server Directory Server
Hardware Platform Layer	PDA WAP phone	Sparc Unix			Mainframe Storage devices/SAN

Quality of Services Analysis Matrix

The Quality of Services matrix shown in Table 4–2 shows how each component can support different "ilities" in different tiers and layers. This is particularly useful for identifying areas for improving scalability and availability. The "ilities" column shows a list of Quality of Services attributes, such as performance, throughput, and scalability. The other columns show different technology options that can be used to design the Quality of Services attributes under different tiers. For instance, reliability and availability for a UDDI Service Registry can be done by clustering the Service Registry hardware. Under a clustered Service Registry, if the master Service Registry has a hardware failure, it will fail over to the secondary Service Registry, without disrupting the lookup service (there may be a short failover lead time of less than 10 minutes though). This can meet around-the-clock service level (7 days × 24 hours). The technical details can be referred to the pattern "High Availability Service Registry" discussed in the following Web Services design pattern section.

Table 4–2 Quality of Services Analysis Matrix

"ilities"	Client Tier	Presentation Tier	Business Tier	Integration Tier	Resource Tier
Performance, throughput, and scalability		HTTP-based load balancing for SOAP servlet SOAP/XML cache	Vertical scaling Horizontal scaling	HTTP-based load balancer for Service Registry SOAP/XML cache	Federated Directory Server
Reliability and availability	Reliable and clustered hardware platform	Reliable and clustered hardware platform Clustered messaging servers	Reliable and clustered hardware platform Clustered Application Server	Clustered Service Registry	Master-slave Directory Server for HA Parallel database server Standby database server Reliable and clustered hardware platform
Security	HTTPS VPN gateway	HTTPS VPN gateway	HTTPS	XML security (e.g., DSIG, WS-security)	XML security standards (e.g., SAML, XACML) Trusted Solaris OE
Manageability	System management tools	System management tools	System management tools	System management tools	System management tools

Table 4–2 Quality of Services Analysis Matrix—*continued.*

"ilities"	Client Tier	Presentation Tier	Business Tier	Integration Tier	Resource Tier
Flexibility		Decoupling presentation from business (e.g., XML for data, HTML for presentation)		Update URL end-point in Service Registry without re-binding run-time (re-compilation)	
Reusability			SOAP-enabled business services	SOAP-enabled business services	SOAP-enabled business services

4.5 Web Services Architecture Principles

The following architecture principles present a high-level discussion of how to architect Web Services solutions. Some of these guiding principles are similar to architecting any IT solution, but they are discussed in Web Services technology context. They can be used as a checklist prior to reviewing a Web Services project proposal or a design artifact. In this section, the ground rules (aka corollary) refer to the extension of the associated high-level architecture principles, or any proposition inferred from the principle.

4.5.1 General Principles

Principle 1. You should build a Web Services-based solution to satisfy user requirements at the time of delivery, where user requirements may evolve with a better understanding of the system and integration capability. You should use iterative requirements analysis techniques to avoid rigid requirements. You must drive integration and interoperability requirements from the business vision. You should not create the impression that you are implementing the idea for technology's sake. Rather, you should focus on broader architecture items and system reusability.

Some architects kick off Web Services projects without a business vision. They may start from a technical perspective, wanting to be in the state-of-the-art technology areas (gimmick). These Web Services projects may not have any supporting user requirements. For example, developers may modify an existing sample wireless Web Services program as a proof of concept. However, they may overlook the architecture complexity of wireless security, the memory constraints, and any associated performance issues of the mobile device (that is, the broader architecture items).

Principle 2. You should achieve business results through a series of successes by breaking down any large and high-risk Web Services initiatives into a small and manageable number of pieces. Besides, you can deploy a small series of projects that are cohesive to the bigger picture of the Web Services initiative. Next, you would like to avoid re-engineering the entire business process while achieving a small success. People may perceive the focus as business changes. For example, if the Web Services project is anticipated to be a large-scale application implementation with 24 elapsed months, then it is better to split the project into smaller projects of three to four months' duration (also refer to ground rule 4).

Principle 3. You should mitigate business and technology risks with pilot or reusable prototypes. Traditional development methodology requires lengthy requirements and design processes, before a pilot or prototype can be produced. You may choose to use an iterative development process with appropriate user involvement for feedback (such as a Use Case workshop).

Ground Rule 1. Web Services solution release must deliver quantifiable business value (for example, a Web Services solution to address the market connectivity between brokerage firms to achieve Straight-through Processing should bring cost savings of around $100,000 dollars annually).

Ground Rule 2. The cost of Web Services infrastructure and integration implementation (for example, the implementation cost for UDDI and SOAP server) should not exceed the business value delivered (such as the sum of cost savings or additional revenue generated from delivering all Web Services solutions). This needs to be expanded in the business case justification. For example, it would not make sense to invest in a $10 million Web Services infrastructure implementation of UDDI Service Registry, while the anticipated revenue of deploying a Service Registry is US$10,000 per year.

Ground Rule 3. Architects should avoid time-consuming analysis of current states and interoperability constraints. This is because Web Services implementation is not intended to re-engineer the entire enterprise architecture (which is usually done by analyzing current states and interoperability). The Web Services technology is suitable for exposing business services and system functionality from legacy systems (aka black-box systems) without refactoring or re-engineering them. This enables a fast interoperability solution. For example, it is not recommended to re-engineer the business process of securities trading (for Straight-through Processing) while implementing a new messaging infrastructure using SOAP messaging over JMS. This will add to the project implementation risks.

Ground Rule 4. You should time-box any Web Services into a three- to five-month delivery time window.

Ground Rule 5. You should exploit reusable prototype (with performance benchmarking) to mitigate business and technology risks.

4.5.2   Lower Platform Layer

Principle 4. Web Services technology operates independent of the Operating System or the Lower Platform. However, the availability of Web Services solutions is dependent on the reliability and availability of the Lower Platform (such as hardware and software clustering, High Availability configuration, and system management).

Ground Rule 6. You should always consider and include the hardware and software level's reliability and availability (for example, clustering or hot failover) during the Web Services implementation. Typically, UDDI or ebXML Service Registry and SOAP appliances are examples of service components where the hardware and software's reliability and availability will be of great importance.

4.5.3   Upper Platform Layer

Principle 5. Web Services solutions can run on any Web or servlet container (such as Tomcat), not necessarily on an EJB container. However, it will still be architecturally neat to have the same vendor servlet container for the same operating environment. Most RPC-based SOAP calls do not manage session or state. Keeping track of the states for each call or every child process may not be necessary or desirable for some RPC-based (synchronous) Web Services for performance reasons.

Ground Rule 7. Many Web Services calls are stateless beans making RPC calls. You may still want to store the session information (such as who has initiated a payment request, and when) when you initiate a SOAP call in order to support Single Sign-on and identity management. This will allow the security infrastructure (such as identity server) to track each security session and Web Services management tools to meter the remote business services for billing or performance-monitoring purposes.

Ground Rule 8. You should not store the state of the Web Service if it spans different legacy systems or multiple nodes, as that requires extremely complex application design to support multiphase commit and rollback. For example, if developers want to aggregate account balances from multiple banking systems to provide a consolidated investment portfolio using synchronous Web Services (say, JAX-RPC), they should not persist the session state of each connection to the individual banking system. Otherwise, if one connection fails, the account balance aggregation service may hang up the entire application (thus, performance overhead). If one of the connections with the banking system needs to make a secondary RPC call to perform a business transaction and the secondary RPC call aborts with an exception, should the developer roll back the transactions or not? This may be a complex design issue to address, if the states of each connection or RPC calls are persisted and tracked.

4.5.4   Virtual Platform Layer

Principle 6. The message exchange between the SOAP Service Provider and the SOAP consumer can be one-way (asynchronous) or two-way (synchronous), bound to the data transport such as HTTP, SMTP, JMS, and so forth. The choice of synchronous messaging is appropriate for the RPC application model. Asynchronous messaging is appropriate for sending or receiving XML documents and can be supplemented by SOAP-JMS binding for guaranteed message delivery.

Business transactions and business process orchestration often require reliable messaging infrastructure to support. Without reliable messaging, Service Requesters do not know the requests have been received and processed by the Service Provider. This will result in potential financial loss.

Ground Rule 9. If guaranteed message delivery is required, then use asynchronous SOAP calls with SOAP-JMS binding (SOAP messages bind to a reliable messaging layer using JMS). This addresses the issue of the reliability of SOAP messaging over HTTP. There are vendor products that provide JMS bridge functionality to bind SOAP messages to JMS; developers need not build this functionality from scratch.

4.5.5   Application Platform Layer

Principle 7. It is easier to wrap a legacy system with a SOAP client proxy. However, be coarse-grained, and do not wrap every functional call. Some SOAP calls can be cached with a time period if the data is relatively static within the predefined time period.

Ground Rule 10. The Web Services calls should be coarse-grained when defining new business services from an existing system. For instance, if an EJB has 100 methods of inquiring about a customer account, it will not be practical to expose all 100 methods as Web Services. A coarse-grained approach to exposing business functionality as Web Services may suggest three to five Web Services calls, where similar account information can be encapsulated into one Web Services call.

4.6   Supporting Software Tools

4.6.1   Web Services Development Platform

TCPTunnel. This is a utility that listens to the TCP/IP port, say, port 8080 for SOAP messages. It comes with Apache SOAP Axis, which you can download from *http://xml.apache.org/axis.*

SOAP Debugger. An example is XMLSpy, which is an XML editing utility with some SOAP debugging capability. You can download a trial copy from *http://www.xmlspy.com.*

4.6.2   Web Services Deployment Platform

Unit Testing. An example is jTest, which is a Java-based unit testing tool.

Stress/Load Testing. An example is Mercury Interactive's LoadRunner, which is an application stress test tool. Refer to *http://www.mercuryinteractive.com* for details.

Regression Testing. An example is Rationale Test Studio, which provides regression testing capability.

SOAP Testing/Performance Testing. Examples are Empirix's FirstAct (commercial product that simulates end-user SOAP client's testing; refer to *http://www.empirix.com*), PushtoTest (a SOAP testing utility; refer to *http://www.pushtotest.com*), and SOAPTest (a public utility for generating stress testing for SOAP clients; refer to *http://www.parasoft.com/jsp/products/home.jsp?product=SOAP*).

Web Services Management/Network Services. These vendors provide routing of Web Services for different versioning and also network management tools for remote Web Services. Examples are *http://www.flamenconetworks.com/* and *http://www.talkingblocks.com/.*

4.6.3   Infrastructure Tools

Version Management. Version management tools keep track of different versions of your SOAP applications. Examples are CVS and Rational ClearCase.

Release Control. Release control tools help when deploying, by upgrade or fallback, a specific version of your SOAP applications to the target platform. An example is Rational ClearCase.

Application Server Analyzer. Application server analyzer helps analyzing the performance and different components (for example, states or cookies) of the J2EE application server. Examples are WebSphere Web Site Analyzer from Altaworks (*http://www.altaworks.com*) and Omegamon XE from Candle (*http://www.candle.com*).

Systems Management Tools. These tools provide infrastructure support and health check for the platform. Examples are BMC Patrol and OpenView.

Performance Tuning. There are performance tuning methods and tools for Unix, NT platform, vendor-specific database tuning tools, and Java application tuning tools.

Middleware Monitoring Tools. If middleware is used, these tools help monitor the middleware components such as the queue management. These are vendor-specific middleware administration control and monitoring tools.

4.6.4   Security Infrastructure

Certificate Management. If digital certificates are used for generating digital signatures, then a certificate management server will be essential. An example is Sun ONE certificate manager server.

Hardware Encryption. Hardware encryption tools may include SSL accelerator for HTTPS connectivity and Hardware Security Module (HSM) for storing the public and private keys. There are various vendor-specific products for hardware encryption and HSM.

Policy Server. A policy server that integrates different directory servers and provides Single Sign-on is essential. An example is Netegrity's Siteminder.

Directory Server. A directory server provides authentication and entitlement services for applications. It is also a core component for network identity management. An example is Sun ONE Directory Server and Identity Server.

4.6.5   Web Services Open Standards

Major Web Services security standards are SOAP-SEC (SOAP security using XML digital signature), XML Key Management Services (XKMS), Security Access Markup Language (SAML), and XML Access Control Mark-up Language (XACML). Please refer to Chapter 3, Web Services Technology Overview for an introduction and Chapter 7, Web Services Security for details.

4.6.6   Product Architecture

J2EE Application Server Platform. These are typically application servers, and they usually come with many useful development tools. Examples are Sun ONE Application Server, IBM WebSphere, and Microsoft .NET Server.

Edge Products. These products provide peripheral utilities that enhance performance (for example, caching product) and scalability (for example, load balancing). An example is Progress eXcelon XIS (aka XML/SOAP Cache).

4.7   Inside Web Services

4.7.1   SOAP Architecture

This section discusses the characteristics of the SOAP architecture, their architecture implications, and the outlook of the technology. W3C's XML Protocol working group is currently incorporating SOAP 1.2 as part of the new XML Protocol. Details can be referenced at *http://www.w3.org/2000/xp/Group/*.

Characteristics. Applications built on the SOAP architecture share the following characteristics:

- They are built on loosely-coupled message-based architecture.
- They have two modes of communication: synchronous (request–reply, RPC), and asynchronous (document, one-way).
- The transport and message levels are decoupled.

SOAP 1.2 does not mandate SOAPAction in the HTTP header; thus the SOAP message can be decoupled from the HTTP header. Also refer to Chapter 3, Web Services Technology Overview.

Architecture Implication. The underlying transport HTTP is stateless. In other words, synchronous communication simulates request–reply on stateless HTTP by storing the state. We need different SOAP message constructs to handle synchronous and asynchronous modes. We cannot use the same client to handle both modes. The security needs to be handled by a mixture of transport-, message-, and application-level protection. The configuration files and WSDL stored in the SOAP server are in clear text, and this may have security implications.

SOAP Constraints and Beyond. The protocol itself does not provide guaranteed message delivery or message-level Quality of Service. For instance, SOAP-RPC invokes remote application calls but it does not assure the call is always successful. It cannot specify Quality of Service priority (that is, high, critical, guaranteed delivery) when passing messages. The protocol cannot support polymorphism, for example, based on the parameter to invoke different methods. It does not provide workflow integration capability.

Technology Outlook. HTTPR (*http://www-106.ibm.com/developerworks/webservices/library/ws-httprspec/*) is a proprietary extension to HTTP proposed by IBM, which enhances the transport-level security. It is not yet clear whether it has gained any strong traction in the industry yet.

SOAP-JMS binding provides guaranteed message delivery or Quality of Service depending on the quality of the underlying JMS vendor. The reliability of SOAP messaging is gaining more attention from developers. There are some vendor products that address the reliability issue of SOAP messaging by providing a JMS Bridge (such as Progress SonicXQ) and some vendors are beginning to support ebMS (such as TIBCO).

The business process model applied to Web Services is preliminary. Further convergence with ebXML is expected (for example, BPEL4WS proposal (*http://www-106.ibm.com/developerworks/webservices/library/ ws-bpel/*) is a step toward workflow integration). It is anticipated that W3C and OASIS will take a more proactive role in working toward a common standard for business process orchestration using Web Services technology.

DCOM, CORBA, and Web Services. Wahili, Tomlinson, Zimmermann, Deruyck, and Hendriks have noticed some interesting comparisons between DCOM, CORBA, and Web Services (see Table 4–3). Table 4–3 shows a comparison of DCOM, CORBA, and Web Services, where Web Services technology provides more flexibility using XML and a loosely coupled client–server computing approach. Interestingly, IBM's UDDI registry was developed by the CORBA development team, who reuse many of the CORBA objects previously developed.

Table 4–3 Comparing DCOM, CORBA, and Web Services

	DCOM	CORBA	Web Services
End-point naming	OBJREF	Interoperable object reference (IOR)	URL/URN
Interfaces	Single	Multiple	Multiple—WSDL
Payload types	Binary	Binary	Text
Payload parameter value format	Network data representation (DR)	Common data representation	XML
Server address resolution	Directory	Naming service	IP routing, URN
Message dispatcher	ID-based	ID-based	Namespace, and parameter types
Client–server coupling	Tight	Tight	Loose

4.7.2 UDDI Architecture

This section discusses the design of the UDDI Service Registry and its architecture implications to developers. Most UDDI implementations today use version 2.0, and are targeted as a private Service Registry, not a public Service Registry. UDDI version 3.0 (*http://www.oasis-open.org/committees/uddi-spec/tcspecs.shtml#uddiv3*) is currently available. Nevertheless, the commercial implementation is still maturing.

Information Model. UDDI has a sound business information model, tModel, to represent business service information. Business and service information is cross-referenced by service keys.

Access Design. UDDI Service Registry is intended to be like DNS (for IP address for domains). The UDDI browser plug-in is available for client browsers. The service look-up performance and UDDI server security depend on the vendor implementation.

Architecture Implication. You do not need to look up the service endpoint by service keys in order to invoke the Web services. UDDI look-up provides the benefits of central repository of services information and run-time bindings (instead of hardcoding). Every user is able to browse and access the UDDI Service Registry, provided that it has access. Vendor-specific implementation may provide additional security (for example, UDDI implemented on a LDAP server).

Differentiator. The key differentiator for UDDI implementation is the availability of a powerful, algorithmic-based, search engine to navigate and locate Service Provider information faster. Another feature is the browser-based GUI to create multiple levels of tModel relationships and Service Provider product hierarchy. A user-friendly GUI administration wizard to guide defining GUID and service end-points would be essential, as it does not require users to understand the nitty-gritty of tModels. It is also useful to have a test UDDI prior to publishing it, tight integration to any developer work-bench, and a built-in UDDI browser plug-in available for Web browsers.

All in all, there should be robust local UDDI security features (for example, RDBMS security, Access Control Levels for different UDDI levels, and capability to support LDAP authentication). The UDDI implementation should not lock in any underlying vendor product infrastructure or software platform.

Constraints. The reliability and scalability of UDDI implementation is vendor-specific. UDDI does not address trading partner profiles and communications contracts like CPP and CPA in ebXML. Thus, there is no constraint or service agreement in client–server or server–server data exchange.

Technology Outlook. The private UDDI Service Registry seems to be more easily accepted than a public UDDI. UDDI will evolve to address trading partner agreement, tangent to ebXML's CPP and CPA. Should trading partner's work flow information (for example, BPEL4WS) be stored in UDDI as well?

4.7.3   ebXML Architecture

This section discusses the design features of ebXML, the architecture implications, and their constraints. This technology is gaining more industry support (*http://www.ebxml.org/endorsements.htm*) with increasing vendor support and commercial implementations since 2001.

Characteristics. There are plenty of ebXML business and conceptual architecture documents available from the official Web site (*http://www.ebxml.org/specs/index.htm*). In summary, ebXML architecture, which now supports Web Services, has the following characteristics:

- They should have loosely-coupled message-based architecture.

- Similar to SOAP, ebXML decouples transport and message level and supports synchronous and asynchronous communication.
- They have sophisticated business process models, and some of them reflect previous EDI data exchange paradigms (many OASIS participants and contributors are EDI veterans).

Architecture Implication. The architecture foundation is good, though commercial offerings are still maturing. The Collaboration Partner Profile and Collaborative Partner Agreement (aka the service contract between trading partners) need to be agreed upon between trading partners. This is more complicated to implement than WSDL-UDDI-SOAP technology because ebXML can be used to support complex Web Services for workflow processing and collaboration.

ebXML Message Service (ebMS) allows guaranteed delivery of messages even if the recipient is not online temporarily. It requires a message provider class that ensures messages are delivered after the recipient is back online. Nowadays, the SOAP message service can be made more reliable by binding it to Java Message Service (JMS). It is sometimes called SOAP-JMS binding for message services. This requires using a JMS bridge to intercept a SOAP message, with a message provider delivering the message to the recipient using the underlying middleware infrastructure. Nevertheless, SOAP-JMS binding technology is not part of the SOAP or JMS specification yet.

Constraints. The complexity of the business process model makes design and implementation difficult. Thus, it may take longer for architects and developers to implement complex workflow processing using ebXML. In contrast, WSDL-UDDI-SOAP technology is not mature enough to implement complex workflow processing, though the recent Business Process Execution Language for Web Services (BPEL4WS) and Web Services Choreography Interface (WSCI) are examples of new initiatives that address these requirements.

Industry support and implementation for ebXML is growing slowly. There are also a number of customers holding a "wait-and-see" position regarding ebXML technology, perhaps because the concept of implementing complex Web Services with workflow capability is still young and maturing.

Technology Outlook. We are seeing further convergence of ebXML and SOAP technology. OASIS recently changed its strategy in ebXML standards development. Sun's Web Services Developer Pack will expedite and shape future evolution of ebXML implementation. Sun will continue to support ebXML, especially in providing reference implementation such as ebXML Service Registry.

4.8   Web Services Design Patterns

The term Design Patterns is now a buzzword that denotes some reusable framework or objects. Design Patterns show a structure that can be applied if certain conditions are met. They are best practices and are accumulated from past implementation experience.

The early use of the term by the so-called Gang of Four (Gamma, Helm, Johnson, and Vlissides) describes the relationship of objects and components in application design in the categories of creational patterns (for example, factory methods), structural patterns (for example, facade, proxy) and behavioral patterns (for example, observer, visitor). Here, the Web Services design patterns lean toward structural design pattern, in the context of deploying an end-to-end architecture with Quality of Services.

We have identified a few design patterns:

- **Scalability Patterns**—SOAP cache, JMS Bridge, multiple servlet engines, HTTP load balancer
- **Reliability Patterns**—State management, SOAP logger
- **Manageability Patterns**—Publish/unpublish/discover Web Services, managing different versions of Web Services deployment with Service Registry, registry content management
- **Availability Patterns**—High Availability for UDDI
- **Security Patterns**—UDDI deployment patterns

The following sections describe some Web Services design patterns associated with designing a high level of Quality of Services. Each design pattern will start by defining the context (background or requirements), problem (problem statement), force (design factors to be considered, or when to use the pattern), solution (proposed solution depicted in Use Cases and sequence diagrams), risks (design or implementation risks, and the risk mitigation), and any relevant examples.

There are also design guidelines and best practices associated with designing and deploying Web Services, which are contributed by many practitioners. They will be recapitulated at the end of this section.

4.8.1   SOAP Cache

Context

In a Service Registry environment, Service Requesters dynamically look up a business service by finding the business organization name and service category (such as NAICS) to locate a service key. With a service key, they can retrieve the service endpoints URI and bind the URI to the remote business service using a client SOAP proxy. This dynamic service look-up is beneficial to managing business services within a large user community (such as millions of content providers and mobile phone subscribers), where business services and content are usually added or modified in real-time. It will not be practical to store a predefined URI or network address of the remote business service in the client's front-end, because every change in the business service information or the URI will require a program recompilation at the client front-end.

Although dynamic service look-up allows flexibility in managing changes in service information, it has a system performance overhead. The SOAP client front-end that looks up a Service Registry may take up to a few seconds' overhead (an extreme example is six seconds response time) to invoke a remote Web Service call. This will not be acceptable to many customers.

One solution is to reduce the service look-up overhead by caching frequently accessed Web Services at the SOAP client's side. Another solution is to cache the frequently accessed Web Services at the SOAP server's side. Caching the result from frequently accessed Web Services can improve performance of the services if the result contains static information (such as a code look-up table) that is valid within a given time window.

Problem

Every time a SOAP client looks up the service end-point URL from the Service Registry, there is a performance overhead. Sometimes, the response time may take half a second to two seconds, depending on the infrastructure set-up and application design. Frequently accessed transactions, such as stock quotes or common data look-up, take a considerable amount of CPU cycles and network I/O.

Force

For high transaction volume and high performance applications, there is a strong requirement to process a large quantity of SOAP requests during peak hours. If a normal distribution curve is extracted from the SOAP requests and there is a considerable number of frequently accessed service end-point URLs (that is, these frequently accessed service end-points are in the center of the bell curve), then this SOAP cache pattern will be useful to address the performance overhead of dynamic service look-up.

Client-side SOAP caching is desirable if it can be deployed to the Service Requester's side in a manageable manner. For example, if the Service Requester uses a Java-rich client, then the client-side SOAP cache can be implemented and updated easily with Java Web Start (that comes with JDK 1.4). Server-side SOAP caching is desirable if the Service Requester is using a browser or mobile device and loading cached processing logic in an applet is difficult due to performance constraints.

Solution

Use Case Modeling

Figures 4–6 through 4–8 depict the logical process with Use Cases and sequence diagrams for SOAP Cache. They help elaborate the context, and how the solution can address the dynamic service look-up overhead. In Figure 4–6, a SOAP client intends to initiate an RPC call to a remote business service. Instead of dynamically looking up the service end-point URL from a Service Registry, the SOAP client accesses a SOAP cache first. The SOAP cache can be implemented as a hash table stored in the physical memory of the SOAP client or the SOAP server for fast access. If the service end-point URL is available in the cache and the cached data is not yet expired, then the SOAP client will bind the service end-point URL. If the cached data is already expired (or there is no cached data available), the SOAP client will look up the Service Registry. The new service information (including service end-point URL) will be stored in the SOAP cache for faster retrieval with an expiry time frame. The expiry time frame is arbitrary. For example, a public portal service supporting a non-real-time stock quote or foreign exchange rate inquiry can set the expiry time to be every 15 minutes.

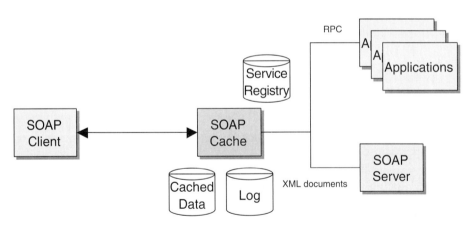

Figure 4–6   SOAP Cache

Figure 4–7 describes four business scenarios, or Use Cases, around managing a SOAP cache. A SOAP client looks up the cached data from a SOAP cache and retrieves business service information (such as service end-point URLs) from the cached data. If the cached data is available, then the SOAP client does not need to look up the Service Registry, which will reduce the dynamic service look-up overhead. It will then bind to the service end-point URL and invoke the remote business service via by the SOAP server. If the cached data is not available (or expired), the SOAP

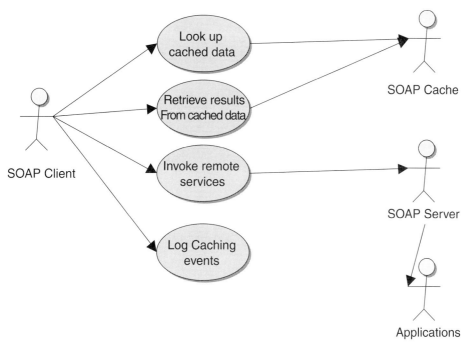

Figure 4–7   SOAP Cache Use Cases

client will perform a dynamic service look-up from the Service Registry. Newly fetched business service information can be added or updated to the SOAP cache, and this will be logged for event tracking.

Figure 4–8 elaborates some details of the Use Cases discussed earlier. The SOAP client needs to look up a service end-point URL to invoke a remote business service. It checks whether the nature of the remote business service supports cached business service information. For instance, an indicative foreign exchange rate inquiry is a good example of using SOAP cache. It will then access the SOAP cache, which may be implemented as a hash table stored in the physical memory of the SOAP client. If the cached data is available and is still timely, the SOAP client will retrieve the business service information from the SOAP cache. The business service information may show the binding information of the service end-point URL. Retrieving cached data (or even cached transaction information such as foreign exchange rates) from the physical memory is speedy and does not require routing the service look-up request to a Service Registry that may reside on another network. This will reduce CPU and network resources considerably.

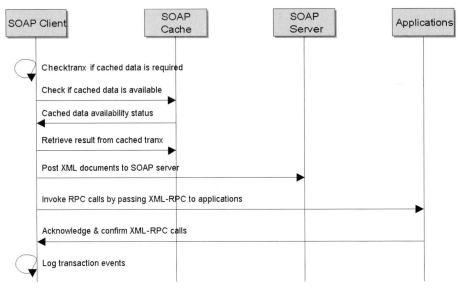

Figure 4–8   SOAP Cache Sequence Diagram

The SOAP client will then generate a SOAP request in an XML document and send it to the SOAP server (RPC router servlet). The SOAP server will initiate an RPC call to the application providing the business services. Using a synchronous Web Services call, an acknowledgement and the inquiry details (or transaction information) will be returned to the SOAP client. Both the caching event and the business transaction will be logged for tracking and management purposes.

Detailed Design

Transaction Cache Creation. Predefined transaction types can cache transaction contents and results. Cached data can be stored in serialized data objects, databases, XML cache (edge products), and LDAP with time stamp, version, and transaction type/id. Cache data (read-only) can be represented in XML structure and can be parsed/retrieved via DOM, SAX, JDOM, or Xpath.

There is a time-to-live time window. New and updated versions of cache data can be indicated by version and time stamp, whereas outdated/obsolete data can be decommissioned upon creation. If cached data is unavailable (for example, if it is corrupted, or being updated or removed), transaction contents need to be refetched and recached.

Retrieval of Cached Data. The SOAP Cache can be configured to intercept a normal SOAP request, check whether the transaction has been cached, before retrieving the cached data or passing through to applications or the SOAP server. A hash key can be generated to determine whether the transaction cache data is available. Data synchronization is critical, otherwise obsolete data is retrieved.

Implementation. SOAP Cache can be home-grown (such as Leavson's Professional Java SOAP), or off-the-shelf using an XML database (such as Progress eXcelon's XIS). Leavson's book provides some sample code (*http://www.wrox.com/dynamic/books/download.aspx?isbn=1861006101# downloads*) to implement a SOAP Cache, and it is a good reference point. The logical steps are outlined as follows:

Read in XML-RPC request

Check if cache is available against the cache hash table

Locate the relevant cached data (XML file)

If available, read cached data, identify the cached result by key

    Present result

Else

    format XML-RPC request

    send to SOAP server

End-if

Benefits

Some frequently accessed real-time (within a time window) or off-line applications can cache their transactions to boost performance and to reduce network traffic. Cached transaction results can be placed in memory and/or in edge products, instead of fetching the same requests from the application servers or from the database.

Risk

- **Transaction Integrity and Data Synchronization.** If the application contents are updated or changed, then how does this impact the cached data (for example, automatic/timed data synchronization)?

- **Design Complexity.** Intercepting transactions and applications requests by SOAP Cache requires additional application design and is often complex to implement.

- **Recovery of Cached Data.** If cached data is corrupted or being replaced, how should the application handle the recovery (for example, high availability of the cached data, refetch and cache the transactions)?

Example

Progress eXcelon's XIS (*http://www.exln.com/products/*) is an example of using an XML database to implement SOAP Cache, but it needs to be customized. Spiritsoft's jcache (*http://www.spiritsoft.com/products/jms_jcache/overview.html*) provides similar capability.

4.8.2   JMS Bridge

Context

Java Message Service (JMS) is part of the J2EE technology to provide reliable messaging for business transactions. It provides a set of high-level abstraction APIs to abstract connectivity and message delivery and is implemented using a middleware product or by reusing a J2EE application server infrastructure. It also allows richer and more flexible mechanisms (such as using Java Connector Architecture together) to integrate with other system components.

However, one trading partner (such as an investment manager) cannot send business transactions using a specific JMS vendor product to another trading partner (such as a sales trader or broker) who uses another JMS vendor product. This is because the underlying data transport implementation for the two JMS vendor products is different. A messaging bridge capability (such as JMS bridge using SOAP messaging) will be required to exchange business transactions and documents in a common format that can be understood by different JMS vendor implementations.

Reliable messaging using Web Services technology is critical to delivering financial messages or high-value transactions. An example is the case of an investment manager placing a trade order with a brokerage firm (see Figure 4–9). Both trading partners have JMS implementations in their back-office infrastructure. If the investment manager is placing a trade order of 10,000 lots of high-value technology stocks with the brokerage firm and his portfolio management system uses JMS to exchange trade orders, then the two different JMS vendor implementations cannot exchange messages directly. This is because they have different underlying data transport. The trading partners may want to utilize the benefits of SOAP messaging as a standards-based integration and interoperability technology, which is very useful for cross-institution interoperability or B2B integration. One solution approach is to use a JMS bridge for SOAP messaging, so that the trading partners can benefit from easier integration and interoperability using Web Services technology and JMS. This design pattern describes what a JMS bridge is, and how it can be implemented.

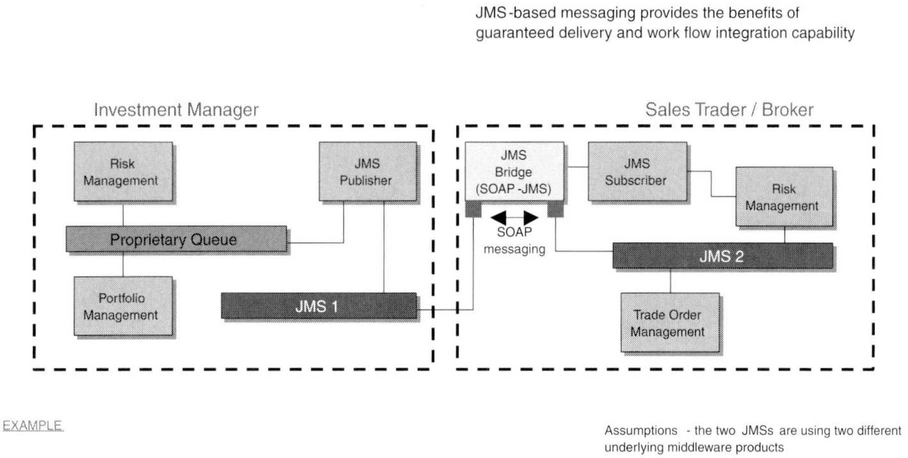

JMS-based messaging provides the benefits of
guaranteed delivery and work flow integration capability

EXAMPLE

Assumptions - the two JMSs are using two different
underlying middleware products

Figure 4–9   JMS Bridge

Problem

JMS is an integration technology that provides good Quality of Service and reliability for business transactions. However, different JMS vendor implementations are not interoperable, as the underlying transport and application protocols are different.

Force

JMS provides reliable message delivery within one application infrastructure. To interoperate with another infrastructure or other institutions, it is essential to build a JMS bridge between two different JMS vendor products. SOAP messaging is a flexible and standards-based interoperability technology and can be bound to JMS in the data transport layer to offer reliable message delivery. This design pattern is useful to business scenarios where there is a need to interoperate between two different JMS vendor products or two different middleware products.

Solution

Use Case Modeling

Figures 4–10 and 4–11 depict the logical process with Use Cases and sequence diagrams for a JMS bridge. Figure 4–10 describes five business scenarios or business cases. A trading partner (say, an investment manager, who is also a JMS publisher) wants to send business transactions to another trading partner (say, a sales trader, who

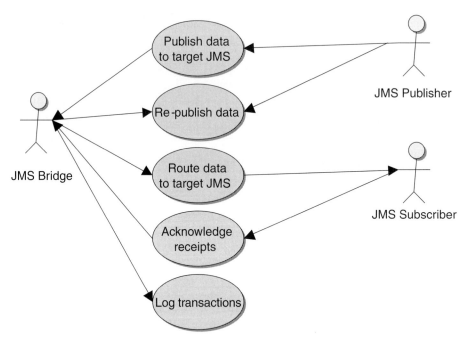

Figure 4–10 JMS Bridge Use Cases

is also a JMS subscriber). The JMS publisher publishes the business transaction information to a predefined JMS topic using the same JMS vendor implementation (say, JMS product 1). The JMS bridge picks up the business transaction information from the JMS queue, routes it, and resends it to the JMS subscriber under another specific JMS topic using a common JMS vendor implementation (say, JMS product 2).

Basically, the JMS bridge has two components, one of which (JMS bridge component 1) works with JMS product 1 and another (JMS bridge component 2) which works with JMS product 2. The two components exchange the business transaction information via SOAP messaging. Upon successful message delivery to the JMS subscriber, the JMS bridge returns an acknowledgement to the JMS publisher. It also logs transaction and exception events for monitoring and audit trail purposes.

Figure 4–11 elaborates some details of the Use Cases discussed earlier. The JMS publisher publishes business transaction information to a predefined JMS topic, where JMS bridge component 1 can pick up. The JMS publisher and JMS bridge component 1 are sharing the same JMS vendor implementation. The JMS bridge component 1 then serializes the content into a SOAP message and sends it to JMS bridge component 2. There is a built-in control mechanism to ensure the SOAP messages will be resent if JMS bridge component 2 has not received the content under the

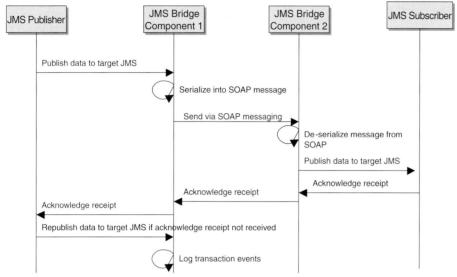

Figure 4–11 JMS Bridge Sequence Diagram

same JMS bridge. For instance, the business transaction information can be persisted in an XML cache, where JMS bridge component 1 can resend it later, even if JMS bridge component 2 is unavailable temporarily.

The JMS bridge component 2 deserializes the SOAP message and publishes to another JMS topic, where the JMS subscriber subscribes to using the same JMS vendor implementation. Upon successful delivery of the message to the JMS subscriber, the JMS subscriber will return an acknowledgement receipt to the JMS bridge. The JMS bridge will then acknowledge receipt with the JMS publisher. It will also log the messaging events for tracking purposes. This completes the entire life cycle of interoperating with two different JMS implementations.

In case any component is unavailable, the business transaction information is encapsulated in SOAP messages and is persisted in an XML cache (or a relational database). If the JMS subscriber is not available online, the JMS publisher can persist the message on the queue and republish the SOAP messages when the JMS subscriber resumes online.

Detailed Design

Creating a JMS Bridge. The topics/queue names of the target JMS need to be registered in the JMS bridge. A JMS bridge client listens to the target topics/queue names, unmarshals the data objects or messages from the original JMS, serializes them into a SOAP message, and then posts it to the recipient JMS bridge client. Data is also stored in XML cache for audit logging and for message recovery. If there is no message acknowledgement, then it recovers the message from the XML cache and resend.

Receiving Messages. The JMS bridge recipient listens to any SOAP messages (synchronous or asynchronous); it acknowledges receipt of messages. Received messages will be also stored in XML cache for audit logging and message recovery. Based on the previous SOAP message routing information, the JMS bridge recipient will act as a JMS publisher to publish the message content to the target JMS. The JMS bridge recipient (JMS publisher) will republish from the XML cache if necessary to provide guaranteed message delivery.

Benefits

There is no need to develop or implement a vendor-specific adapter to bridge two underlying middleware vendors. Caching XML data between two JMSs can provide availability and interoperability. There are existing edge products (such as XML database) to cache XML data from one JMS that can be passed to another JMS (that is, JMS bridge or JMS-SOAP bindings). A JMS bridge is vendor/JMS-independent. Guaranteed messaging between two JMSs.

Risk

- **Real-time Support.** A small lead time is required to bridge two JMSs using asynchronous messaging. System overhead is incurred to provide guaranteed messaging. Application security of XML cache is vendor-dependent.

Example

There are many vendors providing JMS Bridges to bind SOAP messages to JMS for reliable messaging. Two examples are Progress eXcelon (*http://www.exln.com/using XIS*), and Spiritsoft (*http://www.spiritsoft.com/products/jms_ jcache/overview.html*).

4.8.3   Multiple Servlet Engines

Context

A SOAP server handles incoming service requests from SOAP clients. If there are an increasing number of SOAP service requests, a single SOAP server may become a bottleneck. If a SOAP server cannot handle the large influx of incoming service requests, the Service Requester may experience events such as a browser hanging up while waiting for an HTTP connection, HTTP connection drops, and SOAP messaging results. These exception events are examples of a poor service level, even though the service availability of the SOAP server still appears to be high.

A SOAP server is primarily a set of servlets running on top of a Web container (servlet engine). By scaling the SOAP servers vertically on the infrastructure level, architects are able to improve the Quality of Services easily without changing the application.

Problem

A large influx of incoming SOAP service requests during peak hours may deteriorate the performance of SOAP servers. Adding more machines configured as SOAP servers (horizontal scaling) to meet a high volume of SOAP service requests is usually expensive due to additional hardware and maintenance cost. Besides, a single SOAP server on a single Unix machine may underutilize the capacity of the CPU and memory of the operating platform.

Force

Vertically scaling the SOAP server platform is desirable if there is excessive processing capability in the same machine hosting the SOAP server. This is usually implemented by using additional physical memory, disk space, and network adapter cards.

Solution

To horizontally scale up a servlet engine (Web container), multiple instances can be added to the same Unix (or Windows) machine. For an entry-level Unix machine, it is feasible to configure two or more servlet engines (such as Apache HTTP server). This is usually done by installing multiple instances of the servlet engine under different directories. Administrators also need to modify the configuration parameters (such as defining separate IP ports for each servlet engine instance and adding different environment variables or paths). A SOAP server is a set of servlets running on top of the servlet engine. Each SOAP server uses a separate IP port number. This is usually well documented in the servlet engine administration guide (for instance, *http://httpd. apache.org/docs-2.0/vhosts/*) and the SOAP server installation guide.

Figure 4–12 depicts a scenario with four instances of SOAP servers, each of which uses a separate IP port number (ports 8060, 8070, 8080, 8090 respectively). As there are four instances running on the same Unix machines, there are a few hardware requirements, including sufficient physical memory allocated to each virtual host, an individual network adaptor for each virtual host, and more CPUs. A separate hardware capacity sizing plan exercise is essential.

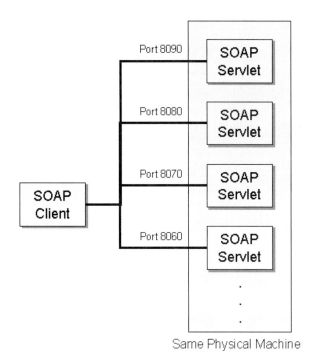

Figure 4–12   Multiple Servlet Engines

Detailed Design

Administering Multiple Servlet Engines. Install multiple servlet engines; installation and configuration varies by vendor implementation. For example, Tomcat 4.x requires creating the variables CATALINA_HOME, CATALINA_BASE, and CATALINA_OPTS to reference to the base instance. Different ports need to be defined in the server.xml of the $CATALINA_HOME/conf directory.

Configuring Servlet Engines. You can assign different priorities and resources to different servlet engines on Unix, just like any Unix processes. You can have different configurations for different servlet engines in the server.xml file, or equivalent—for example, different services and resources mapping.

Application Partitioning. Different instances of servlet engines can be dedicated to support specific applications.

Benefits

Vertical scaling optimizes existing computing capacity by running multiple instances of the SOAP servlet engines. Multiple servlet engines can support application partitioning for better performance and scalability.

Risk

There are initial administrative overheads for application partitioning; this is not ideal for frequently changed partitioning criteria (for example, servlet A handles cities A to K this month, but handles cities A to P next month). Multiple SOAP servlet engines on the same machine are competing for network I/O or memory, though there are ways to compensate them (such as adding additional network adapter cards for each port to compensate for network I/O competition).

Example

Multiple SOAP engines (which are physically servlets) can be created and run on the same machine. For example, a Windows PC can run two instances of Tomcat servers, and each instance can run a separate SOAP engine.

4.8.4   HTTP Load Balancer (SOAP Server Farm)

Context

A SOAP server handles incoming service requests from SOAP clients. Vertically scaling up SOAP servers with multiple instances on the same Unix machine allows handling a large number of incoming service requests from SOAP clients simultaneously. However, vertical scaling can easily come to a saturation point, where a single machine becomes a bottleneck, perhaps a single point of failure.

Horizontal scaling of SOAP servers is usually implemented by connecting multiple SOAP servlets with a number of HTTP load balancers. The HTTP load balancers allow any incoming SOAP service request to be allocated to an available SOAP server instantly. To increase the processing power of SOAP service requests during peak hours, an additional SOAP server machine can be added and attached to the subnet connecting to the HTTP load balancers. This does not impact the existing SOAP messaging or HTTP requests routing operations. Besides, there is no need to cluster the SOAP servers, because if one SOAP server dies, the HTTP load balancers will allocate workload to another SOAP server automatically.

A SOAP server is primarily a set of servlets running on top of a Web container (servlet engine). By scaling the SOAP servers horizontally on the infrastructure level, architects are able to improve the Quality of Services easily without changing the application.

Problem

Massive volumes of SOAP service requests are not easily handled and processed by a single SOAP server machine, even if it is configured with multiple instances. A single SOAP server machine is exposed to the risk of single point of failure. In case one single instance of a SOAP server causes any system failure, the entire machine may need to be rebooted. This will be disruptive to the service operation, impacting the service level.

Force

Horizontal scaling of SOAP servers is considered appropriate for a large user community with numerous SOAP service requests simultaneously. The traffic volume requirement is multiple times greater than the case in a single SOAP server machine with vertical scaling.

The implementation consideration for horizontal scaling is the server consolidation strategy. Although horizontal scaling can be implemented with low-cost machines (such as blade servers and Linux machines) and load-balancing switches, maintaining a SOAP server farm denotes considerable administrative and maintenance cost.

Solution

Figure 4–13 depicts a scenario using three SOAP server machines connected to a HTTP load balancer. One of the SOAP server machines has two instances of SOAP servers. Load balancers and switches can be used to balance the HTTP load for SOAP requests and responses. This is useful in building a SOAP server farm (with HTTP Load Balancer), when the Web Services network traffic increases.

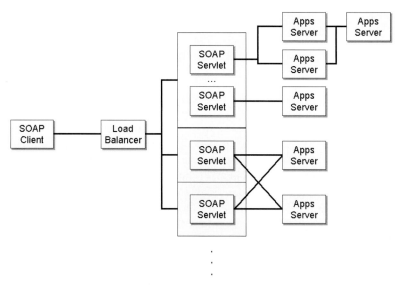

Figure 4–13   HTTP Load Balancer

SOAP RPC router (aka SOAP server) is primarily a servlet running on a Web container (for example, Apache Tomcat, Sun ONE Web Server, or WebSphere Application Server). Architects and developers can run multiple instances of SOAP RPC routers on a physical machine (for example, a multiple-domain machine such as Sun

Fire 6800) for vertical scaling or run multiple instances on separate machines as a SOAP server farm for horizontal scaling. There is no fixed rule about whether architects and developers should start with vertical or horizontal scaling first. As in the HTTP load balancing design, HTTP traffic and SOAP RPC routing are better managed by horizontal scaling because each instance of the server farm has a separate network adapter and if one is unavailable, the other instance can take over the processing.

Architecturally, the SOAP RPC router can be installed on a Sun ONE Web Server (Web Container) and a J2EE Application Server (Web container and EJB container) in the same operating environment. It is always a good architecture design practice to decouple the Web Tier from the Application Tier for security and scalability reasons. It is recommended that it be installed on the Web Tier (that is, Sun ONE Web Server) because of the following considerations:

Security Considerations

There is no business logic in the Web Tier. SOAP RPC router is acting as the SOAP message router behind the DMZ (Demilitarized Zone) firewall. If there is any security attack such as Denial of Service, this will not affect the business logic.

Better Scalability

With the use of load balancers, architects and developers can scale up better with horizontal scaling of the SOAP RPC routers (aka SOAP server farm) if the SOAP RPC routers reside on the same machine as the HTTP Server. If SOAP RPC routers reside on the same machine with the application server, this will allow only vertical scaling by creating multiple instances within a Unix machine (for example, multidomain Solaris OE).

Benefits

SOAP requests can be evenly spread out to different SOAP servers during the peak hours. No additional programming is required in the application or server side.

Risk

Load balancers usually do not support session management; thus if a HTTP session dies, the SOAP request will be lost.

Example

SOAP server farm can be implemented by combining SOAP servers with the Web servers and HTTP load balancers as Web Services appliances (or edge devices).

4.8.5   State Management

Context

A complex business transaction may consist of a chain of remote business services, where each RPC-based Web Services call is dependent on one another. Architects are often tempted to persist the state of each RPC call, so that they can roll back to the previous state in case there is any exception in the midst of the chained RPC calls. If architects keep track of numerous chained Web Services calls, they will create heavy resource overheads, especially when the Web Services call invokes an EJB via RMI/IIOP. Besides, the business rules for any potential rollback are very complicated.

Keeping the session information is different from maintaining the state of each Web Services call. Session information (such as whether a JAX-RPC Web Service is successfully returned with a result) needs to be captured for tracking high-level Web Services calls, for security monitoring, and also for Single Sign-on. In case the JAX-RPC call fails, the client can resend the request based on the session information.

This design pattern suggests a scenario of how states are handled using RPC-based Web Services calls (see Figure 4–14). In this sample scenario, an investment manager wants to place a trader order of 10,000 stocks with the sales trader. The investment manager's SOAP client initiates a trade order Web Service that triggers a chain of Web Services calls. This includes authenticating the user credential for Single Sign-on, checking the access rights to place a trade order, checking the account balance for risk exposure, and placing the trade order. Most of the business functionality resides on the legacy mainframe system. Each Web Services call is dependent on the others.

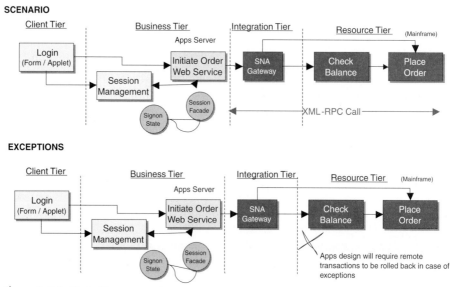

Figure 4–14   State Management

In a stateless RPC-based Web Services call scenario, the session management module creates a login session, and authenticates the user credential. Upon successful log in, the system redirects the user to the order booking page. By filling in the trade order details, the SOAP client is able to invoke the high-level trade order Web Services call. A session facade is used to perform three things: check the access rights, check the account balance, and place the trade order. Each RPC call is dependent on another. In this normal scenario, the investment manager is a valid user with access rights to place a trade order. Each RPC-based Web Services call is successful, and the session facade confirms that the trade order is placed successfully. During the RPC-based Web Services calls to the mainframe system, no state information is captured. Only the return code of each call is logged and tracked.

If this is a stateful RPC-based Web Service, each of the Web Services calls will capture the state information. There will be code customized to handle every possible exception. In this sample scenario, if the Web Services call to place a trade order fails, the system will roll back to the previous Web Services call (check balance). Practically, the process "check balance" does not process any business transaction and is simply an inquiry. Capturing the business logic to handle roll back and exceptions will be redundant and resource-intensive. The design can be simpler to reinitiate the trade order Web Services, if there is any exception during the chain of Web Services calls.

Problem

Some architects maintain states for remote transactions because they can reinitiate the remote transactions if there are any exceptions. However, maintaining states incurs system overhead and heavy resources. Should state or session be maintained for RPC-based Web Services? Can a Web Service be recovered if there is a failure in the midst of the remote XML-RPC call?

Force

RPC-based Web Services calls can be stateful or stateless. Stateful RPC-based Web Services calls denote persisting the states of every remote call, but this is very resource expensive. Sometimes, a stateful EJB can be created to initiate a chain of Web Services calls. This is also called EJB Web Services, and developers need to design what state information is captured and how to use it. Stateless RPC-based Web Services calls are simply remote procedure calls implemented in a Java program or a servlet. They do not capture any state, and therefore there is no mechanism to roll back any transaction. In both cases, the return code of the Web Services calls can be captured and logged. The choice of stateful or stateless Web Services is dependent on business requirements and operating environment constraints. Typically, if the remote business services are provided by legacy mainframe applications via RPC-based Web Services calls, it would be difficult to capture the states without changing the back-end mainframe applications.

The session information (for example, the user, date, and time) tracked during a session is useful for logging and exception handling. Architects should consider what session information is necessary to support security session control or event tracking. This should be separate from maintaining states.

Solution

Use Case Modeling

Figures 4–15 and 4–16 depict the logical process with Use Cases and sequence diagrams for state management. Figure 4–15 describes six business scenarios or Use Cases. A SOAP client initiates a chain of RPC-based Web Services calls. The SOAP server creates a session to track the Web Services calls. The Web Services calls invoke the remote business applications via XML-RPC. The remote business applications process requests from each RPC call. Upon completion of the current RPC call, the RPC call will return to the SOAP server (or the parent Web Services call), which will initiate the next Web Services call. After all RPC calls are completed, the application will commit transactions. The session will be killed. The SOAP server can also reinvoke the RPC call if any exception is encountered.

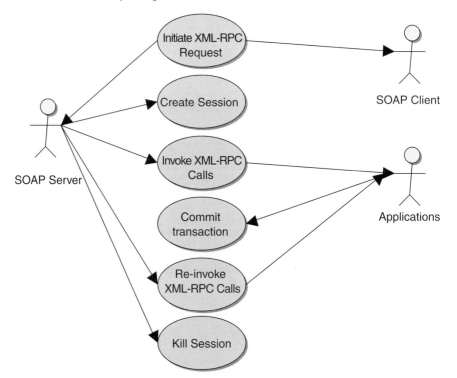

Figure 4–15 State Management Use Cases

Figure 4–16 elaborates the details of the previous Use Cases. The SOAP client initiates a stateless RPC-based Web Services call by passing an XML-RPC request to the SOAP server. The SOAP server uses a session facade, creates a sign-on session, and builds up a chain of RPC-based Web Services calls. For each RPC call, the session facade tracks the session information for the calls, and invokes the back-end mainframe applications. The back-end business application acknowledges the RPC call and processes the service request. If the service request is successful, then the application will return the requested business information. If there is any exception, the application will handle error recovery or roll back. The session facade will then reinvoke the RPC call.

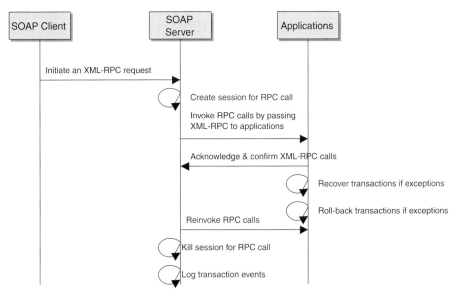

Figure 4–16   State Management Sequence Diagram

Upon successful completion of all RPC calls, the session facade will kill the session and log the transaction events to the logger.

Detailed Design

SOAP Client. XML-RPC from a SOAP client can create a session variable, but cannot track states remotely for several reasons. For example:

- State cannot be updated and tracked remotely.
- Multiple phase commit will create many wait states and is overly complex and therefore problematic.
- Remote RPC is usually functionally like a black box and may not support state management.

Remote Applications. They are likely to be black box processes, which may or may not support state management or transaction roll-back/roll-forward. Upon completion of the Web Services call and success return code, the SOAP client can kill the session; otherwise, the SOAP client should assume the RPC call fails and needs reinvocation.

In case of exception in the midst of the XML-RPC call, the SOAP client may not like to reinvoke automatically for various reasons; therefore, do not make design assumptions to reinvoke automatically.

Benefits

Session control is in place for XML-RPC Web Services, where remote transactions can be reinvoked if the session dies or fails over. There is also a clear demarcation of recovery. Remote applications should be responsible for transaction roll-back or roll-forward for recovery, while Web Services should handle invocation only, not provide recovery. Architects can reuse the session facade pattern (use of session bean to encapsulate the complexity of interactions between the business subjects participating in a workflow) in designing state management. This pattern (refer to Alur, Crupi, and Malks, *Core J2EE Patterns*, 2001, pp. 291–309 for more details) provides a uniform coarse-grained service access layer to clients without overloading the system performance by storing states for each tier.

Risk

We cannot know whether a session dies, fails over, or recovers if there is no session or state management at all. Many remote applications may not support states or session recovery.

Example

The session facade pattern (refer to Alur, Crupi, and Malks, *Core J2EE Patterns*) has provided good guidelines in state management and are applicable to developing Web Services applications.

4.8.6   SOAP Logger

Context

Transaction logging is essential for troubleshooting, audit trail, and billing. Service providers often need transaction logging information for metering service levels or billing, if they provide a variety of Web Services calls to Service Requesters.

High-level Web Services call information can be easily captured in the SOAP server level, using the logging infrastructure provided by the Web container (for example, Java logging API from J2SE version 1.3.x/1.4). This will considerably reduce application developers' efforts to capture Web Services calls.

Problem

SOAP request–reply does not support logging. Apache SOAP server does not provide sufficient logging capability for audit trail or for billing purposes. Developers need to add customized Web Services call transaction logging functionality or to rely on the application server platform that runs J2SE version 1.3.x/1.4 to provide logging.

Force

JAX-RPC-based Web Services may not support transaction logging if the remote business services cannot generate logging events. Thus, the support of transaction logging depends on two factors: the logging infrastructure (as provided by the Web container or customized logging facilities) and the capability of remote business services to generate logging events.

Solution

Use Case Modeling

Figures 4–17 through 4–19 depict the logical process with Use Cases and sequence diagrams for a SOAP logger. Figure 4–17 presents a scenario where the SOAP server (SOAP reply) generates a logging event before it initiates a SOAP-RPC call or a document-based Web Services call. This is based on the logging provider class provided by J2SE 1.4 or the logging facility in Apache AXIS.

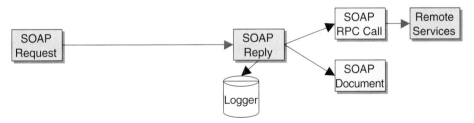

Figure 4–17 SOAP Logger

Figure 4–18 depicts four business scenarios, or Use Cases, about transaction logging. A SOAP client initiates a document-based or an RPC-based Web Services call by sending an XML document to the SOAP server. The SOAP server, using the logging provider class, logs the transaction events, and binds the service end-point URL to the remote business applications.

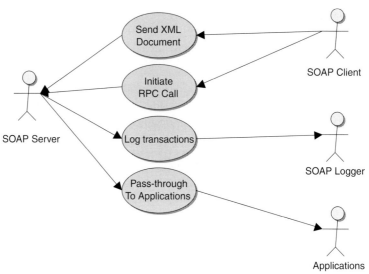

Figure 4–18   SOAP Logger Use Cases

Figure 4–19 elaborates the Use Cases with more details using sequence diagrams. Once the SOAP client initiates a SOAP service request, the SOAP server will unmarshal the sender information from the SOAP envelope and the session information. It logs the sender and session information in the logger using the Java API for logging. The SOAP server will then invoke RPC calls with the remote business applications. The date/time and usage will be logged in the logger as well. Upon successful invocation of the remote business services, the SOAP server will acknowledge with a return code or an exception. The information captured in the logger should be sufficient for basic usage analysis and per-call-based billing.

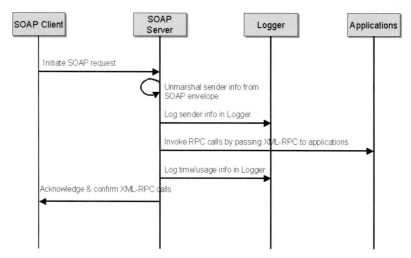

Figure 4–19   SOAP Logger Sequence Diagram

Detailed Design

Logger Design. J2SE 1.3.x or 1.4 has a logger API that can be used for logger design. Unmarshal the SOAP envelope to acquire the sender information and time stamp for logging.

Time Services. If time services are required for remote RPC calls, the start time and the end time for the RPC call invocation need to be tracked for logging purpose.

Persistence and Storage. The choice of persistence and storage (for example, LDAP, RDBMS, XML Cache, or flat file) will determine the quality of data security of the logging information. Though the logging information may not contain sensitive financial information, it is useful for audit tracking and perhaps for billing. Therefore, the logger needs to be protected in the server for access control (for example, file access restricted to server administrators only).

There needs to be a proper archive strategy, and backup/restore procedure for the logger (such as daily backup or archive every 30 days).

Benefits

Logs of SOAP replies (requester, request time stamp, or service request) can be captured for audit trail or for billing purpose. The built-in features of Java logging can be leveraged.

Risk

Requester information is not reliable or easily authenticated; the SOAP envelope is the only source. The service time is not usually available from the RPC call, if time-based billing is required.

Example

Apache Axis has a logging feature based on log4j (also incorporated in J2SE 1.4) using the log handler. Every time a business service is invoked (for example, via JAX-RPC), the log handler will track the usage for application monitoring and troubleshooting. The following deployment description shows an example of how the log handler is specified (see Figure 4–20). In this example, the transaction events are logged by the log handler LogTestService in a file MyService.log whenever the samples.userguide.example4.Service is invoked.

```
<deployment xmlns="http://xml.apache.org/axis/wsdd/"
            xmlns:java="http://xml.apache.org/axis/
wsdd/providers/java">

 <!— define the logging handler configuration -->
 <handler name="track"
type="java:samples.userguide.example4.LogHandler">
  <parameter name="filename" value="MyService.log"/>
 </handler>

 <!— define the service, using the log handler we just
defined -->
 <service name="LogTestService" provider="java:RPC">
  <requestFlow>
   <handler type="track"/>
  </requestFlow>

  <parameter name="className"
value="samples.userguide.example4.Service"/>
  <parameter name="allowedMethods" value="*"/>
 </service>

</deployment>
```

Figure 4–20 Deployment Descriptor for Log Handler (aka SOAP Logger)

4.8.7   High Availability of Service Registry

Context

Service Requesters that use dynamic service look-up for Web Services are heavily dependent on the availability of the Service Registry. High availability of the Service Registry denotes the Service Registry is always available, even though one of the instances may fail or be hacked.

Problem

Dynamic service look-up requires the Service Registry to always be available. If there is any downtime, no SOAP client (Service Requester) can access remote business services. Although the Service Registry functionality is based on the UDDI or ebXML standard, each vendor implementation varies, and there is no standard mechanism to support high availability. How do we make the Service Registry highly available?

Force

The provision of a high availability Service Registry requires a resource cost (for example, redundant hardware platform or redundant network switch).

Solution

The Service Registry can be made resilient by clustering the hardware platform that runs the Service Registry. Figure 4–21 depicts a scenario of clustering the hardware platform of multiple Service Registries, and the contents of these Service Registries are also synchronized using the underlying database replication or proprietary Service Registry replication utilities (such as Systinet's UDDI registry).

Detailed Design

General. Follow the rule of three. This means that architects should have at least three instances of the Service Registry running in production. These instances can be clustered to provide a better level of service availability. Always have three. If one is down, then you have two clustered as backup.

Hardware Level. Hardware level clustering of all UDDI servers is useful to provide machine-level availability. Hardware-level failover may have a short lead time to switch from one UDDI server to another (for example, 10 minutes); thus, this must go hand in hand with the software level.

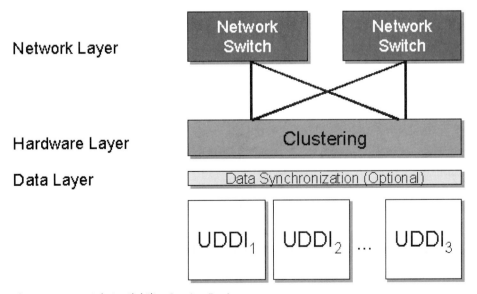

Figure 4–21   High Availability Service Registry

Network Level. Network-level resilience is important when UDDI service look-up becomes critical. Dual network link or cross-network switch is fairly standard.

Software Level. Software-level availability of UDDI servers depends on the physical implementation such as—RDBMS, LDAP, or proprietary. RDBMS can have a parallel database server (data synchronization); yet the I/O overhead to synchronize data in real time is fairly high; thus the machine resources and costs are higher.

Another RDBMS variation is to have standby database mode, where the secondary database is replicated. LDAP can be set up as master-slave replication; thus when one fails, the slave (secondary LDAP) will take over. Proprietary implementation may make use of mirrored disks and manual switch over; but the service level is unpredictable.

Benefits

$7 \times 24 \times 365$ high availability enables service lookup running nonstop (not disruptable).

Risk

The quality of high availability of the UDDI Service Registry depends highly on the UDDI implementation (for example, RDBMS or LDAP). Hardware-level-only clustering of the UDDI server has a short recovery time (for example, 10 minutes). Parallel database server implementation of UDDI has expensive I/O overhead to synchronize the databases.

Example

The Service Registry can be clustered on a redundant hardware platform such as Sun Fire mid-frame series (*http://www.sun.com/servers/midrange/sunfire/*), which has redundant power supply, redundant system boards, and network adapters. This will enable better availability.

4.8.8   UDDI Deployment

Context

The Service Registry is a key piece of architecture that enables service look-up and accessing remote business services. External or internal security attacks may intrude into the Service Registry and cause denial of service. The Service Registry (either UDDI or ebXML Service Registry) should be deployed with appropriate firewall protection. It is important to understand the appropriate deployment strategy on which the UDDI Service Registry should be placed.

Problem

In which tier (outer tier, DMZ, or inner tier) should the UDDI Service Registry be placed? Public and private Service Registries have different security requirements, and they do not necessarily have the same deployment and security protection strategy.

Force

Potential security attacks on the Service Registry will be a major threat to the discovery and invocation of Web Services. They will impact the service availability.

Solution

Figure 4–22 depicts the deployment scenarios for both a public UDDI Service Registry and a private UDDI Service Registry. Public UDDI Service Registries are usually vulnerable to outside security attack. The security attack usually takes the form of a penetrating agent (aka Trojan horse) and intrudes into internal resources once access to the internal network is gained. Thus, it is better to place the UDDI Service Registry in front of the Demilitarized one next to the Web server with a standby instance. This is similar to placing the DNS server in front of the DMZ.

Private UDDI Service Registries are primarily intended for internal use. They have different security risks when compared to public UDDI Service Registries. It is recommended that private UDDI Service Registries be placed behind the DMZ. An optional standby instance may be installed. However, private UDDI Service Registries are open to insider security attacks.

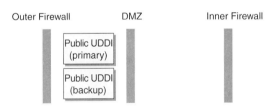

Public UDDI is vulnerable to outside security attack as an agent to intrude into internal resources, thus it is better to be placed in front of the DMZ (next to the public HTTP web server) with a backup instance

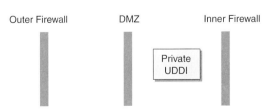

Private UDDI can be placed behind the DMZ, & may have an optional standby backup instance. However, private UDDI is open to insider security attack,

Figure 4–22   UDDI Deployment

Detailed Design

Deployment Architecture. There are many types of UDDI Service Registries, but there is no need for an individual deployment architecture for each type. The UDDI deployment architecture usually varies for public UDDI and private UDDI.

Benefits

Reduction of security risk for the UDDI Service Registry if it is placed in the appropriate tier.

Risk

Firewall port administration—the UDDI port (port 8080) needs to be defined and opened in the firewall policy.

Example

A Public Service Registry is always deployed in the demilitarized zone behind the outer firewall. A private Service Registry is usually deployed behind the DMZ.

4.8.9   Publish, Unpublish, and Discover Web Services

Context

The Service Provider (developers and architects) needs to register, publish, and unpublish a business service to a Service Registry for consumers (endusers and trading partners) to utilize. Each Service Registry vendor product usually has its own set of APIs and utilities to manage publishing and unpublishing business services and service information, though all of these products support a Service Registry standard. Thus, there is a design and management issue for architects and developers who must determine the best strategy for managing different vendor product implementations.

Problem

Different Service Registry vendor products have different APIs to publish and unpublish. Thus, if architects and developers have multiple Service Registry vendor products, they may need to maintain different sets of programs to register and publish Web Services.

Force

Different vendor implementations of Service Registries have their own set of APIs to publish or unpublish business service information. This has a major impact to developers if they decide to migrate from one vendor product to another. Developers may consider standardizing APIs (such as using JAXR, or creating an abstract layer on top of the vendor-specific Service Registry APIs) to publish and unpublish Web Services to the Service Registries for easy maintenance and high usability.

Solution

The recommendation is to use JAXR (JAX Pack from *http://java.sun.com*) to access UDDI. This enables developers to switch to other UDDI vendor products seamlessly without rewriting their code. They simply need to replace the query.url and publish.url entries in the `registry.properties` file (see Figure 4–23) to denote the specific UDDI vendor product APIs (refer to the following excerpts). There is no need to recompile or rewrite the code if a new Service Registry product is used.

```
query.url=http://uddi.ibm.com/ubr/inquiryapi
publish.url=https://uddi.ibm.com/ubr/protect/publishapi
```

Figure 4–23 Sample registry.properties File Used by JAXR Client

```
        /*
         * Define connection configuration properties.
         * To publish, you need both the query URL and
         * the publish URL.
         */
        Properties props = new Properties();

props.setProperty("javax.xml.registry.queryManagerURL",
        queryUrl);

props.setProperty("javax.xml.registry.lifeCycleManager
URL",
        publishUrl);
    ...
```

Figure 4–24 Sample JAXR Program Excerpt

The Java Web Services Developer Pack 1.01 Tutorial (*http://java.sun.com/webservices/ downloads/webservicestutorial.html*) contains a sample JAXR publisher (see Figure 4–24) that can be reused as a standard template. Developers can use a registry.properties file to specify the query.url and publish.url for the specific Service Registry. The same JAXR publisher and registry.properties can be customized as standard Web Services utilities that can be reused for implementation in a different country. Architects and developers can customize their JAXR Publisher utility in the Proof of Concept stage or future phases.

Risk

There are implementation and migration risks when migrating from one Service Registry to another because they use different publish and unpublish APIs. Switching from one Service Registry vendor to another often incurs intensive testing and regression testing. To mitigate the risk, architects and developers can adopt the JAXR standard using the registry.properties file to work with any Service Registry vendor product. This approach does not require retesting as JAXR can work with both UDDI and ebXML Service Registry vendor products without rewriting the APIs.

Example

Some of the common and infrastructural services, even including authentication and authorization services, can be published in the Service Registry. JAXR provides a common and standardized mechanism to browse and invoke these services. If architects and developers determine to transition to a new Service Registry vendor product or to split the services to multiple Service Registries, this JAXR approach will not require developers to migrate or redo any integration testing.

Alternatively, architects and developers may provide a standard set of B2B Web Services APIs using JAXR to their trading partners. With these standards-based APIs, trading partners do not need to worry about the client platform or back-end integration with the invocation APIs, as the same invocation APIs (URIs) using JAXR will work with any platform.

4.8.10 Managing Different Versions of Web Services Deployment With Service Registry

Context

Many Service Providers (such as retail banks) have deployed legacy customer front-ends and systems around the world. Once they adopt Web Services for customer integration, it is necessary to integrate with these legacy customer front-ends and systems. However, these systems provide the same business service functionality, but they likely run on different platforms with multiple versions. It is rather challenging to standardize the software versions simultaneously in terms of management and upgrade cost.

These Service Providers need to deploy and manage different versions of Web Services in a structured and manageable manner. The Service Registry can be used as an administration tool to centralize managing different versions of Web Services deployment.

Problem

There are different versions of business services available to support different platforms, different customers (customized for specific customers), and different countries. There is a need to easily manage different versions when publishing (and even discovering) business services from the Service Registry.

Force

Different variants of clients or software versions of the interfaces are deployed in parallel. Administering and managing different versions for the same client or trading partners is complex.

Solution

Different versions of business services can be registered in the Service Registry under the same Service Provider as different service bindings (that is, URLs) and service binding descriptions. This enables running variants of the business services globally in parallel. Figure 4–25 depicts how different versions of the same business service can be defined in a UDDI Service Registry.

Publishing different versions of business services requires planning ahead of the versions (for example, creating a product version roadmap). The Service Registry can act as a tool to track all versions and can be supplemented by Web Services network Service Providers such as Flamenco Network and Talking Block. These vendors provide services that can route the client request to different versions of the remote Web Services based on their profile.

There should be a synergy between the service versioning development best practice (for example, specifying the service version in the SOAP message header attribute) and this best practice. Practically, the service version should tie to (or equate to) the "Service Bindings" and their associated service end-points (or service bindings access URI). They collaborate to provide manageability of deployed Web Services. Refer to Figure 4–25 for an example.

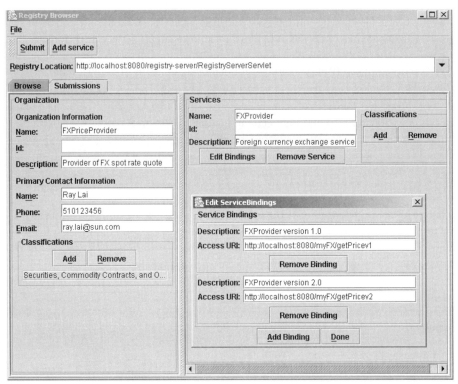

Figure 4–25   Different Web Services Versioning Can Be Managed as Different Service Bindings

Risk

Using URLs in the service bindings to manage versions is currently a manual process, prone to careless human errors (for example, during staff changeover). Web Services network tools that provide an administrative tool to track versions and to deploy URLs can supplement it. Alternatively, architects and developers can develop some utilities to publish different versions of business services.

Example

Historically, customers may have many commercial off-the-shelf applications deployed in local countries. Some of them have similar functionalities, and some have many software versions deployed in parallel.

4.8.11 Registry Content Management

Context

Service Providers (developers) need to manage the contents of Web Services globally to provide timely access and update of the service end-point URLs. Being able to create, publish, and access timely information for a large user community is crucial. The timeliness of service information affects the quality of Web Services.

A large user community may generate a large volume of service information. As the number of content providers or Service Providers increases, the process of updating the content of the Service Registry becomes more complicated to manage. There needs to be a well-defined Service Registry content management process to manage the timeliness of the service information. If there are multiple Service Registries deployed, there needs to be a deployment strategy to synchronize them.

Problem

The nature of the Service Registry is to allow dynamic updates of the business services and related service information. As the service information size is small and the update is instantaneous, developers may assume that a Web Services client performing a dynamic service look-up is able to discover that the service has just been removed or upgraded. However, there is always the risk of synchronization issues, as in the case of DNS management.

Forces

There are two major factors affecting the content management strategy for Service Registries: the business rules and the data volume. Local business rules of updating and replicating the business service information (for example, service end-point URLs) need to be established.

The data volume (size of the business service information) and the number of Service Registry instances need to be updated and managed.

Solution

Immediate Recommendation

It is not recommended to dynamically update the Service Registry on the production platform. Doing so exposes the risk of synchronization problems when any Web Services client is looking up the service end-point. Besides, there is no fallback if the production master Service Registry is updated directly. There should be operational processes defined and reinforced to ensure updates are accurate and timely. This can be addressed in future phases.

Short-Term Recommendation

A staging Service Registry is highly recommended, where administrators can perform updates. There should be scheduled replications (for example, every hour) to synchronize the master Service Registry with the staging Service Registry. Administrators can also push replication in real-time, if necessary. The replication implementation should be synchronizing the "delta." The replication schedule is dependent on the number and volume

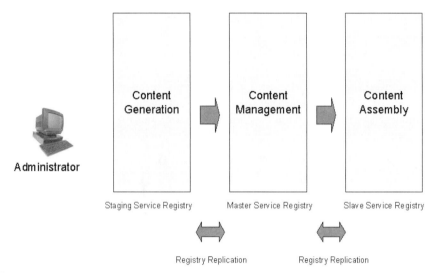

Figure 4–26   Staging Service Registry

of the changes. It can be increased as the volume goes up. There should be also scheduled replications (such as every 8 hours or every 24 hours) to synchronize the master Service Registry with the slave Service Registries. Refer to Figure 4–26 for an example.

For emergency (ad hoc with high priority) updates, it is recommended that administrators push the update to the master Service Registry (that is, nonscheduled), which will also push the updates to the next tier of the slave Service Registries in realtime.

Removing a business service entails removing the entry instantaneously from the Service Registry. Typically, the deprecated or decommissioned business service will be made unavailable before the update of the Service Registry. During service discovery, Web Services clients should be able to get a return code from the Service Registry indicating that the service is unavailable, and the client's exception handling routine should be able to display an error message.

Risk

Upgrading a business service entails removing the entry and adding a new entry in the Service Registry. However, customers may need to run multiple versions in parallel, without decommissioning older versions immediately. As service discovery is designed to bind the business service at runtime, the chance of binding to the old business service during the update is slim because the update is instantaneous. It may be helpful to check the version from the SOAP message header. If a different version is found, then the Web Services client can reinvoke the business service again for the upgraded business service.

Example

Many financial institutions have decentralized applications and services running in different regions. These business services can be registered in the centralized Service

Registry, while copies (slave Service Registries) can be replicated for better performance and availability.

4.8.12 Design Consideration

JNDI Look-up versus UDDI. JNDI look-up can be performed in place of UDDI look-up. The benefits of doing this include:

- There is no dependency on an additional UDDI server.
- Established Java programs already use JNDI.
- It alleviates the complexity involved implementing and tuning UDDI servers.
- JNDI provides a better paradigm of dynamic discovery (Jini!).

Web Services Troubleshooting Approach. SOAP calls debugging tools are available to trace each step invoked (for example, XMLSpy). SOAP load testing tools are emerging. The general troubleshooting approach is to identify the first-tier bottleneck (for example, memory, I/O, or network), and perform load testing with different transaction volumes and at different times see whether the problem is related to load or time.

Performance Tuning. Performance tuning of SOAP calls is like tuning and scaling up a servlet (SOAP is a servlet). Tuning an XML-RPC call is difficult, as there may be multiple processes beneath and very often the remote applications are wrapped as a SOAP-based Web Service (black box processes).

Trace the SOAP calls to narrow down the potential problem areas and isolate the problem by trial-and-error testing (for example, repeat the first-tier bottleneck testing or load testing).

4.8.13 Other Design Guidelines for Web Services

Coarse Grained. There is a general understanding among Web Services architects that Web Services calls need to be coarse grained, while leaving EJBs or Java beans fine grained. In other words, a customer may start with one single coarse-grained Web Service, where different services can be invoked by passing parameters in the Web Service call (either an XML-RPC or an XML message). Architects can also expose the business service using a coarse-grained uniform access point such as a business delegate or a session facade (refer to Alur, Deepak, and Crupi, *Core J2EE Patterns* for details).

Performance. Raghu Varadan, in his presentation "Patterns for eBusiness—Design Guidelines for Web Services," has pointed out that the notion of Web Services being slow because of transmitting or XML parsing is unfounded—a myth. He quotes a GeSC test, which shows that the response time for a simple transaction on an IBM F40 machine with no load yields 8 ms. The same transaction on an IBM F80 machine can yield over 300 transactions per seconds. XML parsing can be addressed by using XML parsing library calls. The live implementation of Hewitt Associates' managed HR services using Web Services, according to Hilgenberg and Hansen, yields similar results. Hewitt Associates' Web Services implementation can support up to 4 million transactions per day.

Distributed Events. Geysermans and Miller have identified design patterns for managing distributed events using a Distributed Event-based Architecture (DEBA). DEBA patterns make use of state machine concepts and callback design patterns (visitor and observer). This allows an easy implementation of a dynamic workflow model. Currently, DEBA patterns include multiple observables (aka providers) and observers (aka requesters) as well as distributed state machine, router, workflow, and composite patterns.

4.9　Perspectives

4.9.1　Highlights

- Web Services products usually come with specific product architecture. For example, the UDDI Service Registry must run on a specific RDBMS vendor product. These Web Services vendors do not usually provide a framework or architecture methodology for defining, customizing, and implementing enterprise architecture solutions using a combination of Web Services products.

- A structured Web Services architecture framework not only provides a structured methodology to define Web Services components, but also helps select appropriate tools for meeting different Quality of Services ("ilities") during the development and deployment life cycle.

- Web Services design patterns can be accumulated as you gain experience from deployment. It is useful to maintain a catalog of customized Web Services within the enterprise for future reuse.

4.9.2　Best Practices and Pitfalls

Best Practices

Keep a high-level session variable for each XML-RPC Web Services call to track who is making the call and when. This will help track the security session and Web Services performance monitoring.

Always do stress testing in different time periods before deploying Web Services.

Pitfalls

Use fine-grained Web Services that attempt to expose all APIs as Web Services.

Use the same deployment architecture and support strategy for public and private UDDI registries.

High availability for Web Services is achieved by simply clustering all hardware machines.

Always use one Web Service to embrace multiple back-end sources across different machines (difficult to troubleshoot and isolate the problem sources).

4.9.3   Paper and Pencil

Objective

To use the SOAP local message provider with JAXM to send an XML message.

Exercise

Using the JAXM concept in the chapter Web Services Overview, you are to write a servlet to send an XML message (in fact, this is a Foreign Exchange option message using fpML). The XML message is shown in Figure 4–27 for reference.

```
<?xml version="1.0" encoding = "UTF-8" ?>
<!DOCTYPE trade
  [
    <!— DTD declarations omitted  -->
  ]>

<trade>
  <tradeHeader>
    <partyTradeIdentifier>
      <partyReference href = "#XYZ"/>
    </partyTradeIdentifier>
    <partyTradeIdentifier>
      <partyReference href = "#ABC"/>
    </partyTradeIdentifier>
    <tradeDate>2002-01-15</tradeDate>
  </tradeHeader>
  <fxSimpleOption>
      <productType>Nondeliverable Option</productType>
      <buyerPartyReference href = "#XYZ"/>
```

Figure 4–27   Foreign Exchange Option Message in XML

```
        <sellerPartyReference href = "#ABC"/>
        <expiryDateTime>
            <expiryDate>2002-04-09</expiryDate>
            <hourMinuteTime>1000</hourMinuteTime>
            <businessCenter>USNY</businessCenter>
        </expiryDateTime>
        <exerciseStyle>European</exerciseStyle>
    </fxSimpleOption>
    <party id = "XYZ">
        <partyId>CHASUS33</partyId>
        <partyName>XYZ BUYER BANK</partyName>
    </party>
    <party id = "ABCN">
        <partyId>ABCANL2A</partyId>
        <partyName>ABC Seller Bank</partyName>
    </party>
</trade>
<!- end of DTDs -->
```

Figure 4–27 Foreign Exchange Option Message in XML—*continued.*

The source files `ReceivingServlet.java` and `SendingServlet.java` are located on the accompanying CD-ROM in the Chapter 4 labs sub-directory. They are also presented as follows for reference.

Step 1: Write the SendingServlet.java
The sender client `SendingServlet.java` creates a connection to the message factory. It uses standard JAXP to construct the SOAP header and body. The SOAP message contains the XML message as shown in Figure 4–28.

```
package mySimple.sender;

import java.net.*;
import java.io.*;
import java.util.*;

import javax.servlet.http.*;
import javax.servlet.*;

import javax.xml.soap.*;
```

Figure 4–28 SendingServlet.java Sends an XML Message in SOAP Messaging With JAXM

```java
import javax.activation.*;
// import javax.naming.*;


import org.apache.commons.logging.*;


public class SendingServlet extends HttpServlet {
    static Log
    logger =
LogFactory.getFactory().getInstance("Samples/mySimple"
);

    String to = null;
    String data = null;
    ServletContext servletContext;

    // Connection to send messages.
    private SOAPConnection con;

    public void init(ServletConfig servletConfig)
throws ServletException {
        super.init( servletConfig );
        servletContext =
servletConfig.getServletContext();

        try {
        SOAPConnectionFactory scf =
SOAPConnectionFactory.newInstance();
            con = scf.createConnection();
        } catch(Exception e) {
            logger.error("Unable to open a
SOAPConnection", e);
        }

        InputStream in
        = servletContext.getResourceAsStream("/WEB-
INF/address.properties");

        if (in != null) {
            Properties props = new Properties();
```

Figure 4–28   SendingServlet.java Sends an XML Message in SOAP Messaging With JAXM—*continued.*

```
            try {
                props.load(in);

                to = props.getProperty("to");
                data = props.getProperty("data");
            } catch (IOException ex) {
                // Ignore
            }
        }
    }

    public void doGet(HttpServletRequest req,
HttpServletResponse resp)
    throws ServletException {

        String retval ="<html><H1>FX Option Order
Receipt</H1><body><H4>";

        try {
            // Create a message factory.
            MessageFactory mf =
MessageFactory.newInstance();

            // Create a message from the message
factory.
            SOAPMessage message = mf.createMessage();

            //  SOAP message body
            SOAPPart soapPart = message.getSOAPPart();
            SOAPEnvelope envelope =
soapPart.getEnvelope();

            javax.xml.soap.Name name =
envelope.createName("trade" , "fx",

"http://www.nextfrontiers.com/fxOption/");
            SOAPBody body = envelope.getBody();
            SOAPBodyElement trade =
body.addBodyElement(name);
            SOAPHeader header = envelope.getHeader();
```

Figure 4–28 SendingServlet.java Sends an XML Message in SOAP Messaging With
JAXM—*continued.*

```
                SOAPHeaderElement headerElement =
header.addHeaderElement(name);
                // create tradeHeader
                Name childName =
envelope.createName("tradeHeader");
                SOAPElement tradeHeader =
trade.addChildElement(childName);

                childName =
envelope.createName("partyTradeIdentifier");
                SOAPElement partyTradeIdentifier =
tradeHeader.addChildElement(childName);

                childName =
envelope.createName("partyReference");
                SOAPElement partyReference =
partyTradeIdentifier.addChildElement(childName);
                childName = envelope.createName("href");
                partyReference.addAttribute(childName,
"#XYZ");

                Name childName2 =
envelope.createName("partyTradeIdentifier");
                SOAPElement partyTradeIdentifier2 =
tradeHeader.addChildElement(childName2);

                childName2 =
envelope.createName("partyReference");
                SOAPElement partyReference2 =
partyTradeIdentifier2.addChildElement(childName2);
                childName2 = envelope.createName("href");
                partyReference2.addAttribute(childName2,
"#ABC");

                // create fxSimpleOption
                Name childName3 =
envelope.createName("fxSimpleOption");
                SOAPElement fxSimpleOption =
trade.addChildElement(childName3);
```

Figure 4–28   SendingServlet.java Sends an XML Message in SOAP Messaging With JAXM—*continued.*

```
            childName3 =
envelope.createName("productType");
            SOAPElement productType =
fxSimpleOption.addChildElement(childName3);
            productType.addTextNode("Nondeliveable
options");

            childName3 =
envelope.createName("buyerPartyReference");
            SOAPElement buyerPartyReference =
fxSimpleOption.addChildElement(childName3);
            childName3 = envelope.createName("href");

buyerPartyReference.addAttribute(childName3, "#XYZ");

            childName3 =
envelope.createName("sellerPartyReference");
            SOAPElement sellerPartyReference =
fxSimpleOption.addChildElement(childName3);
            childName3 = envelope.createName("href");

sellerPartyReference.addAttribute(childName3, "#ABC");
            childName3 =
envelope.createName("expiryDateTime");
            SOAPElement expiryDateTime =
fxSimpleOption.addChildElement(childName3);
            childName3 =
envelope.createName("expiryDate");
            SOAPElement expiryDate =
expiryDateTime.addChildElement(childName3);
            expiryDate.addTextNode("2002-04-09");
            childName3 =
envelope.createName("hourMinuteTime");
            SOAPElement hourMinuteTime =
expiryDateTime.addChildElement(childName3);
            hourMinuteTime.addTextNode("1000");
            childName3 =
envelope.createName("businessCenter");
            SOAPElement businessCenter =
expiryDateTime.addChildElement(childName3);
```

Figure 4–28   SendingServlet.java Sends an XML Message in SOAP Messaging With JAXM—*continued.*

```
            businessCenter.addTextNode("USNY");

            childName3 =
envelope.createName("exerciseStyle");
            SOAPElement exerciseStyle =
fxSimpleOption.addChildElement(childName3);
            exerciseStyle.addTextNode("European");

            // create party information
            Name childName4 =
envelope.createName("party");
            SOAPElement party =
trade.addChildElement(childName4);
            childName4 = envelope.createName("id");
            party.addAttribute(childName4, "XYZ");

            childName4 =
envelope.createName("partyId");
            SOAPElement partyId =
party.addChildElement(childName4);
            partyId.addTextNode("CHASUS33");

            childName4 =
envelope.createName("partyName");
            SOAPElement partyName =
party.addChildElement(childName4);
            partyName.addTextNode("XYZ BUYER BANK");

            Name childName5 =
envelope.createName("party");
            SOAPElement party2 =
trade.addChildElement(childName5);
            childName5 = envelope.createName("id");
            party2.addAttribute(childName5, "ABCN");

            childName5 =
envelope.createName("partyId");
            SOAPElement partyId2 =
party2.addChildElement(childName5);
            partyId2.addTextNode("ABCANL2A");
```

Figure 4–28   SendingServlet.java Sends an XML Message in SOAP Messaging With JAXM—*continued.*

```
            childName5 =
envelope.createName("partyName");
            SOAPElement partyName2 =
party2.addChildElement(childName5);
            partyName2.addTextNode("ABC Seller Bank");

            StringBuffer urlSB=new StringBuffer();
            urlSB.append(req.getScheme()).append
(":://").append(req.getServerName());
            urlSB.append( ":" ).append(
req.getServerPort() ).append( req.getContextPath() );
            String reqBase=urlSB.toString();

            if(data==null) {
                data=reqBase + "/index.html";    //
this sets the URL for accessing this web service
            }

            // Want to set an attachment from the
following url.
            //Get context
            URL url = new URL(data); // URL to access
this web service

            AttachmentPart ap = message.create
AttachmentPart(new DataHandler(url));

            ap.setContentType("text/html");

            // Add the attachment part to the message.
            // You can attach an EDI (UN/EDIFACT or
ANSI X12) message, image or digital signature
            message.addAttachmentPart(ap);

            // Create an endpoint for the recipient of
the message.
            if(to==null) {
                to=reqBase + "/receiver";
            }

            URL urlEndpoint = new URL(to);
```

Figure 4–28   SendingServlet.java Sends an XML Message in SOAP Messaging With JAXM—*continued.*

```
            System.err.println("Sending message to
URL: "+urlEndpoint);
            System.err.println("Sent message is logged
in \"sent.msg\"");

            retval += " Sent message (check
\"sent.msg\") and ";

            FileOutputStream sentFile = new
FileOutputStream("sent.msg");
            message.writeTo(sentFile);
            sentFile.close();

            // Send the message to the provider using
the connection.
            SOAPMessage reply = con.call(message,
urlEndpoint);

            if (reply != null) {
                FileOutputStream replyFile = new
FileOutputStream("reply.msg");
                reply.writeTo(replyFile);
                replyFile.close();
                System.err.println("Reply logged in
\"reply.msg\"");
                retval += " received reply (check
\"reply.msg\"). </H4> </body></html>";

            } else {
                System.err.println("No reply");
                retval += " no reply was received.
</H4> </html>";
            }

        } catch(Throwable e) {
            e.printStackTrace();
            logger.error("Error in constructing or
sending message "
            +e.getMessage());
            retval += " There was an error " +
```

Figure 4–28　SendingServlet.java Sends an XML Message in SOAP Messaging With JAXM—*continued.*

```
                    "in constructing or sending message. </H4>
</html>";
        }

        try {
            OutputStream os = resp.getOutputStream();
            os.write(retval.getBytes());
            os.flush();
            os.close();
        } catch (IOException e) {
            e.printStackTrace();
            logger.error( "Error in outputting servlet
response "
            + e.getMessage());
        }
    }

}
```

Figure 4–28   SendingServlet.java Sends an XML Message in SOAP Messaging With JAXM—*continued.*

The recipient client `ReceivingServlet.java` creates a connection to the Message Factory class. The underlying messaging still uses SOAP messaging via JAXM. The source code is shown in Figure 4–29.

```
package mySimple.receiver;

import javax.xml.soap.*;
import javax.xml.messaging.*;
import javax.servlet.*;
import javax.servlet.http.*;

import javax.xml.transform.*;

import javax.naming.*;

import org.apache.commons.logging.*;
```

Figure 4–29   ReceivingServlet.java Receives an XML Message Using JAXM

```
public class ReceivingServlet
    extends JAXMServlet
    implements ReqRespListener
{
    static MessageFactory fac = null;

    static {
        try {
            fac = MessageFactory.newInstance();
        } catch (Exception ex) {
            ex.printStackTrace();
        }
    };


    static Log
        logger =
LogFactory.getFactory().getInstance("Samples/mySimple"
);

    public void init(ServletConfig servletConfig)
throws ServletException {
        super.init(servletConfig);
        // Not much there to do here.
    }

    // This is the application code for handling the
message.. Once the
    // message is received the application can
retrieve the soap part, the
    // attachment part if there are any, or any other
information from the
    // message.

    public SOAPMessage onMessage(SOAPMessage message)
{
        System.out.println("On message called in
receiving servlet");
        try {
            System.out.println("Here's the message:
");
```

Figure 4–29   ReceivingServlet.java Receives an XML Message Using JAXM—*continued.*

```
            message.writeTo(System.out);

            SOAPMessage msg = fac.createMessage();

            SOAPEnvelope env =
msg.getSOAPPart().getEnvelope();

            env.getBody()

.addChildElement(env.createName("Response"))
                .addTextNode("This is a response");

            return msg;
        } catch(Exception e) {
            logger.error("Error in processing or
replying to a message", e);
            return null;
        }
    }
}
```

Figure 4–29   Receiving Servlet.java Receives an XML Message Using JAXM—*continued.*

Step 2: Write the build.xml File

An ANT build script (`build.xml`) is created to compile the Java source codes (servlets) and deploy the servlets in war files under the Web Container. It reads in a property file `jaxm.properties` to set the variables and paths. The `build.xml` file can be found under `/opt/mySimple/build.xml`.

Step 3: Compile Source Codes

To compile the source codes (the project name inside the build file is called mySimple), you may execute the following commands at a command prompt (Windows platform) or a Unix terminal (Unix platform). Figure 4–30 shows the script and the result when executed on a Windows machine.

```
D:\opt\mySimple>ant
Buildfile: build.xml

set.available:
```

Figure 4–30   Compile mySimple Source Codes

```
check.jaxm:

check.saaj:

check.appname:

check.servlet:

checks:

build.dir.webapps:

build.dir.local:

init:
     [[echo]] ———— Building mySimple to /opt/temp

prepare.build:

prepare:

compile:
    [[javac]] Compiling 2 source files to
\opt\temp\mySimple\WEB-INF\classes

main:

BUILD SUCCESSFUL
Total time: 11 seconds
```

Figure 4–30   Compile mySimple Source Codes—*continued.*

Step 4: Deploy as war Files

To deploy the compiled servlets (the project name inside the build file is called mySimple), you may execute the following commands at a command prompt (Windows platform) or a Unix terminal (Unix platform). Figure 4–31 shows the script and the result when executed on a Windows machine.

The war file created is placed under D:\opt\temp\war\mySimple.war. This needs to be copied to the webapps directory of your Web Container (for example, D:\Dev\WSDP\webapps).

```
D:\opt\mySimple>ant war
Buildfile: build.xml

set.available:

check.jaxm:

check.saaj:

check.appname:

check.servlet:

checks:

build.dir.webapps:

build.dir.local:

init:
     [[echo]] ——— Building mySimple to /opt/temp

prepare.build:

prepare:

compile:
    [[javac]] Compiling 2 source files to
\opt\temp\mySimple\WEB-INF\classes

main:

war:
     [[jar]] Building jar:
D:\opt\temp\war\mySimple.war

BUILD SUCCESSFUL
Total time: 6 seconds
```

Figure 4–31 Deploy mySimple Servlets

Step 5: Test Run

The Tomcat engine needs to be started. On a Windows machine, you may start the Tomcat server by clicking `Start | Java Web Services Developer Pack 1_0_01 | Start Tomcat` on the desktop. On Unix, you may start by issuing the command `./startup.sh` from your Java Web Services Developer Pack installation location (for example, `/opt/jwsdp/bin`).

From a Web browser, issue the URL *http://localhost:8080/mySimple/index.html*. You should see the screens shown in Figures 4–32 and 4–33.

4.9.4   References

Sun ONE Architecture and SunTone Architecture Methodology

Sun ONE Architecture Guide.
   http://wwws.sun.com/software/sunone/docs/arch/index.html

Sun ONE Architecture Implementation—Zefer.
   http://dcb.sun.com/practices/devnotebook/webserv_refarch.jsp

SunTone Architecture Methodology.
   http://www.sun.com/service/sunps/jdc/suntoneam_wp_5.24.pdf

Unified Process/Rational Unified Process

Enterprise Unified Process. *http://www.enterpriseunifiedprocess.info.*

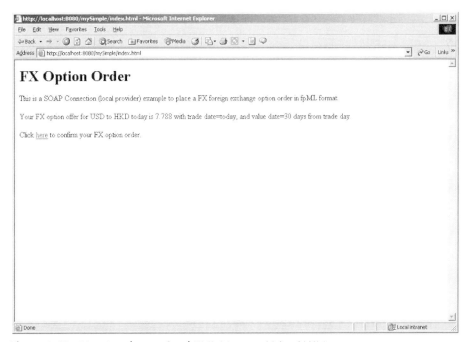

Figure 4–32   User Interface to Send XML Message Using JAXM

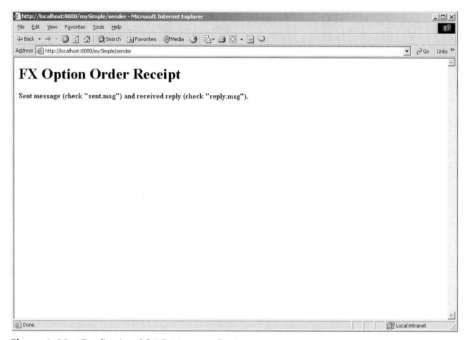

Figure 4–33 Confirming SOAP Message Sent

Rational. *Rational Unified Process* (CD-ROM media). Version 2001.03.00. Rationale, 2001.

Web Services Architecture

Judith M. Myerson. "Web Services Architectures." Tech, 2001.

Ueli Wahili, Mark Tomlinson, Olaf Zimmermann, Wouter Deruyck, and Denise Hendriks. "Web Services Wizardry with WebSphere Studio Application Developer." IBM Red Books, October 2001.

Web Services Design Patterns and Best Practices

Francis Geysermans and Jeff Miller. *"Implementing Design Patterns with Web Services."* IBM developerWorks Live! 2002 Conference.

Tim Hilgenberg and John A. Hansen. *"Building a Highly Robust, Secure Web Services Architecture to Process Four Million Transactions per Day."* IBM developerWorks Live! 2002 Conference.

Raghu Varadan. *"Patterns for eBusiness—Design Guidelines for Web Services."* IBM developerWorks Live! 2002 Conference.

Others

Alur Deepak, John Crupi, and Dan Malks. *Core J2EE Patterns*. Prentice Hall, 2001.

Chapter 5

MAINFRAME INTEGRATION AND INTEROPERABILITY

5.1 Chapter Summary

- The capability to reuse existing business functionality via Web Services technology, instead of system rewrite, is attractive in terms of total implementation cost, integration effort, and risks.

- Business functionality developed on IBM legacy mainframe platforms can be integrated by exposing the business service (for example, from existing CICS screens, SNA LU 6.2 verbs, and COMMAREA) via SOAP client proxy and XML-RPC technology.

- There are a few interoperability approaches to expose the business functionality of the legacy mainframe platform: CICS Transaction Gateway, APPC adapter, EAI adapter for mainframe, Linux 390 / z/OS, WebSphere/390, and SOAP proxy on z/OS. Each of these approaches requires additional software to be installed and thus have different architecture impacts. These approaches assume a long-term commitment to using a legacy mainframe.

- The alternatives to interoperating with a legacy mainframe assume a stop-gap measure to integrate with the mainframe systems using Web Services technology, while migrating the business functionality to the Open Standards in parallel. The migration can be done using transcode, recompile, rehost, and refront technology.

5.2 Chapter Objectives

- To identify the major mainframe interoperability approaches using Web Services technology and when to use them.
- To identify the alternatives to mainframe-based interoperability approaches and their associated benefits.

5.3 Background to Mainframe Interoperability

5.3.1 Current Mainframe Technology Update

The New IBM Mainframe

The IBM z/Series mainframe is a new product line of legacy S/390 mainframe hardware that provides backward compatibility for previous legacy operating systems using logical partitions (LPARs). The operating system z/OS provides support for multiple operating systems, including MVS, VSE, Linux, and OS/390 Unix Services.

OS/390 can be emulated on a notebook running Linux with a USB dongle and a valid license key. Fundamental Software has produced a Linux package called FLEX-ES *(http://www.funsoft.com/index-technical.html)* that developers may use as a development platform or for unit testing.

Under the z/OS, the management console is still based on TSO for managing jobs and executing console commands interactively. The System Authorization Facility (SAF) manages the security requests by integrating with the Resource Access Control Facility (RACF), and collaborates with LDAP/390 (previously SecureWay Security Manager LDAP Server) to provide Directory Server with some proprietary extensions. Understanding the architecture of z/OS and different mainframe integration options is crucial to building Web Services from legacy applications.

Figure 5–1 shows IBM's z/OS mainframe that has two logical partitions sharing a common high-performance filing system called HFS. Both logical partitions are connected to a Workload Manager and a System Logger, which will allocate workload and service requests to the business applications running on the logical partitions. Each logical partition is a virtual host, running its own operating system with multiple CICS regions, a J2EE application server, a Directory Server, and so forth. Business data is stored in the HFS, and thus it can be shared among different logical partitions. The shared business data is protected under RACF and can be accessed by CICS APPC calls, WebSphere MQ, or other customized data access methods such as VSAM (Virtual Sequential Access Method).

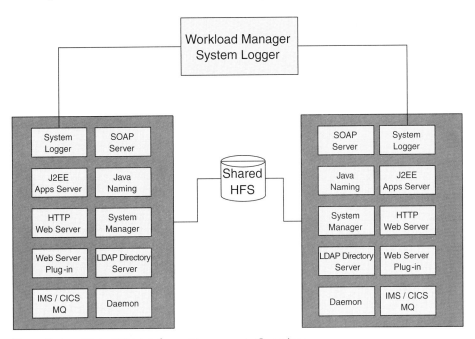

Figure 5–1   IBM z/OS Mainframe Components Overview

The modernized z/OS includes the WebSphere application development environment, where developers can share the same physical mainframe hardware and data resources. WebSphere version 4 is certified to be J2EE-compliant. The legacy database, such as VSAM and IMS, which were only accessible via COBOL/CICS before, can be accessed using a thin client browser. IBM provides Java classes (in jar files) under the CICS Transaction Gateway.

Typically, in a mainframe environment, Web server and application server instances are deployed in the same physical machine or even in the same logical partition. Nevertheless, these instances can be deployed in multiple logical partitions and even interoperate with other Web servers or application servers outside the mainframe.

Linux on Mainframe

The Open Source Linux distribution can be installed in a logical partition under z/OS (this is also known as Linux/390). Applications developed and run on Linux need to be recompiled under z/OS. Under Linux/390, developers can run WebSphere or other Linux-based J2EE application servers. Applications developed under Linux/390 can also access legacy data stored under an MVS partition, for instance, using shared HFS file systems and the Java classes of the CICS Transaction Gateway.

Figure 5–2 describes how the Linux/390 partition can interoperate with other logical partitions (such as MVS operating system) within a z/OS mainframe. As long as the data objects under the Linux operating system are stored in the shared filing system HFS, z/OS is able to provide data access and connectivity to any operating system of other logical partitions within the physical mainframe. Of course, the data access needs to be granted by RACF. Under HFS, if the business data is stored by a Linux application in a relational database such as IBM's Universal Database (previously, DB2), then a CICS/DB2 application from the MVS partition will be able to access the data. If the business data is stored in a proprietary or vendor-specific format, then the business data may look like a blob of binary data to other logical partitions, even though data access right is granted.

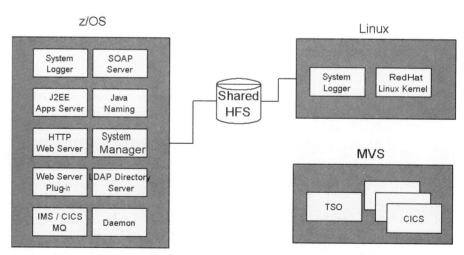

Figure 5–2   Linux/390 Interoperating With z/OS and MVS

IBM has been evangelizing Linux on mainframe for the past two years, but there is a limited installation base so far. *www.linux390.com* provides a good resource regarding the compatibility and implementation issues of Linux on mainframe.

5.3.2   Integration Technology for Legacy Mainframe

There are two different types of integration technology for legacy mainframe systems. The first type is asynchronous messaging, where all service requests and transactions are represented in business documents, and they can be sent via a message-oriented middleware such as WebSphere MQ or a JMS-compliant middleware product. The business documents can be then wrapped in a SOAP envelope and delivered via SOAP messaging over MQ or JMS. The second type is synchronous messaging, where all service requests and transactions are initiated using CICS ECI, EPI, or ESI calls. A server-side SOAP component (SOAP tier or skeleton) can be created to initiate the remote business transactions on the mainframe via these ECI, EPI, or ESI calls. There are a few integration options available, and they will be discussed with some details in this section.

Asynchronous messaging for mainframe integration (such as WebSphere MQ or previously IBM MQ Series) is queue-based messaging, and it does not support real-time processing. Details of WebSphere MQ can be found at *http://www-3.ibm.com/software/ts/mqseries/*.

In two different books (see "References" at the end of this chapter), Phil Wakelin and his colleagues have identified a few legacy mainframe integration options based on different infrastructure configurations. The business functionality provided by these legacy applications can be wrapped as Web Services using the XML-RPC approach. Wakelin, Benedete, et al. (2002, pp. 13–61) and Wakelin, Keen, Johnson, and Diaz (2002, pp. 9–33) have identified different mainframe integration options. The key implications of the architecture design and how Web Services can be applied will be elaborated in the following sections. There are more resources that discuss different technology options to initiate remote calls to CICS transactions via synchronous messaging in the "Reference" section at the end of this chapter.

Many customer environments do not support a message-oriented middleware infrastructure. Integrating with mainframe systems may be restricted to remote calls to CICS transactions. Thus, this section will cover some details of mainframe integration using synchronous messaging and RPC-based Web Services.

CICS Transaction Gateway

Design Features

The CICS Transaction Gateway (CTG), currently in version 3.1, has the following components:

- **Gateway Daemon**—A gateway function that listens to a specified TCP/IP port using TCP, SSL, HTTP, or HTTPS, for Java clients to access CICS applications.

- **Client Daemon**—Provides client–server connectivity to CICS applications via External Call Interface (ECI), the External Presentation Interface (EPI), and the External Security Interface (ESI) calls.

- **CTG Java Class Library**—ctg.jar is a set of Java classes used to initiate ECI, EPI, and ESI calls and to access VSAM and IMS datasets.

- **Configuration Tool**—Is a graphical user interface to configure the properties for the Gateway Daemon and Client Daemon in the CTG.INI file.

- **Terminal Servlet**—A Java servlet that emulates the 3270 CICS application.

According to Wakelin, Benedete, et al. (2002) in *Revealed! Architecting Web Access to CICS* (pp. 13–61), CTG can be deployed in three possible design configurations based on the application architecture (for example, whether the Web server, the application server, and back-end CICS systems are on the same machine), integration strategy (for example, direct connection to CICS with no intermediate component), and performance constraints (for example, whether multiple ports are required to connect to the target CICS applications). The deployment configuration is likely to depend on whether an architects' long-term strategy is to extend the mainframe usage (for example, deploy all Web servers, application servers, and back-end applications on one single mainframe) or to use the mainframe as a Resource Tier (which may allow more technology options to scale up the application services and interoperate the mainframe applications with applications running on other platforms).

Same Platform.   A servlet uses the underlying CICS-proprietary EXCI/MRO protocol, which utilizes a subset of ECI calls, to invoke a remote CICS application. CTG cannot make EPI or ESI calls. The communication between the EXCI program and the target CICS region is a typical SNA connection. The target CICS region must be the CICS Transaction Server version 1.2 or higher. It is not aware that the client request comes from a Java application.

This design configuration is useful when the HTTP Web server, application server, and CICS region reside on the same z/390 machine. It also gives the benefit of invoking native business functions from the existing CICS applications with minimal impact on the back-end architecture design.

Figure 5–3 depicts the design of a CTG running on the same z/390 platform with CICS and the Web server. In this scenario, a SOAP client (using a browser) can initiate a Web Services functionality (such as my mortgage account balance inquiry) provided by the J2EE application server. The remote business service is provided by the back-end CICS application via ECI calls. There is a Java class that exposes the ECI call as a service end-point URL. The SOAP client can initiate an RPC call to the remote business service by looking up the service end-point URL via a Service Registry and invoking it.

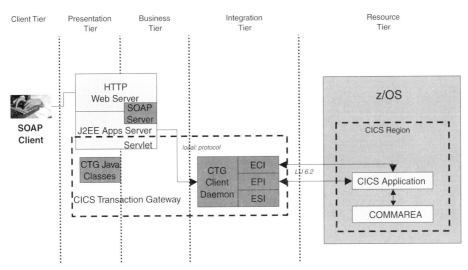

Figure 5–3   CTG—Same Platform Design Configuration

Under the same platform configuration, all architecture components residing in the Presentation Tier (such as HTTP Web Server), Business Tier (such as J2EE application server), Integration Tier (such as CTG), and Resource Tier (such as are within the same z/OS machine). (Chapter 4 of this book introduces how to architect service components in different tiers and platform layers.) The reliability, availability, and scalability for each component will be also dependent on the z/OS platform. For instance, the flexibility of the z/OS platform configuration will have a major impact to administrators if they want to increase the physical memory for the J2EE application server only.

Distributed Platforms.   A servlet initiates an SNA APPC or LU 6.2 connection using the CTG Client Daemon with ECI, EPI, or ESI calls. The HTTP Web Server, Application Server, and CICS region reside on different machines. The connection between CTG Client Daemon and the target CICS region is SNA LU 6.2, not TCP/IP.

This design configuration is useful to integrate Web and application servers running on Unix platforms with legacy mainframe CICS. It is also suitable for the design constraint where the legacy mainframe platform cannot be modified or enhanced. The benefit is better scalability for different applications in each tier, and developers do not need to build every component in the same mainframe platform.

Figure 5–4 depicts the design of a CTG running on a different host that communicates with CICS applications on a z/OS host. In this scenario, a SOAP client (using a browser) can initiate a Web Services functionality (such as my mortgage account balance inquiry) provided by the J2EE application server under the Business Tier. The remote business service is provided by the back-end CICS application via ECI, EPI, or ESI calls. There is a Java class that exposes the ECI/EPI/ESI call as a service end-point URL. The SOAP client can initiate an RPC call to the remote business service by looking up the service end-point URL via a Service Registry and invoking it.

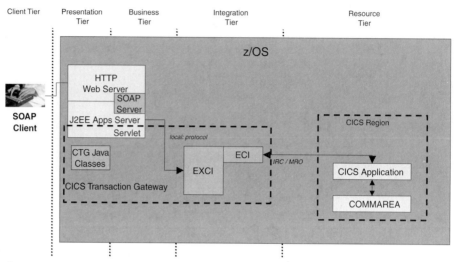

Figure 5–4   CTG—Distributed Platform Design Configuration

Under the distributed platform configuration, HTTP Web server resides in the Presentation Tier, and J2EE application server resides in the Business Tier. If the data traffic increases, architects can scale up these components vertically (for instance, by adding CPUs) or horizontally (for instance, by adding other server instances). This allows less complexity and more flexibility to manage scalability and performance tuning on individual server components, when compared to scaling multiple server components within the same mainframe platform.

Figures 5–5 and 5–6 show a Java Front Controller servlet initiating ECI calls and EPI calls, respectively. (Front Controller handles presentation logic, and can be used to initiate Web Services calls. The term Front Controller is discussed in Alur, Crupi, and Malks [2001, pp. 172–185], *Core J2EE Patterns.*) These program excerpts are extracted and slightly modified from CTG samples for illustration. In the first sample ECI program (Figure 5–5), the objective is to invoke a CICS transaction id, which will return the response in the COMMAREA. Developers need to specify the CTG gateway URL, SSL class name, SSL password, user id, password, server name, and program (transaction id here is PHALL). Then the command ECI Request will initiate the target CICS transaction id (shown in bold). The data and program response can be retrieved from the variable COMMAREA. The rest of the code is similar to a servlet. The sample ECI program (that is modified from the sample programs provided in the CTG software) can be modified slightly and wrapped as an RPC-based Web Services call.

```
import javax.servlet.*;
import javax.servlet.http.*;
import java.io.*;
import java.util.*;
import com.ibm.ctg.client.*;

public class myECI extends HttpServlet
{
    ...
    public void init(ServletConfig sc) throws
ServletException
    {
        super.init(sc);
        // specify the gateway URL
        gatewayURL = sc.getInitParameter
("GatewayURL");

        if (gatewayURL == null)
        {
            gatewayURL = DEFAULT_URL;
        }

        gateway = new JavaGateway();

        // specify the SSL class name and password
        String sslClassName = sc.getInitParameter
("SSLClassname");
        String sslPassword = sc.getInitParameter
("SSLPassword");

        if (sslClassName != null && sslPassword !=
null)
        {

SslJavaGateway.setKeyRing(sslClassName.trim(),
sslPassword.trim());
        }
    }
```

Figure 5–5   Sample CTG ECI Call

```
    public void destroy()
    {
        try
        {
            if (gateway!=null)
            {
                if (gateway.isOpen())
                {
                    gateway.close();
                }
            }
        }
        catch (IOException e)
        {
            StringWriter exceptionOut = new
StringWriter();
            e.printStackTrace(new
PrintWriter(exceptionOut ));
            String trace = exceptionOut.toString();
            log(trace);
        }
    }

    public void doGet(HttpServletRequest request,
HttpServletResponse response)
    throws ServletException, IOException
    {
        HttpSession session =
request.getSession(true);
        response.setContentType("text/html");
        try
        {
            synchronized(this)
            {
                if (!gateway.isOpen())
                {
                    gateway.setURL(gatewayURL);
                    gateway.open();
                }
            }
            this.displayInitialPage(session,
response);
        }
```

Figure 5–5 Sample CTG ECI Call—*continued.*

```
        catch (IOException e)
        {
            this.displayException(e, response,
session);
        }
    }

    private void displayInitialPage(HttpSession
session, HttpServletResponse response) throws
IOException
    {
      ...
    }

    private void getServers(PrintWriter out) throws
IOException, Exception
    {
        ECIRequest eci = ECIRequest.listSystems(99);
        int returnCode = gateway.flow(eci);

        this.checkReturnCode(returnCode, eci);

        Vector servers = eci.SystemList;

        if (eci.numServersReturned > 0 && servers !=
null)
        {
            int serverListLength = servers.size();
            boolean display = true;

            out.println("Server:<BR><SELECT NAME =
\"Server\">");
            for (int i = 0; I<serverListLength; i++)
            {
                if (display)
                {
                    out.println("<OPTION VALUE = \"" +
servers.elementAt(i)
                                + "\" >" +
servers.elementAt(i));
                    display = false;
                }
```

Figure 5–5 Sample CTG ECI Call—*continued.*

```
                      else
                      {
                           display = true;
                      }
                }
                out.println("</SELECT>");
                out.println("<BR>");
           }
      }

   public void doPost(HttpServletRequest request,
                          HttpServletResponse response)
throws ServletException, IOException
      {
           HttpSession session = null;

           try
           {
                session = request.getSession(true);
                response.setContentType("text/html");

                this.runTransaction(session, request);
                this.displayOutput(response, session);
           }
           catch (Exception e)
           {
                this.displayException(e, response, session);
           }
      }

   private void runTransaction(HttpSession session,
HttpServletRequest request)
      throws IOException, Exception
      {
           String userId = request.getParameter
("UserId");
           // Replace the UserId with your CICS server id
           String password = request.getParameter
("Password");
           // Replace the Password with your CICS server
password
```

Figure 5–5 Sample CTG ECI Call—*continued.*

```
        String server = request.getParameter
("Server");
        //  Replace the Server with your CICS server
name
        String program = request.getParameter
("Program");
        //  Replace the Program with your CICS server
program name

        int commAreaSize;
        if (program.equals(PHALL))
        {
            commAreaSize = 50;
        }
        else
        {
            try
            {
                commAreaSize =
Integer.parseInt(request.getParameter("CommAreaSize").
trim());
            }
            catch (NumberFormatException e)
            {
                commAreaSize = DEFAULT_SIZE;
            }

            if (commAreaSize>MAX_COMMAREA_SIZE)
            {
                commAreaSize = MAX_COMMAREA_SIZE;
            }

            if (commAreaSize<MINIMUM_SIZE)
            {
                commAreaSize = MINIMUM_SIZE;
            }
        }

        byte[[]] commArea = new byte[[commAreaSize]];
        ECIRequest eci = new ECIRequest
(ECIRequest.ECI_SYNC,
```

Figure 5–5   Sample CTG ECI Call—*continued.*

```
                                                server.trim(),
                                                userId.trim(),
                                              password.trim(),
                                               program.trim(),
                                               null,
                                               commArea,
                                               commAreaSize,

ECIRequest.ECI_NO_EXTEND,

ECIRequest.ECI_LUW_NEW);

        int returnCode = gateway.flow(eci);
        this.checkReturnCode(returnCode, eci);
        session.putValue("SESSION_ECI_OBJECT", eci);
    }

    private void checkReturnCode(int returnCode,
ECIRequest eci)
    throws Exception
    {
        if (returnCode!=0)
        {
            if (eci.getCicsRc()==0)
            {
                throw new Exception("Gateway
exception: Return code number:"
                                        + returnCode
                                        + " Return code
String: "
                                        +
eci.getRcString());
            }
            else
            {

                if
(eci.getCicsRc()==ECIRequest.ECI_ERR_SECURITY_ERROR
                    || (eci.Abend_Code != null
                            &&
eci.Abend_Code.equalsIgnoreCase("AEY7")))
```

Figure 5–5   Sample CTG ECI Call—*continued.*

```
                    {
                        throw new Exception("Server is
unable to validate " +
                                        "UserId or
password");
                    }
                    else
                    {
                        throw new Exception("CICS
exception: Return code number:"
                                        + returnCode
                                        + " Return
code String: "
                                        +
eci.getCicsRcString());
                    }
                }
            }
        }
}
```

Figure 5–5   Sample CTG ECI Call—*continued.*

In the following CTG EPI program excerpt (that is modified from the sample programs in CTG software) in Figure 5–6, the objective is to invoke a 3270-based CICS transaction id. The flow events govern the manipulation of data fields and interaction. Developers need to specify the 3270 terminal parameters in the EPIRequest.addTerminal method (shown in bold). Then they initiate the target 3270 screens using the method startTran. Because EPI calls require a series of screen actions and event manipulation, developers can customize the actions in the flowRequest and obtainEvent classes. This may be tedious if many 3270 screens are invoked. The sample EPI program can be modified slightly and wrapped as an RPC-based Web Services call. However, due to the nature of EPI calls, any change in the user interface (such as screen position or screen name) will break the RPC call. Thus, this approach to wrapping EPI calls is not architecturally elegant.

```
import java.io.*;
import com.ibm.ctg.client.*;

public class myEPISample {

    ...
   public static void main(String[[]] args) {
      try {
         ...
         javaGatewayObject = new JavaGateway(myUrl,
myPortNumber);
         ...
         flowRequest(myEPIRequest);
         myEPIRequest =
         EPIRequest.addTerminal(myCICSServerName,
//CICS server
                                    null,
//CICS terminal resource name
                                    null);
//CICS terminal model name
         flowRequest(myEPIRequest);
         myEPIRequest.startTran(null,      // this is
the CICS Transid
                                    mybyteArrayData,
//Byte array of 3270 datastream
                                            //
(CANNOT be null)
                                    7);       //Size
of datastream to be passed
                                            // to
Transaction, in bytes
         flowRequest(myEPIRequest);
         obtainEvent(myEPIRequest);

         while (myEPIRequest.getEvent() !=
EPIRequest.EPI_EVENT_END_TERM) {
            if (myEPIRequest.getEvent() ==
EPIRequest.EPI_EVENT_END_TRAN) {
               System.out.println(" End of
transaction; end reason "
                                    + myEPIRequest.get
EndReasonString()
```

Figure 5–6   Sample CTG EPI Call

```
                                + "\n");
            myEPIRequest.delTerminal();
            flowRequest(myEPIRequest);
        } else {
            dumpDatastream(myEPIRequest.data,
bDebug);
        }
        obtainEvent(myEPIRequest);
    }
    System.out.println(" Terminal deleted; end
reason "
                            +
myEPIRequest.getEndReasonString() + "\n");
    if (myEPIRequest.getEndReason() !=
EPIRequest.EPI_TRAN_NO_ERROR) {
        System.out.println(" EPI returned: "
                        + myEPIRequest.get
EndReturnCodeString());
    } else {
        System.out.println(" Event type "
                        + myEPIRequest.get
EventString()
                        + " Received from
CICS.");
        dumpDatastream(myEPIRequest.data, bDebug);
    }

    // Now terminating EPI session

    if (javaGatewayObject.isOpen() == true) {
        javaGatewayObject.close();
    }

} catch (UnsupportedEncodingException
exceptCode) {
    System.out.println("The " + strEncoding + "
format is not "
                        + "supported.");
} catch (Exception exceptCode) {
    exceptCode.printStackTrace();
}
}
```

Figure 5–6   Sample CTG EPI Call—*continued.*

```
    private static void flowRequest(EPIRequest
myRequest) {
      try {
          int iRc = javaGatewayObject.flow(myRequest);

          switch (myRequest.getCicsRc()) {
          case EPIRequest.EPI_NORMAL:
             if (iRc != 0) {
                System.out.println("\nError from
Gateway ("
                                        +
myRequest.getRcString()
                                        + "), please correct
and rerun this sample");
                if (javaGatewayObject.isOpen() == true)
{
                   javaGatewayObject.close();
                }
                System.exit(0);
             }
             return;

          case EPIRequest.EPI_ERR_MORE_EVENTS:
             if (myRequest.getEvent() ==
EPIRequest.EPI_EVENT_END_TERM) {
                return;
             }
             if (myRequest.getEndReason() !=
EPIRequest.EPI_TRAN_NO_ERROR) {
                System.out.println(" EPI returned: "
                                        +
myRequest.getEndReasonString());
             }
             return;
          }
          System.out.println("\nEPI returned: "
                                +
myRequest.getCicsRcString());
          if (javaGatewayObject.isOpen() == true) {
             javaGatewayObject.close();
          }
          System.exit(0);
```

Figure 5–6   Sample CTG EPI Call—*continued.*

```
      } catch (Exception exceptCode) {
         exceptCode.printStackTrace();
         System.exit(0);
      }
      return;
   }


   private static void obtainEvent(EPIRequest
myRequest) {
      try {
         myRequest.getEvent
         (EPIRequest.EPI_WAIT, //Wait for event
          iBufferSize);          //MAXIMUM size of data
to be returned, in bytes
         int iRc = javaGatewayObject.flow(myRequest);
         switch (myRequest.getCicsRc()) {
         case EPIRequest.EPI_NORMAL:
            if (iRc != 0) {
               System.out.println("\nError from
Gateway ("
                                    +
myRequest.getRcString()
                                    + "), please correct
and rerun this sample");
               if (javaGatewayObject.isOpen() == true)
{
                  javaGatewayObject.close();
               }
               System.exit(0);
            }
         case EPIRequest.EPI_ERR_BAD_INDEX:
         case EPIRequest.EPI_ERR_FAILED:
         case EPIRequest.EPI_ERR_MORE_EVENTS:
         case EPIRequest.EPI_ERR_MORE_DATA:
         case EPIRequest.EPI_ERR_NO_EVENT:
         case EPIRequest.EPI_ERR_NOT_INIT:
         case EPIRequest.EPI_ERR_WAIT:
         case EPIRequest.EPI_ERR_NULL_PARM:
         case EPIRequest.EPI_ERR_IN_CALLBACK:
            System.out.println(" Event type "
```

Figure 5–6   Sample CTG EPI Call—*continued.*

```
                                    + myRequest.get
EventString()
                                    + " Received from
CICS.");
          }

      } catch (Exception exceptCode) {
         exceptCode.printStackTrace();
      }
   }

   private static void dumpDatastream(byte[[]] data,
boolean debug) {
      try {
         int total = data.length;
         if (debug == false) {
            System.out.println("\n Data returned: " +
                               new String(data, 2,
(total - 2), strEncoding));
            return;
         }
         int row = 0;
         int column = 0;
         int character = 0;
         int width = 16;
         System.out.println("\n Datastream
returned:");
         for (row = 0; character < total; row++) {
            System.out.print("   ");
            while ((column < width) && (character <
total)) {
               if (data[[character]] != 0) {
System.out.print(Integer.toHexString(data[[character]]
));
               } else {
                  System.out.print("  ");
               }
               character++;
               column++;
            }
            System.out.print("    " +
```

Figure 5–6   Sample CTG EPI Call—*continued.*

```
                                new String(data,
(row*width), column, strEncoding)
                               + "\n");
            column = 0;
        }

      } catch (UnsupportedEncodingException
exceptCode) {
          System.out.println("The " + strEncoding + "
format is not "
                               + "supported.");
      } catch (Exception exceptCode) {
          exceptCode.printStackTrace();
      }
    }
}
```

Figure 5–6   Sample CTG EPI Call—*continued.*

Remote CTG.   This is a variant of the previously discussed distributed platforms configuration. The servlet can invoke CICS applications using TCP/IP, SSL, HTTP, or HTTPS protocol. The Gateway Daemon, which resides on the same machine as the target CICS region, will process and forward client requests to the target CICS applications via EXCI. The Gateway Daemon reformats the client requests using the Java Native Interface (JNI).

This design configuration is desirable for achieving a pure TCP/IP-based connectivity (using TCP/IP, SSL, HTTP, or HTTPS) between the client and the server. The benefit is that CTG can configure to work with multiple TCP/IP ports and balance client requests across multiple CICS regions for better scalability if available.

Figure 5–7 depicts the design of a remote CTG, where the CTG Gateway Daemon resides in the remote z/OS platform. In this scenario, a Java server-side program invokes the remote CICS applications in the mainframe via CTG Java classes. It uses an HTTP (or HTTPS) connection to the CTG Gateway Daemon. The CTG Gateway Daemon looks up the configuration context via JNI and invokes the CICS executable EXCI. EXCI is able to route ECI, EPI, or ESI calls to the relevant CICS applications. The data parameters for the CICS calls, or the transaction result fetched after the CICS calls, can be placed in the common area region COMMAREA.

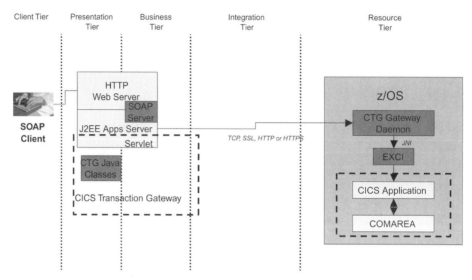

Figure 5–7   Remote CTG Design Configuration

Implication

CTG provides wider integration options for architects who do not desire the Web-based functionality tightly coupled with the legacy CICS platform. Architects can deploy CTG on Unix or Windows platforms with a distributed server topology (n-tier architecture). This enables more options to scale up the capacity. Invoking legacy CICS applications using ECI calls with CTG can shield off complex SNA LU 6.2 protocols from developers. This does not require architects and developers to have an in-depth knowledge of the legacy mainframe systems.

The choice of CTG configuration depends on the server topology (same platform, distributed platforms, or remote CTG). Architects need to make conscious design decisions up front when choosing which CTG configuration to use, as switching to other configuration in the midst of or after deployment could be painful.

To enable Web Services using CTG, architects and developers need to generate an XML-RPC call (for example, using Java Web Services Developer Pack's wscompile or Apache Axis's `org.apache.axis.wsdl.wsdl2 java` utility; refer to the exercises in the chapters Web Services Technology Overview and The Next Frontiers for details) from a Java client that initiates ECI, EPI, or ESI calls. If they are using ECI calls, they need to identify the target CICS transaction id and check out whether any modification to the existing CICS applications or COMAREA is required. If they are using EPI calls, they may need to ensure the data fields in the legacy 3270 screens have not changed, otherwise they must update the EPI calls. If the legacy mainframe functionality is likely to be reused by multiple parties, it is more scalable and reusable to use Java technology approach (such as EJB or JCA) to enable them as Web Services.

CICS Web Support

Design Features

ICS Web Support (CWS) comes with CICS Transaction Server for OS/390 or VSE version 1.3. These are CICS-supplied programs, which provide ASCII-to-EBCDIC code page conversion (Web Attach Processing programs CWXN, DFHCNV, and Analyzer), conversion between 3270-based screens and HTML pages (3270 Web Bridge), decode/encode for Web page presentation logic (Alias Transaction program including CWBA), and analysis of HTTP requests to invoke CICS applications (Alias Transaction program or Business Logic Interface).

There are three different design configurations when using CWS, as shown in Figure 5–8:

Direct Connection. A client browser can directly connect to CICS applications via the CICS Web Support programs CWXN (Web Attach Transaction) and CWBA (Alias Transaction). This requires the installation of an OS/390 Communications Server and assumes the use of the CICS TCP/IP Listener (CSOL) to be running under the CICS region, which intercepts HTTP requests over TCP/IP via a CICS Socket. The HTTP request header and input data need to be converted to EBCDIC using the DFHCNV conversion program. The Analyzer program will then process the incoming HTTP request to look up the alias name (the default CWBA transaction code is DFHWBA), the converter program, the user id, and the user program of the target CICS region (refer to Figure 5–9).

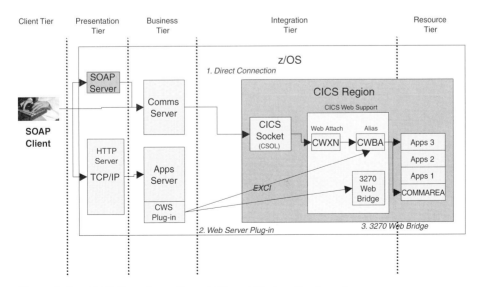

Figure 5–8   CWS Overview—Three Different Design Configurations

This design configuration is appropriate when developers do not require an HTTP Web Server but use the CICS TCP/IP Listener to process HTTP requests. The benefit is that there is no architecture change in the legacy CICS applications on the VSE platform in order to invoke legacy CICS applications from a client browser. The current limitation is that CICS Web Support only allows a maximum of 32KB of data to be received and utilized by the application. With direct connection to CICS without a Web Server, compliance with Open Standards and subsequent integration would be difficult.

Figure 5–9 elaborates the process of direct connection with more details. The browser client issues an HTTP request to access a Web server, which will route the HTTP request to the communications server. The communications server determines that this is a request to access CICS resources in the Resource Tier. It intercepts the CICS resource requests from the CICS Socket (CSOL). The Web Attach program CWXN and the Alias program CWBA (these are CICS programs running in the same CICS region) handle the conversion of the code page from ANSI to EBCDIC (which the mainframe can understand). The DFHCNV process converts input data from the HTTP request to ASCII, which will then be converted to EBCDIC. The CWXN analyzer will look up the alias name, converter, user id, and user program before passing the CICS request to the Alias program CWBA (default is DFHWBA, and the alias program can be customized). The Alias program CWBA functions as a converter, which encodes and decodes CICS data. It then invokes the appropriate user application program to process the CICS requests. It receives the presentation logic decoded in CICS format. It sends the CICS results in encoded data that can be handled by the presentation logic (such as HTML Web pages).

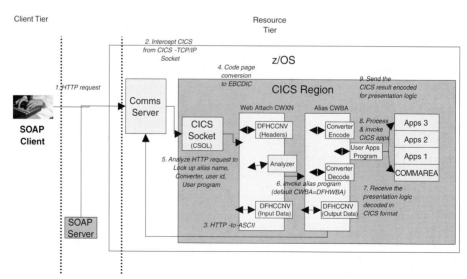

Figure 5–9   CWS Direct Connection

A SOAP server-side component (also called the SOAP tier or SOAP skeleton) can be created to wrap the CICS request using a CICS Socket and the CICS Web Support programs. This approach is suitable if there are browser-based programs currently accessing the back-end CICS resources via a CICS Socket. It can also create a new information aggregation Web Service (such as aggregating my personal wealth portfolio from different bank accounts) by collaborating with Web Services information aggregation tools (such as bowstreet). Nevertheless, the CICS Web Support technology heavily relies on 3270 screens (via 3270-to-HTML conversion), and it may not be a scalable approach to extend new functionality.

A sample DFHCNV ASCII-to-HTML code page conversion configuration may look like the following (see Figure 5–10):

```
DFHCNV TYPE=INITIAL
*
DFHCNV TYPE=ENTRY,RTYPE=PC,RNAME=DFHWBHH,USREXIT=NO,
SRVERCP=037,CLINTCP=8859-1
DFHCNV TYPE=SELECT
DFHCNV
TYPE=FIELD,OFFSET=0,DATATYP=CHARACTER,DATALEN=32767,
LAST=YES
*
DFHCNV TYPE=ENTRY,RTYPE=PC,RNAME=DFHWBUD,USREXIT=NO,
SRVERCP=037,CLINTCP=8859-1
DFHCNV TYPE=SELECT
DFHCNV
TYPE=FIELD,OFFSET=0,DATATYP=CHARACTER,DATALEN=32767,
LAST=YES
*
DFHCNV TYPE=FINAL
END
```

Figure 5–10 Sample DFHCNV Conversion Configuration

CICS Web Server Plug-in.   Figure 5–11 depicts the interaction process between components when using the CICS Web Server Plug-in. The proprietary program DFHWBAPI, a CICS Web Server Plug-in, runs on top of the IBM HTTP Server. It performs the same functionality as the previously mentioned Web Attach Transaction, which invokes the ASCII-to-EBCDIC code page conversion routine. It also builds an EXCI request, decodes the HTTP requests into CICS transactions, and passes the HTTP data stream to the Business Logic Interface for CICS applications in the COMMAREA.

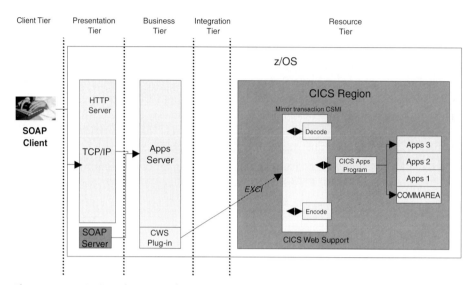

Figure 5–11 CTG Web Server Plug-in

This design configuration is useful when the HTTP Web Server and the target CICS region reside on the same machine and the same sysplex, and developers do not want to add another middleware such as the CICS Transaction Gateway. It has similar advantages and disadvantages as other CWS design configurations.

A server-side Web Services component can be created to invoke remote business functionality residing in the back-end CICS region via DFHWBAPI. The SOAP server tier (or SOAP skeleton) can initiate the EXCI call. It is a simpler architecture to access CICS resources compared with the previous direct connection or the 3270 Web Bridge depicted below.

3270 Web Bridge. Figure 5–12 depicts the interaction process between components using the 3270 Web Bridge. HTTP requests from the client browser can be processed via the Web Attach Transaction and Alias Transaction (that is, Direct Connection design configuration), or the CICS Web Server Plug-in. If these requests and responses need to be formatted and presented in 3270 screen maps or HTML, then 3270 Web Bridge is a flexible solution for 3270-to-HTML conversion using a 3270 HTML conversion program and an HTML template rule database. 3270-based CICS applications (in this example, myapps1) can then be invoked by a URL directly from the host mycics.nextfrontiers.com using port 8080 (for example, *http://mycics.next frontiers.com:8080/cics/cwba/dfhwbtta/myapps1*).

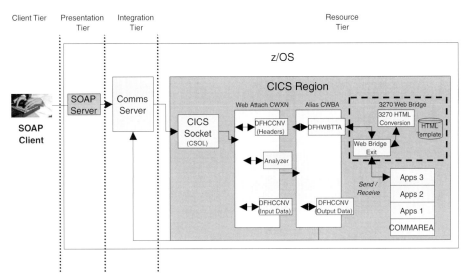

Figure 5–12   CWS—3270 Web Bridge

The excerpt in Figure 5–13 shows a sample BMS mapset definition using the DFHWBOUT and DFHMDX macros (highlighted in bold). The DFHMDX macro maps 3270 data fields to the HTML data fields and attributes.

For 3270 screen mapset and HTML mapping, Eugene Deborin and his colleagues (1999, pp. 257–308) discuss the details of how to define the mapping using a DFHMAPT procedure with the mapset definition macros DFHWBOUT, DFHMDX, DFHMDI, DFHMDF, and DFHMSX.

This design configuration is useful to facilitate easy mapping between 3270 screen maps to HTML conversion using an HTML template rule engine. Nevertheless, the screen mapping is tedious and unavoidably labor-intensive. Chris Smith (2001) has identified a few restrictions on the 3270-to-HTML conversion capability (for example, no dynamic modification of attribute bytes and BMS paging not supported, among others).

Similar to the scenario of using a CICS direct connection, a server-side Web Services component can be created to wrap the CICS request using a CICS Socket and the 3270 Web Bridge. This approach is suitable if there are browser-based programs currently accessing the back-end CICS resources via a CICS Socket and a 3270 Web Bridge. It can also create a new information aggregation Web Service (such as aggregating my home and utility phone bills from different service providers) by collaborating with Web Services information aggregation tools (such as Bowstreet). Nevertheless, the 3270 Web Bridge technology heavily relies on 3270 screens (via 3270-to-HTML conversion), and it may not be a scalable approach to extend new functionality.

```
TITLE 'Testing display with 3270 bridge '
PRINT ON,NOGEN
PHALLGRP DFHMSD
TYPE=MAP,LANG=COBOL,MODE=INOUT,STORAGE=AUTO,SUFFIX=
TITLE 'BMS: PHALLPNL PHALLPNL '
PHALLPNL DFHMDI
SIZE=(24,80),MAPATTS=(COLOR,HILIGHT),DSATTS=(COLOR),  *
COLUMN=1,LINE=1,DATA=FIELD,TIOAPFX=YES,OBFMT=NO
* --------------------------------
DFHWBOUT 'DFHWBOUT places text in the HTML header and
adds text to HTML page'
*
DFHMDX MAPSET=PHALLGRP,MAP=PHALLPNL, X
TITLE='3270 Web bridge Test Transaction', X
BGCOLOR=#F4CEC4, X
PF3=EXIT, X
ENTER=SUBMIT, X
RESET=NO, X
SUPPRESS=((23,1),(24,1))
* --------------------------------
DFHMDF
POS=(1,1),LENGTH=8,INITIAL='JUL/2001',ATTRB=(ASKIP,NOR
M*
)
DFHMDF
POS=(1,63),LENGTH=16,INITIAL='ACBJ3270.PHALLPNL',  *
ATTRB=(ASKIP,NORM)
DFHMDF POS=(2,34),LENGTH=13,INITIAL='Prentice Hall',  *
ATTRB=(ASKIP,BRT),COLOR=RED
DFHMDF POS=(4,25),LENGTH=31,  *
INITIAL='Java Web Services Book',ATTRB=(ASKIP,B*
RT),COLOR=NEUTRAL
DFHMDF POS=(6,25),LENGTH=32,  *
INITIAL='3270 Web bridge Test
Transaction',ATTRB=(ASKIP,*
NORM)
DFHMDF POS=(11,29),LENGTH=9,INITIAL='Option
=>',ATTRB=(ASKIP,N*
ORM)
```

Figure 5–13 Sample 3270 Mapset-to-HTML Mapping

To use the 3270 Web Bridge, developers need to configure some specific parameters during the CICS Transaction Server system setup (for example, TCPIP=YES, WEBDELAY=(terminal-wait-time, state-data-keep-time)) and increase EDSA storage. Most of the CICS-related configuration is lengthy but straightforward. A basic knowledge of Web servers and HTML is essential. However, not all CICS applications may work unchanged. Please refer to Chris Smith (2001) for more details.

Implication

CWS provides a simple pan-CICS design approach to Web-enabling legacy CICS applications from a URL. This technology does not require installing additional application servers or gateway components, and thus it is lightweight. Nevertheless, the integration capability will be constrained by 3270 screen-based or EPI-based technologies. In other words, if developers want to manipulate any data or to invoke a specific business function where there is no CICS screen available, then they have to modify the back-end applications or perhaps create a new CICS screen.

There is a misconception that any browser-based application is a Web Services solution. With CWS and SNA gateway technology, it is possible to access mainframe applications from a browser. CWS technology handles the conversion from CICS to HTML Web pages. This is not a real Web Services solution because CWS does not generate an XML message containing the data contents required from the legacy systems. Architects and developers need to wrap the HTML data fields in a SOAP message or create another XML-RPC to wrap the data contents generated from CWS. Thus, it would be more flexible to use Java technology to enable Web Services.

Java Technology

Design Features

IBM has implemented the Enterprise Java Bean (EJB) Server in the CICS Transaction Server version 2.1. The EJB environment includes TCP/IP Listener, request receiver (DFHIIRRS), request models, request stream directory (DFHEJDIR), request processor, EJB container, object store (DFHEJOS), Java Virtual Machine, CORBA server, and deployed JAR files. Wakelin, Benedete, et al. (2001, pp. 32–34) have details depicting the EJB server components in CICS, and how it operates. Using Java technology to integrate and interoperate with legacy mainframe applications is simpler and architecturally cleaner. The following sections discuss variants of Java technology that can be wrapped as Web Services.

EJB Support. The use of EJB enables a legacy CICS application to be delivered as a session bean and legacy data to be accessed or updated as an entity bean. The EJB container manages the life cycle of the beans. In other words, it provides session management, ensures data integrity, and enables database connection pooling for better performance and scalability. With the support of EJB, a client browser can invoke a servlet (usually presentation logic), which in turn initiates session beans from the local server or a remote CICS region (CICS Transaction Server EJB Server). (See Figure 5–14).

Figure 5–14 shows that architects can create an EJB Web Service, which can be a stateless EJB (either a session bean or an entity bean) invoking RPC calls to CICS resources via CICS Transaction Server version 2.1 EJB Server. The EJB handles the session information using session beans, manages business data residing in the back-end database (such as DB2) using entity beans, and communicates with other service components using a Message Driven Bean (MDB) and Java Messaging Service (JMS). Entity beans from the J2EE application server can exchange business data with another entity bean residing on the EJB server of the back-end mainframe via the RMI/IIOP protocol. The benefit of using EJB Web Services is that EJB has built-in functionality to manage the life cycle of the session, business data with connection pooling, and session failover. This is appropriate for handling business transactions.

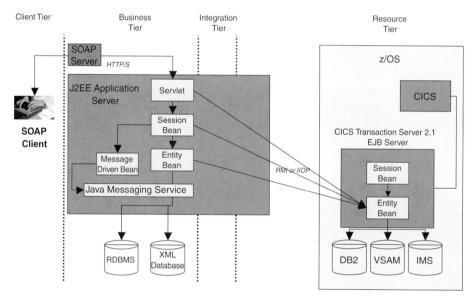

Figure 5–14   CICS EJB Support

Java Connector for CICS.   The Java Connector Architecture (JCA) is a more structured way to provide Open Standards-based connectivity to legacy systems and database resources. For each connection, the Java connector establishes a "service contract" with the target legacy systems. This standardizes the effort to customize different legacy systems, as well as reduces the development effort for proprietary interfaces. Please refer to the chapter Enterprise and Cross-Enterprise Integration for more details.

Legacy mainframe systems can be wrapped as Web Services by using Java Connectors. For instance, a SOAP client (or an EJB Web Service) can invoke a stateless EJB that handles online bill payment for telephone services and utilities. The stateless EJB is connected to a back-end mainframe CICS application using a Java Connector. The benefit is that Java Connector is a standards-based connectivity with legacy back-end systems, and developers do not need to build proprietary extensions to integrate with legacy technologies such as CICS applications.

The excerpt in Figure 5–15 is extracted and modified from sample EJB programs from IBM CICS Transaction Gateway using Java Connector for CICS. It illustrates a stateless session bean that initiates "ECIInteractionSpec" with key methods highlighted in bold. In essence, the connection to CICS using ECI calls requires creating an ECIInteractionSpec instance. Once the ECIInteractionSpec instance is created with the required attributes set (for example, setCommaLength, setReplyLength), the CICS transaction id (in this example, PHALL) will be invoked. Developers can customize their provider class and connection factory methods under getConnection().

```
import com.ibm.connector2.cics.*;
import javax.resource.cci.*;
import java.rmi.RemoteException;
import javax.resource.*;
import javax.ejb.*;

public class myEJBwithECI implements SessionBean {
    private javax.ejb.SessionContext mySessionEJB;
    transient private Connection eciConn;
    transient private Interaction eciInt;
    transient private ECIInteractionSpec eciSpec;

    public void ejbCreate() throws
javax.ejb.CreateException, java.rmi.RemoteException {
        eciSpec = new ECIInteractionSpec();
    }
    ...
    public String execute() throws ResourceException,
Exception {

        getConnection();

        JavaStringRecord jStringRec = new
JavaStringRecord();

        eciSpec.setCommareaLength(20);
        eciSpec.setReplyLength(20);
        eciSpec.setFunctionName("PHALL");  // CICS
transaction id
       eciSpec.setInteractionVerb(ECIInteraction
Spec.SYNC_SEND_RECEIVE);
```

Figure 5–15 Sample Java Connector for CICS Using ECI Calls

```
        try {
            eciInt.execute(eciSpec, jStringRec,
jStringRec);
        }
        catch (ResourceException resEx) {
            ...
        }
        dropConnection();
        return jStringRec.getText();
    }
    ...

    private void getConnection() throws Exception {

        ConnectionFactory connFactory = null;

        try {
            javax.naming.Context iContext = new
javax.naming.InitialContext();
            connFactory =
(ConnectionFactory)iContext.lookup("java:comp/env/ECI"
);
        }
        catch (Exception resEx) {
            ...
        }
        ...
    }

    private void dropConnection() {

        try {
            eciInt.close();
            eciConn.close();
        }
        catch (Exception resEx) {
            resEx.printStackTrace();
        }
        eciInt = null;
        eciConn = null;
    }
}
```

Figure 5–15   Sample Java Connector for CICS Using ECI Calls—*continued.*

Web Services Support. Legacy CICS applications using CTG and/or CICS EJB Server can be easily enabled as Web Services. Developers need to identify the business functionality as coarse-grained Web Services. In other words, not all methods or APIs need to be exposed as XML-RPC. Do not define each CICS transaction id or program name as an individual Web Service call. It is a good practice to define a few Web Services, where different methods or APIs can be invoked by passing parameters to the Web Services call. The same principle holds when creating EJBs—it is not necessary to map each EJB to an individual Web Services call.

Wrapping Java beans or methods using CTG and/or CICS EJB Server on a mainframe platform as XML-RPC Web Services calls is similar to doing so on a Unix or a Windows platform. Examples of the tools include the Java Web Services Developer Pack's xrpcc and Apache Axis's wsdl2java.

Implication

Unfolding the mystery of mainframe integration and interoperability can facilitate and ease enabling Web Services on legacy CICS applications. Hewitt Associates (U.S.), as reported in Hilgenberg and Hansen (2002), dedicated two to three architects to enable Web Services for their legacy HR services on z/OS within three to four months. They note that the critical success factor is the right architecture that can be scalable and reliable to support up to 4 million transactions per day.

SOAP Proxy on Mainframe

It is possible to enable legacy CICS applications as Web Services without using any of the three technology options. The Sun ONE Integration Server EAI edition (previously Forte 4GL for OS/390) has utilized Apache SOAP and a customized transaction adapter to provide SOAP messaging.

Design Features

Figure 5–16 depicts the high-level application architecture. Apache SOAP (SOAP proxy) must be installed under the Unix Services of the OS/390. For instance, the Sun ONE Integration Server has a customizable adapter (known as the Forte Transaction Adapter), which runs under the MVS of the OS/390, and communicates with local or remote CICS, VSAM, and IMS resources using the LU 6.2 protocol. There is a server portion of the adapter (the application proxy with a transaction adapter) running under the OS/390 Unix Services partition, which acts as an APPC client to the CICS applications of the local or remote CICS. The Forte Transaction Adapter (acting as an APPC client) receives data in a data buffer (aka COMMAREA) from the APPC conversation and provides a proxy function that can be accessed from the client browser. The proxy can be exposed as a SOAP proxy using Apache SOAP (or Apache Axis) to support XML and SOAP messaging.

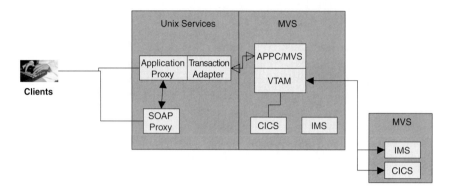

Figure 5–16 SOAP Proxy on Mainframe

The Sun document *Using Forte 4GL for OS/390* (2000, pp. 49–74), provides four sample programs for illustration. The excerpt in Figure 5–17 depicts the Forte Transaction Adapter establishing an APPC conversation with the remote CICS application FR02 using the method APCApiSO.NewConversation. Upon successful connection, it initiates an APPC conversation verb or data request in the data buffer using the method conv.Write. Under the synchronous APPC conversational programming, the remote CICS application will respond by placing the response or data contents in the data buffer. The transaction adapter can simply retrieve the data using the method conv.Read, and close the conversation.

```
--
-- Step 1:
-- Create an APPC session
conv = APPCApiSO.NewConversation();

-- Create COBOL buffer and COBOL field objects
buf : COBOLBuffer = new;
cobAddress: COBOLField = new;
cobAmount: COBOLField = new;
cobComment: COBOLField = new;
cobDate: COBOLField = new;
cobName: COBOLField = new;
cobNum: COBOLField = new;
cobPhone: COBOLField = new;
cobRecStat: COBOLField = new;
```

Figure 5–17 Sample Program Excerpt for Forte Transaction Adapter for a Remote CICS Transaction

```
cobStatus: COBOLField = new;

-- Define COBOL record layout
loc =
cobStatus.Define(location=0,picture='X',usage='DISPLAY
');
loc =
cobNum.Define(location=loc,picture='X(6)',usage='DISPL
AY');
loc =
cobName.Define(location=loc,picture='X(20)',usage='DIS
PLAY');
loc = cobAddress.Define(location=loc,picture='X(20)',
usage='DISPLAY');
loc =
cobPhone.Define(location=loc,picture='X(8)',usage='DIS
PLAY');
loc =
cobDate.Define(location=loc,picture='X(8)',usage='DISP
LAY');
loc = cobAmount.Define(location=loc,picture='X(8)',
usage='DISPLAY');
loc = cobComment.Define(location=loc,picture='X(9)',
usage='DISPLAY');
loc =
cobRecStat.Define(location=loc,picture='X',usage='DISP
LAY');
reclen = loc;

-- Step 2:
-- Establish APPC conversation with target CICS
dest = 'FRTCEXSI'; — must match your symbolic
destination name
tp = 'FR02'; — must match your CICS transaction name
conv.Open(dest=dest,tp=tp);

-- Step 3:
-- Send input data to CICS
len = custRec.NUM_LENGTH;
conv.Write(dataBuffer=custRec.Num,writeLength=len);
```

Figure 5–17 Sample Program Excerpt for Forte Transaction Adapter for a Remote CICS Transaction—*continued.*

```
-- Step 4:
-- Receive data response from CICS
len = reclen;
conv.Read(dataBuffer=buf,readLength=len);
```

Figure 5–17   Sample Program Excerpt for Forte Transaction Adapter for a Remote CICS Transaction—*continued.*

Implication

IBM has been dominant in providing mainframe integration and interoperability technology tools. The Sun ONE Integration Server provides an alternative approach to using Apache SOAP and APPC technology. Tracking the history, Forte 4GL and its application proxy have been around since before SOAP was available. Architecturally, Forte 4GL and its Application Proxy are similar to the SOAP proxy concept, and the Forte Application Proxy can be exposed as a SOAP proxy using Apache SOAP (or Axis). This has provided a more open platform approach to addressing the mainframe interoperability challenge.

5.4   Integration Points

5.4.1   Architecture Perspectives

Different mainframe integration designs have different integration points, which may span multiple tiers and layers. This allows flexibility and options in choosing the integration point that can accommodate local technical requirements and constraints. Table 5–1 recapitulates a list of technology approaches used to wrap back-end mainframe applications as Web Services. It also identifies what architecture components need to be installed in the Business Tier (on top of the application server), Integration Tier (middleware), and Resource Tier (in the back-end legacy system). These architecture components can act as an integration point where Java servlets or EJBs can be a "delegate" or a broker (refer to section 6.7.6) that initiates a SOAP service request for the back-end business services running on the mainframe platform.

CICS Transaction Gateway provides a middleware solution in the Integration Tier, where the server-side SOAP component can invoke a remote Web Service via ECI, EPI, or ESI calls to the back-end CICS applications. There is no additional component to be added to the application server (Business Tier), or the back-end legacy system (Resource Tier). The integration point with the mainframe is via the Integration Tier.

CICS Web Support is a technology solution residing in the back-end CICS region to Web-enable 3270-based CICS applications. A server-side SOAP component can in-

Table 5–1   Integration Points for Mainframe Interoperability

Technology Approach	Business Tier (Application Server)	Integration Tier	Resource Tier (Back-End Legacy System)
CICS Transaction Gateway		CICS Transaction Gateway—use of ECI, EPI, and ESI calls	
CICS Web Support			CICS Web Support—using CWS to Web-enable 3270-based CICS applications
Java	Enterprise Java Beans—abstracting business functionality from legacy systems	Java Connector Architecture—standardizing connectors to legacy systems	CICS EJB Server—EJB container to support EJB
SOAP Proxy on Mainframe		Forte Transaction Adapter—building Application Proxy for back-end resources	Forte Transaction Adapter—server side for APPC conversation

voke a remote Web Service that accesses 3270-based CICS screens. There is no additional component needed in the Business Tier or the Integration Tier. The integration point is via the Resource Tier.

Java technology is a multi-tier architecture approach to integrate with the back-end legacy system. A server-side SOAP component (such as EJB Web Service) can be created to integrate with the back-end via the Business Tier, the Integration Tier (using Java Connector), or the Resource Tier (using RMI/IIOP to invoke another EJB).

The SOAP proxy on mainframe approach uses an application proxy with a transaction adapter to enable SOAP messaging. Forte Transaction Adapter needs to be installed and configured in the Integration Tier and the Resource Tier. The integration point is with the Forte Transaction Adapter.

Figure 5–18 shows the same list of integration points under different tiers. CICS Transaction Gateway resides in both the Business Tier and the Integration Tier. CICS Web Support resides in the Resource Tier. Java technology supports multi-tier architecture design, and thus Java components span different tiers.

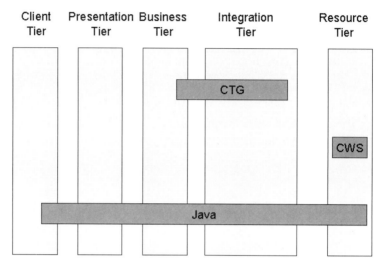

Figure 5–18   Integration Points by Tiers

A conscious design decision to pick an appropriate integration point should include consideration for future extension and scalability. Some integration points can be difficult to scale up or may incur higher integration costs.

5.4.2   Functional Perspectives

Web Services integration can be initiated from a business function. In other words, a Web Service call may embed multiple function calls that come from different sources. These function calls may be EJBs or CICS transaction ids. In Figure 5–19, we show an example of how to open a private banking account. We need to create a Web Service call (Account Opening Web Service under the Business Tier) that consists of three Web Services calls, including credit checking, account opening in the Customer Master, and linking to existing bank products if available. In some instances, these Web Services calls may span different tiers and may require more than one integration technology. One Web Services call (such as credit checking) may be using a SOAP proxy in the Integration Tier, which will invoke a CICS transaction using CTG. Another Web Services call (such as account opening in the Customer Master) may be using a SOAP proxy to invoke a CICS transaction via CICS Web Support. The last Web Services call may be using an EJB Web Service that invokes the back-end CICS transaction wrapped as an EJB in the Resource Tier. These examples show that there are multiple integration points where developers can create Web Services to integrate with the back-end mainframe system. The design consideration may be based on the specific business functionality, which may reside in a specific tier (such as in the Business Tier or the Integration Tier).

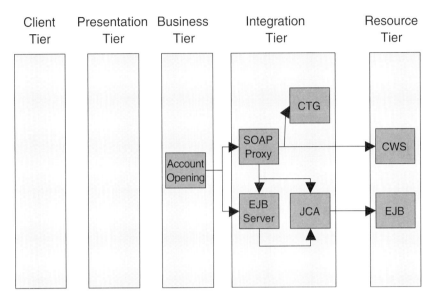

Figure 5–19 Integration Points by Functions

5.4.3 Mainframe Integration and Interoperability Patterns

There are two major mainframe integration and interoperability patterns discussed in this chapter. Synchronous or RPC-based Web Services can be designed by creating a server-side component that invokes CICS transactions via any of the integration components discussed earlier (such as CICS Transaction Gateway and CICS Web Support). Asynchronous or document-based Web Services can be designed by encapsulating existing WebSphere MQ (or JMS) messages in a SOAP envelope. The data content will then be sent using SOAP messaging over WebSphere MQ or JMS. The following section introduces these two patterns based on the mainframe technology options discussed earlier.

Chapter 3, Web Services Technology Overview, discusses synchronous (or RPC-based) and asynchronous (or document-based) Web Services technology. A discussion of integration patterns is also provided in Chapter 6, Cross-Enterprise Integration.

Synchronous Mainframe Web Services Pattern

Context

Many mainframe applications are developed in COBOL running under CICS. As these applications are running in a proprietary operating environment, it is rather difficult for developers to reuse them or to interoperate with them from other front-ends or systems. Currently, the COBOL programs, after compilation, can be accessed via

CICS ECI, EPI, or ESI calls. There are also some Web-enabling tools, such as CICS Web Support, that allow these CICS transactions and resources to be accessible from a browser. If combined with SOAP messaging, these tools can help create reusable Web Services that can invoke remote CICS transactions.

For many financial institutions and service providers, legacy mainframe systems have been processing business transactions for many years, and there are very few system changes. However, the business functionality is not easily accessible from, or integratable with, the Java platform. Synchronous mainframe Web Services can be created to expose these business functionalities as a remote procedural call, and this does not require any application rewrite. In such a way, business functionality can be reused, and made available to different client devices (such as a mobile phone) and platforms (such as the Unix platform).

Problem

Online transactions developed in COBOL running in CICS are proprietary and cannot be easily integrated and interoperated with other platforms. To provide the same functionality on open systems to ease integration and interoperability with other systems, developers need to migrate to other platforms or perhaps rewrite the applications in other programming languages. This may have a long lead time in order to rebuild the same functionality. It would also be risky to the implementation, because many legacy applications do not have any technical documentation for the rewrite design.

Force

The technical considerations that affect the use of synchronous mainframe Web Services is the existing mainframe configuration and legacy system infrastructure. If the current operating environment does not support the use of any mainframe integration component such as CICS Transaction Gateway and CICS Web Support, it would not be viable to implement synchronous mainframe Web Services. For instance, older versions of the IBM mainframe (such as VSE) do not support CICS Transaction Gateway. If developers want to expose CICS transactions as Web Services, they need to upgrade their mainframe to z/OS from older operating systems.

Solution

There are a few mainframe integration products available from IBM and other mainframe vendors such as Jacada (*http://www.jacada.com*). These products help to build synchronous mainframe Web Services without rewriting the back-end CICS applications. They are like middleware that can expose CICS transactions via ECI, EPI, or ESI calls, which can then be wrapped as Web Services calls. It addresses the concern of long lead time in migrating the legacy applications to open systems or rewriting the applications on open systems.

Figure 5–20 summarizes the different mainframe integration and interoperability options. A SOAP client invokes the remote business service by binding to a service end-point URL (via XML-RPC). The service end-point will be processed by the SOAP server-side component (SOAP tier or skeleton), which will initiate an ECI/EPI/ESI call. If an EJB component is used, the CICS EJB server will initiate an RMI/IIOP to invoke another EJB residing in the target CICS region. If a SOAP proxy is used, the application proxy will initiate an APPC program call to the remote CICS resources. The previous sections discussed the architecture and the technical processes for each technology option.

This pattern is useful when there is a business requirement to access and process online CICS transactions by wrapping them as Web Services. Besides, it is appropriate when the current IT operating environment does not allow building a messaging or middleware infrastructure (such as JMS-compliant middleware) due to time and cost constraints.

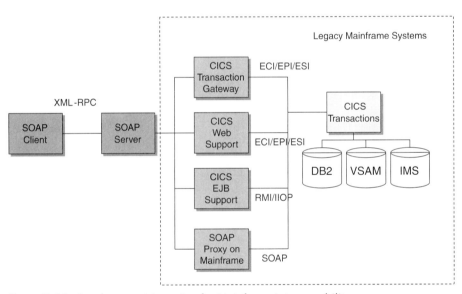

Figure 5–20   Synchronous Messaging for Mainframe Interoperability

Risk

Configuring the mainframe integration components and exposing legacy applications as Web Services require some knowledge and experience of the IBM mainframe platform. The technologies behind these components are often proprietary in nature, and there are not very many experienced architects in the market. This is a risk to the implementation, because the implementation requires a high level of technical skills and support experience in mainframe integration and Web Services technology.

Example

Hewitt Associates uses CICS Transaction Gateway to wrap back-end mainframe systems as Web Services (also refer to Chapter 2, The Web Services Phenomenon and Emerging Trends). This enables employee benefits system functionality to be available and reusable to a large number of business partners. The development took three to four months to complete, and there was no need to modify the back-end CICS programs.

Asynchronous Mainframe Web Services Pattern

Context

Some customers who operate many business applications on legacy mainframe systems may also have a message-oriented middleware infrastructure (such as WebSphere MQ). Such messaging infrastructure enables business information to be encapsulated in a business document and routed to different applications for sharing and for further data processing. However, to be able to make use of common business information, developers need to build a custom adapter for each front-end or application system, because each may support its own data format only. Thus, the custom adapter needs to translate the data content into a format that can be understandable by the front-end or application system.

Another issue is that if the common business information needs to be exchanged with external trading partners (that is, Business-to-Business integration), there is no common middleware or messaging mechanism that can be easily agreed upon between two trading partners. A similar business scenario occurs when exchanging business data between two internal systems within an enterprise, where each system runs on different application platforms and the systems do not share a common middleware infrastructure.

Asynchronous mainframe Web Services would be a good solution here, because it can wrap an existing business message in a SOAP envelope and exchange with multiple trading partners over different data transport or middleware (such as SOAP over MQ, and SOAP over JMS). SOAP messaging accommodates the issue of different connectivity requirements (using SOAP over different data transports) and different data format requirements (using XML parsers for easier data transformation). This becomes a time-to-market solution to expose business data messages as reusable Web Services that are encapsulated in proprietary mainframe systems and middleware infrastructures.

Problem

Common business data from the back-end mainframe systems that are encapsulated in existing message-oriented middleware are usually shared between multiple application systems in the mainframe. How can architects and developers expose the business data in a Web Service that can be accessible to other systems or external trading partners?

Force

There are two dependencies to support asynchronous mainframe Web Services: the availability of a common business data message used by the back-end mainframe systems and the availability of a message-oriented middleware infrastructure that connects to the back-end mainframe systems.

The common data message is usually shared by multiple back-end mainframe applications or different software versions of the same business functionality. It can be used as an input service request or output business transaction data. For instance, an account balance inquiry data message is shared by multiple versions of retail banking systems.

The availability of an existing message-oriented middleware infrastructure is important because Web Services technology can leverage on the current infrastructure to integrate and interoperate with the back-end mainframe systems. Building a huge middleware infrastructure that can connect to the back-end mainframe systems from scratch is very expensive and time consuming.

Solution

Major message-oriented middleware vendors support SOAP messaging today, with additional provider classes that enable SOAP messaging over different data transports including WebSphere MQ and JMS. This does not require building customized adapters or programs in the legacy mainframe systems to wrap the business data in a SOAP envelope. By enabling the WebSphere MQ or JMS queue manager to support SOAP messaging, business data encapsulated in the back-end mainframe systems and in the message-oriented middleware can be reused for data interchange between trading partners and systems. It is a cost-effective solution approach to Business-to-Business integration and internal system integration.

Figure 5–21 depicts a scenario where service requests can be encapsulated in a WebSphere MQ format, wrapped in a SOAP envelope, and written to a MQ queue or JMS queue that can be processed by the back-end mainframe systems. A SOAP client sends a service request in a SOAP message to the SOAP server-side component. The SOAP server-side component (SOAP tier or skeleton) will then bind the messaging to the underlying data transport layer using WebSphere MQ or JMS. The WebSphere MQ or JMS queue manager needs to support SOAP messaging. Currently, WebSphere MQ version 5.0 or higher supports SOAP messaging over WebSphere MQ. There are also some JMS vendor products (such as Progress SonicXQ) that support SOAP messaging over JMS. Upon receiving the SOAP message, the queue manager will then unmarshal the SOAP envelope and retrieve the message payload in native MQ or JMS format. It can then route the message to the target queue residing in the mainframe CICS region. The same process applies to both WebSphere MQ and JMS technologies.

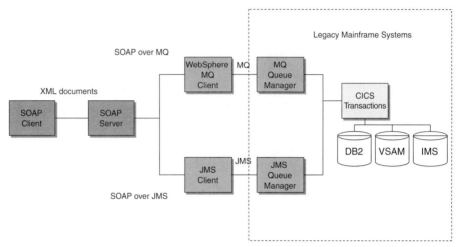

Figure 5–21   Asynchronous Messaging for Mainframe Interoperability

This pattern is a simple solution to Web Services enable an existing messaging infrastructure using WebSphere MQ or JMS. It is useful when there are different CICS transactions that need to be accessed and there is no standard way to invoke them (for instance, one CICS transaction may require an ECI call and another an EPI call). By consolidating these heterogeneous CICS transactions and online interfaces into a single message, developers do not need to build different program invocation or data access methods for each CICS transaction. Future enhancement to the application functionality will be more flexible and dynamic (for instance, it will be easier to add or aggregate new information elements to the remote CICS transactions without changing the back-end applications.) In addition, it does not require installing additional components to support asynchronous or document-based Web Services.

Risk

There is a high design complexity in normalizing a common data message for multiple back-end mainframe applications. There may be a temptation for architects to simply use all existing data interfaces as the SOAP message payload. The risk is that irrelevant data in the SOAP message payload will increase data processing and XML data parsing time, which impacts the performance.

Example

Progress SonicXQ is an example of SOAP messaging over WebSphere and JMS and can be used to implement this pattern.

5.4.4   Design Considerations

Security

Usually, either user id/password or SSL is used for authentication. Nevertheless, form-based or HTTP-based authentication may not be sufficient for today's Web security. Architects and developers need to understand that security should not be viewed as user id authentication only. Chapter 7, Web Services Security, has more discussion on this topic.

Authentication Design

RACF is the legacy mainframe security infrastructure for authentication of user identity and credentials for mainframe resources. It is now enhanced to register SSL certificates (which requires some specific APARs or service packs) and can integrate with LDAP/390. To use SSL certificates, architects need to configure the AUTHENTICATE parameter in the TCPIPSERVICE resource definition of the CICS. This is a feature in CWS called *CWS Certificate Auto-registration*. Upon successful registration of SSL certificates in RACF, CICS can retrieve the user id from the EXEC CICS EXTRACT CERTIFICATE USERID command. This design approach can leverage on and integrate with the existing security infrastructure of the legacy mainframe environment.

The design dilemma is whether architects should use a Directory Server on Open Platform (Unix) rather than a legacy mainframe platform. One argument is that architects can scale up multiple Directory Servers on the Unix platform for better scalability. This can support federated Directory Servers (which is also known as Network Identity). There are a few factors to consider: total cost of ownership, scalability and extensibility of the platform, and whether any proprietary extended security features are used. A common misconception is that the total cost of ownership is usually the cost of obtaining the software license. In reality, the total cost of ownership also includes the cost of upgrading hardware (for example, the existing mainframe needs to upgrade to a G5 processor in order to run z/OS), the one-off and ongoing support or maintenance costs, additional hardware and software costs (such as additional Unix servers to host the Directory Servers, additional software required to run LDAP/390) to install and customize the authentication features, one-off and ongoing implementation costs for SSL- or PKI-based authentication and authorization, and integration costs. In addition, the business constraints and IT strategy for integrating with the legacy mainframe platform are important considerations. Thus, there is no easy answer to the design dilemma.

EBCDIC Conversion

The mainframe interprets EBCDIC code pages but not ASCII. Java uses Unicode. Thus it is important to ensure that the mainframe integration technology includes EBCDIC conversion. For example, the CICS Transaction Gateway translates EBCDIC and ASCII into Unicode.

5.5 Alternatives to Mainframe Interoperability

Architects may want to consider alternatives to mainframe interoperability other than building on top of the mainframe architecture. This interest is usually driven by lower total cost of ownership (such as operating cost and service support cost for legacy COBOL applications), transition strategy to move away from obsolete COBOL technology to Open Standards and J2EE technology, and more importantly, easier integration and interoperability using Java technology.

By migrating legacy application code to Java, architects and developers can then determine whether they would like to use document-based (asynchronous) or RPC-based (synchronous) Java Web Services. This will allow more flexibility in customizing the business functionality to accommodate local requirements of synchronous or asynchronous transactional processing.

5.5.1 Technology Options

Transcode

The term *transcode* refers to translating and converting from one program language structure to another using intelligent rule engines, without rewriting from scratch.

Architecture

There are more than two COBOL-to-Java Transcoder products currently available. The product architecture shown in Figure 5–22 shows an example from Relativity. Relativity's RescueWare consists of intelligent parsers that can parse COBOL programs and CICS/IMS screens into Java objects (including classes, methods, or even Java beans). This provides a convenient way to turn legacy COBOL programs into reusable objects. Java objects can then be exposed as Web Services.

Typically, COBOL-to-Java transcoding tools should provide the following functionality:

- The automated migration tool set should provide tools to analyze the dependency and components hierarchy of the COBOL programs, and support automated (unattended or nonmanual) code conversion, preferably with some "conversion patterns." It should also allow platform environment parameters (for example, JCL parameters or dataset names on the mainframe) to be changed "intelligently" to the new target environment.

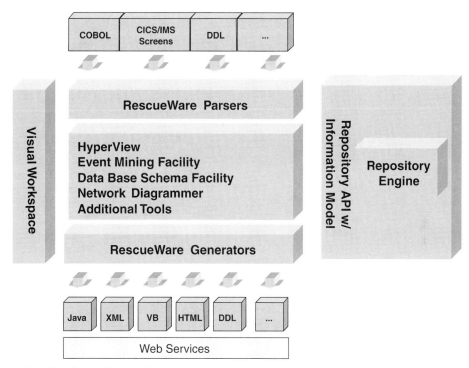

Figure 5–22 Relativity's RescueWare Architecture

- Some tools may have better integration with software version control tools (such as ClearCase, CVS). MIS reporting should be available for code changes, version changes, and audit logging.
- There should be intelligent screen display code migration from 3270-like screen to SWING. There will be lots of usability anomalies that need to be resolved or supported.

After the COBOL codes are transcoded into Java classes or EJBs, developers can create a server-side SOAP component to invoke these Java classes or EJBs. This approach provides a more flexible solution architecture for integrating with other systems and for extending the system functionality.

Solution Stack

The developer's platform relies on a PC, typically a Pentium 3, with 256MB RAM and at least 20GB storage running Windows 2000 or XP. The deployment hardware depends on the processing capacity requirements of the applications. Typically, they may range from Sun Fire mid-frame series (model 3800 to 6800) to the high-end Sun Fire 15K series.

Relativity's RescueWare, a developer tool, provides a comprehensive developer workbench, COBOL program analyzer, COBOL transcoding utilities, and data migration utilities.

Benefits

Automated and intelligent transcoding from COBOL to Java will expedite the migration effort. The COBOL program analyzer can help developers to identify dead code and to factor legacy business logic into reusable EJBs components.

Recompile

The term *recompile* refers to cross-compiling the source program language structure (such as COBOL) to a target program language structure (such as Java byte-code) using an intelligent language cross-compiler without changing the application program logic.

Architecture

Figure 5–23 depicts the architecture of cross-compiling COBOL programs to Java byte-codes using the LegacyJ product. Legacy COBOL programs can be refactored and cross-compiled to Java byte code using intelligent COBOL business rules. Structured procedures can then be transcoded into Java beans or EJBs. Data access routines to a legacy database such as VSAM or IMS can be also translated into the Java Naming Convention via the CICS Transaction Gateway Java classes or the like. However, the constraint is that both the Java Virtual Machine and the original CICS need to reside on the same physical machine.

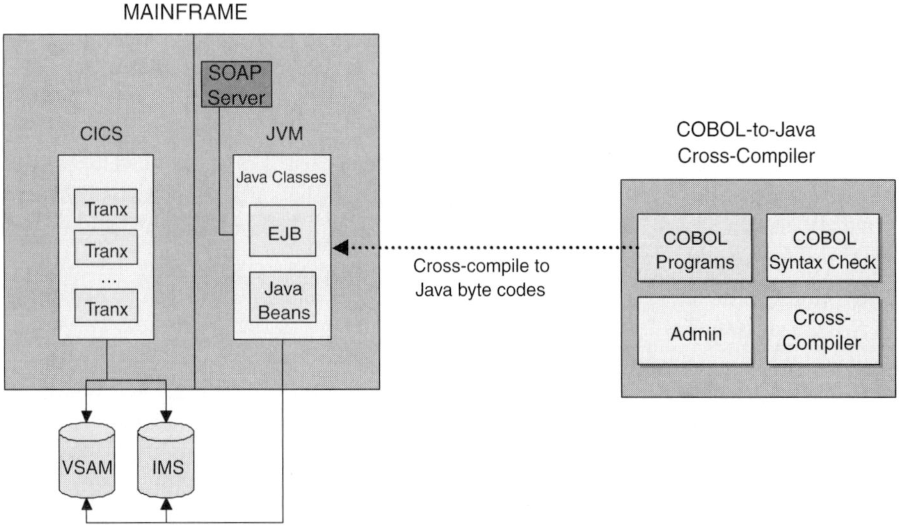

Figure 5–23   LegacyJ Architecture

Once the COBOL programs are cross-compiled as Java classes, beans, or EJBs on the mainframe, developers can expose them as Web Services using tools such as Java Web Services Developer Pack or Apache Axis. This approach is conceptually elegant because it does not require vendor-specific middleware components (such as CICS Web Support) in the mainframe.

Solution Stack

The developer's platform relies on a Windows NT/2000 Pentium-based PC, typically of 256MB RAM and at least 40GB of storage. The deployment hardware is assumed to be the legacy platform such as IBM mainframe OS/390 R1.x or OS/400 R4.x. On the OS/390 platform, IBM Java Virtual Machine (or Java Run time version) 1.3 or higher needs to be installed and configured on the OS/390 Unix Service partition. Similarly, IBM JVM 1.3 or higher needs to be installed and configured on the OS/400 platform.

LegacyJ's PerCOBOL—A developer tool built on top of Eclipse open source that provides a COBOL-to-Java byte code cross-compilation functionality. Several COBOL variants are supported. When the COBOL code is being compiled, a syntax check is also performed. Developers need to ensure the original COBOL source code is tested and deployed on the legacy system first, and then copied to the workbench for cross-compilation. Upon successful compilation, the code needs to be copied to the target platform for running.

Java Classes on Legacy System—IBM requires installing and loading relevant VSAM or IMS Java classes in order to access VSAM/IMS datasets. These files should come with the OS or are downloadable from IBM's Web site.

Benefits

Legacy COBOL programs can be cross-compiled to run on a Unix Service partition of the legacy system and can be called like Java. The cross-compilation capability enables external systems to access legacy system functionality via Java calls. These Java calls can be also wrapped as SOAP Web Services (XML-RPC) without changing the system infrastructure. This provides fast system interoperability, while leaving more room to re-engineer or migrate the legacy systems to an open platform in the long run.

Rehost

The term *rehost* refers to migrating the original program code from one platform to another without rewriting the program business logic. This may require some minor modifications to the language syntax owing to platform variance.

Architecture

Rehosting legacy COBOL applications on a mainframe usually results in porting the original COBOL source code to a Unix platform. This requires the use of a flexible COBOL environment that can accommodate variants of ANSI COBOL that run on the legacy mainframe, such as COBOL II and HOGAN COBOL. Apart from legacy COBOL programs, the rehosting environment also supports porting JCL (Job Control Language) or REXX, which are batch or scripting languages for both online and batch transaction processing.

The following logical architecture in Figure 5–24 shows a multi-tier architecture that corresponds to different components of a typical mainframe environment.

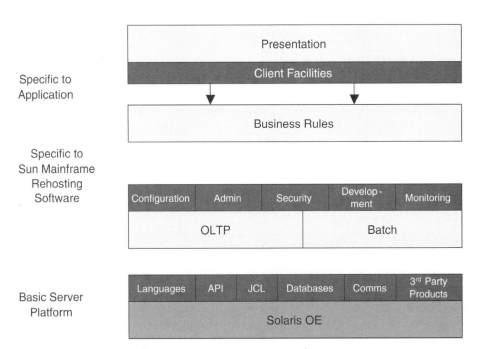

Figure 5–24   Sun's Mainframe Transaction Processing Architecture

Solution Stack

The hardware depends on the processing capacity requirements of the applications. Typically, they may range from the Sun Fire 3800–6800 series to the high-end Sun Fire 15K series.

Sun's Mainframe Transaction Processing Software (MTP) (previously In-Join's TRANS)—This provides a CICS-like environment for processing COBOL applications. MTP now supports MicroFocus COBOL applications. Some COBOL variants may need to be modified to run on MicroFocus COBOL applications under the MTP environment. There is a VSAM-compatible database for COBOL-VSAM implementation.

Sun's Mainframe Batch Manager (MBM) (previously InJoin's BATCH)—This provides a batch-oriented environment similar to MVS/JCL. This will supplement COBOL applications with any batch job control language in the operating environment.

It is possible to use Sun ONE Integration Manager EAI edition to expose COBOL programs as Web Services. This is similar to building a SOAP proxy on the mainframe, as depicted in the previous section (see Figure 5–16). However, it may not be cost-effective if the primary goal is to expose legacy COBOL programs as Web Services, because the total cost and effort of migrating COBOL programs from a mainframe to a Unix system may be higher than using other mainframe integration technologies.

Benefits

Legacy COBOL applications can be ported to a Unix environment with minor modifications to the MicroFocus COBOL syntax. This provides a low-risk, low-impact, minimal-change alternative to rehost COBOL applications on Unix, with potential integration with open platform using Java or another open technology. This solution approach does not need to re-engineer dead code from legacy COBOL applications.

Refront

The term *refront* here refers to rewriting the legacy program code in the Java language. This usually results in redeveloping or redesigning the front-end and perhaps refactoring the business logic into reusable components.

Architecture

Refronting legacy COBOL applications denotes rewriting and rebuilding the business logic. This requires re-engineering the business logic as well as the application architecture, say, using Java and Web Services. J2EE provides a flexible framework and application architecture (see Figure 5–25) that can be scalable in an n-tier architecture. Developers can design JSPs, servlets, or EJBs to invoke Web Services. This is a neater and more long-term architecture solution and is not constrained by any legacy system components.

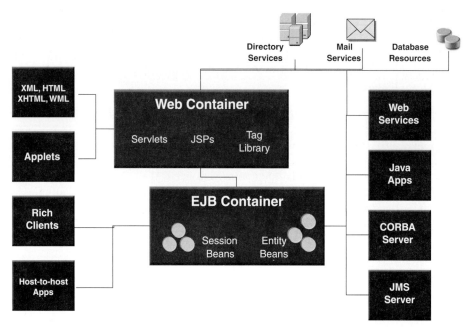

Figure 5–25   Refactoring Legacy Systems Using J2EE Architecture

Solution Stack

The developer's environment runs on Solaris OE™ version 8 or higher (for example, on Ultra-10 workstation), Windows 2000, or XP Pentium-based PC, typically of 256MB RAM and at least 20GB of storage. The deployment hardware depends on the processing capacity requirements of the applications. Typically, they may range from the Sun Fire midframe (such as Sun Fire 3800 or Sun Fire 6800) to the high-end Sun Fire 15K series.

Sun ONE Studio, a developer tool, provides a powerful developer workbench to develop, test, and deploy Java programs. There are extensive libraries (such as NetBeans) and J2EE patterns (from *http://developer.java.sun.com/developer/technicalArticles/J2EE/patterns/* and *http://www.sun.com/solutions/blueprints/tools/*) available for software reuse.

> **Sun ONE Application Server.** A J2EE-compliant application server, provides Web and EJB containers to develop and execute Java servlets and EJBs. It also supports session, state, and connection pooling for transaction processing.

JAX (Java API for XML Pack). A publicly available bundle of XML-related Java APIs to develop XML-based transforming and Web Services. It includes JAXP, JAXB, JAXM, JAXR, and JAX-RPC modules.

Java Web Services Developer Pack. An all-in-one Web Services developer kit available to the public; it includes JAX, Tomcat, ANT, SOAP, and an application deployment tool.

Benefits

J2EE is an industry-acceptable Open Standard that enables better system interoperability and reusability. The legacy system and any dead code (legacy program codes that are inefficient or poorly designed) can be re-engineered. It also provides a good opportunity to refactor inefficient code into reusable components and to tune up the performance of some bottleneck modules. This results in better application Quality of Services, such as better performance, throughput, and reusability of program modules, after re-engineering the inefficient code.

5.5.2   Design and Implementation Considerations

When to Use

Table 5–2 outlines some pros, cons, and when-to-use guidelines for legacy code migration implementation. They may not be applicable to all scenarios, as each real-life customer scenario is complex. There are many batch and off-line programs that do not require interactive response. There is no mixture of asynchronous or synchronous modes of messaging or communication.

Migration Framework

In addition to sound architecture strategy and appropriate tools, a structured migration framework is critical to migrating legacy applications to Java and Web Services. The following is a migration framework to migrate legacy COBOL applications to Java for a commercial bank scenario. It provides an example of how to use Web Services to integrate with mainframe systems and transition to a J2EE platform in the long term. The migration framework should be reusable for most industries.

Multiphase Customer Relationship Management

At present, the bulk of customer information is stored in the current Customer Master (also known as Customer Information File or CIF) on the mainframe. Different delivery channels or touch points (such as the call center/Internet banking, securities

Table 5–2 Some Considerations for When to Use Legacy Codes Migration Tools

Migration Approach	When to Use	Pros	Cons
Transcode	Existing legacy applications have a low complexity. This applies to both off-line and batch processing.	The legacy code conversion can be automated and thus there is a low change impact for COBOL code written in a general well-documented programming style.	There are manual changes needed for high-complexity programs with dead code.
Recompile	This is suitable for stable legacy system functionality where there is no anticipated change or no strategy for future enhancement or re-engineering.	There is minimal impact to the existing architecture. There is no need to migrate the back-end database resources.	The application requires upgrading the legacy operating system to z/OS and installing a Java Virtual Machine in an LPAR for run time. Thus, architects and developers cannot decouple the business functionality from the legacy platform.
Rehost	This applies to many batch and off-line programs.	It has a lower impact of changes.	This is not ideal for online legacy systems as this may incur considerable changes to the hardware and software environment.
Refront	This allows re-engineering of business logic incrementally.	Developers can take the chance to clean up dead code.	There is a high risk of re-engineering business logic.

products, credit card application, or loan processing application) have also captured some customer information and preferences, but there is no single customer information repository to aggregate them in real-time for customer analysis and business intelligence. We propose to adopt a multiphase approach to migrating the existing CIF and various customer information sources to a new customer database to support Customer Relationship Management (CRM).

In Stage 1 (see Figure 5–26), a new CRM business data model needs to be defined and customized. Customer information will be extracted from existing CIF and delivery channels (such as ATM channel and teller platform). The data extraction will be one-way data synchronization using the existing middleware or messaging infrastructure. Nonintrusive adapters or Web services need to be implemented.

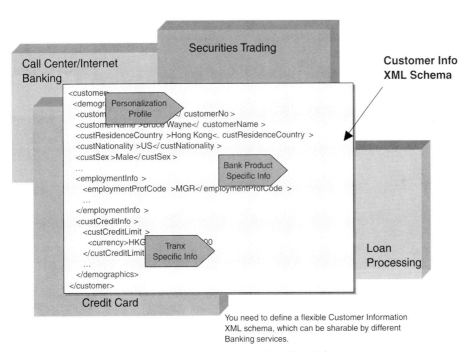

You need to define a flexible Customer Information XML schema, which can be sharable by different Banking services.

Figure 5–26   Stage 1—Creating Customer Information XML Schema

In Stage 2 (see Figure 5–27), we recommend building a two-way simultaneous data synchronization between the new customer database and various data sources.

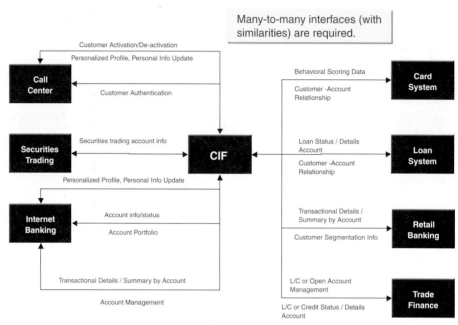

Figure 5–27 Stage 2—Synchronizing All Interfaces

In Stage 3 (see Figure 5–28), the legacy CIF and old CIF interfaces can be decommissioned and dynamic customer analysis, segmentation, and cross-selling/up-selling can be supported using OLAP (Online Analytical Processing) and a data warehouse/business intelligence infrastructure. A single customer view can be consolidated easily.

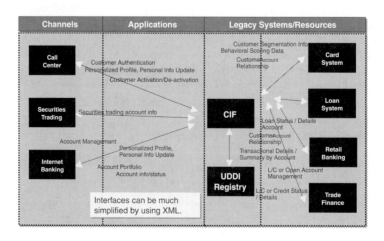

Figure 5–28 Stage 3—Consolidating into a Single Customer View Using Web Services

Data Migration

Similar to multiphase CRM, legacy data files or databases (VSAM or DB2) can be migrated from the mainframe to an Open Platform in Stages 2 and 3, in conjunction with the initiatives to off-load mainframe loading. There are existing utilities that can rehost VSAM files to a Unix platform (for example, Sun's MTP). Alternatively, data can be extracted to flat files and reimported into an RDBMS.

Data migration will depend on a business data model, data extraction, data cleansing, data transformation, and the subsequent administration (for example, backup, archive, and restore). The current middleware or messaging infrastructure will provide a core infrastructure for the data migration processes.

Legacy Application Migration

Legacy COBOL applications can be off-loaded from the mainframe by any or a combination of the following migration approaches: rehosting on Unix with COBOL, recompile COBOL to Java byte codes, transcode COBOL to Java, or rewrite in J2EE.

Approaches to COBOL-to-Java Migration

This may be a big bang approach with complete code-level conversion. All code will run on Java with a new database platform running on Unix. This is a complete detachment and cut-off from the mainframe. This is the ideal case.

Another approach is a parallel run, which is a transition strategy where the new Java code/database will be run in parallel with the legacy system. Thus, how does the data synchronization operate? For example, if the Java code will retrieve historic data from the legacy system via JDBC, how would it handle mainframe integration online (or off-line)?

Partial migration, where legacy code coexists with Java, is the most complicated approach, as the majority of the code will be converted to Java, while some of it may need to access historical data or legacy resources (such as QSAM files on mainframe or DB2 via JDBC). The migration tool should be able to support direct access to legacy resources via JDBC or some other mainframe integration means (for example, translate database access codes to JDBC). This is the worst scenario.

Code Conversion Methodology

A systematic methodology for handling code conversion is very useful for the delivery. This includes packaging all JCL/COBOL programs in the source directory, scanning the original programs to analyze the program hierarchy or dependency, and scanning the programs for the appropriate programming models or conversion patterns. There may be a need to refactor the business logic into reusable components such as EJBs (Alur, Crupi, and Malks, 2001, *Core J2EE Patterns* and *http://www.refactoring.com* introduce the concept of refactoring).

Developers may then start converting the code to Java, start manually fixing the dead code, or re-engineering some code. This is followed by retrofitting the new EJBs or components into a design pattern or Java library for future use and testing the code with GUI or test data feeds.

Integration With Development Life Cycle

The entire migration needs to integrate with the development platform management. The tool should be able to migrate converted code to a virtual or temporary development platform for code testing (for example, automated software migration to a "partitioned" or logical development platform where developers can modify their code with their IDE front-end).

It should also integrate with the back-end resources management. The migration tool should be able to handle changes in the system environment parameters in the original COBOL code, MVS/JCL, embedded SQL code, or EXEC CICS code easily, without manually changing these parameters in many places. It also needs potential simulation of legacy systems or transient storage devices (for example, the devices DB2, COMMAREA, and the temporary DD units used in the SORT utilities need to be simulated).

For testing platform management, the finished Java code should be "packaged" (for example, recompiling a set of J2EE .ear files) and tested in a "partitioned" or logical testing platform for unit testing or integration testing. The tool should allow test feeds to be input for testing. This will entail another software migration process (via scripting, if necessary) to a testing platform, which may be on the same physical machine with a logical partition or a separate machine.

For production platform management, this is similar to the testing environment platform management, except that this is a production platform. There should be a fire-fighting production mirror platform where high severity production bugs can be fixed right away, before migrating to production.

Conclusion

Banking customers are risk-averse to migrating their legacy systems to an open platform, as banking services are highly critical to customer services and financial risks. As a result, it is important to adopt a low-risk approach to mitigate technology and implementation risks.

The critical success factors for migrating core banking systems are expertise, process, and technology skills. Therefore, getting people with the right experience to customize the appropriate migration methodology is worthwhile and risk-aversive. Aside from that, doing a Proof of Concept or pilot also helps.

Architecture Implications and Design Considerations

Different migration design options will impose certain architectures. For example, a rehosting architecture requires porting the entire application to a new open platform, which requires a different technology skill set than the mainframe skill. This is on top of the migration hardware and software cost. Architects and developers need to be conscious of each design decision made.

On the other hand, transcoding technology may render different Java code design. For instance, some transcoding tools may render the same COBOL procedure into a lengthy if–then statement or a structured case loop. This may impact the maintainability and performance tuning of the Java source code. Some intelligent transcoding tools can refactor dead code into EJBs. This will obviously make the design more flexible and extensible if developers want to add more service components to the EJBs.

Risks and Their Mitigation

In order to migrate COBOL applications to Java, there are several technical risks that may impose constraints to the implementation. They may require a mixture of software solution sets and migration processes to mitigate these risks. This section will introduce a few major migration models that mitigate specific technology risks.

Most legacy systems are traditionally built from years of experience and testing. It is unrealistic to wait for years for the new system to be rebuilt. In order to meet changing market needs, it is crucial to build systems using automated migration tools (for example, recompile COBOL to Java byte codes) with shorter development life cycles and faster to-market times.

COBOL programs have a relatively longer development life cycle (for example, long program construct and longer testing cycle) and many variants (such as ANSI COBOL and COBOL II, for example). By nature, they were not designed to handle memory management, message processing, and system interoperability. Thus, rewriting the applications in Java can address these language constraints.

Many COBOL-based applications have dead code or proprietary extensions. Some of them do not have design documentation, which makes re-engineering difficult. They may require some form of re-engineering. Thus, transcoding tools may provide a neater way to analyze and rebuild business logic based on COBOL source code.

Many COBOL programs rely on system-specific interface methods (such as EXEC CICS on an IBM mainframe) to interoperate with external systems. This may impose a major constraint to application migration, as this is platform-dependent and often requires some re-engineering. However, this may open up the opportunity to re-engineer the legacy system interface as an asynchronous message or simply expose the system interface as re-usable Web Services.

5.6   Perspectives

5.6.1   Highlights

- New integration technologies have enabled exposing legacy system functionality on a mainframe to be reusable as Web Services. Architects and developers can enjoy faster implementation and easier interoperability using Open Standards. This becomes attractive to many customers because Web Services can leverage on legacy systems without rewriting them.

- Existing mainframe integration design approaches include using CICS Transaction Gateway, CICS Web Support, Java technology (such as EJB Server for CICS), and SOAP proxy to enable legacy CICS applications as Web Services. A server-side SOAP component can be created to invoke the remote CICS transactions via any of these mainframe integration components. Different design approaches have certain architecture implications, and architects need to make conscious design decisions based on the cost-benefits.

- The alternative to wrapping legacy system functionality as Web Services is to migrate legacy code to Java and enable them as Web Services later. This is a more flexible strategy that brings long-term benefits. At present, architects and developers can transcode, re-compile, rehost, or refront legacy application code. Examples of success stories include the U.S. Air Force (using RescueWare) and Access International's Global Product Suite for Straight-through Processing (using BluePhoenix's AppBuilder).

5.6.2   Best Practices and Pitfalls

- *Prerequisites of Enabling Web Services on Legacy Mainframe.* Implementing Web Services on a legacy mainframe platform may require hardware and software upgrades on the legacy mainframe to z/OS, which may be extremely expensive. Architects and developers may wish to check out the prerequisites of each integration option to the hardware and software, as well as the architecture implications.

- *Coarse-Grained Web Services.* Do not create a Web Services call for each individual legacy system functionality. This is because there will be scalability and maintainability issues to support too many Web Services calls on the legacy mainframe systems. Architects and developers can also consider passing parameters to coarse-grained Web Services.

- *Mainframe Interoperability When to Use.* Architects and developers may not need to integrate with all legacy mainframe functionality. Some of the legacy functionality may be available via existing messaging. Some of them are dead codes and thus deserve re-engineering. Therefore, it will not be sensible to wrap them as Web Services. Architects and developers may wish to consider the cost-benefits of building Web Services, such as the costs associated with internal implementation, external consultancy, or mentoring service.

- *Using Web Services Mentoring Service.* Some case studies show that architects and developers can jumpstart a Web Services implementation if experienced Web Services consultants are brought in. Architects and developers may wish to consider piloting a Web Services architecture workshop to define a pilot scenario, develop a Proof of Concept, and pilot a small system. This will enable transfer of skills and lessons learned about implementation pitfalls.

5.6.3   References

OS/390 or z/OS

IBM Redbook. *S/390 Partners in Development: Thinkpad Enabled for S/390.* *http://publib-b.boulder.ibm.com/Redbooks.nsf/RedbookAbstracts/ sg246507.html* OpenJava on S/390 resources. *http://www.s390java.com/*

OS/390 resource portal. *http://ronmas.virtualave.net/*

S./390 Mainframe Emulation on Notebook - FLEX-ES. *http://www.funsoft.com/index-technical.html*

Mainframe Integration

Eugene Deborin, Anita Ekstedt, Jim Hollingsworth, Takeo Machida, Antonius Inggil Paripurnanto, and Norbert Verbestel. *CICS Transaction Server for OS/390 Version 1 Release 3: Web Support and 3270 Bridge.* San Jose: IBM Redbooks, November, 1999.

http://www.redbooks.ibm.com/pubs/pdfs/redbooks/sg245480.pdf

Chris Smith. "CICS Transaction Server for VSE/ESA: CICS Web Support Technical Overview." London: IBM UK, July 2001.

http://www-3.ibm.com/software/ts/cics/pdfs/cictsvse_cwsovw.pdf

Sun Microsystems. *Using Forte 4GL for OS/390: Release 3.5 of Forte 4GL.* Palo Alto: Sun Microsystems, October 2000.

http://docs.sun.com/db?p=/doc/806-6665-01 (under Sun ONE Integration Server EAI Edition).

Phil Wakelin, Antonio C. Benedete, Jr., Phil Cartwright, John Holland, Jim Hollingsworth, Daniel McGinnes, Satish Tanna, and Bart Verboven. *Revealed! Architecting Web Access to CICS.* San Jose: IBM Redbooks, 2002.

http://publib-b.boulder.ibm.com/Redbooks.nsf/RedbookAbstracts/sg245466.html

Phil Wakelin, Martin Keen, Richard Johnson, and Daniel Cerecedo Diaz. *Java Connectors for CICS: Featuring the J2EE Connector Architecture.* San Jose: IBM Redbooks, March 2002.

http://publib-b.boulder.ibm.com/Redbooks.nsf/RedbookAbstracts/sg246401.html

Case Studies

Tim Hilgenberg and John A. Hansen. *"Building a Highly Robust, Secure Web Services Architecture to Process Four Million Transactions per Day"* IBM developerWorks Live! 2002 conference.

Mainframe Integration Vendors

Blue Phoenix. *http://www.bluephoenixsolutions.com/index.cfm*

Jacada. *http://www.jacada.com*

LegacyJ. *http://www.legacyj.com/*

Sun Microsystems. *http://www.sun.com*

A list of J2EE Connectors vendors. *http://java.sun.com/j2ee/connector/industry.html*

Other

Alur Deepak, John Crupi, and Dan Malks. *Core J2EE Patterns.* Prentice Hall, 2001.

Chapter **6**

ENTERPRISE AND CROSS-ENTERPRISE INTEGRATION

6.1 Chapter Overview

- Enterprise Application Interface (EAI) and Web Services technology have many similarities. Rather than either–or, Web Services technology can be a good complementary approach to integrating business functionality and legacy systems between business partners.
- Enterprise and cross-enterprise integration requires integration at different tiers—from security, data transport, middleware, and data to business processes.
- A catalog of Business-to-Business integration patterns is introduced to illustrate how Java Web Services and EAI technology are collaborated.

6.2 Chapter Objectives

- To identify some emerging Web Services technology appropriate for enterprise integration and to differentiate Enterprise Application Integration from Web Services.
- To outline how Web Services technology can ease enterprise and cross-enterprise integration with integration patterns.

6.3 Background

Business-to-Business integration (B2Bi) has primarily involved many host-to-host interfaces, personalized commerce services, and business process collaboration. As we have discussed in earlier chapters, private labeling has become more popular to leverage the infrastructure of the service provider for low-cost B2Bi. Time-to-market and personalized service information are key business drivers. With increasing organizational restructuring, consolidation, and mergers, many corporations are seriously looking into B2Bi technology options that can deliver results speedily.

The ability to provide personalized service information and Single Sign-on to private labeling clients is essential. This enables the clients to enjoy the same business functionality provided by the private labeling Service Provider, while keeping their own branding and integrating with their existing back-office systems. It is a key service differentiation factor.

Technology is changing frequently. It would be good risk mitigation for architects and developers to adopt a mature technology and adhere to a technology standard to integrate and interoperate with other business partners. Today, the integration technology options for many architects and developers include deploying proprietary interfaces, adapting an Enterprise Resource Planning (ERP) product as their integration infrastructure, using a specific Enterprise Application Integration (EAI) product, and adopting Web Services technology for integration. These options are like a spectrum with two polarity ends—proprietary and open technology.

Table 6–1 outlines a high-level comparison of these integration technology options:

Table 6–1   Different B2Bi Integration Technology Options

	Pros	Cons	Risks
Proprietary interfaces	Proprietary interfaces are highly customized to meet local business and technology requirements. Interfaces and message formats can be standardized across the enterprise without depending on external parties.	They are not easily reusable and extended for other similar requirements. They may require complex changes or re-engineering in order to integrate and interoperate with external business partners.	These interfaces may work like a black box, and thus the technology has high maintenance issues.
ERP	Companies that have deployed an ERP system can leverage the ERP infrastructure to integrate with their front-end systems. ERP systems usually have J2EE and XML connectors and interfaces that can communicate with other systems.	Only newer versions of ERP systems support J2EE and XML connectors. It may be very complicated and expensive to develop a new connector for the ERP system. The required ERP integration expertise is scarce.	There is a risk of vendor lock-in with the ERP infrastructure. The scalability and extensibility of the integration architecture is impacted by the legacy architecture of the ERP system. In some cases, any change is dependent on the availability and capability of the ERP system.
EAI	EAI adapters (connectors) can be customized to accommodate different requirements of each system. Complex business process and workflow requirements can be integrated using Message-Oriented Middleware (MOM) and Integration Manager. This allows more flexibility and extensibility.	EAI is usually expensive to implement. Workflow changes may require business process re-engineering, which may complicate the implementation. Different EAI products are not interoperable.	Adopting a specific middleware to implement EAI may lock in with a specific vendor architecture and technology. It is fairly painful to switch to another vendor technology.

Table 6–1   Different B2Bi Integration Technology Options—*continued.*

	Pros	Cons	Risks
Web Services	Web Services technology has emerged as an Open Standard technology option for B2Bi. It is a light-weight technology option and can be used without EAI. Java Web Services technology collaborates with and complements J2EE-based EAI to provide B2Bi.	WSDL-UDDI-SOAP Web Services does not support business process and workflow integration. (ebXML Web Services technology does though through BPSS, the Business Process Spec Schema)	The business process and workflow integration capability of WSDL-UDDI-SOAP technology is still evolving. ebXML technology offers a more sophisticated Web Services alternative to address the B2Bi requirements.

6.4   Web Services and EAI—Friends or Foes?

Enterprise Application Integration (EAI) is an established technology used to integrate different business processes. It can link one application to another sequentially or, based on a predefined pattern (workflow), perform certain business functionality. Thus, different chains of events can be related together seamlessly without manual intervention or disruption. These events can also be programmed to handle different conditions with a rule engine (that is, Business Process), instead of hard-coding with specific conditions.

Another key feature of EAI is its integration with existing applications and legacy back-end systems, including mainframe and ERP systems. The value of EAI technology is that it provides seamless interoperability between systems across different platforms without rebuilding the business functionality. Many legacy back-end systems run on an IBM mainframe, a Tandem mainframe, a DEC platform, and a PC platform. Most of these systems store data in legacy databases and do not have interfaces or APIs for integration with external systems. To standardize a single interface or API on all these platforms would not be pragmatic. Many architects and developers will opt to utilize an EAI product to accommodate different data formats in each system and convolute into a single data format centrally.

EAI technology is often implemented using middleware products. Middleware can be point-to-point, queue-based, or publish-subscribe models. Typically, middleware products require building customized adapters for each system. The adapter is usually platform-specific. It is designed to transform data from a proprietary format to another for a specific application (Data Transformation). Data from one system is transformed and exchanged with another system via the customized adapters (Messaging).

If using EAI and CORBA technology together, customized EAI adapters can expose legacy business functionality by wrapping existing interfaces with an Interface Definition Language (IDL). IDLs provide a self-describing structure for the data and service provided (Service Definition). Client stubs will be generated from IDLs in order to access remote business functionality. They will look up a naming server in order to locate and bind the local or remote business service (Service Discovery). The physical business service may reside on another machine or at a remote data center in another country. This provides a more dynamic environment to bring together different business functionality within the enterprise. However, only CORBA-based EAI technology products require IDLs and naming servers.

EAI technology using Message-Oriented Middleware (MOM) is able to scale up with the use of a hierarchy of topics or queues (Manageability). Different topics or queues (hierarchical subject namespace that indicates the message category or application areas, such as PROD.TREASURY.FX, PROD.TREASURY.OPTION, and DEV.TREASURY.FX), can be managed and segregated to specialize in processing specific categories of transactions. Queues can also be clustered to provide message-level load balancing and resilience. In other words, the workload can be shared between queues under the same cluster. When the transaction volume goes up, architects and developers simply add more queues in the same machine or in another machine (that is, a choice of vertical and horizontal scaling). A queue can fail over to another queue under the same cluster automatically, if there is any message level anomaly. This is a better option than using proprietary interfaces or APIs.

Web Services technology has emerged as an enabling technology for B2Bi. Is it a subset of EAI technology or a competing technology? If we take the broader meaning of EAI, we can categorize Web Services and J2EE technology as part of EAI technology, as they provide different technology implementations for enterprise integration. If we take the narrow meaning of EAI, where EAI is often associated with MOM middleware, then we may see many similarities between EAI and Web Services.

We learned from previous chapters that Web Services technology has a self-describing service definition (WSDL). Clients may discover different business services from a Service Registry, whether a UDDI or an ebXML Service Registry. Once the business service is found, clients can send service requests to the Service Provider using SOAP messaging. Java technology has extended the current WSDL-UDDI-SOAP-based Web Services technology to provide XML data transformation using JAXP and XSLT. To address guaranteed message delivery and manageability, architects and developers can leverage the Java Messaging Service (for example, SOAP-JMS) to collaborate with SOAP messaging. Java technology also eases legacy mainframe or ERP system integration with Java Connector Architecture, which provides a service contract for better Quality of Service and transactional integrity. ebXML's Business Process Specification Schema (BPSS, *http://www.ebxml.org/specs/ebBPSS.pdf*), Web Services Choreography

Interface (WSCI, *http://wwws.sun.com/software/xml/developers/wsci/wsci-spec-10. pdf*), Business Process Execution Service Definition Language for Web Services (BPEL4WS, *http://www.oasis-open.org/cover/bpel4ws.html*), XML Processing Description Language (XPDL, *http://www.simonstl.com/projects/xpdl/*), and Enterprise Distributed Object Computing (EDOC, *http://www.omg.org/cgi-bin/doc?ad/99-03-10*) are Web Services technology extensions to provide better enterprise and cross-enterprise integration. They can collaborate with existing EAI vendor products for cross-enterprise or B2B integration. This addresses the issue of interoperability between multiple EAI products.

Carol Murphy (2002) has summarized the differences and similarities between EAI and Web Services technology concisely (see Table 6–2). Murphy shows that both EAI and Web Services technology can provide service definition, service discovery, and messaging capability to support exposing remote system functionality as reusable services components. We can see that Web Services technology is extending more to cover data transformation, Business Process Management, and manageability. We are beginning to see more commercial Web Services products with Business Process Management capability (such as Progress eXcelon's BPM) in the market. In essence, current Web Services technology is a lightweight integration option and collaborates very well with or complements existing EAI products.

Table 6–2   Similarities Between EAI and Web Services Technology

Functionality offered in each architecture	EAI					
	Web Services					
Functionality Required → ↓ Usage Required	Service Definition	Messaging	Service Discovery	Data Transformation	Business Process Management	Manageability
Exposing existing application functionality	X	X	X	X		X
Exposing new application functionality	X	X	X			X
Combining multiple applications into an integrated business process (composite application)	X	X	X	X	X	X
Exposing an integrated business process	X	X	X		X	X
Managing a heterogeneous environment	X	X	X		X	X

Remarks

The ebXML Message Service is tied to business processing through BPSS (*http:// www.ebxml.org/specs/ebMS2.pdf*) and Collaboration Protocol Profile/Agreement *http://www.ebxml.org/specs/ebTA.pdf*). There are similar initiatives to address business processes in BPEL4WS (*http://www-106.ibm.com/developerworks/webservices/ library/ws-bpelcol1/?dwzone=webservices*) and in similar ways. This has made the boundary between EAI and Web Services more difficult to differentiate.

6.5   Cross-Enterprise Integration Framework

An integration framework is essential to define different integration tiers and basic components or enabling technology for enterprise and cross-enterprise integration. It also outlines how each integration tier communicates with the other. The integration framework does not build on top of existing EAI vendor products. It can mix-and-match implementing any EAI vendor products with Web Services technology.

There are five different tiers of integration that need to be considered. Figure 6–1 provides a sample scenario where a user accesses Web Services functionality provided by a series of legacy back-end systems to perform a fund transfer. A client user has a unique network identity using a digital certificate with a user id and password to access business services from a number of Service Providers. The client user performs a Single Sign-on using his Network Identity (step 1), where his credential is authenticated against a series of PKI infrastructure and Directory Servers under a federated identity management environment. This process will invoke the authentication and the associated entitlement services to determine whether the client is a valid user, and whether he is authorized to access the fund transfer service (step 2). All client requests for the fund transfer Web Services are represented in SOAP messages, which are carried over HTTPS in this scenario (step 3). SOAP messages can also be carried over other data transport, such as SMTP or FTP. The legacy back-end systems are wrapped as XML-RPC Web Services using Java Connector Architecture. Chapter 5, Mainframe Integration and Interoperability, discusses the details of how legacy mainframe systems can be wrapped as Web Services using XML-RPC. Upon receipt of the SOAP service request, the server-side SOAP component (SOAP tier or skeleton) will then invoke the remote back-end mainframe system functionality via XML-RPC (step 4). The Java Connector is a J2EE-based integration technology to connect the Web Services client request to the back-end legacy mainframe systems (step 5). The client user has a synchronous Web Services session to retrieve account profile, perform account balance enquiry, and transfer cash from one account to another account. There are complicated back-end business processes that require sophisticated business process

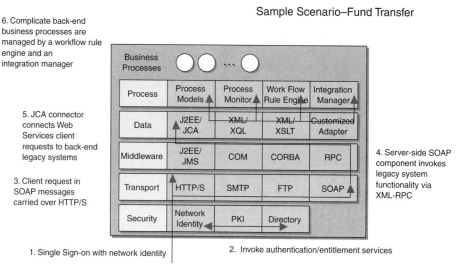

6. Complicate back-end business processes are managed by a workflow rule engine and an integration manager

5. JCA connector connects Web Services client requests to back-end legacy systems

3. Client request in SOAP messages carried over HTTP/S

4. Server-side SOAP component invokes legacy system functionality via XML-RPC

1. Single Sign-on with network identity

2. Invoke authentication/entitlement services

Figure 6–1   Integration Framework

collaboration and monitoring. The "fund transfer" processes are being managed by a workflow rule engine and an Integration Manager hosted by the financial portal Service Provider (step 6). All workflow processes are being monitored with all transactions logged for audit purposes.

6.5.1   Security Integration

The notion of Network Identity is to provide a unique identity for accessing business services over the Internet, where users just need to sign on once for multiple Service Providers. Sometimes, this is also associated with Single Sign-on (SSO) technology. Network Identity often assumes the use of security tokens such as X.509v3 digital certificates or a Kerberos ticket with Public Key Infrastructure. The Network Identity process will also retrieve the user profile and access rights from one federated Directory Servers and validate against the credentials. SAML (and its extension), under the Project Liberty specification, may be used as the underlying security messaging specification. The client requester will initiate a SAML access right assertion to the federated Directory Servers. Upon successful validation, the client requester will be granted access to the authorized business services stored in the user profile.

6.5.2   Data Transport Integration

SOAP over TCP/IP is the underlying messaging transport. It can be carried over HTTP, HTTPS, SMTP, or FTP. The SOAP 1.1 specification defines SOAP over HTTP. For SOAP-SMTP and SOAP-FTP binding, developers need to write their own provider class for the SOAP bindings.

6.5.3   Middleware Integration

The integration framework allows multiple middleware integration options with the back-end systems. Typically, middleware products can communicate with the back-end systems using Java Message Service (JMS). If there is a need to communicate between the client and the back-end systems using two middleware products, even though they may be using JMS, they still require a JMS bridge that binds JMS to the underlying data transport such as SOAP. This is sometimes known as SOAP-JMS binding.

With Java technology, developers can also use COM (for example, using a Java-COM bridge), CORBA (for example, using RMI-IIOP or a Java-CORBA bridge), and Remote Procedure Call (or RPC, such as XML-RPC). Using Web Services technology, either of these middleware integration options will use SOAP over HTTPS as the transport. This decouples the middleware from the data transport integration, making interoperability easier.

6.5.4   Data Integration

At the data level, business data objects that are encapsulated in existing relational databases can be accessed and retrieved by XQL (XML Query Language or SQL-like XML notation). If the data are persisted in proprietary format and a customized adapter has been built, then developers may wrap the customized adapter as Web Services functionality.

At the presentation level, if data need to be transformed, developers can use the XML Style Sheet Processor (XSLT) to translate and render data into another format, such as delimited text, proprietary text format, or PDF.

Legacy systems data can be also accessed using the Java Connector Architecture (JCA). Developers can also build custom JCA connectors using an off-the-shelf JCA connector software development kit or Java class library.

6.5.5   Process Integration

Using an EAI product, complex business processes can be modeled as Process Models with a Workflow Rule Engine and an Integration Manager. Process Models are an encapsulation of a series of actions, where specific actions will be taken if certain events take place. The Workflow Rule Engine manages a list of business rules defined to describe and execute predefined Process Models when different events take place. To monitor the current or historic events, Process Model actions, or which business rules are fired, we need to administer them by a Process Monitor for performance and audit purpose.

Table 6–3 summarizes the integration components and enabling technology by tiers versus layers. You will notice that certain components span different tiers and platforms. Therefore, it is important to remember that enterprise and cross-enterprise integration covers components by components, across tiers and layers. This does not stop at any component level.

Table 6–3   Integration Framework Components by Tiers Versus Layers

	Client Tier	Presentation Tier	Business Tier	Integration Tier	Resources Tier
Application Layer				Process Models Process Monitor Workflow Rule Engine Integration Manager	
Virtual Layer		XSLT	XML	JMS RPC COM CORBA	JCA XQL
Upper Layer	HTTPS SOAP	HTTPS SOAP SMTP FTP	SOAP		
Lower Layer	Network Identity/ Single Sign-on PKI Directory server	Network Identity/ Single Sign-on PKI Directory server	Network Identity/ Single Sign-on PKI Directory server	Network Identity/ Single Sign-on PKI Directory server	Network Identity/ Single Sign-on PKI Directory server

6.5.6   How to Use the Integration Framework

In order to utilize the integration framework, architects and developers may wish to define their integration requirements and map to the five tiers of the integration framework. Then they need to identify their integration approach and model and consider reusing any existing B2Bi integration patterns (refer to the next section). Always customize and adapt your integration methodology for each business case.

To customize the integration architecture, architects and developers may wish to start with Use Case modeling. Remember to be customer-centric. Always consider reusability (for example, build a library of repeatable services, codes, and integration tools) and how to lower Total Cost of Ownership (TCO). Place the big picture first, and do not focus on the interfaces or APIs yet. Integration design also needs to cover many aspects of security, processes, data, and business services. Wherever possible, always decouple transport from the message contents or structure.

6.5.7   Benefits

With a comprehensive integration framework, architects and developers can customize their own structured processes and methodology, which can reduce technology and implementation risks. They can focus on their success, as they may find it easier to set their priorities on the critical integration areas.

The integration framework also provides a reusable structure to customize and fine-tune the customer's integration architecture. This sets the big picture or blueprint for its target architecture. The technology options are Open Standards compliant, which eases future extension and interoperability. The integration framework also comes with some best practices that describe when to use specific integration patterns.

6.6   Emerging Integration Technology

6.6.1   Java Connector Architecture

Java Connector Architecture (JCA) provides a standard architecture for connecting to Enterprise Information Systems such as mainframe legacy systems and Enterprise Resource Planning systems. Figure 6–2 shows a high-level architecture. Java Connector provides a Resource Adapter that enables J2EE application components to connect to Enterprise Information Systems (EIS) or legacy mainframe systems. Any J2EE application component needs to establish application contracts with the Resource Adapter. The Resource Adapter provides Common Client Interface (CCI) to connect the EIS. When an established system contracts with the J2EE application server and the application contracts with the J2EE application components, the Resource Adapter can ensure reliable data connectivity and messaging with the EIS. The Java Connector Architecture has been maturing since J2EE 1.3.

A server-side SOAP component (SOAP tier or skeleton) can initiate service requests to the EIS via the relevant J2EE application component, which will create a connection with the EIS via the Resource Adapter. The Resource Adapter will also handle connection pooling and session failover. The business transaction result will be returned in a SOAP message to the SOAP client via the SOAP server. The JCA design can support both synchronous and asynchronous Web Services.

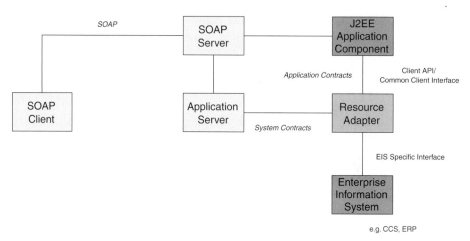

Figure 6–2   Java Connector Architecture Overview

We also see growing numbers of commercial implementations, such as CICS and SAP. JCA 2.0 adds the features of asynchronous resource adapters (for example, supporting inbound and outbound directions for complex integration scenarios), Java Message Service API provider pluggability (that is, treating JMS API as a resource adapter), XML support in CCI (for example, JAXP and JAXB support), and CCI metadata support (for example, providing meta information such as input and output record types). This has significantly enriched the legacy system integration.

The core component in JCA is the Resource Adapter. It provides connectivity to the Enterprise Information Systems where the client (J2EE application components) uses a Common Client Interface (CCI) to invoke enterprise system functionality or to retrieve customer information (using Enterprise Information System's input and output record types). The key benefits of the JCA Resource Adapter are to address previous integration issues of scalability, asynchronous communication between the client and Enterprise Information Systems, pluggability with a standard J2EE container, and transactions and security integration issues. One major implication is that the JCA Resource Adapter provides a "system contract" with the J2EE application server and an "application contract" with the J2EE application components. The contract denotes connection management, transaction management, and security management (refer to the next section on "Resource Adapter Architecture"). This allows a better quality of service and transaction integrity.

Resource Adapter Architecture

One key benefit of the Resource Adapter is the system contract between the J2EE application server and the Resource Adapter, which provides reliable connection management, transaction management, and security management. Figure 6–3 depicts the connection management process taking place in the Resource Adapter. The boxes denote the Java class objects (such as `ConnectionFactory` and `ConnectionManager`) that need to be used for connection management. Figure 6–4 depicts the transaction management processes, where the `TXManager` object manages the business transactions using the `LocalTransaction` class as per the system contracts in the `XAResource` object.

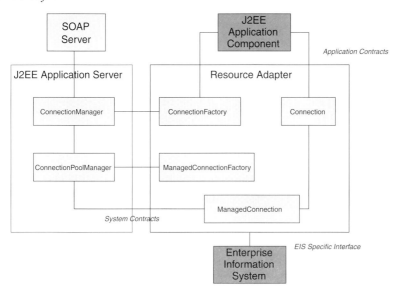

Figure 6–3   JCA Connection Management

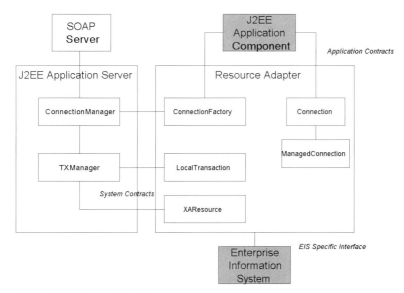

Figure 6–4   JCA Transaction Management

Common Client Interface

Figure 6–5 shows how Common Client Interface is being created for a legacy Enterprise Information System (CICS application). The `ConnectionManager` object initializes the connection, specifies the user id and password for security, sets the remote application id (in this case, CICS transaction id), and invokes the remote functionality. The `InteractionSpec` object denotes the remote CICS transaction id. The result is then returned at the end in the `ResultSet` object.

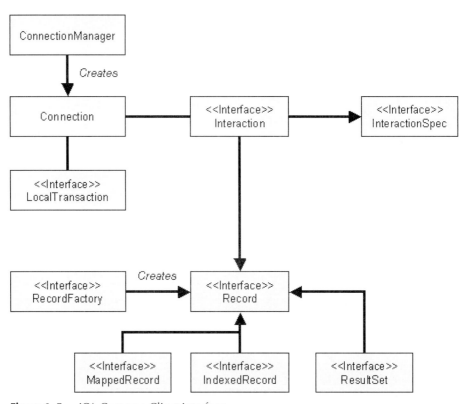

Figure 6–5 JCA Common Client Interface

Figure 6–6 shows a program excerpt using CCI to place an FX trade order by connecting to the back-end EIS. It invokes the remote CICS transaction "`PHALL`" by specifying the InteractionSpec object and initiating the method "`execute`" (as in `ix.execute(ispec, custRec, resultRec)`). The transaction result is returned in the `ResultSet` object (as in `resultRec`).

```
import com.ibm.connector2.cics.*;
import javax.naming.Context;
import javax.resource.cci.*;
...

public int placeFXTradeOrder(int accountNumber,String
fxCode,int amount, String homeCurrency, date
valueDate)
{

ECIConnectionSpec cspec =  new
ECIConnectionSpec("myUserID", "myPassword");
//  ID and password for CICS sign-on

//  Get a connection to CICS
Context nc = new InitialContext();
ECIConnectionFactory cf  =
(ECIConnectionFactory)nc.lookup(
"java:comp/env/eis/ECIConnectionFactory");  // Java
naming context lookup

Connection cx = cf.getConnection(cspec);

// Prepare for interaction CICS via ECI

ECIInteractionSpec ixSpec = new ECIInteractionSpec();
ixSpec.setFunctionName("PHALL");  // PHALL is a CICS
transaction id for processing FX trade order
ixSpec.setInteractionVerb(InteractionSpec.SYNC_SEND_
RECEIVE);

// Prepare records - custom records implement
javax.resource.cci.Record
CustomerInfoRecord custRec = new CustomerInfoRecord();
// Input
ResultInfoRecord resultRec = new ResultInfoRecord();
// Result

// specify any parameters for the CICS transaction
function if necessary
...
```

Figure 6–6   Sample CCI Program Excerpt

```
// Execute the remote CICS transaction
Interaction  ix = cx.createInteraction();
ix.execute(ispec, custRec, resultRec);

// Close the connection
cx.close();

// Retrieve results from the result record
int fxTradeStatus = resultRec.placeFXTradeOrder();
return fxTradeStatus;


}
```

Figure 6–6   Sample CCI Program Excerpt—*continued.*

Figure 6–7 shows a client proxy that the Java client needs to invoke. The service endpoint "fxPlaceOrder" from the SOAP Router will invoke the method placeFX-TradeOrder, which may be an EJB, Java bean, or a legacy system function from the legacy mainframe applications. The return code of the call is placed in the resp variable.

```
import java.io.*;
import javax.xml.soap.*;
import javax.xml.messaging.*;
import java.net.URL;
import java.rmi.RemoteException;
import java.util.*;
...

public class fxTradingClientProxy
{
  private Call call = new Call();
  private URL url = null;
  private String SOAPActionURI = "";
  private SOAPMappingRegistry smr =
call.getSOAPMappingRegistry();

  public fxTradingClientProxythrows MalformedURLException
  {
    call.setTargetObjectURI("urn:fxPlaceOrder");

call.setEncodingStyleURI(Constants.NS_URI_SOAP_ENC);
```

Figure 6–7   Sample Client Proxy for the FX Web Services Call

```
    this.url = new
URL("http://localhost:8080/test/servlet/rpcrouter");
    this.SOAPActionURI = "urn:fxPlaceOrder";
  }

  // Customize here for your business services
  public synchronized int
    placeFXTradeOrder(int accountNumber,String
fxCode,int amount, String homeCurrency, date
valueDate) throws Exception
  {
    if(url == null)
    {
     throw new SOAPException(Constants.FAULT_CODE_CLIENT,
      "URL must be specified via " +
"fxTradingClientProxy.setEndPoint(URL).");
    }

    call.setMethodName("placeFXTradeOrder");

call.setEncodingStyleURI(Constants.NS_URI_SOAP_ENC);
    ...

    // invoke Java Web services via SOAP here
    Response resp = call.invoke(url, SOAPActionURI);

    //Check the result
    if (resp.generatedFault())
    {
      Fault fault = resp.getFault();
      throw new SOAPException(fault.getFaultCode(),
fault.getFaultString());
    }
    else
    {
      Parameter refValue = resp.getReturnValue();
      return (refValue.getValue());
    }
  }
}
```

Figure 6–7   Sample Client Proxy for the FX Web Services Call—*continued.*

The Java client invoking the Web Services may look like this (see Figure 6–8):

```
import java.io.*;
import java.net.URL;
...

// Create an instance of the Java Web services client
proxy
fxTradingClientProxy myFxTradingWebServices = new
fxTradingClientProxy();

// Invoke the Java Web Services method
int fxTradeStatus =
myFxTradingWebServices.placeFXTradeOrder(accountNumber
,fxCode,amount, homeCurrency, valueDate);
```

Figure 6–8   Sample Java Client Invoking the FX Web Services Call

Commercial Implementation of Resource Adapter

With the growing implementation of J2EE-based technology, there are increasing numbers of commercial implementations of Resource Adapter for legacy mainframe systems and Enterprise Resource Planning. Figures 6–9 and 6–10 depict the Resource Adapter implementation for CICS and SAP R/3, respectively.

Figure 6–9 shows the components of a CICS Resource Adapter, which consists of an ECI Resource Adapter, an EPI Resource Adapter, and an ESI Resource Adapter. These adapters accommodate all types of CICS communication calls (that is, ECI, EPI, and ESI calls), depending on how the client invokes the back-end CICS transactions. The data result is placed in the common area COMMAREA. The CICS Resource Adapter currently comes with the CICS Transaction Gateway software package.

Figure 6–10 depicts the components of an SAP Resource Adapter. The back-end SAP resources and business functionality are currently accessible by a proprietary RFC library (RFC Lib). The SAP Resource Adapter provides an abstraction layer called JCo (Java Connector) to invoke RFC lib calls.

Wakelin et al. (2002, pp. 17–32) have a detailed elaboration of the Java Connector for CICS. Juric and colleagues (2001) have a good summary of the SAP R/3 Resource Adapter with some code examples.

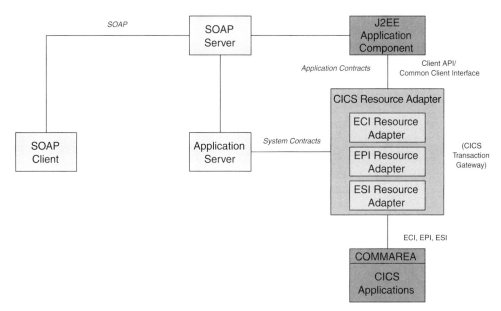

Figure 6–9   CICS Resource Adapter

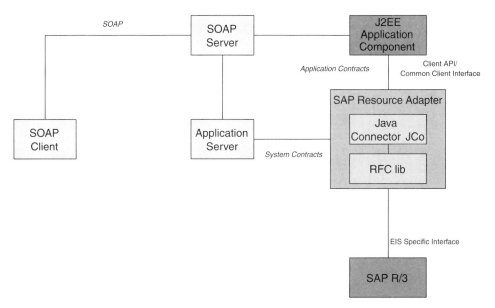

Figure 6–10   SAP R/3 Resource Adapter

6.6.2   ebXML Business Process Management

Business Process Management is a key element in enterprise and cross-enterprise integration. It entails unified process automation and workflow models. It requires a direct model execution and manipulation. It should also support state management, time-based exception handling, robust process monitoring and analysis, nested model support, and concurrent model support. Architecturally, systems supporting Business Process Management should be highly reliable, highly available, and scalable. They should be also Open Standards compliant.

ebXML Web Services technology provides a good integration option to managing business processes. Please refer to Chapter 3, Web Services Technology Overview, for a brief description of ebXML. An example of Business Process Management using ebXML Web Services technology is Progress eXcelon's Business Process Manager (BPM). BPM is designed to support B2Bi using ebXML's Business Process Management. BPM has three key components: Process Flow Engine (business rules encapsulating event process flow and collaboration rules in CPP documents), Integration Framework (a set of adapters and listeners that connects system components and supports SOAP-JMS, as well), and Business Document Repository (a Service Registry and a directory of XML documents).

Figure 6–11 illustrates how BPM can be used to implement a Straight-through Processing presettlement matching solution using ebXML Web Services technology. Fund managers and traders initiate a trade order with the Business Process Manager (that is, BPM's Process Flow Engine). The Business Process Manager administers a series of business rules regarding how a trade order should be validated and processed. It then exchanges trade order information between the Portfolio Management System, the Trade Order Management System, and the Risk Management System from multiple parties via the Enterprise Service Interface (that is, BPM's Integration Framework). There will be a series of workflow events to be triggered and processed. The trade order documents are stored in XML within the BPM's Document Repository.

Web Services technology can be used as a better alternative to automate and exchange trade order information (such as order initiation, order, notice of execution [NOE], and matching trades) between different trading partners. The underlying messaging infrastructure adopts ebXML Message Service, which provides a reliable messaging for business transactions. In case of any system failure in the applications at the fund manager, trader, broker/dealer, or custodian level, ebXML messaging is able to resend the business documents once it resumes operations. This is critical to the Straight-through Processing for capital market customers.

Upon a successful trade order execution, the Business Process Manager will initiate presettlement matching. This will require many interfaces between Broker/Dealer, the Virtual Matching Utility (or VMU; for example, GSTPA or Omgeo), and Custodian. The Business Process Manager will resolve any settlement exceptions based on the business rules defined in the Process Flow Engine.

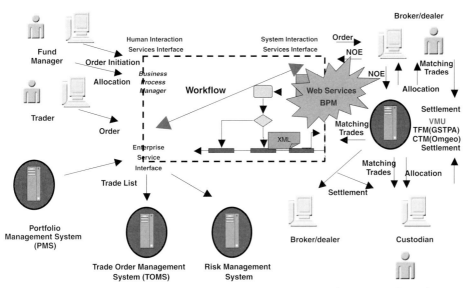

Figure 6–11 Using Progress eXcelon's Business Process Manager for Straight-through Processing (Courtesy of Progress eXcelon)

6.6.3 SOAP-JMS Integration

Although Java Message Service (JMS) is a messaging standard for middleware products, developers cannot exchange data from one JMS to another because JMS depends on the underlying physical data transport. For example, data objects encapsulated by TIBCO JMS implementation will not be able to be exchanged with an IBM MQ JMS implementation. This is particularly significant for cross-enterprise integration when both trading partners claim to support JMS but technically cannot exchange data using a JMS implementation.

The alternatives include using a proprietary middleware bridge (such as TIBCO's TIB2MQ) and a JMS bridge. The JMS bridge is a generic term for integrating JMS together using a XML cache solution (for example, Progress eXcelon's XIS) or implementing a SOAP-JMS bridge to utilize SOAP messaging over different JMS implementations.

The SOAP-JMS bridge simply refers to extending the SOAPTransport class to customize a SOAP-to-JMS Transport class that can create a JMS queue session, create a queue message from the SOAP header, and extract and decode the SOAP message. Ahmed Kal and his colleagues have a working example in *Professional Java XML* (2001, pp. 831–861).

6.6.4 Integrating Different Data Sources

Without XML support in the database, architects and developers need to write JDBC calls to encapsulate business data objects and extract and transform them into XML messages. They probably end up writing lengthy entity beans and complex data handling methods. The alternative may be using legacy database warehousing techniques to extract data into a data mart for processing. However, this will require off-line processing for data extraction, transformation, and database loading.

Major database vendors have now added SQL-to-XML mapping and native XML format storage support to their database technology. For example, developers can use an add-on utility (such as XML extender or servlet) to extract a relational database and transform into XML messages from DB2 or Oracle 8i. This has eased accessing and updating data from a real-time Web Services calls and reduced the development effort considerably.

Several XML-related database initiatives such as XQL (SQL-like XML query language) and DADX Web Services (Mapping SQL to DTD or XML Schema) are evolving. XQL is designed to be used as a query language in XML syntax. This reduces the development effort to parse relational database data results to XML and vice versa. Details of XQL can be referenced at *http://www.w3.org/TandS/QL/QL98/pp/flab.txt* and *http://www.ibiblio.org/xql/xql-tutorial.html.* DADX is a proprietary implementation to combine a SOAP service request with SQL calls. It is currently generated and managed from WebSphere Application Developer and can only work with DB2. Details of DADX Web Services can be referenced at *http://www7b.software.ibm.com/ dmdd/library/techarticle/0212yu/0212yu.html?t=gr,lnxw07=DB2-NET-WS.* Some of these technologies are implemented with proprietary databases. Reed (2002) and Haggarty (2002) have some good examples of SQL queries rendering XML SQL queries and transforming them into XML messages.

6.7 Integration Design Patterns

Here is a collection of B2B integration design patterns. Some of the integration pattern names and concepts are modified from Yee and Apte (2001, pp. 30–41), *Integrating Your e-Business Enterprise,* and expanded to cover Web Services technologies.

In each of the integration design patterns, a scenario is presented where the design pattern may be applied, followed by a sequence diagram to depict how Web Services technology can be implemented. Each integration design pattern will start by defining the context (background or requirements), problem (problem statement), force (design factors to be considered or when to use the pattern), solution (proposed solution depicted in Use Cases and sequence diagrams), risk (design or implementation risks, and the risk mitigation), and any relevant examples.

6.7.1 Application-to-Application Pattern

Context

It is fairly common to have ad hoc requirements for a point-to-point interface with another trading partner. For instance, Figure 6–12 depicts a scenario where a corporate institution (Customer B) wants to automate the Foreign Exchange trade order process by sending an electronic interface to the broker (Securities Firm A). Customer B is a large corporate customer, and it prefers to use a mutually agreed interface format or perhaps a standard data exchange format. Trading partners may use a customized adapter to transform business data from existing back-end systems to exchange with the trading partner (either synchronous or asynchronous).

Problem

Different trading partners' applications have local and proprietary data formats. These applications do not share a common data format, and thus they require customized data transformation. If a trading partner (such as Customer B) needs to send transaction data to another trading partner (such as Securities Firm A), it either customizes the data mapping and transformation or sends in a preagreed format before exchanging data. If the number of application interfaces increase, the customization effort for the data transformation or customization would be very expensive and inefficient.

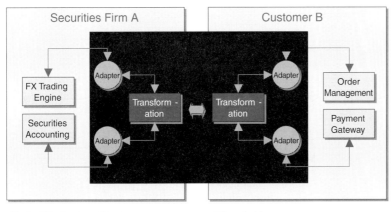

Typical Technology Used
Customized adapter
Preagreed interface format/standard
EDI translator

When to Use
Point-to-point exchange, tight
integration
Limited number of trading partners
Relatively static data formats

EXAMPLE   Based on: Yee & Apte. Integrating Your e-Business Enterprise. SAMS, 2001.

Figure 6–12 Application-to-Application Pattern

Force

Different trading partners have different data formats that require customized data transformation. It may not be viable to standardize a single data format that can be used to exchange data with all trading partners. Thus, the use of a flexible data format (such as XML) and a standards-based messaging (such as SOAP messaging) is very crucial to facilitating application-to-application integration.

Solution

In this sample scenario (in Figure 6–12), Customer B wants to send a Foreign Exchange trade order directly from its back-end Order Management system in an fpML message format. Its current Order Management system does not process fpML message types. A custom adapter is used to extract and transform trade orders in fpML (for example, using JAXP). It then exchanges the fpML messages with the trading partner. The trading partner, Firm A, has a legacy FX trading engine and securities accounting back-office systems and does not support fpML. However, Firm A uses a custom adapter to receive the fpML message from Customer B and passes it to its Message Broker (aka EDI translator) to transform the data contents to a proprietary format that its back-office systems can understand. fpML is a market message standard, which is initially agreed upon between the two trading partners.

Figure 6–13 elaborates the details of the data exchange using Web Services. Firm A extracts and renders the data contents from the back-end applications. The Message Broker (the data transformation engine) then transforms the data into XML using JAXP. It uses a hashing algorithm to generate the digital signature (DSIG), attaches to the SOAP envelope, and sends the SOAP message using JAXM. Upon receipt of the SOAP message, Customer B's Message Broker (the data transformation engine) will unmarshal the SOAP envelope and retrieve the message content. It will also need to use the public key pair to decode the message content and transform the XML using JAXP into a format that is understandable by the back-end applications. Once the message processing is done, Customer B's Message Broker will then prepare an acknowledgement message (SOAP reply message), encode and sign with a digital signature, and return to Firm A's Message Broker. Upon receipt of the acknowledgement message, Firm A's Message Broker will notify the back-end application that a message reply has been received.

This Web Services integration pattern makes use of JAXP for flexible data transformation and JAXM for heterogeneous platform connectivity. It addresses the issues of proprietary data format and connectivity for point-to-point application interfaces discussed earlier. The "adapter" becomes a standards-based implementation and can be highly reusable for other trading partners.

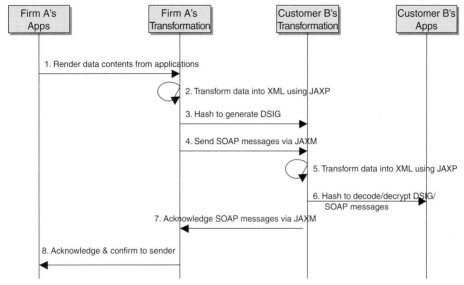

Figure 6–13 Application-to-Application Pattern Sequence Diagram

When to Use. This Application-to-Application integration pattern is suitable for point-to-point exchanges where tight integration is required. There are limited numbers of trading partners. The message format is relatively stable.

EAI Versus Web Services. With an EAI implementation, architects and developers are likely to use an EDI translator (Message Broker) together with customized adapters. With a Web Services implementation, they may use JAXP to transform data from the back-end systems and JAXM to exchange fpML messages between the trading partners.

Risk

Not all trading partners are technologically ready to customize the data transformation engine to support SOAP messaging. Many customers are using proprietary EAI products for data transformation. It requires a long-term strategy to migrate all interfaces to support SOAP messaging.

Example

Many investment banks are taking online trade orders from large corporations or investment managers using a customized data transformation approach. For instance, RandomWalk's retail brokerage system, using its WOLF framework (*http://www.randomwalk.com/*) is able to send a SOAP message to the trading partner. The SOAP message is used to encapsulate the trade order status or account balance. At the SunGard user conference 2001, SunGard (*http://www.sungard.com/*) also announced that its system is able to exchange its trade information with OM products (*http://www.om.com/*) using SOAP messages. These are examples of application-to-application data exchange. This pattern will be useful to streamline the order management process to support Straight-through Processing.

SOAP messaging using JAXM is a way to encapsulate business data in a SOAP envelope and send message acknowledgements to the trading partner. The "Paper and Pencil" exercise at the end of this chapter illustrates how to send a Foreign Exchange option using JAXM.

6.7.2   Standard Build Pattern

Context

One of the challenges of a massive global rollout of business applications is the complexity of software service versions to support the heterogeneous platforms used by different users or trading partners. For instance, in the banking industry, home banking and cash management systems are two typical examples in which different versions of user front-ends are deployed to the market. Supporting different software versions that run on heterogeneous platforms (such as Windows 95 and Windows 98) could be a nightmare.

Architects and developers may design and deploy a standard build gateway for both trading partners to exchange business data (either synchronous or asynchronous). All data formats and APIs are standardized on the same platform.

Problem

There are many variants (or versions) of application interfaces for different trading partners, even though these interfaces share many similarities. As the number of application interface variants increase, the maintenance and support effort will be immense and difficult to manage.

Force

Standardizing all data interfaces and gateways that handle data exchange will ease software deployment and management. However, many customers' business operating or deployment environments require localized requirements, thus deploying standard builds may not be easy or feasible in some cases.

Solution

Figure 6–14 depicts a scenario where both trading partners have agreed on a common interface with a standard API library build version 1.3. Securities Firm A has managed the deployment of a Standard Build Gateway product that can handle the data exchange using the standard API library build version 1.3. In this sample scenario, Customer B uses the APIs provided by the Standard Build Gateway, say version 1.3, to extract business data and transform the data in a standard message format. Then the Standard Build Gateway will exchange with the trading partner, who is also using the same Standard Build software with the same message format.

The Standard Build Gateway can be built in any arbitrary programming language and platform. Each of the back-end systems makes use of the common API library to extract data and send it to the Standard Build Gateway.

Figure 6–15 elaborates the details of the previous process of the standard build using Web Services. Firm A extracts and renders the data contents from the back-end applications. The Message Broker (the data transformation engine) then transforms the data into XML using standard build APIs. It uses a hashing algorithm to generate the digital signature (DSIG), attach it to the SOAP envelope, and send it the SOAP message using a customized SOAP-to-Standard-Build-Gateway protocol binding.

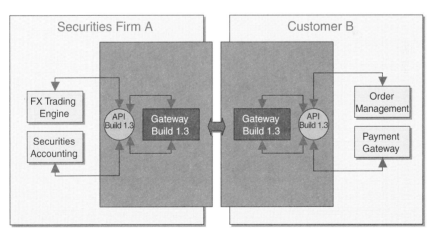

Typical Technology Used
Standardized home-grown/customized adapter
Standardized interface format/API standard
EDI translator/EAI or middleware

When to Use
Strong urge for standard build
Point-to-point exchange, tight integration

EXAMPLE

Figure 6–14 Standard Build Pattern

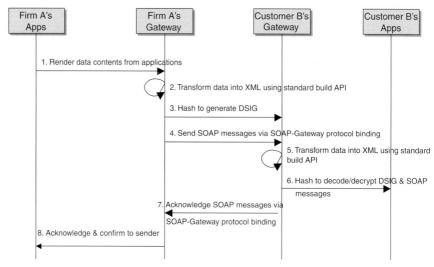

Figure 6–15   Standard Build Pattern Sequence Diagram

Upon receipt of the SOAP message, Customer B's Message Broker (the data transformation engine) will unmarshal the SOAP envelope and retrieve the message content. It will also need to use the public key pair to decode the message content and transform the XML using standard build APIs into a format that is understandable by the back-end applications.

Once the message processing is done, Customer B's Message Broker will then prepare an acknowledgement message (SOAP reply message), encode and sign it with a digital signature, and return it to Firm A's Message Broker. Upon receipt of the acknowledgement message, Firm A's Message Broker will notify the back-end application that a message reply has been received.

The Standard Build Gateway may be a customized version of any existing communications gateway or a SOAP server with a customized set of APIs for data transformation, authentication, or exception handling. It is not necessary that a proprietary implementation be built from scratch. The customized SOAP-to-Standard-Build-Gateway protocol binding refers to the binding of SOAP messages to the underlying data transport of the Standard Build Gateway. If the Standard Build Gateway uses a JMS server, the SOAP-to-Standard-Build-Gateway protocol binding would simply denote SOAP messaging over JMS data transport. If the Standard Build Gateway uses a proprietary data transport implementation, then developers need to write their own data transport provider classes for the SOAP server to perform the SOAP-to-Standard-Build-Gateway protocol binding.

This Web Services integration pattern provides a standard build approach to address heterogeneous platform deployment issues. It is useful for the business scenario where the trading partners and their underlying applications are tightly coupled.

When to Use.   This Standard Build Integration pattern is suitable for trading partners who have a strong desire to standardize all message formats and interface programs on the same platform. The Standard Build Gateway can also be deployed in a large number of sites. This allows tight integration between the trading partners and their underlying applications.

EAI Versus Web Services.   With an EAI implementation, architects and developers are likely to develop some proprietary APIs and the Standard Build Gateway using the underlying EAI infrastructure. With a Web Services implementation, they may expose the common library as Web Services calls for the back-end systems to invoke. Similar to the Application-to-Application pattern, the Standard Build pattern uses JAXP to transform data from the back-end systems and uses JAXM to exchange fpML messages between the trading partners.

Risk

Although Standard Build deployment can standardize data format and interfaces, it also requires versioning management. The versioning of Web Services can be implemented by adding a version attribute in the XML message header and registering different software versions as different service bindings under the same business service in the Service Registry. Please refer to Chapter 4, Web Services Architecture and Best Practices, for more details.

Example

The Standard Build pattern has been widely used in highly centralized business environments such as the Treasury departments of international banks. For example, a top-tier British international bank deploys a Java-based Foreign Exchange system to its Treasury units worldwide. All data interfaces are provided by a Standard Build Gateway, which is deployed to the customer's site. Corporate customers (such as corresponding banks) can use their Foreign Exchange platform to connect to FXall exchange (*http://www.fxall.com*) via the Standard Build Gateway.

6.7.3   EAI Patterns

EAI Patterns are designed to provide some best practices that can be reusable for integrating with multiple systems within an enterprise. There are three variants of the EAI Patterns: Hub-Spoke Replication Pattern, Federated Replication Pattern, and Multi-Step Application Integration Pattern. They have many similarities in their approaches to resolving application integration issues. Very often, they implement the solution using a message-oriented middleware product.

Hub-Spoke Replication Pattern

Context

Large international firms or Application Service Providers often have numerous country offices around the world, each running an instance of the back-office systems. Typically, common reference data and business logic residing in these back-office systems need timely replication. The head office usually has all the customer and trade data as the master copy, and the local country offices act as spokes where the customer and trade data will be replicated. Figure 6–16 depicts a business scenario where common reference data and business transactions are replicated using a Hub-Spoke Replication Pattern.

Architects and developers can replicate business transactions to a remote trading partner or an affiliate's Web site (usually asynchronous). This assumes that the Service Provider hosts the business transactions centrally on behalf of its trading partners, affiliates, or remote country office, as in an Application Service Provider scenario. The replicated data is for local retrieval or convenience purposes.

Problem

Architects and developers need to extend the Business-to-Business integration to a larger number of trading partners (or remote country offices). Different trading part-

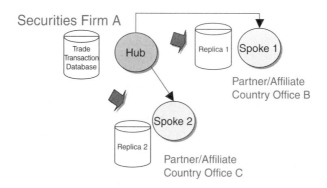

Typical Technology Used	When to Use
Synchronous/asynchronous database replication (push-pull)	Highly centralized business applications
Database/message centric applications	No geographical location constraints
EAI/Messaging middleware (e.g., RV-TX JMS with JMS Bridge or JMS-SOAP)	Local spokes are for backup/ performance benefits (e.g., faster access, MIS)

EXAMPLE

Figure 6–16   Hub-Spoke Replication Pattern

ners or remote country offices run different systems on heterogeneous platforms. The Web Services deployment needs to be highly available to different users and to cater to the heterogeneous connectivity between the systems.

Force

Large-scale deployment of Web Services to a number of different trading partners (or remote country offices) requires a scalable Hub-Spoke Replication model. If all the customer and trade data reside in a relational database, then a database replication technology can be used to replicate and synchronize all hub-spoke instances. However, if the customer and trade data reside in different systems and none of them is sharing the same underlying storage platform, then Web Services technology would be a good solution to replicate and synchronize them from the hub to all the spoke instances.

Solution

In this sample scenario, Firm A receives a business transaction. It processes the transaction and stores it centrally in the master repository. It then publishes the transaction in messages to the remote spokes.

Figure 6–17 elaborates the details using Web Services to replicate the business and trade data from the hub to the spokes. A SOAP client (also acting as the transaction client) wants to update certain customer and account data to the hub. In this example, it is assumed that the SOAP client sends a SOAP service request with XQL calls to the hub and the hub replicates the business data with the spokes using SOAP messaging. The SOAP client sends a service request to update some account information to the hub using an XQL (or JDBC) call wrapped in a SOAP message. It establishes a messaging connection with the JMS queue manager and writes the business data to the predefined queues. It also uses a hashing algorithm to generate a digital signature (DSIG) with a pair of public and private keys and wraps the business data contents in a SOAP envelope using JAXM and/or JAXP. The business data (business transactions in SOAP messages) are then published to the hub using SOAP messaging over JMS. The publishing event will be logged for tracking purposes.

Upon receipt of the business data in SOAP messages, the hub unmarshals the SOAP envelope and extracts the data contents. It needs to verify the digital signature for authenticity of the sender's credentials using the public key. It will also notify the JMS queue manager that the hub is ready to update the business transaction. The hub transforms the data contents into its local repository or database. Now the customer and account data are updated in the hub, and the hub can start replicating the contents to the spokes.

The hub starts publishing the business data to the associated spokes. If the hub-spoke connectivity is done via a relational database, then the hub can initiate a database replication process. If the hub-spoke connectivity is done via an LDAP Directory Server, then the hub can initiate LDAP-based replication based on the current LDAP

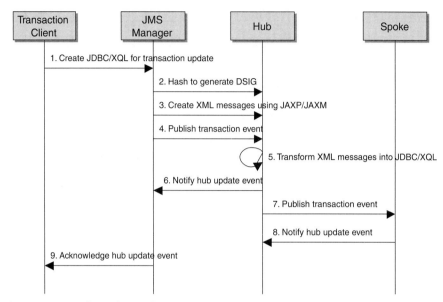

Figure 6–17   Hub-Spoke Replication Pattern Sequence Diagram

configuration settings. If the hub-spoke connectivity is heterogeneous (the spokes do not operate on the same platform), then the hub can send a SOAP message to all spokes that contains the new business data. Each spoke will then update its back-end database with the new business data. Upon completion, the spokes will return an acknowledgement SOAP message to the hub. The hub can also optionally send an alert notifying the SOAP client that the hub-spoke replication is completed.

This Web Services integration pattern provides a flexible replication solution to synchronize the hub and the spokes. It addresses the complexity of hub-spoke connectivity and the underlying platform interoperability. It is useful for central management of resources and business information.

When to Use.   The Hub-Spoke Replication Pattern is suitable for highly centralized business applications under no geographical location constraints. The local spokes are set up for backup, faster access, or MIS for better performance.

EAI Versus Web Services.   With an EAI implementation, architects and developers can use a multicast publish-subscribe model to simultaneously publish the transactions for all remote spokes to persist locally. Alternatively, they can use a database replication approach where remote spokes can pull from the centralized hub. With a Web Services implementation, they can use SOAP-JMS binding (for example, client initiating a SOAP message that contains the transaction, which is bound to a JMS client to publish or subscribe for the remote spokes or the ebXML Web Services technology (for example, Business Process Management).

Risk

Hub-Spoke Replication Pattern does not easily accommodate differences or variants in localized requirements.

Example

Many global organizations, such as computer manufacturing firms, have adopted this Hub-Spoke Replication Pattern to implement their global business operations.

UDDI Service Registry is a simplified example of the Hub-Spoke Replication Pattern. A SOAP client can update the business services and service details using JAXR. The hub (master UDDI Service Registry) can then be replicated to the spokes using the underlying platform technologies, such as DB2 database replication or LDAP replication. In this example, the SOAP client does not need to use complicated JDBC/XQL calls or JMS messaging because the JAXR is a high-level abstraction API that shields off the complexity of the underlying database or storage platform or the underlying hub-spoke replication mechanism.

Federated Replication Pattern

Context

Large international firms or Application Service Providers often have numerous country offices around the world, with each of them running similar back-end systems on different platforms. Typically, shared customer and account information in these back-office systems need to be synchronized in a timely manner to support CRM and cross-border trading. Figure 6–18 depicts a business scenario where shared customer and trade data are synchronized using a Federated Replication Pattern.

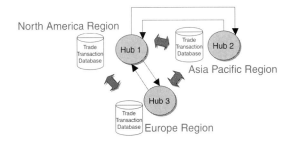

Typical Technology Used	When to Use
Synchronous/asynchronous database replication (push-push) Database/Message centric applications EAI/Messaging middleware, (e.g., RV-TX JMS with JMS Bridge or JMS-SOAP)	Highly distributed business applications with local control Geographical location constraints Partition different hubs for different products or transaction types, where replications are for back-up purpose

EXAMPLE

Figure 6–18 Federated Replication Pattern

Architects and developers replicate business transactions to peer hubs (usually asynchronous) hosted by the trading partner or affiliate's Web site. This assumes that the Service Providers and the trading partners are both hosting the business transactions.

Problem

Local market requirements cannot be easily accommodated by a highly centralized deployment strategy. Local offices and trading partners always have different requirements that need flexibility.

Force

Time to market and the need to meet local requirements are the key business drivers for the Federated Replication Pattern.

Solution

Figure 6–18 depicts a scenario where there are distributed hubs in different countries. The customer and account data need to be synchronized across the hubs. In this sample scenario, Firm A receives a business transaction. It processes the transaction and stores it centrally in its local repository. Then it publishes the transaction in messages to the peer hub for synchronization or backup.

Figure 6–19 elaborates the process with more details using Web Services to replicate the business and trade data between the hubs. The assumptions are similar to the scenario in Figure 6–17, except that the JMS queue manager will publish the business data to each hub in order to synchronize all hubs. A SOAP client (also acting as the transaction client) wants to update certain customer and account data to the federated hubs. In this example, it is assumed that the SOAP client sends a SOAP service request with XQL calls to each hub via the JMS queue manager and that the hub synchronizes the business data using SOAP messaging over JMS.

The SOAP client sends a service request to update some account information to the first hub using an XQL (or JDBC) call wrapped in a SOAP message. It establishes a messaging connection with the JMS queue manager and writes the business data to the predefined queues. It also uses a hashing algorithm to generate a digital signature (DSIG) with a pair of public and private keys and wraps the business data contents in a SOAP envelope using JAXM and/or JAXP. The business data (business transactions in SOAP messages) are then published to the hub using SOAP messaging over JMS. The publishing event will be logged for tracking purposes.

Upon receipt of the business data in SOAP messages, the first hub unmarshals the SOAP envelope and extracts the data contents. It needs to validate the digital signature for authenticity of the sender's credentials, using the public key. It will also notify the JMS queue manager that the first hub is now updated. The first hub will then transform the data contents into its local repository or database.

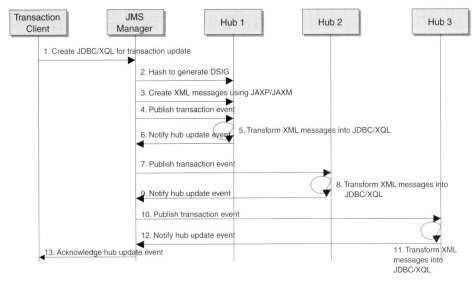

Figure 6–19 Federated Replication Pattern Sequence Diagram

Now the customer and account data are updated in the first hub, and the JMS queue manager can start publishing the business data to the other hubs. Each hub will perform similar hub processing. Upon completion of updating the business data content in the local hub, each hub will notify the JMS queue manager. When all hubs are synchronized, the SOAP client (the transaction client, or the client that initiates the transaction) will be notified.

This Web Services integration pattern provides a flexible replication solution to synchronize the federated hubs. It addresses the complexity of synchronizing different systems where customer and account data are updated in different times locally. It is useful for decentralized management of resources and business information, where a centralized hub may not be viable for various business reasons.

When to Use.   This Federated Replication Pattern is suitable for highly distributed business applications. There may be geographical constraints for the distributed applications, and sometimes architects may prefer to partition different hubs for different transaction types. The federated hubs have autonomy of their own data. However, the originating hub owns the transaction while the other hubs are replicated with a copy.

EAI Versus Web Services.   With an EAI implementation, architects and developers can use a multicast publish-subscribe model to simultaneously publish the transactions for all hubs to persist locally. Alternatively, they can use a database replication approach where remote hubs can pull from the originating hub. With a Web Services implementation, they can use SOAP-JMS binding (for example, a client initiates a

SOAP message that contains the transaction, which is bound to a JMS client to publish or subscribe for the remote hubs) or ebXML Web Services technology (for example, Business Process Management).

Risk

A highly federated operating environment will result in many variants and software versions. This will make manageability of Web Services applications challenging. Versioning of Web Services will be particularly useful to a federated operating environment. Please refer to Chapter 4, Web Services Architecture and Best Practices, for more details.

Example

Many decentralized business environments (such as regional offices of investment banks in the United States, Europe, and Asia Pacific) implement Federated Replication Pattern, as they require highly flexible operations to accommodate local market requirements in a timely manner.

Multi-Step Application Integration Pattern

Context

For complicated application processing (such as trade financing or order fulfillment with logistics management), there are multiple steps or processes to be done in order to complete a business transaction. Each process may be performed by one application. These applications may also be sharing common business data and processing partial content at different stages of the life cycle. There may be dependencies between each application, so an Integration Manager would be useful to manage these processes and enable some common processes and customer data that can be reusable by these processes. Web Services technology can be used as the lynchpin to bind these processes together and share common customer data.

Figure 6–20 shows an example of the trade-financing scenario, where there are multiple steps to process a Purchase Order and a Letter of Credit. In step 1, Publisher 1 begins to publish a Purchase Order document (Message A) to the Information Bus (the messaging infrastructure). Subscriber 1 subscribes the trade data and sends to the Message Broker (step 2) to transform the content into a format (Message B) that can be understandable by the target recipient (for example, the seller who supplies the merchandise to the buyer). In step 3, Publisher 2 is responsible for sending the business document to the target recipient via the appropriate delivery channel. Subscriber 2 subscribes to the newly transformed data in Message C (in step 4). The process in step 5 will render and transform the business data into the email delivery channel.

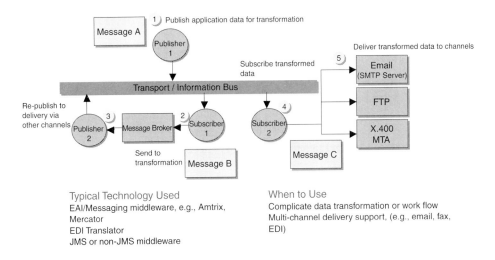

Typical Technology Used
EAI/Messaging middleware, e.g., Amtrix, Mercator
EDI Translator
JMS or non-JMS middleware

When to Use
Complicate data transformation or work flow
Multi-channel delivery support, (e.g., email, fax, EDI)

EXAMPLE

Figure 6–20   Multi-Step Application Integration Pattern

Architects and developers implement a Multi-Step Application Integration scenario (usually asynchronous) where there are dependencies between processes, and applications may be distributed in different locations.

Problem

Some Web Services applications have dependencies, which are complex transaction workflows, and have multi-step routing rules for message processing. Similar processes (such as data transformation) need to be abstracted and made sharable to reduce duplicating efforts.

Force

There may be complex processing rules or routing rules for different types of XML messages. Some of the similar processing rules can be refactored. Web Services technology can be used to expose the common processing rules so that different applications can apply during the life cycle of the business transaction.

The Multi-Step Application Integration pattern is useful for complicated data transformation or workflow and for multichannel delivery support, which requires a chain of Web Services to be invoked.

Solution

Figure 6–21 elaborates the details of the processes to manage Multi-Step Application Integration using Web Services. The seller has delivered the goods to the buyer and is ready to collect his money from the sales with the Letter of Credit collection letter. A SOAP client (the seller) initiates a service request to apply for a Letter of Credit collection and invokes a trade finance collection Web Service that triggers a chain of business services. The trade finance collection Web Service will transform the collection letter into a financial EDI message and send to the remitting bank (the seller's bank) about the receipt of a collection letter. This will allow the remitting bank to validate the relevant trade and shipping documents, confirm release of the Letter of Credit documents, and enable the applicant (the seller) to collect the money via remittance.

In this example, the SOAP client submits a transaction message (for example, a Letter of Credit collection letter document) to the Service Provider. It transforms the transaction request into XML and publishes the transaction request to the Integration Manager. The Integration Manager manages multiple processes needed to handle the entire business transaction (in this case, processing the Letter of Credit collection). It will then publish a service request to the Message Broker via the information bus to transform the business data (Letter of Credit collection letter document) into an email format that can be sent to the trading partner (in this case, the corresponding bank that handles the Letter of Credit collection letter).

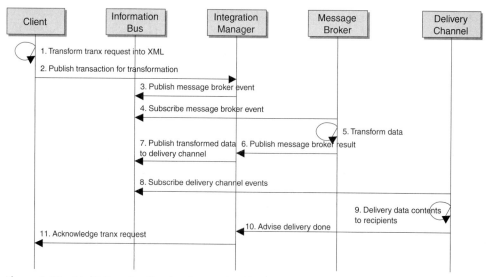

Figure 6–21 Multi-Step Application Integration Pattern Sequence Diagram

The Message Broker is a business application that transforms business documents from one format to another. It subscribes to any data transformation service request from the Information Bus. If there is a data transformation service request event from the Information Bus, the Information Bus will extract the business document and transform it into the format requested. Upon successful data transformation, the Message Broker will publish the transformed business document to the Integration Manager, who will relay it to the target delivery channel (in this case, it is an EDI message to notify the corresponding bank about the Letter of Credit collection letter).

This Web Services integration pattern eases the workflow management of complicated multi-step processes by using flexible messaging and data transformation. It also reuses existing similar processes and turns them into Web Service components. It is useful for complicated data transformation and for multichannel delivery support.

When to Use.   This Multi-step Application Integration pattern is suitable for complicated data transformation with simple workflow requirements. There are also requirements for multichannel support to render the data contents to different formats simultaneously.

EAI Versus Web Services.   With an EAI implementation, architects and developers can build custom adapters for the Message Broker component to subscribe to data transformation job orders and publish the transformed data contents back to the Information Bus. They will also need adapters for each of the different delivery channel components to subscribe to the transformed data contents. These delivery channel components include SMS gateways, WAP gateways, or EDI mailboxes. With a Web Services implementation, architects and developers can use SOAP-JMS integration similar to the previous EAI Integration Patterns.

Risk

Current Web Services workflow-related specifications (such as WSCI and BPEL4WS) are still maturing to handle complex multi-step application integration.

Example

Some B2B Exchanges (for example, Standard Chartered Bank's eXonomy) are implemented with this Multi-Step Application Integration pattern. eXonomy uses an ebXML manifest to encapsulate business documents (such as a Purchase Order or Letter of Credit) that can be passed to multiple applications within the enterprise. They have complex routing rules for processing a Purchase Order, for instance, and the order status needs to be delivered in multiple delivery channels such as email, a PDA, or a WAP phone.

6.7.4   Data Exchange Pattern

Context

Regional or international customers who open up their application platform to exchange trade data with other trading partners often require flexibility and scalability in handling multiple data formats and in interoperating with heterogeneous interface requirements from the trading partners. They also have to cater to high volumes of business transactions. This is especially complex and challenging if the customers want to provide white labeling services (aka act as an Application Service Provider for other customers), where they need to have a standards-based data exchange standard and an agile data connectivity (or exchange gateway).

Figure 6–22 shows a scenario where Securities Firm A has deployed a variety of order management systems (such as TIBMercury for Foreign Exchange trading) and a settlement system (such as SunGard STN). Customer B is a corporate customer of Firm A. Customer B places a Foreign Exchange trade order with Firm A. Firm A executes the trade order on behalf of Customer B. Upon successful execution, Customer B pays and settles with Firm A. At the end of the day, Firm A also needs to send an electronic file to reflect the daily trading activities, so that it can update its back-end account system (SAP/FI module).

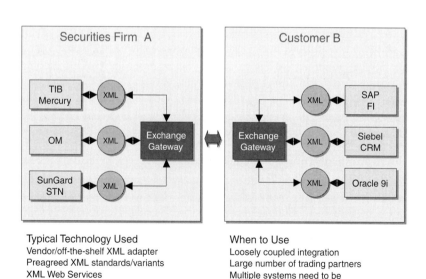

Typical Technology Used
Vendor/off-the-shelf XML adapter
Preagreed XML standards/variants
XML Web Services

When to Use
Loosely coupled integration
Large number of trading partners
Multiple systems need to be integrated

EXAMPLE

Based on: Yee & Apte. Integrating Your e-Business Enterprise. SAMS, 2001.

Figure 6–22 Data Exchange Pattern

These are a series of data exchange activities between the two trading partners. Each data exchange requires a different data format. It would be ideal to use a common Exchange Gateway to handle all required data formats and various connectivity requirements. One common way to achieve the goal of interoperability is to encapsulate the business data in XML and wrap them in SOAP messages. In other words, architects and developers need to normalize all data from the back-end applications to XML and exchange the business transaction with the trading partner in XML (either synchronous or asynchronous).

Problem

Different trading partners and back-end systems require specific data format and database connectivity. The more trading partners a customer has, the more complex the data format and the connectivity will be. Thus, there is a need to simplify the development and management of the data format and connectivity between the trading partners.

A high volume of transactions using asynchronous Web Services needs to be handled during peak hours. Thus, the scalability and throughput of the data exchange is a key challenge.

Force

The Data Exchange Integration pattern is desirable for loosely coupled processes where multiple systems need to be integrated. It is good for a large number of trading partners, where system interfaces and service components can be reusable.

XML data format provides a flexible data format where proprietary data formats can be converted. Together with an XML parser, many systems can extract and transform their proprietary data into XML, which can facilitate data exchange with other trading partners.

Scalability and reliability of SOAP messaging using asynchronous Web Services is critical to the service level.

Solution

Figure 6–23 elaborates the details of business processes to support the Data Exchange pattern using Web Services. In this sample scenario, Customer B extracts and normalizes business transactions (for example, an FX trade order) in XML, transforms the business transactions into XML using JAXP, wraps the data content with a SOAP envelope, and then sends the data content in SOAP messages to Firm A's Exchange Gateway. Firm A's Exchange Gateway handles the network connectivity and the message

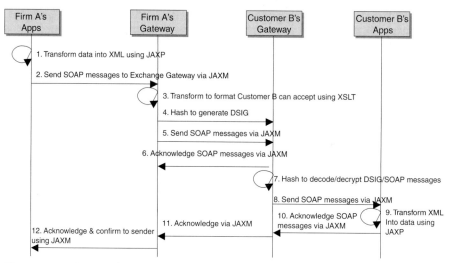

Figure 6–23 Data Exchange Pattern Sequence Diagram

exchange functions. It transforms the data content, using JAXP and XSLT, to a format that Customer B's applications can understand. Upon successful data transformation, Firm A's gateway will use a hashing algorithm to generate a digital signature (DSIG), attach it to the SOAP envelope, and send the data content in SOAP messages to Customer B's gateway using JAXM. When Customer B's gateway receives the SOAP messages, it will return with an acknowledgement.

Customer B's gateway will verify the digital signature with a public key and use a hashing algorithm to decode the data content. Upon successful verification, it will send the data content to the back-end applications in SOAP messages using JAXM. Customer B's back-end applications will perform any necessary data transformation using JAXP. Then it will return acknowledgement to Customer B's gateway, which will also return acknowledgement to Firm A's gateway and Firm A's applications.

This Web Services integration pattern allows a flexible data transformation and connectivity for a large number of trading partners who operate on heterogeneous applications and platforms.

When to Use.   This Data Exchange pattern is suitable for loosely coupled systems where there are large numbers of trading partners, and multiple applications need to be integrated simultaneously. It resembles the stock exchange-style architecture.

EAI Versus Web Services.   With an EAI implementation, architects and developers can build custom adapters for each of the back-end applications to handle message transformation. As the trading partners may be using different network connectivity, architects and developers may wish to use different Exchange Gateways that handle different network connectivity, such as SMTP, EDI, or proprietary network connectivity (as in existing stock exchanges). With a Web Services implementation, the XML data transformation is usually implemented by JAXP and XSLT, and the Exchange Gateway is implemented using SOAP messaging and/or SOAP-JMS integration.

Risk

SOAP messaging without reliable and guaranteed message delivery is a key concern for delivering high-volume transactions in the Data Exchange pattern.

Example

Equities stock trading applications and stock exchanges are candidates for implementing this Data Exchange pattern. With the increasing interest in achieving Straight-through Processing in the capital market, many brokerage firms would like to adopt a standards-based data exchange mechanism, such as using XML to exchange trade order and settlement information. ISO 15022 XML is a classic example of trade data that are represented in XML and exchanged between trading partners using a private network (such as SWIFT) or the Internet. Web Services technology using the Data Exchange Integration pattern would be a good solution approach because it provides a standards-based data exchanging mechanism and does not require both ends of the trading partners to adopt any proprietary infrastructure.

There are increasing numbers of capital market vendors supporting SOAP or ebXML messaging for B2B integration and data exchange. Examples are TIBCO's ActiveEnterprise solutions for capital markets (*http://www.tibco.com/solutions/industry_ solutions/finance/capmarkets.jsp*).

6.7.5 Process Integration Patterns

There are two variants of the Process Integration pattern: the Closed Process Integration pattern and the Open Process Integration pattern. Both have many similarities.

Closed Process Integration Pattern

Context

Business-to-Business integration often involves managing business workflow processes between trading partners. Some business processes do not need to depend on another. These are often called *closed processes.*

Figure 6–24 depicts a business scenario where each trading partner has a number of workflow processes to process the business transactions, prior to sending or receiving the business documents. Each trading partner uses a local workflow engine (Process Broker) to manage workflow and process integration. In this example, Customer

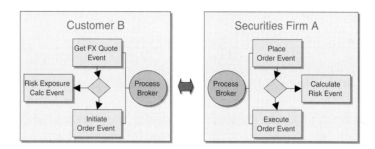

Typical Technology Used
Customized work flow integration tools
Preagreed message formats/APIs

When to Use
Tightly coupled integration
Small number of trading partners
Strong business service integration needs

EXAMPLE

Based on: Yee & Apte. Integrating Your e-Business Enterprise. SAMS, 2001.

Figure 6–24   Closed Process Integration Pattern

B wants to get a Foreign Exchange rate quote from Securities Firm A. Upon receiving a rate quote from Firm A, Customer B calculates the risk in his portfolio management system and initiates a trade order. Firm A receives the trade order and calculates the risk based on Customer B's credit risk profile. Upon approval of Customer B's risk exposure, Firm A will execute the trade order. There is no dependency of Customer B's workflow events for Firm A's workflow events.

Business process collaboration is often done by using both SOAP messaging and workflow-enabled processing tools. It also requires reliable messaging between trading partners. ebXML, using JAXM, provides more reliable messaging than SOAP messaging. It can help closed process workflow process because it has message provider classes that can provide message acknowledgement and resend messages later if the recipient is not available online.

Problem

There are complex workflow events within closed business processes. Simple SOAP messages may not be sufficient to handle workflow processing.

Force

Closed Process Integration refers to workflow processes that do not need to depend on one another. It is useful when there is tightly coupled integration between trading partners and there is a strong need for business service integration. Such Closed Process Integration is also ideal for a small number of trading partners creating some tightly coupled business services.

Solution

In this sample scenario, Customer B requests an FX quote from Firm A. Firm A responds with an FX quote. Upon Customer B's acceptance of the FX quote, Firm A will initiate a series of workflow events for account profile retrieval, risk exposure calculation, and credit checking. There is no dependency between two different sets of processes of each trading partner.

The Process Broker denotes intelligent business processes that can handle different workflow events and actions, as well as network connectivity and messaging with the corresponding Process Broker of the trading partner.

Figure 6–25 elaborates the details of the Closed Process Integration pattern using Web Services. Customer B publishes a workflow event (such as getting a Foreign Exchange rate quote) to his Process Broker. The Process Broker starts to process the workflow events and creates a service request using SOAP messaging. It uses a hashing algorithm to generate a digital signature, attaches to the SOAP envelope, and sends the SOAP messages to Firm A's Process Broker via JAXM.

Firm A's Process Broker receives the service request. It verifies the digital signature with the public key and decodes the SOAP message using a hashing algorithm. It then publishes the associated workflow events (such as check risk exposure). Upon completing the series of workflow events at Firm A, the Process Broker returns an acknowledgement to Customer B's Process Broker and Customer B respectively.

ebXML messaging using JAXM is a good technology option to handle Closed Process Integration between two trading partners. Reliable messaging between trading

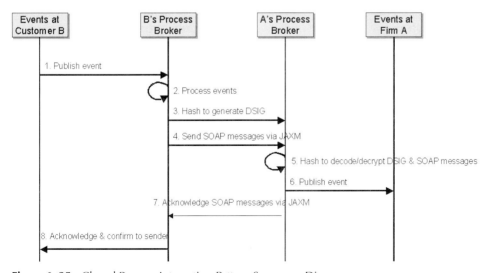

Figure 6–25 Closed Process Integration Pattern Sequence Diagram

partners is particularly important for business transactions containing high financial values. This Web Services pattern provides reliable messaging for business transactions, so that each trading partner can focus on managing its internal processes.

When to Use.   This Closed Process Integration pattern is suitable for tightly coupled integration with a small number of trading partners and strong business service integration needs.

EAI Versus Web Services.   With an EAI implementation, architects and developers can use customized workflow integration tools and preagreed message formats (or APIs) for exchange between the two trading partners. With a Web Services implementation, they can use ebXML Business Process Management tools.

Risk

Current Web Services workflow-related specifications (such as WSCI and BPEL4WS) are still maturing to handle complex multi-step application integration.

Example

Exception management for next-day settlement in the securities trading industry may be a good example. In order to manage better data quality for account information and trade transactions to support Straight-through Processing, there are many dependencies (such as account name validation and risk exposure) that need to be performed while settling a trade order transaction.

Sabre (*http://www.sabre.com*) is an example of this Closed Process Integration pattern. Sabre provides airline reservation services for a number of airlines. It uses an ebXML-based workflow engine to implement business process collaboration among its trading partners. Details can be referenced in Milo, Malks, and *MacDonald Architecting and Delivering ebXML-based Collaborative Web Services* (2003).

Open Process Integration Pattern

Context

Complex B2B integration often requires multiple business workflow processes with dependencies. Workflow processes that may depend on one another are called *open processes*. Sometimes, an external party, rather than either one of the two trading partners, handles workflow events (or shared public events), such as a call center or a managed Service Provider. In such a case (see Figure 6–26), the business documents that are exchanged between the trading partners need to reflect some information of the workflow event and the relevant workflow status. This would enable the intermediary (or the Process Broker) to route and process the workflow event accordingly.

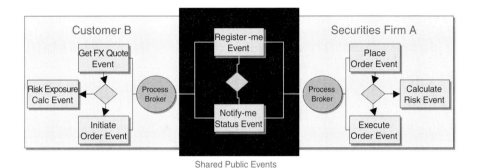

Figure 6–26   Open Process Integration Pattern

Classical messaging approaches, such as EAI and SOAP messaging, are good for exchanging business documents. However, open process collaboration requires more sophisticated workflow processing and reliable messaging. Business process collaboration is often done by using both SOAP messaging and workflow-enabled processing tools. It also requires reliable messaging between trading partners. ebXML Business Process and BPEL4WS are examples of specifications to support workflow processing.

Problem

There are complex workflow events within open business processes. Open business processes can brand sophisticated business service offerings as one single service from one Service Provider, instead of silo processes from each of the Service Providers. This will depend on two key factors: reliable messaging to handle business transactions and business process collaboration that handles complicated workflow processes. Simple SOAP messages may not be sufficient to handle workflow processing.

Force

There are workflow processing rules and sequences for different Web Services applications. Trading partners may have workflow processes that may depend on one another.

Solution

The open process scenario has many similarities with the closed process scenario. In this sample scenario, Customer B registers customer profile with Firm A ("Register-me" event.) Customer B cannot initiate any FX transactions without completion of the registration ("Notify-me" status event).

The Process Broker denotes an intelligent business process that can handle different workflow events and actions, as well as network connectivity and messaging with the corresponding Process Broker of the trading partner.

Figure 6–27 elaborates the details of Open Process Integration pattern using Web Services. Customer B publishes a workflow event (such as get a Foreign Exchange rate quote) to his Process Broker. The Process Broker starts to process the workflow events and creates a service request using a SOAP message. It uses a hashing algorithm to generate a digital signature, attaches to the SOAP envelope, and sends the workflow events using ebXML Business Process (BPSS) or BPEL4WS to Firm A's Process Broker via JAXM.

Firm A's Process Broker receives the service request. It verifies the digital signature with the public key and decodes the SOAP message using a hashing algorithm. It then publishes the associated workflow events (such as check risk exposure). Upon completing the series of workflow events at Firm A, the Process Broker returns an acknowledgement to Customer B's Process Broker and Customer B, respectively.

This Web Services pattern supports the use of business process collaboration using ebXML BPSS or BPEL4WS. ebXML BPSS or SOAP messaging using JAXM can provide reliable messaging for processing business transactions. These technologies support business transactions with high financial values using reliable message services and address the issue of implementing complex workflow processes between trading partners.

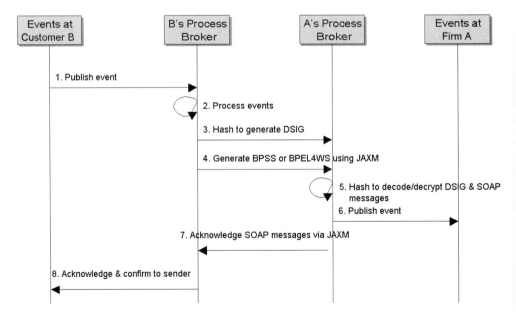

Figure 6–27   Open Process Integration Pattern Sequence Diagram

When to Use. This Open Process Integration pattern is suitable for tightly coupled processes and technical integration with a small number of trading partners. The business scenario usually denotes a strongly "co-branded" service where there is some interdependency among the different sets of business processes of each trading partner.

EAI Versus Web Services. With an EAI implementation, architects and developers can use customized workflow integration tools and preagreed message formats (or APIs) for exchange between the two trading partners. With a Web Services implementation, they can use ebXML Business Process Management tools.

Risk

Current Web Services workflow-related specifications (such as WSCI and BPEL4WS) are still maturing to handle complex multi-step application integration.

Example

A private labeled online trading service (for example, a brokerage firm offering online trading services using its trading partner's existing online trading service and application infrastructure, but with its own branding) may be a good candidate. For instance, there are open business processes (such as customer registration and risk exposure checking) that depend on one another, as the private labeled Service Provider (in this example, the brokerage firm) owns the customer account information. The underlying application infrastructure depends on the provision of the customer account information from the private labeled Service Provider.

6.7.6 Broker Integration Patterns

There are two variants of the Broker Integration Patterns: Service Consolidation–Broker Integration pattern, and Reverse Auction–Broker Integration pattern. Both have many similarities.

Service Consolidation–Broker Integration Pattern

Context

There are increasing numbers of intermediaries (aka information brokers) who offer portal services that consolidate or aggregate different business services. Content or Service Providers may be integrating with the portal service via URL rewriting, data exchange using XML and Web Services, or application-to-application interfaces (see Figure 6–28). Typically, a Partner Directory will be created (aka Yellow Pages) to list all business services. UDDI or ebXML Service Registry are usually used to implement the Partner Directory. Users (or subscribers) navigate in the Partner Directory and invoke relevant Web Services.

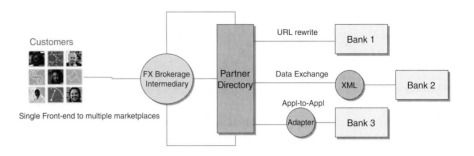

Typical Technology Used
Hyrbrid integration methods
Pre-agreed message formats/APIs
XML Web Services
HTTP/S GET or POST

When to Use
Brokering similar services with a single front-end
(service–provider neutral)
Loosely coupled process & technical integration
Large number of trading partners

EXAMPLE

Figure 6–28   Service Consolidation-Broker Integration Pattern

Architects and developers consolidate business services from a number of service providers in order to provide an added-value service. Web Services technology can be used best to aggregate business information from different information sources or content providers. This enables users to have a single front-end to access multiple marketplaces. It would be a killer application to create user-stickiness.

Problem

Different sources of Web Services need to be consolidated to present a hybrid business service with added values.

Force

Different Service Providers have different integration and security requirements. Some Service Providers have lower service-level requirements (for example, their service is not around the clock), and some have very proprietary technology that cannot be easily integrated or scaled up.

Solution

In this sample scenario, customers search and discover a variety of FX trading services from the FX Brokerage Intermediary portal's Partner Directory. The FX Brokerage Intermediary aggregates information from different sources and consolidates it for customers for better customer service. There are a variety of integration points with different local technical integration constraints.

Figure 6–29 elaborates the details of Service Consolidation–Broker Integration pattern using Web Services. A Service Requester initiates a service request from the information broker (portal). The information broker performs a UDDI service lookup for the specified business service. The UDDI Service Registry returns the URI (service end-point) to the information broker. The information broker then invokes the business service. The remote business service provided by the Service Broker (Service Provider or content provider) requires authentication. The Service Requester will then submit credentials for authentication to the information broker and the Service Broker, respectively. Upon successful authentication, the information broker will send the service request in SOAP messages using JAXM. The Service Broker will acknowledge the SOAP messages and return with the business information as requested. The information broker consolidates the business information and returns the result to the Service Requester using JAXM.

This Web Services pattern is useful for portal integration with multiple Service Providers or content providers. Traditional point-to-point partner integration requires complex technical customization for each partner's back-end application infrastructure. Using Web Services technology can lower the cost of partner integration because SOAP messaging is relatively flexible and less costly to implement. It can also accommodate different data formats and platform connectivity. Business information can easily be aggregated from multiple sources to create user-stickiness for the portal service.

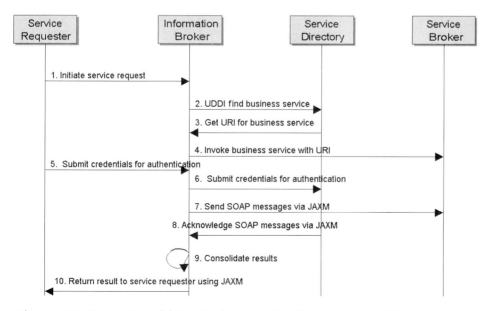

Figure 6–29   Service Consolidation–Broker Integration Pattern Sequence Diagram

When to Use.   This Service Consolidation–Broker Integration pattern is suitable for a brokerage service with a single front-end. The Brokerage Intermediary is Service-Provider neutral. The integration approach is designed to cater for loosely coupled processes with a large number of trading partners.

EAI Versus Web Services.   With an EAI implementation, architects and developers can use customized workflow integration tools to cater for different proprietary integration requirements and message formats (or APIs). With a Web Services implementation, they can use ebXML Business Process Management tools. Both XML document (asynchronous data exchange) and XML-RPC (synchronous data exchange) will be used.

Risk

The interoperability of different legacy technology used by the target service providers may be very challenging.

Example

Many emerging intermediaries, such as a third-party bill presentment service bureau, are examples of the Service Consolidation–Broker Integration pattern. Bumiputra Commerce Bank has deployed a portal service where SOAP messaging helps to extract the account information from different back-end information sources, then consolidates and delivers it to the bank's portal (refer to *http://www.sun.com/finance/docs/bumiputra.pdf*). In the recent Worldwide Analyst Conference (February 2003), Sun demonstrated a Proof of Concept developed for a brokerage firm, where RPC-based Web Services technology is used to consolidate account balance and transaction details from various banks to create an aggregated financial portfolio (aka wealth management). These are good examples illustrating the Service Consolidation–Broker Integration pattern.

SOAP messaging with JAXM is a powerful messaging API to consolidate and aggregate different information sources to implement the Service Consolidation-Broker Integration Pattern. The "Paper and Pencil" exercise at the end of this chapter will provide practice on how to send an FX option using reliable ebXML Message Service via JAXM.

Reverse Auction–Broker Integration Pattern

Context

Architects and developers consolidate business services from a number of Service Providers in order to provide the lowest-priced service. This is a reverse auction-like service brokerage (refer to Figure 6–30).

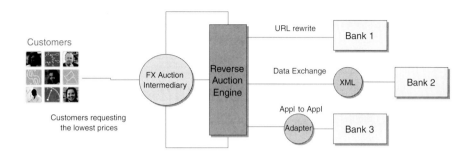

Typical Technology Used

Hyrbrid integration methods
Preagreed message formats/APIs
XML Web Services
HTTP/S GET or POST

When to Use

Brokering lowest price of similar services with a
single front-end (Service-Provider neutral)
Loosely coupled process & technical integration
Large number of trading partners
Price-sensitive & homogeneous products

EXAMPLE

Figure 6–30 Reverse Auction–Broker Integration Pattern

Problem

The reverse auction business model requires real-time messaging and integration capability to different Service Providers' back-end systems and the client's capability to respond to the offered price or services.

Force

Real-time messaging capability is required to support this auction-style business model.

Solution

In this sample scenario, customers do not need to search each Service Provider one by one from the FX Brokerage Intermediary portal's Partner Directory. They specify a criterium for the lowest FX transaction service from the FX Brokerage Intermediary. The FX Brokerage Intermediary aggregates information from different sources, then consolidates and filters information in order to locate the lowest-cost service. There are a variety of integration points with different local technical integration constraints.

Figure 6–31 elaborates the details of Reverse Auction–Broker Integration pattern using Web Services. A Service Requester initiates a service request from the information

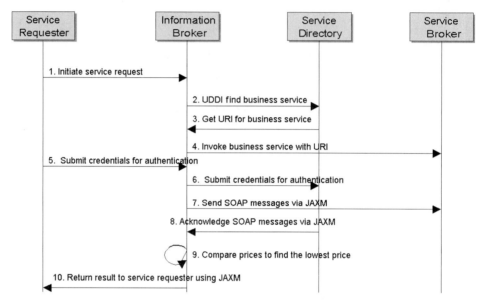

Figure 6–31   Reverse Auction–Broker Integration Pattern Sequence Diagram

broker (portal). The information broker performs a UDDI service lookup for the specified business service. The UDDI Service Registry returns the URI (service end-point) to the information broker. The information broker then invokes the business service. The remote business service provided by the Service Broker (Service Provider or content provider) requires authentication from users. The Service Requester will then submit user credentials for authentication to the information broker and the Service Broker, respectively. Upon successful authentication, the information broker will send the service request in SOAP messages using JAXM. The Service Broker will acknowledge the SOAP service request and return with business information as requested. Finally, the information broker compares the prices to find the lower price and returns the result to the Service Requester using JAXM.

This Web Services pattern is useful for reverse-auction style portal integration with multiple Service Providers or content providers. Traditional reverse auction requires highly customized point-to-point partner integration and real-time processing capability. Using Web Services technology can lower the cost of partner integration because SOAP messaging supports heterogeneous platform connectivity and real-time information processing (such as price comparison) at a lower implementation cost.

When to Use. This Reverse Auction–Broker Integration pattern is suitable for a reverse auction-like brokerage service with a single front-end. The Brokerage Intermediary is Service-Provider neutral. The integration approach is designed to cater for loosely coupled processes with a large number of trading partners. The services provided are price sensitive, time sensitive, and homogeneous.

EAI Versus Web Services. With an EAI implementation, architects and developers can use customized workflow integration tools to cater to different proprietary integration requirements and message formats (or APIs). With a Web Services implementation, they can use ebXML Business Process Management tools. Both XML document (asynchronous data exchange) and XML-RPC (synchronous data exchange) will be used.

Risk

Real-time and online Web Services can be very challenging to consolidate prices from this auction model.

Example

Auction-style Service Providers (such as eBay and Integral's CFOWeb) are potential candidates for this Web Services integration pattern.

6.7.7 How to Use Integration Patterns

In order to optimize the integration patterns, you may wish to define your integration requirements with Use Case modeling (for easier communication with vendors and partners) and chart your big picture with prioritized targets. This may not be easy as the more details you articulate, the more you see gaps and required changes.

Next, you may wish to look into the "When to Use" sections and map your integration requirements to each integration pattern to see which one is relevant Integration patterns are not mutually exclusive. Thus, you may need a hybrid or a mix-n-match of patterns.

Always use the integration framework as a guideline to identify components or areas of integration, and the protocols or standards to be used. Examine technology options for the technology used in the integration patterns. Once the integration architecture is ready and defined, you can begin to customize your integration methodology in details.

Table 6–4 and Table 6–5 recapitulate the discussion of the different integration scenarios and design patterns.

Table 6–4   Integration Patterns Summary 1

Integration Patterns	When to Use	Benefits	Consideration
Application to Application	Point-to-point exchange	Tight integration	Limited scalability
Standard Build	Strong branding Strong urge to standardize	Reduce deployment effort Standardized service, faster deployment with no customization	Consensus on standard builds
Hub-Spoke Replication Federated Replication Multi-step Application Integration	Hub-spoke business model Intra-enterprise integration	Flexible workflow integration Reliable and consistent multi-step application integration	Inter-enterprise integration with many customization options
Data Exchange	Large number of partners to integrate with heterogeneous platforms & standards	Accommodating differences in standards/interfaces	Emerging standards and technology
Closed Process Integration Open Process Integration	Shared business processes Workflow-oriented services	Richer support for process integration Cohesive and tightly integrated services	Complexity for partners to agree and implement
Service Consolidation– Broker Integration Reverse Auction– Broker Integration	Single front-end for multiple Service Providers	Added values and Service-Provider neutral	Handling service failure of partners

Table 6–5   Integration Patterns Summary 2

Integration Patterns	Typical Technology Used	Typical Standards Used	Examples
Application to Application	Customized adapters EDI translator	Proprietary XML variants	Ariba Commerce One
Standard Build	Proprietary	Proprietary	Hexagon

Table 6–5   Integration Patterns Summary 2—*continued.*

Integration Patterns	Typical Technology Used	Typical Standards Used	Examples
Hub-Spoke Replication Federated Replication Multi-step Application Integration	EAI solutions, such as Amtrix, Mercator, and TIBCO	JMS, SOAP-JMS binding	eXonomy
Data Exchange	XML Web Services	XML and SOAP, UDDI, WSDL	AIG Visa Commerce
Closed Process Integration Open Process Integration	EAI solutions or middleware, such as Sun ONE Integration Server EAI edition, XML Web Services technology	BPEL4WS	
Service Consolidation– Broker Integration Reverse Auction– Broker Integration	Hybrid of any integration technology	Hybrid of any integration standards	Yahoo! Digilogistics (obsolete) CFOWeb Vcheq (obsolete) Bumiputra Commerce Bank

6.8   Perspectives

6.8.1   Highlights

- Both EAI and Web Services technology provide similar capabilities of easier integration between systems, abstracting complex systems into simpler business services, good manageability of interfaces and infrastructure, preserving existing IT investments, and accommodating open technology standards evolution.

- Integrating data from multiple data sources across heterogeneous database vendor environments and database technology can be done using Java Web Services and XML. Several database-related XML initiatives such as XQL and DADX Web Services are still evolving. However, major database vendors have now added SQL-to-XML mapping (for example, XML extender) and XML object store (storing XML as native format in the database) support to their databases.

• We are seeing a growing trend in which many EAI vendors rebrand their legacy middleware products as Web Services. There are more choices for SOAP-JMS integration and workflow products. Needless to say, ebXML Web Services technology is becoming stronger in this space.

6.8.2   Best Practices and Pitfalls

Best Practices

• Strong business proposition (and clearly defined requirements) for service integration.

• Always start with a big picture and prioritized targets.

• Use Open Standards (such as XML Web Services) wherever possible.

• Keep the integration requirements and processes simple.

• Decouple data contents or messages from the underlying transport to ease interoperability and integration.

Pitfalls

• The integration approach and technology are too complex or too difficult to understand.

• The integration architecture has a single point of failure.

• The integration architecture is a proprietary black box.

• It requires many system changes to accommodate integration, which then affect system stability.

• It has so many point-to-point interfaces.

6.8.3   Challenge

An international investment bank, which is a key member of FXAll trading portal, is providing a private labeling online Foreign Exchange service for some small securities firms in Asia. The small securities firms do not have presence in Asia. By adapting the white labeling service, these securities firms can provide online FX trading services to their local customers using the international investment bank's infrastructure and delivery channels, but under the label of their own brands. The international investment bank has spent six months integrating with FXAll. The bank's IT management indicates to the securities firms that the white labeling integration service for the next securities firms should be three to five months.

The international investment bank is traditionally a legacy mainframe shop, with limited integration experience with Unix and external customers. Its FX trading platform is an off-the-shelf package implemented on a Unix platform using a proprietary publish-subscribe message-oriented middleware. Assuming most small-size securities firms are not sophisticated in technology and that they run either a Unix-based or a Windows-based application platform, what integration technology (EAI or Web Services) would you recommend to the international bank?

Hint: Use one of the Broker Patterns.

6.8.4   Paper and Pencil

Background

ebXML messaging is often used as the underlying technology for business process collaboration and reliable business transactions. This is particularly important to Business-to-Business integration. The following exercise will illustrate how to use JAXM to write simple ebXML messaging to place a Foreign Exchange option order.

Objective

To use the ebXML message provider using JAXM to send an XML message.

Exercise

Using the JAXM concept in Chapter 3, Web Services Technology Overview, you are to write a servlet to send an XML message (in fact, this is a Foreign Exchange option message using fpML). ebXML messaging using JAXM is almost identical to SOAP messaging using JAXM, except that ebXML messaging requires ensuring that the support profile is ebXML-based (that is, `supportedProfiles[i].equals("ebxml")`). The XML message is listed in Figure 6–32 for reference:

```
<?xml version="1.0" encoding = "UTF-8" ?>
<!DOCTYPE trade
   [
     <!- DTD declarations omitted  - ->
   ]>
```

Figure 6–32 Foreign Exchange Option Message in XML

```
<trade>
  <tradeHeader>
    <partyTradeIdentifier>
      <partyReference href = "#XYZ"/>
    </partyTradeIdentifier>
    <partyTradeIdentifier>
      <partyReference href = "#ABC"/>
    </partyTradeIdentifier>
    <tradeDate>2002-01-15</tradeDate>
  </tradeHeader>
  <fxSimpleOption>
      <productType>Nondeliverable Option</productType>
      <buyerPartyReference href = "#XYZ"/>
      <sellerPartyReference href = "#ABC"/>
      <expiryDateTime>
          <expiryDate>2002-04-09</expiryDate>
          <hourMinuteTime>1000</hourMinuteTime>
          <businessCenter>USNY</businessCenter>
      </expiryDateTime>
      <exerciseStyle>European</exerciseStyle>
  </fxSimpleOption>
  <party id = "XYZ">
      <partyId>CHASUS33</partyId>
      <partyName>XYZ BUYER BANK</partyName>
  </party>
  <party id = "ABCN">
      <partyId>ABCANL2A</partyId>
      <partyName>ABC Seller Bank</partyName>
  </party>
</trade>
<!- end of DTDs ->
```

Figure 6–32 Foreign Exchange Option Message in XML—*continued.*

The source files `ReceivingServlet.java` and `SendingServlet.java` can be found in the CD-ROM accompanying this book under /labs/ch6. They are also listed here for reference (refer to the excerpts in Figures 6–33 through 6–39).

Step 1: Write the SendingServlet.java
The sender client `SendingServlet.java` (see Figure 6–33) creates a connection to the Message Factory using an ebXML support profile (highlighted as follows). It uses standard JAXP to construct an ebXML Manifest, a SOAP header, and a body. The SOAP message contains the XML message from Figure 6–32.

```
package myRemote.sender;

import java.net.*;
import java.io.*;
import java.util.*;

import javax.servlet.http.*;
import javax.servlet.*;

import javax.xml.messaging.*;
import javax.xml.soap.*;

import javax.activation.*;
import com.sun.xml.messaging.jaxm.ebxml.*;


import org.apache.commons.logging.*;

public class SendingServlet extends HttpServlet {
    private static Log logger =
LogFactory.getLog("Samples/myRemote");

    private String from
="http://www.wombats.com/remote/sender";
    private String to =
"http://www.wombats.com/remote/sender";
    private String data =
"http://127.0.0.1:8080/myRemote/index.html";

    private ProviderConnectionFactory pcf;
    private ProviderConnection pc;
    private MessageFactory mf = null;

    private static final String providerURI =

"http://java.sun.com/xml/jaxm/provider";

    public void init(ServletConfig servletConfig)
throws ServletException {
        super.init( servletConfig );
```

Figure 6–33 SendingServlet.java Sends an XML Message in ebXML Using JAXM

```
        try {
        pcf = ProviderConnectionFactory.newInstance();
        pc = pcf.createConnection();
        } catch(Exception e) {
            logger.error("Unable to open connection to
the provider", e);
        }

        InputStream in =
servletConfig.getServletContext().
                getResourceAsStream("/WEB-
INF/address.properties");

        if (in != null) {
            Properties props = new Properties();

            try {
                props.load(in);

            String from = props.getProperty("from");
                String to = props.getProperty("to");
                String data =
props.getProperty("data");
            if (from != null)
                this.from = from;
                if (to != null)
                    this.to = to;
                if (data != null)
                    this.data = data;
            } catch (IOException ex) {
                // Ignore
            }
        }
    }

    public void doGet(HttpServletRequest req,
HttpServletResponse resp)
        throws ServletException

    {
        try {
```

Figure 6–33   SendingServlet.java Sends an XML Message in ebXML Using JAXM—
continued.

```
            // Create a message factory.
        if (mf == null) {
            ProviderMetaData metaData =
pc.getMetaData();
            String[] supportedProfiles =
metaData.getSupportedProfiles();
            String profile = null;

            for(int i=0; i < supportedProfiles.length;
i++) {
                if(supportedProfiles[i].equals("ebxml")) {
                    profile = supportedProfiles[i];
                break;
                }
            }
                mf = pc.createMessageFactory(profile);
        }


            // Create a message from the message
factory.
            EbXMLMessageImpl ebxmlMsg =
(EbXMLMessageImpl)mf.createMessage();

        ebxmlMsg.setSender(new Party(from));
        ebxmlMsg.setReceiver(new Party(to));

        Service service = new
Service("FXOrderProcessing");
        ebxmlMsg.setRefToMessageId("20001209-133003-
28572@example.com");

ebxmlMsg.setCPAId("http://www.nextfrontiers.com/cpas/
ourcpawithyou.xml");
        ebxmlMsg.setConversationId("20001209-133003-
28572");
        ebxmlMsg.setService(service);
        ebxmlMsg.setAction("NewFXSpotOrder");
        Manifest manifest = new Manifest("manifest",
"1.0");
```

Figure 6–33   SendingServlet.java Sends an XML Message in ebXML Using JAXM—
continued.

```
        Reference ref = new Reference("pay01",
"cid:pay01",
                "http://regrep.org/gci/fxOrder");

        Schema schema = new Schema(
                "http://regrep.org/gci/fpML.xsd",
                "1.0");

        ref.setSchema(schema);

        Description desc = new Description("en-us");
        desc.setText("FX Spot Rate Order for Next
Frontiers Ltd.");
        ref.setDescription(desc);
        manifest.addReference(ref);
        ebxmlMsg.setManifest(manifest);

        SOAPPart soapPart = ebxmlMsg.getSOAPPart();
        SOAPEnvelope envelope =
soapPart.getEnvelope();

        Name name = envelope.createName("trade" ,
"fx",
            "http://www.nextfrontiers.com/fxOption/");
        SOAPBody body = envelope.getBody();
        SOAPBodyElement trade =
body.addBodyElement(name);
        SOAPHeader header = envelope.getHeader();
        SOAPHeaderElement headerElement =
header.addHeaderElement(name);
        // create tradeHeader
        Name childName =
envelope.createName("tradeHeader");
        SOAPElement tradeHeader =
trade.addChildElement(childName);

        childName =
envelope.createName("partyTradeIdentifier");
        SOAPElement partyTradeIdentifier =
tradeHeader.addChildElement(childName);
```

Figure 6–33   SendingServlet.java Sends an XML Message in ebXML Using JAXM— *continued.*

```
            childName =
envelope.createName("partyReference");
            SOAPElement partyReference =
partyTradeIdentifier.addChildElement(childName);
            childName = envelope.createName("href");
            partyReference.addAttribute(childName,
"#XYZ");

            Name childName2 =
envelope.createName("partyTradeIdentifier");
            SOAPElement partyTradeIdentifier2 =
tradeHeader.addChildElement(childName2);

            childName2 =
envelope.createName("partyReference");
            SOAPElement partyReference2 =
partyTradeIdentifier2.addChildElement(childName2);
            childName2 = envelope.createName("href");
            partyReference2.addAttribute(childName2,
"#ABC");

            // create fxSimpleOption
            Name childName3 =
envelope.createName("fxSimpleOption");
            SOAPElement fxSimpleOption =
trade.addChildElement(childName3);

            childName3 =
envelope.createName("productType");
            SOAPElement productType =
fxSimpleOption.addChildElement(childName3);
            productType.addTextNode("Nondeliverable
options");

            childName3 =
envelope.createName("buyerPartyReference");
            SOAPElement buyerPartyReference =
fxSimpleOption.addChildElement(childName3);
            childName3 = envelope.createName("href");
            buyerPartyReference.addAttribute(childName3,
"#XYZ");
```

Figure 6–33   SendingServlet.java Sends an XML Message in ebXML Using JAXM—
continued.

```
         childName3 =
envelope.createName("sellerPartyReference");
         SOAPElement sellerPartyReference =
fxSimpleOption.addChildElement(childName3);
         childName3 = envelope.createName("href");
         sellerPartyReference.addAttribute(childName3,
"#ABC");

         childName3 =
envelope.createName("expiryDateTime");
         SOAPElement expiryDateTime =
fxSimpleOption.addChildElement(childName3);
         childName3 =
envelope.createName("expiryDate");
         SOAPElement expiryDate =
expiryDateTime.addChildElement(childName3);
         expiryDate.addTextNode("2002-04-09");
         childName3 =
envelope.createName("hourMinuteTime");
         SOAPElement hourMinuteTime =
expiryDateTime.addChildElement(childName3);
         hourMinuteTime.addTextNode("1000");
         childName3 =
envelope.createName("businessCenter");
         SOAPElement businessCenter =
expiryDateTime.addChildElement(childName3);
         businessCenter.addTextNode("USNY");

         childName3 =
envelope.createName("exerciseStyle");
         SOAPElement exerciseStyle =
fxSimpleOption.addChildElement(childName3);
         exerciseStyle.addTextNode("European");

         // create party information
         Name childName4 =
envelope.createName("party");
         SOAPElement party =
trade.addChildElement(childName4);
         childName4 = envelope.createName("id");
         party.addAttribute(childName4, "XYZ");
```

Figure 6–33   SendingServlet.java Sends an XML Message in ebXML Using JAXM—
continued.

```
        childName4 = envelope.createName("partyId");
        SOAPElement partyId =
party.addChildElement(childName4);
        partyId.addTextNode("CHASUS33");

        childName4 = envelope.createName("partyName");
        SOAPElement partyName =
party.addChildElement(childName4);
        partyName.addTextNode("XYZ BUYER BANK");

        Name childName5 =
envelope.createName("party");
        SOAPElement party2 =
trade.addChildElement(childName5);
        childName5 = envelope.createName("id");
        party2.addAttribute(childName5, "ABCN");

        childName5 = envelope.createName("partyId");
        SOAPElement partyId2 =
party2.addChildElement(childName5);
        partyId2.addTextNode("ABCANL2A");

        childName5 = envelope.createName("partyName");
        SOAPElement partyName2 =
party2.addChildElement(childName5);
        partyName2.addTextNode("ABC Seller Bank");

        URL url = new URL(data);

        AttachmentPart ap =
            ebxmlMsg.createAttachmentPart(new
DataHandler(url));

        ap.setContentType("text/html");

        // Add the attachment part to the message.
        // You can attach an EDI (UN/EDIFACT or ANSI
X12) message, image or digital signature
        ebxmlMsg.addAttachmentPart(ap);

        System.err.println("Sending FX Spot Order in
fpML to : "+ebxmlMsg.getTo());
```

Figure 6–33 SendingServlet.java Sends an XML Message in ebXML Using JAXM—
continued.

```
        System.err.println("Sent message is logged in
\"sent.msg\"");

        FileOutputStream sentFile = new
FileOutputStream("sent.msg");
        ebxmlMsg.writeTo(sentFile);
        sentFile.close();

        pc.send(ebxmlMsg);
            String retval =
        "<html> <H4> FX Spot Rate Order delivered to
Broker Firm.</H4></html>";
        OutputStream os = resp.getOutputStream();
        os.write(retval.getBytes());
        os.flush();
        os.close();

        } catch(Throwable e) {
        e.printStackTrace();
            logger.error("Error in constructing or
sending message "
                        +e.getMessage());
        }
    }
}
```

Figure 6–33 SendingServlet.java Sends an XML Message in ebXML Using JAXM—*continued.*

The recipient client `ReceivingServlet.java` creates a connection to the Message Factory class using an ebXML implementation. The underlying messaging is still using SOAP messaging via JAXM. The source code is shown in Figure 6–34:

```
package myRemote.receiver;

import javax.xml.messaging.*;
import javax.xml.soap.*;
import javax.servlet.*;
import javax.servlet.http.*;
```

Figure 6–34 ReceivingServlet.java Receives an XML Message Using JAXM

```
import javax.xml.transform.*;

import java.io.*;
import java.util.Enumeration;

import org.apache.commons.logging.*;
import com.sun.xml.messaging.jaxm.ebxml.*;

public class ReceivingServlet extends JAXMServlet
implements OnewayListener {
    private static Log logger =
LogFactory.getLog("Samples/myRemote");

    private ProviderConnectionFactory pcf;
    private ProviderConnection pc;
    private static final String providerURI =

"http://java.sun.com/xml/jaxm/provider";

    //private MessageFactory messageFactory;

    public void init(ServletConfig servletConfig)
throws ServletException {
        super.init(servletConfig);
    try {
        pcf = ProviderConnectionFactory.newInstance();
        pc = pcf.createConnection();
        setMessageFactory(new
EbXMLMessageFactoryImpl());
    }catch (Exception e) {
        e.printStackTrace();
        throw new ServletException(
          "Couldn't initialize Receiving servlet " +
e.getMessage());
    }
    }

    public void onMessage(SOAPMessage message) {
        System.out.println("On message called in
receiving servlet");
```

Figure 6–34 ReceivingServlet.java Receives an XML Message Using JAXM—*continued.*

```
        try {
            System.out.println("Here's the message:
");
        message.saveChanges();
            message.writeTo(System.out);
        } catch(Exception e) {
            logger.error("Error in processing or
replying to a message", e);
        }
    }
}
```

Figure 6–34   ReceivingServlet.java Receives an XML Message Using JAXM—*continued.*

Step 2: Write the build.xml File

An ANT build script (`build.xml`) is created to compile the Java source code (servlets) and deploy the servlets in war files under the Web Container. It reads in a property file `jaxm.properties` to set the variables and paths. The `build.xml` can be found under `/opt/myRemote/build.xml`.

Step 3: Compile Source Codes

To compile the source code (project name inside the build file is called myRemote), you may execute the following commands in a command prompt (Windows platform) or Unix terminal (Unix platform). Figure 6–35 shows the script and the result on a Windows platform.

```
D:\opt\myRemote>ant
Buildfile: build.xml

set.available:

check.jaxm:

check.saaj:

check.appname:

check.servlet:
```

Figure 6–35   Compile myRemote Source Codes

```
checks:

build.dir.webapps:

build.dir.local:

init:
     [echo] ____ Building myRemote to /opt/temp

prepare.build:
    [mkdir] Created dir: D:\opt\temp\myRemote
    [mkdir] Created dir: D:\opt\temp\myRemote\WEB-INF
    [mkdir] Created dir: D:\opt\temp\myRemote\WEB-
INF\src
    [mkdir] Created dir: D:\opt\temp\myRemote\WEB-
INF\classes
     [copy] Copying 4 files to D:\opt\temp\myRemote

prepare:

compile:
    [javac] Compiling 2 source files to
\opt\temp\myRemote\WEB-INF\classes
     [copy] Copying 2 files to
D:\opt\temp\myRemote\WEB-INF
     [copy] Copying 1 file to
D:\opt\temp\myRemote\WEB-INF\classes

main:

BUILD SUCCESSFUL
Total time: 7 seconds
```

Figure 6–35 Compile myRemote Source Codes—*continued.*

Step 4: Deploy as war Files
To deploy the compiled servlets (project name inside the build file is called
myRemote), you may execute the following commands in a command prompt
(Windows platform) or Unix terminal (Unix platform). Figure 6–36 shows the
script and the result on a Windows platform.

The war file created is placed under D:\opt\temp\war\myRemote.war.
This needs to be copied to the webapps directory of your Web Container (for example, D:\Dev\WSDP\webapps).

```
D:\opt\myRemote>ant war
Buildfile: build.xml

set.available:

check.jaxm:

check.saaj:

check.appname:

check.servlet:

checks:

build.dir.webapps:

build.dir.local:

init:
     [echo] ____ Building myRemote to /opt/temp

prepare.build:

prepare:

compile:

main:

war:
      [jar] Building jar: D:\opt\temp\war\myRemote.war

BUILD SUCCESSFUL
Total time: 2 seconds
```

Figure 6–36 Deploy myRemote Servlets

Step 5: Test Run
The Tomcat engine needs to be started. On a Windows platform, start the
Tomcat server by clicking Start | Java Web Services Developer
Pack 1_0_01 | Start Tomcat on the desktop. On a Unix platform, start

by issuing the command `/startup.sh` from your Java Web Services Developer Pack installation location (for example, `/opt/jwsdp/bin`).

From a Web browser, issue the URL *http://localhost:8080/myRemote/index.html.* You should see the following screens in Figure 6–37 and Figure 6–38.

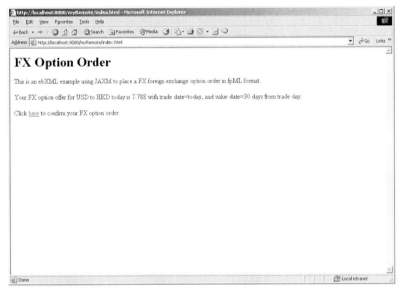

Figure 6–37   User Interface to Send XML Message Using ebXML With JAXM

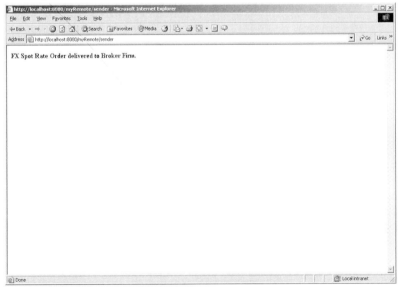

Figure 6–38   Confirmation of Receipt of the XML Message Using ebXML With JAXM

Step 6: Verify Sent Log

The ebXML message provider has sent and received logs. If the XML message is not yet received due to potential system unavailability of the recipient, the ebXML message provider will resend the message when the recipient resumes operations. Figure 6–39 shows the sent log of the ebXML message provider. The receive log is similar.

Figure 6–39   ebXML Message Provider Sent Log

6.8.5   References

Web Services and EAI

Mikhail Genkin and Jin Li. *"Web Services and J2EE Connectors for B2B Integration." http://www-106.ibm.com/developerworks/library/j-conn/index.html*

Matjaz B. Juric, Jeelani Basha, Rick Leander, and Ramesh Nagappan. *Professional J2EE EAI.* Birmingham, UK: Wrox, 2001.

Matjaz B. Juric and Marjan Hericko. "J2EE, EAI and Web Services: New Challenges for your Information Systems." *Web Services Journal,* May 2002.

J. P. Morgenthal. "Web Services for Enterprise Application Integration: What Solutions are Offered for the Enterprise Today." *Web Services Journal,* May 2002.

Carol Murphy. "Will Web Services Mean the End for EAI?" *Web Services Journal,* May 2002.

Gunjan Samtani and Dimple Sadhwani. "J2EE-based Application Servers, Web Services and EAI." *Web Services Journal,* May 2002.

Andre Yee and Atul Apte. *Integrating Your e-Business Enterprise.* Indianapolis, IN: SAMS, 2001.

Emerging Technologies
Java Connector Architecture
Dale Green and Beth Stearns. "J2EE Connector Architecture." *J2EE Tutorial.*

http://java.sun.com/j2ee/tutorial/1_3-fcs/doc/Connector.html

J2EE Connector Architecture version 1.5 specification.

http://java.sun.com/j2ee/download.html#connectorspec

Phil Wakelin, Martin Keen, Richard Johnson, and Daniel Cerecedo Diaz. *Java Connectors for CICS: Featuring the J2EE Connector Architecture.* San Jose, CA: IBM Redbooks, March 2002.

http://publib-b.boulder.ibm.com/Redbooks.nsf/RedbookAbstracts/sg246401.html

ebXML-based Web Services
ebXML technical specification.

http://www.ebxml.org/specs/index.htm#technical_specifications

A list of ebXML products and implementation.

http://www.ebxml.org/implementations/index.htm

Paul Milo, Dan Malks, and John MacDonald. "Architecting and Delivering ebXML-based Collaborative Web Services." SunNetwork Conference, 2003.

SOAP-JMS Integration
Kal Ahmed et al. *Professional Java XML.* Birmingham, UK: Wrox, 2001.

Database and XML Web Services
Joan Hagarty. "XML and WebSphere Studio Application Developer—Part 3: SQL and XML Together." *IBM WebSphere Developer Technical Journal,* February 2002.

http://www7b.software.ibm.com/wsdd/techjournal/0202_haggarty/haggarty.html

Brian C. Reed. "Data—a Key Part of Web Services." *Web Services Journal,* May 2002.

Chapter 7

WEB SERVICES SECURITY

7.1   Chapter Overview

- Many firewall configurations have filtered IP ports that block client applications from invoking applications and EJBs using RMI and RPC. Web Services applications, on one hand, address firewall filtering features by utilizing the default IP port 80 or port 8080 and decoupling the data transport from the physical transport layer. On the other hand, they also open up new areas of security integration requirements, including key management, digital signature generation, authentication between trading partners, and application host (Solaris or Windows) security hardening. Architects and developers may overlook some of these security areas because they usually focus on the SOAP message security alone.

- WS-Security is a new security specification proposed to W3C from IBM, Microsoft, and VeriSign. The design objective is to provide a consolidated security framework to accommodate different security tokens (such as X.509v3 and Kerberos ticket), trust domains, multiple digital signature formats, and encryption technologies. It is intended to supersede the previous SOAP-SEC, WS-Security, WS-license, and various security token and encryption mechanisms.

- Network identity management with Single Sign-on is the key attraction for B2B integration and cross-enterprise integration. Project Liberty is collaborating different XML security initiatives such as SAML to provide industry-wide specifications for Single Sign-on, federated data exchange, B2B transaction support, and a reliable Web Services security framework.
- Today's Web Services security is primarily dealing with SOAP security and digital signature for XML messages. There are also work-in-progress Web Services security initiatives that cover key management (XKMS), security tokens and encryption (WS-Security), Single Sign-on (SAML), and network identity (Project Liberty). However, they are designed to address a specific problem space, not the entire end-to-end security framework for implementing Web Services technology.

7.2 Chapter Objectives

- To outline an end-to-end Web Services security framework that can address the security requirements by establishing a trust model of key management, authentication, and transactional security mechanisms.
- To identify recent initiatives on Web Services security standards, their design features, and the implications of implementing reliable Web Services applications.

7.3 Some Myths and Common Beliefs

Developers and architects who have been tracking Web Services security may have encountered the myth about its weak security capability from various magazines and news organizations. There is a common belief that SOAP calls can pass information in XML clear text across firewalls and servers, and this may expose the risk of hacker attacks and exploits. The myth also claims that the current security protection of using HTTPS is insufficient. If we consider SOAP to be the only Web Services technology, then the myth is a self-fulfilling prophecy. Nevertheless, there is more to Web Services security than simply SOAP.

The followings are examples of some myths about Web Services that are *not true*.

SOAP Security Is *the* Web Services Security. Early Web Services books and articles focused on SOAP security in the context of Web Services security, which may have led to this myth. There are new additional specifications such as SOAP-SEC (SOAP security), XML-ENC (encryption), and XML-DSIG (digital signature), but none of them is designed to cover all aspects of Web Services. Thus, it is unfair to assume that SOAP security alone covers the realm of Web Services security.

Demythicization: Web Services security does not rely on SOAP messaging security alone. Web Services security should cover end-to-end applications and services, from network layer to application layer. SOAP message security is only a part of the end-to-end Web Services security.

HTTPS Is *the* Secure Network Transport for Web Services. The underlying transport of SOAP messages is HTTP and HTTPS. Due to the nature of stateless HTTP/S, synchronous SOAP messages do not support guaranteed message delivery. However, asynchronous SOAP messages can use SMTP or Java Messaging Service (JMS) where message delivery and acknowledgement can be assured. There are different security implications for different underlying transports. HTTPS assures that the connection between the client and the server is reasonably secure with 128-bit SSL. JMS often relies on data encryption and digital signatures for security protection. The SMTP security, if without a digital signature, is generally weaker when compared with HTTPS and JMS.

Demythicization: HTTPS provides data transport security from client browser to the server. To ensure end-to-end security, there are other components of Web Services security data transport that need to be used.

Passing XML Data in Clear Text Is Insecure. It is insecure for financial transactions or if private customer data is transmitted in XML clear text *without encryption,* even though this is within the intranet and behind the demilitarized zone (DMZ). It is easy to sniff into a LAN environment for clear text in SOAP messages. However, as a good practice, the sensitive data in the SOAP messages is typically encrypted and signed with a digital signature to support non-repudiation. Therefore, the SOAP messages can be secure with digital signature and encryption, provided there is no compromise in the key management or exploit in the client or host.

Demythicization: Passing XML data in clear text is insecure *if done without encryption.*

Dependency on PKI Implementation. SOAP messages do not necessarily rely on PKI implementation. Information that is not open to the public, or is not sensitive, can be sent in clear XML text if there is no requirement to encrypt or protect the data contents.

Demythicization: The XML Key Management Specification (XKMS) is an initiative to provide public/private key management services for secure business transactions, without having to invest into an expensive Public Key Infrastructure implementation (such as implementing a Certificate Management Server and setting up processes to be an internal Certificate Authority). Refer to the section on XKMS later in this chapter for more details.

Using Digital Signatures Alone for Web Services Applications Is Secure. SOAP messages can be secured with digital signatures using security tokens such as X.590v3 digital certificates or Kerberos tickets. However, Web Services security requires end-to-end protection, ranging from client, host, network transport, messages, and applications. Key management and network identity management are two other important areas.

Demythicization: Web Services Security is end-to-end. Digital signature is a mechanism to address non-repudiation. There are other aspects of security requirements to be considered.

7.4 Web Services Security Requirements

Security sometimes is an afterthought until something unpleasant happens or a security loophole is reported. Security is a process. The security requirements are the key drivers for the Web Services security framework. They relate the security concerns to different areas of Web Services technology during the initial design and implementation stage. It would be useful to put these requirements into scenarios to get the appropriate perspective.

Authentication.   The client accessing the business services, which may be a Web browser, PDA, or WAP phone, needs to be authenticated with reliable credentials. Reliable credentials may be passwords, X.509v3 digital certificates, Kerberos tickets, or any secure token and are used to validate the identity of the Service Requester. This is paramount to Web Services because the business services, which are provided by a third party or a remote Service Provider from overseas, may incur high monetary value payment transactions using credit cards.

Authorization/Entitlement.   Upon successful authentication, a client requests access to business services, whether locally or remotely. Because Web Services are "programmatic" interfaces, they are harder to monitor for suspicious activities. Therefore, it is crucial that there is proper access control for each business service invoked. In other words, each network identity should be entitled with access rights for the local or remote service and the access level of the Service Requester checked against a list of resource access rights at run time. The access request can be granted and the Web Services invoked upon successful authorization, or denied if insufficient access rights are identified.

Traceability.   Each transactional Web Services call should be logged at the level of Web Services invocation and transport layer. This is in addition to the transaction log taken by the local or remote applications. In such a case, administrators can track and trace the service request at different points within the life cycle. For example, the HTTP/S activities can be tracked from the Web server's audit and log, and the XML-RPC SOAP calls can be traced from the SOAP server log.

Data Privacy and Confidentiality.   Data privacy keeps information confidential, so that only the data owner and the target recipient are able to read it. Data privacy and confidentiality is usually accomplished using encryption. Web Services technology should be able to accommodate different encryption mechanisms (such as RSA-MD2, RSA-MD5, SHA, and NIST) with different key length (which may be subject to some countries' export regulations—for example, 128-bit encryption key for SSL may be restricted to certain countries).

Availability/Denial of Service.   Denial of Service is often employed to attack Web sites and business services that have sophisticated security features. However, no matter how sophisticated these business services are, they may still be vulnerable to a Denial of Service attack. It is useful to profile the loading and capacity for each Web Services call so that appropriate preventive measures, such as load balancing, packet filtering, virus checking, failover, or backup, can be designed to protect from any potential Denial of Service.

Data Integrity.   Transactions and private data, if transmitted in XML clear text, may be intercepted, modified, or tampered with. The use of different encryption mechanisms can protect the data from retrieval. However, if the keys are compromised, then a middleman or a replay attack may tamper with the data. Thus, in addition to encryption, checksums and MAC'ing, as part of the XML elements, are good tools to support data integrity.

Non-repudiation.   Increasing cross-enterprise data exchanges and B2B integration would require support for non-repudiation. It has a legal implication. Digital signature using digital certificates (such as PKI X.509v3) or Kerberos tickets (such as Microsoft PASSPORT) is a key element to provide non-repudiation. Non-repudiation enables users to prove that a transaction has been committed with valid credentials. This prevents any trading partner from claiming that the transaction never occurred. The support of non-repudiation requires logging details of the transactions at each point of exchange (including the application server at both ends), digital signatures along with the transactions, and a mechanism that ensures the logs and credentials are authentic.

7.4.1   The Big Picture

To get the big picture of end-to-end Web Services, it is important for us to understand the security stack of Web Services technology, the security characteristics of each layer, their potential point of attacks, and examples of the commercial implementation. Next, it is important to understand how trust models are built and the related threat profiling, where we can design risk mitigation mechanism.

Web Services Security Stack

The security stack shown in Table 7–1 is ideal for designing Web Services applications. The approach to protecting Web Services security involves using different security technology and tools at each layer.

Table 7–1   Web Services Security Stack

	Security Mechanism	Examples of Security Protection	Security Standards Specifications
Service Negotiation	Identity management Access control and policy management Single Sign-on	Liberty-compliant Identity Server Access control for XML messages Single Sign-on products	*Identity management*— Liberty 1.1, XML Key Management Specification (XKMS), WS-Federation *Entitlement*—SAML, XACML, WS-Authorization *Policy*—WS-Policy *Others*—WS-Secure Conversation, WS-Trust, WS-Privacy
Service Discovery	Service Registry security	UDDI Service Registry security features Protection for WSDL documents	UDDI WSDL
Transaction Routing	Messaging security	Data encryption Digital signature Key management and managing credentials	XML Encryption (XML-ENC) XML Signature (XML-DSIG) WS-Security XKMS

Table 7–1   Web Services Security Stack—*continued.*

	Security Mechanism	Examples of Security Protection	Security Standards Specifications
Transport	Data transport security	128-bit SSL with HTTPS Protocol security for FTP, SMTP, and so forth	HTTPS HTTPR IPSec
Internet	Network connectivity security	Leased line or router-level encryption Virtual Private Network (VPN) gateways	
Platform	Operating system security Penetration testing Key exchanges between hosts	Solaris OE™ hardening Linux Operating System (OS) hardening Windows OS hardening Professional Penetration Testing	

Platform Security

The platform security is essential to protecting the Service Provider and the Requester (Consumer). This is often the target for security attacks or exploitation—for example, a Denial of Service attack for SOAP servers may result in no service available even if the back-end applications are still running. To mitigate the platform security risks, architects and developers may use Operating System security hardening and penetration tests to secure the platform.

Internet or Network Layer Security

The Internet layer is using the TCP/IP protocol. A Virtual Private Network (VPN) gateway is one common way to protect Web Services applications deployed using the public Internet. This is in conjunction with using HTTPS and SSL for secure tunneling between the client and the server. Both trading partners need to establish a VPN tunnel.

Transport Layer Security

HTTPS is an authentication protocol using a secure tunneling between the client and the server. It encodes the transmissions between the client and the server using Secure Sockets Layer (usually 128-bit SSL). As HTML form-based authentication passes user id and password information in clear text, the use of HTTPS addresses the security issue of passing such data in clear text over HTTP. Often, Web Services applications are distributed, and HTTPS alone will not be sufficient to protect distributed Web Services from end to end. HTTPR is a specification from IBM to provide guaranteed message delivery of SOAP messages over HTTPS (*http://www. 106.ibm.com/developerworks/webservices/library/ws-phtt/*). It was not submitted to W3C, but it was being discussed under W3C Web Services discussion forum. The ebXML Message Service (*http://www.ebxml.org/specs/ebMS2.pdf*), which uses SOAP messaging as the transport and routing layer, is another initiative that provides reliable message delivery over HTTPS.

IPSec is another security protocol on top of TCP/IP that protects the IP connectivity between the client and the server at the IP data-packet level. This provides additional transport-layer security, in conjunction with HTTPS. Most operating system platforms, such as Windows 2000/XP and Solaris 8 OE, have built-in IPSec today.

Another useful security protection in conjunction with the network layer is host security hardening. This ensures the network services of the host infrastructure can be hardened and secured.

Transaction Routing

XML encryption, together with digital signatures, is a key means to protect sensitive data during message routing. Users can sign before they encrypt data or encrypt data before they sign. There are a few encryption algorithms supported, such as block encryption and chain mode. XML encryption and digital signatures are covered in both XML-ENC and WS-Security. There are commercial implementations of these standards, including IBM's XML Security Suite, Baltimore's Keytools, Microsoft's CAPICOM, and Sun's J2SE 1.4 security features (JCE, JSEE, Java CertPath, JAAS, and JGSS).

Service Discovery

Web Services are discovered and bound to Web Services Description Language (WSDL) at run time. Many commercial implementations of the Service Registry use LDAP (for example, Sun ONE Registry Server) or RDBMS (for example, IBM UDDI), which require access rights for read access or administrative update. None of the service information is stored in clear text. Web Services can be discovered using a WSDL file, without UDDI. However, WSDL files are often stored in clear text and may be another target for attack. This needs to be addressed by security hardening of the host and a file-protection mechanism.

Service Negotiation

After service discovery, Web Services are negotiated and invoked upon successful authentication. XKMS is one important security initiative to support a managed trust service (key management and identity authentication outsourced to an external trusted authority), as well as a home-grown trust service (customers performing authentication and key management). The security risk will be dependent on the trust level and reliability of the external or internal Trust Authority. Examples of XKMS implementation include VeriSign's Trust Services Integration Kit.

Upon successful authentication, Web Services Service Providers will retrieve the access rights and profile for the Service Requester. SAML and Liberty are cross-enterprise Single Sign-on technologies that enable easier integration between trading partners, independent of the network identity management infrastructure or entitlement service technology used. XACML provides a fine-grained access control capability of the XML data contents. However, without encryption, the SAML and XACML files are in clear text and may be another target of attack.

Figure 7–1 depicts a scenario, using security techniques just discussed, in which a Web Services call requires different layers of security. Both the Service Requester (client) and the Service Provider (server) are assumed to have their platforms secured with operating system security hardening. This refers to the platform security. The following processes illustrate that a Web Services call needs to have different security mechanisms in place to enable end-to-end Web Services.

A Service Requester is connected to the Service Provider via a VPN over the Internet. The VPN makes use of the IPSec protocol to secure the connection between the client and the server (step 1). This refers to the Internet or network layer security. The client also uses HTTPS to secure the connection between the client browser and the server using a 128-bit SSL certificate (step 2). The use of HTTPS with SSL should safeguard the client session. This refers to the transport layer security.

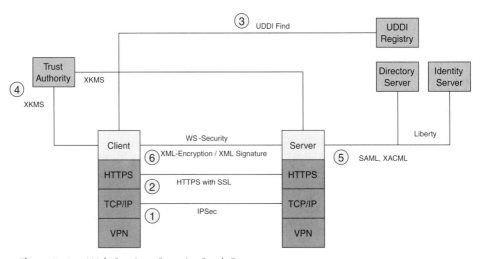

Figure 7–1   Web Services Security Stack Process

Using a secure HTTPS connection, the client browses various business services from a UDDI Service Registry. It finds the relevant business service, and retrieves the service end-point URL (step 3). This refers to the service discovery security.

Upon invoking the business service, the Service Requester (the SOAP client) needs to provide user credentials in order to authenticate himself/herself for using the remote Web Services. The Service Provider is part of a Circle of Trust that is managed by an external Liberty-compliant Identity Provider, which provides an authentication service using the XML Key Management Specification. The client's key is located from the trust authority via XKMS (step 4). The Service Requester then provides a user id and password to authenticate himself/herself. Upon successful authentication, the Identity Provider enables Single Sign-on for the Service Requester using SAML and XACML protocols (step 5). Thus, the Service Requester does not need to log in again to use other Web Services. This refers to the service negotiation security.

When the Service Requester invokes a Web Service, the client side makes use of the public and private keys using XKMS to encrypt the data content in the SOAP message (XML Encryption) and to generate a digital signature (XML Signature) to attach to the SOAP envelope. WS-Security is a message-level security to protect SOAP messages. It is built on top of the XML Encryption and XML Signature specifications. In such a way, the service request and the data content in the SOAP messages are secured by using the WS-Security specification (step 6). This refers to the transaction routing security.

7.4.2 Web Services Security Framework

An end-to-end Web Services implementation not only makes use of encryption and digital signatures appropriately for transactional security, it also requires a structural framework so that none of the development and implementation aspects are missed. There are four key concepts that can describe an end-to-end Web Services security framework: Identity, Trust, Policy, and Threat Profiling. Figures 7–2 and 7–3 relate these concepts in the context of the interaction between Service Requesters, Service Providers, and Service Brokers.

Figure 7–2 depicts a similar scenario to Figure 3–3, where a Service Requester (supplier or buyer) is invoking a remote business service from a Service Provider or a Service Broker in a Business-to-Business (B2B) marketplace. The security concerns for the B2B market are the identity of each marketplace player (in other words, do you trust the identity of the person you are going to do business with, and is he/she reliable for doing business with financially) and the policy (in other words, what business functionality is he/she entitled to). If this is the first time doing business with the trading partner, the Service Requester would often like the Service Provider or the Service Broker to authenticate the identity of the trading partner first. The Service Provider or the Service Broker will also authenticate the identity of every business corporation (trading partner) who publishes business services and service details in its Service Registry. This ensures that the trading partner is not someone with a fake identity or somebody who is masqueraded by a security hacker.

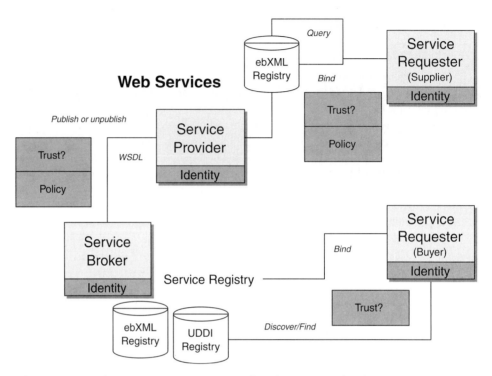

Figure 7–2   Web Services Security Framework in the Context of Web Services Interaction

Figure 7–3 elaborates the security concerns for the same business scenario with details. Security threats may come from different areas to attack the identity and the policy (also refer to the following section on threat profiling). For instance, the identity of the Service Provider can be faked if the user id and password are being hijacked (identity). A man-in-the-middle security attack may modify the service request content (such as modifying the account number in a financial transaction), which affects the reliability of the message security, the data transport security, or the platform security. These security risks may be a result of an overlooked security design or any security implementation pitfalls.

Currently, the platform security (such as operating system security hardening), the data transport security (such as HTTPS), and the messaging security (such as WS-Security, XML Encryption/XML-ENC, and XML Signature/XML-DSIG) are security design elements that address the security concerns regarding the identity of the consumer or Service Provider. Once the identity is established and authenticated, the consumer or the Service Provider would be reliable to do business with.

The next security design element is the reliability of the business transaction between the consumer and the Service Provider. Liberty, together with the SAML specification,

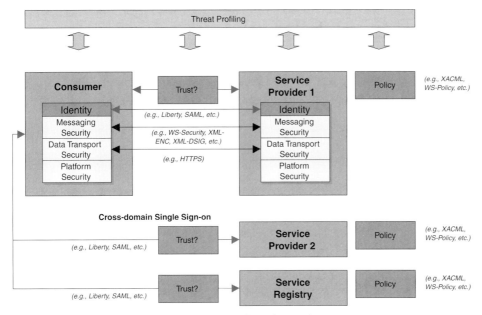

Figure 7–3   Web Services Security Framework With Details

is a security specification to establish a Circle of Trust (cross-domain Single Sign-on) where consumers can sign on once to the B2B marketplace to do reliable business transactions. Within the B2B marketplace, trading partners can also use the messaging security and the data transport security to assure the reliability of the business transactions.

Another security design element is policy. XACML and WS-Policy are examples of security specifications that help govern only authorized users who can access the business transactions or resources. This would safeguard any unauthorized access to sensitive business information between different enterprises (or domains).

The following section discusses the concepts of identity, trust, policy, and threat profiling in the Web Services security framework. *Identity* denotes how to authenticate the valid identity of the Service Requester or user. This requires authentication of the user credentials (security tokens in the form of user id/password, digital certificates, or Kerberos tickets) and platform security.

Trust denotes how to secure the messaging and transactions between two entities (identities). If the two entities (Service Requester and Service Provider) are authentic, the Service Requester is authenticated with the Service Provider, and they are within a secure environment, then they are in a Trust Domain. Service Providers exchanging messages with Service Requesters from an unauthenticated source or over the public Internet are often considered within a Non-trust Domain. In both cases, Web Services applications require the use of different security mechanisms for the complete Web Services security stack (refer to previous section) in order to support transactional security.

This would require a combination of platform security (for example, Operating System security hardening), data transport security (for example, HTTPS), and messaging security (for example, WS-Security) in order to support the requirements of confidentiality, traceability, non-repudiation, data integrity, and availability.

Policy denotes authorization (entitlement) for accessing different resources, policy enforcement, and policy decision.

Threat Profiling denotes profiling the Web Services objects, tools, and applications in order to assist in protecting these resources from potential hacker attacks and unauthorized access. This will involve defining and reinforcing security policies on how to protect and implement security mechanisms for the Web Services objects, tools, and applications on an ongoing basis.

The following structural framework in Table 7–2 covers the core components to establish a Trust Domain, which is suitable for your organization, and what threats and potential risks exist for each Trust Domain.

Table 7–2 Web Services Security Framework

	Security Technology or Standards	Security Requirements
Trust Domains		
Key management	XKMS Host security hardening	Authentication Confidentiality Traceability Non-repudiation
Authentication	Single Sign-on with SAML and Directory Server	Authentication Entitlement Traceability Availability
Transactional security	XML Encryption, XML-DSIG XACML WS-Security Client and host security hardening	Entitlement Confidentiality Availability Data integrity Non-repudiation
Threat Profiling		
Web Services objects	Security hardening for UDDI configuration files and WSDLs	Data integrity Availability
Hacker attack	Profiling of transaction loading/capacity to support availability and scalability Client and host security hardening Virus protection for hosts Intrusion detection testing Patch management for software platform (for example, buffer overflow)	Availability Confidentiality Traceability Authentication Entitlement Non-repudiation

Trust Domains

From a security perspective, a business service and data exchange is reliable only if both parties are "trusted," and are not "John Does" from an unknown place. Trusted parties here do not refer to business trust. The term *trusted* denotes the trust relationship between trading partners (if this is cross-enterprise) or business units (enterprise). A trusted trading partner means that he/she is authenticated with a valid network identity. His/her user credentials are issued and managed by an authorized Identity Provider. Under the management of the authentic Identity Provider, it is secure to exchange business documents between the "trusted" trading partners. Business-to-Business transactions often involve high monetary value transactions (for instance, a Purchase Order containing a monetary value of over $1 million U.S.), and thus authentic identity and a trust relationship are crucial to reliable business services.

This trust relationship may be implemented by a combination of technology and processes. Examples of the technology are Public Key Infrastructure (which involves key management for trading partners), authentication of credentials using Directory Server, use of XML-based encryption, and digital signatures for transaction security.

Different business models of the trust relationship between trading partners, or *Trust Domains*, may influence how these technologies are used. If a business corporation decides to use an external Certificate Authority to issue digital certificates and manage key issuance, this trust service is a *managed trust domain.* However, if the business corporation has a large IT organization and decides to manage its own trust service, including key management, authentication services, and digital certificate operational support, then this is a *client-responsible Trust Domain.* The business may also decide which trust model (hierarchical, distributed, or direct) is suitable to implement its Public Key Infrastructure. In either case, each trust domain has different Use Cases for key management, authentication of client and hosts, and handling of transaction security.

Key Management

Security tokens such as X.509v3 digital certificates are fundamental to generating digital signatures for transactions. They are also the key to authenticating user credentials and network identity. Transactions that are signed with digital signatures are confidential and cannot be repudiated.

XKMS provides a framework for implementing key management. There are a few implementations to support different trust domains. Under the client-responsible Trust Domain, if customers are managing their own PKI infrastructure, they would probably prefer deploying Certificate Management Server together with home-grown key management and call center operation processes (for example, Certification Practice Statement and Certificates Policies).

Under the managed Trust Domain, these security tokens or key pairs are issued and managed by an external trust service such as an external Certificate Authority (for example, UK Post Office or Identrus). Customers need to establish a Web Services call for key retrieval or validation of the key name against the public key.

In either scenario, the server hosting the PKI infrastructure (for example, Certificate Management Server) or the client requesting the XKMS requests needs to be securely hardened. Examples of platform security hardening tools are Titan *(http://www.fish.com/titan/)* and SATAN *(http://www.fish.com/satan/)*. These tools scan and identify different network services and ports that are unused and may be easily exploited by hackers.

Authentication

Form-based (users presenting user id and password in an HTML form) or security token (such as X.509v3 digital certificate) authentication are common means to validate the network identity within an application. For enterprise-wide applications, authentication is usually implemented using security tokens and Directory Server. This requires all applications, including back-end legacy systems, to invoke authentication services (such as LDAP authentication APIs or SAML assertion requests) from the authentication server. Thus, enterprise-wide Single Sign-on is crucial to the user experience and security administration. The capability to sign on once with the partners' systems is also more complex, as the trading partners are unlikely to use the same authentication service or infrastructure.

Historically, Single Sign-on can be implemented by either proprietary authentication APIs on both ends, secure server-side cookies (such as Netegrity's Siteminder), meta-directory (such as Sun ONE Meta-Directory), or PKI implementation using digital certificates. Each of these options has drawbacks.

SAML is a security protocol designed to address Single Sign-on, within an enterprise or across enterprises. It assumes the trading partners do not share the same security infrastructure and authentication mechanism. Using SOAP calls, SAML does not require customers to change the existing security infrastructure. SAML requires the client requester (Relying Party), under either the client-responsible or the managed Trust Domain, to send a request for authentication assertion during login to the Issuing Authority, which returns a SAML Assertion Response.

SAML is dependent on a reliable key management infrastructure and processes, as discussed earlier in a previous section. It is now a core component of the Project Liberty specification.

Transaction Security

Message-level and application-level security provides protection for the transaction. An appropriate choice of encryption algorithm (such as XML encryption or XML-ENC) together with a digital signature (such as XML Signature or XML-DSIG) is essential for the transaction security. XACML attempts to provide a data-level access and addresses issues like sending different subsets of the XML data contents to different groups of users.

The WS-Security specification, dated April of 2002, attempts to define a broader Web Services security framework by consolidating variants of security token and encryption specifications. The interoperability aspects of how Single Sign-on and transaction security are implemented have not yet been articulated.

Different Web Services security specifications have provided a good framework. However, the reliability and scalability of the transaction security really depends on the physical implementation of the security infrastructure and the application design. The reliability and security of the client and host platform requires security hardening. Most hackers do not know these application security aspects, but they are able to hack into the transactions from the platform security loopholes.

Threat Profiling

Web Services Objects

The following objects may become targets of attacks. Understanding how these objects operate will help defend against attacks.

Hosts.   Many servers running Windows 2000 or Solaris OE are installed with default configuration settings. This could be an issue of security threat. For example, default configuration settings in Windows operating systems leave most objects and resources unprotected (for instance, an anonymous id can access these objects). Most customers may not be aware of the need to download and install security patches to the operating system in a timely way. Thus, many unused ports or services, such as RPC or COM+ objects, can be easily exploited.

The example in Figure 7–4 shows a list of risky areas, identified by Titan and NMAP, on a Unix host (IP address 10.4.16.14) running Apache Tomcat and SOAP using the default installation. Please note the interesting ports that may be open to security attacks or exploits.

UDDI Host Scan.   Figure 7–4 is a scan log of the Unix host drip9 (IP address is 10.4.16.19) generated by NMAP. The interesting ports are RPC (which is different from XML-RPC), which are easily exploited.

```
%./nmap -v -sU -sT drip9

Starting nmap V. 2.54BETA34 ( www.insecure.org/nmap/ )
Host drip9 (10.4.16.19) appears to be up ... good.
Initiating Connect() Scan against drip9 (10.4.16.19)
Adding open port 8080/tcp
Adding open port 8081/tcp
...
The Connect() Scan took 1 second to scan 1556 ports.
```

Figure 7–4   UDDI Host Scan

```
Initiating UDP Scan against drip9 (10.4.16.19)
Too many drops ... increasing send delay to 50000
The UDP Scan took 357 seconds to scan 1459 ports.
...
Adding open port 32771/udp
Interesting ports on drip9 (10.4.16.19):
(The 2973 ports scanned but not shown below are in
state: closed)
Port          State        Service
...
21/tcp        open         ftp
22/tcp        open         ssh
23/tcp        open         telnet
...
42/udp        open         nameserver
79/tcp        open         finger
111/tcp       open         sunrpc
111/udp       open         sunrpc
161/udp       open         snmp
512/tcp       open         exec
513/tcp       open         login
514/tcp       open         shell
514/udp       open         syslog
517/udp       open         talk
540/tcp       open         uucp
587/tcp       open         submission
2049/tcp      open         nfs
2049/udp      open         nfs
4045/tcp      open         lockd
...
8080/tcp      open         http-proxy
8081/tcp      open         blackice-icecap
32771/tcp     open         sometimes-rpc5
32771/udp     open         sometimes-rpc6
32772/tcp     open         sometimes-rpc7
32773/udp     open         sometimes-rpc10
32779/tcp     open         sometimes-rpc21

Nmap run completed — 1 IP address (1 host up) scanned
in 360 seconds
#
```

Figure 7–4   UDDI Host Scan—*continued.*

Apache Tomcat/UDDI Host Security Healthcheck.   Figure 7–5 is extracted from a detailed report generated by Titan. Titan also explains the potential risk areas (in this example, they refer to the unused Unix services and IP ports) and makes recommendations to mitigate the risks. These risks, such as login and shell defaults, are common to platform security and thus also applicable to a Web Services implementation. Nevertheless, Titan's findings varied when scanning a Unix host with and without Apache Tomcat, Apache SOAP, and Apache Xindice database (for storing UDDI objects) respectively.

In this excerpt, RPC and IP forwarding are two common risks for Web Services implementation, which may be open to security attack or exploit using buffer overflow.

```
*=*=*=*=* Running modules/disable-L1-A.sh now.....
Output to ../logs/modules/disable-L1-A.sh.V.113340
============================
Abort sequence set to enable - FAILS CHECK

Titan Recommendation: (disable-L1-A.sh -f) This is a
physical access issue. If a person can abort the
current Solaris session, and reboot using an alternate
device, (see eeprom.sh -f) they can access/modify any
file.
Titan sets abort sequence to:

KEYBOARD_ABORT=disable in /etc/default/kbd


========================================================
========
bin shell = - FAILS CHECK

Titan Recommendation: (disable-accounts.sh -f) Set
system accounts defined as:
any accounts less than UID 100 or greater than UID
60000 to /bin/true or to another non-interactive
shell. This keeps bad guy from putting in a
/usr/bin/.rhosts on a NFS exported partition and being
able to rsh/rlogin as user bin.

It is recommended that the Titan binary for noshell be
compiled and used as it notifies the administrator of
access attempts to a reserved system account.
```

Figure 7–5   Titan's Scanning Result of a UDDI Host

```
(see
/tmp/Titan,v4.0BETA2/arch/sol8sun4/bin/src1/noshell.c)


=========================================================
========
Service S88sendmail still active in /etc/rc2.d - FAILS
CHECK

Titan Recommendation: (disable-services.sh -f) Disable
NFS server, NFS client, and *RPC on all systems that
don't require them.
Note - RPC is required on HA systems. Use Ipfilter or
EFS Lite to restrict RPC on these networks.


=========================================================
========
Service S71rpc still active in /etc/rc2.d - FAILS
CHECK

Titan Recommendation: (disable-services.sh -f) Disable
NFS server, NFS client, and *RPC on all systems that
don't require them.
Note - RPC is required on HA systems. Use Ipfilter or
EFS Lite to restrict RPC on these networks. Service
S76snmpdx still active in /etc/rc3.d - FAILS CHECK


*=*=*=*=* Running modules/disable_ip_holes.sh now.....
Output to ../logs/modules/disable_ip_holes.sh.V.113340
============================
Checking kernel settings using ndd
IP source routing is currently set to 1
System allows source routed packet forwarding - FAILS
CHECK

Titan Recommendation: (disable_ip_holes.sh -f) Disable
ip_src_routed, broadcast, and use strict multihoming.
Add to /etc/rc2.d/S69inet:

ndd -set /dev/ip ip_forward_src_routed 0
ndd -set /dev/ip ip_forwarding 0
```

Figure 7–5 Titan's Scanning Result of a UDDI Host—*continued.*

```
ndd -set /dev/ip ip_forward_directed_broadcasts 0
ndd -set /dev/ip ip_ignore_redirect 1
ndd -set /dev/ip ip_strict_dst_multihoming 1


*=*=*=*=* Running modules/fix-cronpath.sh now.....
Output to ../logs/modules/fix-cronpath.sh.V.113340
============================
 File /var/spool/cron/crontabs/root exists; continuing
...
        No cron.allow file - FAILS CHECK
        No at.allow file - FAILS CHECK
```

Figure 7–5   Titan's Scanning Result of a UDDI Host—*continued.*

UDDI Service Registry.   Local configuration or data files for the UDDI Service Registry are potential targets for attack. For example, Apache Xindice, which Java Web Services Developer Pack uses to store the UDDI Service Registry objects, stores data contents under $JWSDP/tools/db/uddi and system access information under $JWSDP/tools/db/system. WSDL files, if they are stored in the Service Registry, are critical files that hackers may locate using the service end-point URL as targets of attack.

Web Container/Application Server.   Some Web Containers or Application Servers store user access files in clear text (for example, Apache Tomcat stores users and passwords in $CATALINA/conf/tomcat-users). Saumil Shah and Shreeraj Shah, in RSA Conference 2002 (refer to *http://www.rsaconference.net/RSApresentations/ pdfs/devthu1015_shah.pdf* for details) identify another area of threat from specific application server implementations, where hackers may exploit the abuse of URL to CLASSPATH mapping, or cause source code disclosure or arbitrary file retrieval by forcing a FileServlet on a JSP file. In most cases, the application server may have a security patch already. They suggest some countermeasures, such as avoiding the use of servlet invocation by URL to CLASSPATH mapping as much as possible, disallowing any meta-characters (for example, ° or .) as part of the URL, unregistering any unused alias mappings, and isolating the system's core servlets from application servlets.

Hacker Attacks

Typical hacker attacks usually start with information gathering by footprinting, scanning, and enumeration. If Web Services applications are implemented with poor security, hackers may simply intrude into the system and access data contents. For security-hardened systems, hackers may attempt Denial of Service or middleman attack.

Denis Piliptchouk and Vince Dovydaitis, in RSA Conference 2002 (refer to *http://www.rsaconference.net/RSApresentations/pdfs/devwed1115_piliptchouk.pdf* for details), compared the security features of .NET with those of Java. Interestingly, they note that both languages have similar capabilities with cryptography, authentication, and authorization services. The key difference is that .NET security design is to enable all features by default, while Java is to disable all features by default. Both .NET CLR and Java provide a sandbox for program execution and store configurations in XML files. Therefore, it is the overall design quality that impacts the security of a Web Services implementation.

Denial of Service.   A common approach to attacking Web Services applications with implementation of key management and digital signatures is a Denial of Service (DoS) attack. This is based on some information gathering about the profiling of the loading and capacity from the service end-point URLs in the WSDL files. One possible countermeasure is to review the "ilities" of the overall architecture and to profile the loading and capacity regularly as preventive measures.

Man-in-the-Middle Attack.   A likely security attack approach, illustrated in the scenario in Figure 7–6, is to spoof service requests to Web Services end-points by reusing previous key information and key name, which are captured from previous footprinting. In this example, a SOAP client is sending a SOAP message that contains a fund transfer request in clear text. The data content includes user id and password. The SOAP message is in unencrypted clear text and is supposed to be signed with a digital signature. It is assumed that SOAP messaging does not need data encryption within an internal proprietary network. Unfortunately, hackers acquire a WSDL document in advance and sniff for a copy of SOAP messages from the internal network. Then, they may modify the SOAP message contents and post it to the target service end-point URL.

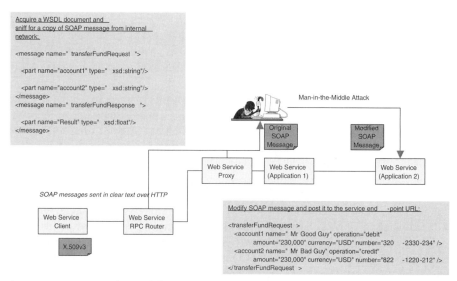

Figure 7–6   Man-in-the-Middle Attack Risk for Web Services Applications

7.5 Recent Web Services Security Initiatives

The following sections summarize the major design features of recent Web Services security initiatives. When reviewing these initiatives for implementation, it is important to consider the ease of the implementation, the stopgap measure if the commercial implementation is not ready, and the migration roadmap from an existing stopgap implementation to the mature standard.

This book does not intend to cover the program code or XML specifications in detail. Examples are given to illustrate the implementation and tools. The resource list at the end of this chapter provides some pointers with details.

7.5.1 WS-Security

Background

IBM, Microsoft, and VeriSign submitted a new Web Services security specification on April 5, 2002, that is intended to consolidate previous security specifications, including Microsoft and IBM's SOAP-SEC, security tokens, encryption specifications, Microsoft's WS-Security, and WS-license (refer to Figure 7–7). From the details of the specification (*http://www-106.ibm.com/developerworks/library/ws-secure/*), it focuses on converging the PKI-based and Kerberos-based authentication and encryption technologies used for SOAP messaging. This addresses the divergence of the current Web Services security implementation using X.509v3 digital certificates and .NET PASSPORT. It stated in Section 1.1.2 that it does not deal with authentication across different exchanges (compare SAML), key exchange, or establishing trust (compare XKMS).

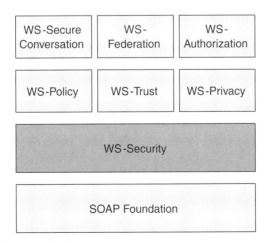

Figure 7–7   WS-Security Roadmap

OASIS's Web Services Security Technical Committee has taken up the ownership to further work on Web Services security based on the WS-Security roadmap (*http://www.oasis-open.org/committees/wss/*). Currently, there are new draft core specifications and profile documents published (for example, *http://www.oasis-open.org/committees/wss/documents/WSS-SOAPMessageSecurity-11-0303-merged.pdf*). OASIS has a concise highlight of the history and changes at *http://xml.coverpages.org/ws-security.html*.

Some vendors have also provided an early release of WS-Security toolkits (such as Microsoft's Web Services Enhancement and IBM's Web Services Toolkit) and demonstrated an interoperability test between them in February of 2003 (*http://www.cbdiforum.com/public/news/index.php3?id=1192*).

Design Features

WS-Security differentiates unsigned security tokens (that is, user name and password) from signed security tokens (that is, X.509v3 certificates and Kerberos tickets). It uses two new tags—`<SecurityTokenReference />` and `<BinarySecurityToken />`—to support different security tokens.

Figure 7–8 is an example modified from the original WS-Security specification. The example shows a stock symbol in a SOAP message, which consists of a SOAP header (with a security token and a digital signature) and a SOAP body (the payload, or the stock symbol itself). The bolded passages highlight some of the changes from the XML Signature specification.

```
<?xml version="1.0" encoding="utf-8"?>
<S:Envelope xmlns:S="http://www.w3.org/2001/12/soap-
envelope"
    xmlns:ds="http://www.w3.org/2000/09/xmldsig#"
    xmlns:wsse="http://schemas.xmlsoap.org/ws/2002/04/
        secext"
    xmlns:xenc="http://www.w3.org/2001/04/xmlenc#">
    <S:Header>
        <m:path xmlns:m="http://schemas.xmlsoap.org/rp">
            <m:action>http://bar.com/getQuote</m:action>
            <m:to>http://bar.com/stocks</m:to>
            <m:from>mailto:foo@bar.com</m:from>
```

Figure 7–8   Sample WS-Security File

```
            <m:id>uuid:61a8f5c2-14be-3a40-a13f-
5b750540abc8</m:id>
      </m:path>
      <wsse:Security>
        <wsse:BinarySecurityToken
                  ValueType="wsse:X509v3"
                  EncodingType="wsse:Base64Binary"
                  Id="X509Token">
              Ksdfjs723ekldfsj...
        </wsse:BinarySecurityToken>
        <ds:Signature>
            <ds:SignedInfo>
              <ds:CanonicalizationMethod Algorithm=
                  "http://www.w3.org/2001/10/xml-
exc-c14n#"/>
              <ds:SignatureMethod Algorithm=
"http://www.w3.org/2000/09/xmldsig#rsa-sha1"/>
              <ds:Reference>
                <ds:Transforms>
                  <ds:Transform Algorithm=
"http://...#RoutingTransform"/>
                  <ds:Transform Algorithm=
"http://www.w3.org/2001/10/xml-exc-c14n#"/>
                </ds:Transforms>
                <ds:DigestMethod Algorithm=

"http://www.w3.org/2000/09/xmldsig#sha1"/>
<ds:DigestValue>UFDYsdf...</ds:DigestValue>
              </ds:Reference>
            </ds:SignedInfo>
            <ds:SignatureValue>
              XMdfihdfdsl...
            </ds:SignatureValue>
            <ds:KeyInfo>
              <wsse:SecurityTokenReference>
                <wsse:Reference URI="#X509Token"/>
              </wsse:SecurityTokenReference>
```

Figure 7–8   Sample WS-Security File—*continued*.

```
            </ds:KeyInfo>
          </ds:Signature>
       </wsse:Security>
    </S:Header>
    <S:Body>
       <myService:StockSymbol
xmlns:myService="http://bar.com/payloads">
          SUNW
       </myService:StockSymbol>
    </S:Body>
</S:Envelope>
```

Figure 7–8   Sample WS-Security File—*continued.*

Figure 7–9 is an example, based on the same contents modified from the XML Signature specification. It is shown here for easy comparison with the WS-Security specification (as in Figure 7–8).

```
<?xml version="1.0" encoding="utf-8"?>
<S:Envelope xmlns:S="http://www.w3.org/2001/12/soap-
envelope"
xmlns:ds="http://www.w3.org/2000/09/xmldsig#"
   <S:Header>
      <Signature Id="myXMLSignature"
xmlns="http://www.w3.org/2000/09/xmldsig#">
         <SignedInfo>
            <CanonicalizationMethod
Algorithm="http://www.w3.org/TR/2001/REC-xml-c14n-
20010315"/>
            <SignatureMethod
Algorithm="http://www.w3.org/2000/09/xmldsig#dsa-
sha1"/>
            <Reference
               URI="http://www.w3.org/TR/2000/REC-
xhtml1-20000126/">
```

Figure 7–9   Sample XML Signature

```
                  <Transforms>
                     <Transform
Algorithm="http://www.w3.org/TR/2001/REC-xml-c14n-
20010315"/>
                  </Transforms>
                  <DigestMethod
Algorithm="http://www.w3.org/2000/09/xmldsig#sha1"/>
<DigestValue>UFDYsdf...</DigestValue>
               </Reference>
            </SignedInfo>
<SignatureValue>XMdfihdfdsl...</SignatureValue>
            <KeyInfo>
               <KeyValue>
                  <DSAKeyValue>
<P>...</P><Q>...</Q><G>...</G><Y>...</Y>
                  </DSAKeyValue>
               </KeyValue>
            </KeyInfo>
         </Signature>
      </S:Header>
      <S:Body>
         <myService:StockSymbol
xmlns:myService="http://bar.com/payloads">
            SUNW
         </myService:StockSymbol>
      </S:Body>
   </S:Envelope>
```

Figure 7–9   Sample XML Signature—*continued.*

Although the digital signature construct <ds:Signature /> is similar to the XML Signature, WS-Security does not use Enveloped Signature Transform or the Enveloping Signature in the XML Signature specification. WS-Security reuses the existing XML Encryption.

When implementing WS-Security, developers need to detect any security threats, such as replays of the SOAP messages with security information. They can incorporate the use of timestamp, sequence numbers, expirations, and message correlations into the application design.

IBM's Web Services Toolkit (WSTK) version 3.3.2 uses Apache Axis's handlers, namely "`com.ibm.wstk.axis.handlers,`" to implement WS-Security XML Signature. The client generates a digital signature by invoking "`org.apache.axis.utils.Admin`" with a Web Services Deployment Descriptor (WSDD).

```
java -cp "%WSTK_CP%" org.apache.axis.utils.Admin
client dsig_client_deploy.wsdd
```

`dsig_client_deploy.wsdd` (extracted from a demo program from WSTK 3.1), as shown in Figure 7–10, contains the target Web Service name and the Axis signer handler. No additional programming needs to be made. This is a good alternative to implement SOAP message-level security.

```
<deployment xmlns="http://xml.apache.org/axis/wsdd/"
xmlns:java="http://xml.apache.org/axis/wsdd/providers/
java">

  <handler name="log"
type="java:org.apache.axis.handlers.LogHandler"/>
  <handler name="signer"
type="java:com.ibm.wstk.axis.handlers.Signer">
    <parameter value="john" name="alias"/>
    <parameter value="keypass" name="keyPassword"/>
    <parameter value="keystore.db" name="keyStore"/>
    <parameter value="wstkdemo"
name="keyStorePassword"/>
  </handler>

  <handler name="verifier"
type="java:com.ibm.wstk.axis.handlers.Verifier"/>

  <service name="urn:xmltoday-delayed-quotes">
    <requestFlow>
      <handler type="log"/>
      <handler type="signer"/>
    </requestFlow>
    <responseFlow>
      <handler type="log"/>
    </responseFlow>
  </service>
</deployment>.
```

Figure 7–10   Sample Digital Signature Client WSDD File

Implication

Beyond WS-Security, IBM and Microsoft in their Web Services security roadmap (*http://www-106.ibm.com/developerworks/webservices/library/ws-secmap/*) have introduced a plan for new security specifications that supports defining policies, establishing trust and ensuring data privacy, secure conversation, federation of identities, and authorization. These new security specifications are also supported by IBM's XML Security Suite (*http://www.alphaworks.ibm.com/tech/xmlsecuritysuite*), IBM's Emerging Technologies Tool Kit or previously Web Services Tool Kit version 3.3.2 (*http://alphaworks.ibm.com/tech/ettk*), and Microsoft's CAPICOM (*http://msdn.microsoft.com/library/default.asp?url=/library/en-us/security/Security/capicom_reference.asp*). Nevertheless, they also overlap with existing security initiatives XKMS and SAML under Project Liberty. Thus, Web Serv-ices security becomes another battlefield between software vendors.

WS-Security cannot be isolated without the context of the big picture from IBM and Microsoft's security roadmap. Though the current roadmap is the first step to defining a comprehensive Web Services security strategy, it has not covered aspects of integration and interoperability between different security standard variants, platform security and security hardening, and threat profiling.

From the customer perspective, the convergence of different security standards is beneficial. Because these new security specifications are still evolving, risk-aversive customers may not be ready to adopt them. Customers face the risk of not implementing PKI-based or Kerberos-based authentication and encryption and the dilemma of painfully migrating to the industry security standard in the future. What may be useful to customers would be a migration technology (such as XML stylesheet mapping) to map different security schema or message constructs of these variant technologies.

Benefits

WS-Security converges two different technology platforms and makes interoperability between .NET and Open Systems much easier. Developers may find WS-Security attractive because there are supporting implementations available to the developer desktop immediately, without waiting for long-due security standard specifications.

7.5.2 XKMS

Background

XML Key Management Service (XKMS) is also considered part of the so-called Second Generation PKI. VeriSign, Microsoft, and webMethods contributed the draft specification to W3C. It is also part of the bigger XML Trust Service initiative (*http://www.xmltrustcenter.org*) sponsored by VeriSign.

XKMS is intended to simplify the integration of PKI and digital signatures with XML applications. This is done by enabling the XML applications to delegate trust-processing decisions to a "specialized trust processor."

Design Features

XKMS is a security specification (*http://www.w3.org/TR/xkms2/*) depicting key registration, key retrieval, key revocation, and validation of key information. It supports different Trust Domains. There are two major components in XKMS: X-KISS and X-KRSS (refer to Figure 7–11).

Figure 7–11 summarizes five tiered models defined in the XKMS version 1.0 specification (http://www.w3.org/TR/xkms/). Tier 0 XKMS denotes there is no trust service. The applications on both ends need to handle the authentication and generation of digital signatures. Under Tier 1 XKMS, the applications on both ends will provide authentication service, and the client will validate the digital signature. Under Tier 2 XKMS, there is a validation service available with service reporting capabilities. The client can issue a query to the trust service in order to validate the key. Tier 3 XKMS will help define a long-term trust relationship to establish and manage assertion service. Tier 4 XKMS will help manage the status of assertions. Tier 3 and Tier 4 XKMS are currently removed from the XKMS version 2.0 specification.

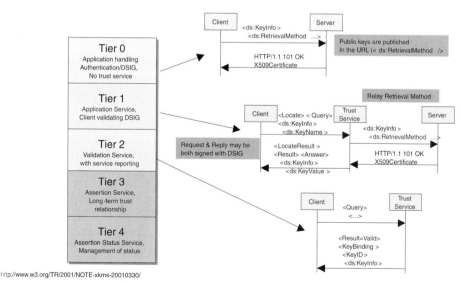

http://www.w3.org/TR/2001/NOTE-xkms-20010330/

Figure 7–11   XKMS Tiered Models

XML Key Registration Service Specification (X-KRSS)

This is a key pair holder to register a key pair. Key pairs can be generated in advance, upon a client request. The registration protocol may be used to recover private keys. These features are important aspects of issuing and managing key pairs stored in security tokens, such as digital certificates.

Before X-KRSS is available, key registration and retrieval are vendor-specific. There are some variations in the details by security token storage devices.

XML Key Information Service Specification (X-KISS)

This is a relying party to locate and validate key information associated with a digital signature. It supports the current Directory Server, Certificate Authority, Registration Authority, and Validation Authority infrastructure. X-KISS allows signers to communicate to a verifier which public key to select, using `<ds:KeyInfo />`, which contains public signing key information (such as key name and key value) within the signature block of the XML message. Besides, it also allows substituting or supplementing `<ds:KeyInfo />` if the property of the key information is cryptographically bound to the digital signature.

Figures 7–12 and 7–13, extracted from the original XKMS specification, show an XKMS key location service request and response for Tier 1 service model (applications perform key information processing). In this scenario, the client sends a locate key request to the trust service with the tag "<Locate>" (Figure 7–12 shows the service request to locate a key). The trust service processes the locate key request, and relays it to the server with the tag "RetrievalMethod." The key is returned to the client with the tag "<LocateResult>" (Figure 7–13 shows the result of locating the key). Figure 7–11 also shows a sequence diagram that illustrates the processes of locating the key and returning the key result.

```
<?xml version="1.0"?>
<soap:Envelope
xmlns:soap="http://schemas.xmlsoap.org/soap/envelope/"
xmlns:soapenc="http://schemas.xmlsoap.org/soap/encodin
g/" xmlns:xsi="http://www.w3.org/1999/XMLSchema-
instance" xmlns:xsd="http://www.w3.org/1999/XMLSchema"
xmlns:ds="http://www.w3.org/2000/09/xmldsig#">
  <soap:Body>
    <Locate xmlns="http://www.xkms.org/schema/xkms-
2001-01-20">
```

Figure 7–12   XKMS Example 1—Locate a Key

```
            <Query>
              <ds:KeyInfo>
                <ds:KeyValue>
                  <ds:RSAKeyValue>

<ds:Modulus>998/T2PUN8HQlnhf9YIKdMHHGM7HkJwA56UD0a1oYq
7EfdxSXAidruAszNqBoOqfarJIsfcVKLob1hGnQ/l6xw==</ds:Mod
ulus>
                    <ds:Exponent>AQAB</ds:Exponent>
                  </ds:RSAKeyValue>
                </ds:KeyValue>
              </ds:KeyInfo>
            </Query>
            <Respond>
            <string>KeyName</string>
        </Respond>
        </Locate>
      </soap:Body>
</soap:Envelope>
```

Figure 7–12   XKMS Example 1—Locate a Key—*continued.*

```
<?xml version="1.0"?>
<soap:Envelope
xmlns:soap="http://schemas.xmlsoap.org/soap/envelope/"
xmlns:soapenc="http://schemas.xmlsoap.org/soap/encodin
g/" xmlns:xsi="http://www.w3.org/1999/XMLSchema-
instance" xmlns:xsd="http://www.w3.org/1999/XMLSchema"
xmlns:ds="http://www.w3.org/2000/09/xmldsig#">
  <soap:Body>
    <LocateResult
xmlns="http://www.xkms.org/schema/xkms-2001-01-20">
      <Result>Success</Result>
      <Answer>
        <ds:KeyInfo>
          <ds:KeyValue>
            <ds:RSAKeyValue>

<ds:Modulus>998/T2PUN8HQlnhf9YIKdMHHGM7HkJwA56UD0a1oYq7Ef
dxSXAidruAszNqBoOqfarJIsfcVKLob1hGnQ/l6xw==</ds:Modulus>
```

Figure 7–13   XKMS Example 2—Return the Locate Key Result

```
                <ds:Exponent>AQAB</ds:Exponent>
              </ds:RSAKeyValue>
            </ds:KeyValue>
          <ds:KeyName>Account 1823945 Key
3</ds:KeyName>
        </ds:KeyInfo>
     </Answer>
   </LocateResult>
 </soap:Body>
</soap:Envelope>
```

Figure 7–13 XKMS Example 2—Return the Locate Key Result—*continued.*

Figures 7–14 and 7–15, extracted from the original XKMS specification, show an XKMS client request and response for Tier 2 service model (use of validation service).

```
<?xml version="1.0"?>`,/kmp:Envelope
xmlns:soap="http://schemas.xmlsoap.org/soap/envelope/"
xmlns:soapenc="http://schemas.xmlsoap.org/soap/encodin
g/" xmlns:xsi="http://www.w3.org/1999/XMLSchema-
instance" xmlns:xsd="http://www.w3.org/1999/XMLSchema"
xmlns:ds="http://www.w3.org/2000/09/xmldsig#">
  <soap:Body>
    <Validate xmlns="http://www.xkms.org/schema/xkms-
2001-01-20">
      <Query>
        <Status>Valid</Status>
        <KeyID/>
          <ds:KeyInfo>
            <ds:KeyValue>
              <ds:RSAKeyValue>

<ds:Modulus>998/T2PUN8HQlnhf9YIKdMHHGM7HkJwA56UD0a1oYq
7EfdxSXAidruAszNqBoOqfarJIsfcVKLob1hGnQ/l6xw==</ds:Mod
ulus>
              <ds:Exponent>AQAB</ds:Exponent>
            </ds:RSAKeyValue>
          </ds:KeyValue>
```

Figure 7–14 XKMS Example 3—Validate a Key

```
              <ds:KeyName>Account 1823945 Key
3</ds:KeyName>
          </ds:KeyInfo>
      </Query>
      <Respond>
          <string>KeyName</string>
          <string>KeyValue</string>
      </Respond>
    </Validate>
   </soap:Body>
</soap:Envelope>
```

Figure 7–14 XKMS Example 3—Validate a Key—*continued.*

```
<?xml version="1.0"?>
<soap:Envelope
xmlns:soap="http://schemas.xmlsoap.org/soap/envelope/"
xmlns:soapenc="http://schemas.xmlsoap.org/soap/encodin
g/" xmlns:xsi="http://www.w3.org/1999/XMLSchema-
instance" xmlns:xsd="http://www.w3.org/1999/XMLSchema"
xmlns:ds="http://www.w3.org/2000/09/xmldsig#">
   <soap:Body>
     <ValidateResult
xmlns="http://www.xkms.org/schema/xkms-2001-01-20">
       <Result>Success</Result>
       <Answer soapenc:arrayType="KeyBinding[[1]]">
         <KeyBinding>
           <Status>Valid</Status>
       <KeyID>http://www.xmltrustcenter.org/assert/
           20000920-3</KeyID>
           <ds:KeyInfo>
             <ds:KeyValue>
               <ds:RSAKeyValue>

<ds:Modulus>998/T2PUN8HQlnhf9YIKdMHHGM7HkJwA56UD0a1oYq7Ef
dxSXAidruAszNqBoOqfarJIsfcVKLob1hGnQ/l6xw==</ds:Modulus>
             <ds:Exponent>AQAB</ds:Exponent>
               </ds:RSAKeyValue>
             </ds:KeyValue>
```

Figure 7–15 XKMS Example 4—Return the Validate Key Result

```
            <ds:KeyName>Account 1823945 Key
3</ds:KeyName>
         </ds:KeyInfo>
         <ValidityInterval>
            <NotBefore>2000-09-20T12:00:00</NotBefore>
            <NotAfter>2000-10-20T12:00:00</NotAfter>
         </ValidityInterval>
       </KeyBinding>
     </Answer>
   </ValidateResult>
  </soap:Body>
</soap:Envelope>
```

Figure 7–15 XKMS Example 4—Return the Validate Key Result—*continued.*

Examples of XKMS implementation include VeriSign's Trust Services Integration Kit (*http://www.xmltrustcenter.org/developer/verisign/tsik/index.htm*) and Evincible's INK. (*http://www.evincible.com/products/ink.asp*).

The following examples are Locate and Validate XKMS services using VeriSign's Trust Service Integration Kit (TSIK) version 1.1 on Windows 2000. To locate the key information, developers can use the method XKMSLocate(keyName, responses) or XKMS Locate(publicKey, responses) and XKMSLocateResponse lr = locate.sendRequest (transport) to return the Locate service response in an XML message.

The Locate XKMS service partial code using TSIK looks like Figure 7–16.

```
    String responses[[]] = {XKMSLocate.KeyName,
XKMSLocate.KeyValue};

    XKMSLocate locate = null;
    if (keyName != null){
        locate = new XKMSLocate(keyName, responses);
    } else {
        locate = new XKMSLocate(publicKey, responses);
    }

    XKMSLocateResponse lr =
locate.sendRequest(transport);
    System.out.println("Response status is
"+lr.getStatus());
```

Figure 7–16 Sample XKMS Locate Client

Running the sample XKMS client to locate key information from the TSIK will render the result as in Figure 7–17.

```
D:\Dev\Test\tsik1_0\samples\xkms>java SampleXKMS
    Client http://interop-xkms.verisign.com/xkms/
    Acceptor.nano locate
"http://xkms.verisign.com/key?jurisdiction=d7ea68c518b
2602ca4bbca895826a7dd&mail_email=valid@xkms.org"
    sending debug output to D:\Temp\xkmsclient.out
    Response status is true
    KeyInfos is
[[com.verisign.xkms.client.XKMSKeyInfoImpl@bd7848]]
```

Figure 7–17   Running Sample XKMS Client to Locate Key Information

To validate the key information, developers can use the method XKMSValidate (keyName, responses) and XKMSValidateResponse vr = validate.sendRequest(transport) to return the validation response in an XML message, as in Figure 7–18.

```
    String responses[[]] = {"KeyName", "KeyValue",
ValidityInterval",
                    "KeyUsage", "Status"};
    XKMSValidate validate = null;
    if (keyName != null) {
        validate = new XKMSValidate(keyName,
responses);
    } else if (cert != null) {
        validate = new XKMSValidate(cert, responses);
    } else {
        validate = new XKMSValidate(publicKey,
responses);
    }

    XKMSValidateResponse vr =
validate.sendRequest(transport);
```

Figure 7–18   Running Sample XKMS Client to Validate Key Information

Running the sample XKMS client to validate key information from the TSIK will render the result in Figure 7–19.

```
   D:\Dev\Test\tsik1_0\samples\xkms>java SampleXKMS
      Client
http://interop-xkms.verisign.com/xkms/Acceptor.nano
validate
"http://xkms.verisign.com/key?jurisdiction=d7ea68c518b
2602ca4bbca895826a7dd&mail_email=valid@xkms.org"
PubKey PrivKey
   sending debug output to D:\Temp\xkmsclient.out
==========
   Caught XKMSException:
com.verisign.xkms.client.XKMSServiceFailureException:
      An X509Certificate was not included in the
      Signature of the Validate request. TransactionID:
      26837070-72df-11d6-a2db-b9a141e81eaa
==========
   Code: XKMS.Validate.Request.MissingCert
   Description: An X509Certificate was not included
      in the Signature of the Validate request.
      TransactionID: 26837070-72df-11d6-a2db-
      b9a141e81eaa
==========
   Stacktrace:
   com.verisign.xkms.client.XKMSServiceFailure
      Exception: An X509Certificate was not included
      in the Signature of the Validate request.
      TransactionID: 26837070-72df-11d6-a2db-b9a141e81eaa
      at
com.verisign.xkms.client.XKMSValidateResponse.<init>(X
KMSValidateResp
   onse.java:63) at
com.verisign.xkms.client.XKMSValidate.processValidateR
esult(XKMSValid
   ate.java:549) at
com.verisign.xkms.client.XKMSValidate.makeResponse(XKM
SValidate.java:
   329) at
com.verisign.messaging.AbstractTransport.sendRequest(A
bstractTranspor
   t.java:672) at
com.verisign.xkms.client.XKMSValidate.sendRequest(XKMS
Validate.java:439)
```

Figure 7–19 Result of Validating Key Information From an XKMS Client

```
        at
SampleXKMSClient.validate(SampleXKMSClient.java:297)
        at
SampleXKMSClient.main(SampleXKMSClient.java:411)
==========
    XML message from exception:
    <?xml version="1.0" encoding="UTF-8"?>

    <xkms:ValidateResult Id="refId_0"
xmlns:xkms="http://www.xkms.org/schema/xkms-20
01-01-20">
    <xkms:Result>Failure</xkms:Result>
    <xkms:ErrorInfo
errorCode="XKMS.Validate.Request.MissingCert">
        <xkms:ErrorDescription>An X509Certificate was
not included in the Signature of the Validate
request.TransactionID: 26837070-72df-11d6-a2db-
b9a141e81eaa</xkms:ErrorDescription>

<xkms:ErrorActor>kiss_onsite/validate_onsite#Validate_
to_XASRequest</xkms:ErrorActor>
    </xkms:ErrorInfo>
    <dsig:Signature
xmlns:dsig="http://www.w3.org/2000/09/xmldsig#">
        <dsig:SignedInfo>
            <dsig:CanonicalizationMethod
Algorithm="http://www.w3.org/TR/2001/REC-xml-c14n-
20010315"/>
            <d:SignatureMethod
Algorithm="http://www.w3.org/2000/09/xmldsig#rsa-sha1"
xmlns:d="http://www.w3.org/2000/09/xmldsig#"/>
            <dsig:Reference URI="#refId_0">
                <dsig:Transforms>
                    <d:Transform
Algorithm="http://www.w3.org/2000/09/xmldsig#enveloped
-signature"
xmlns:d="http://www.w3.org/2000/09/xmldsig#"/>
                    <dsig:Transform
Algorithm="http://www.w3.org/TR/2001/REC-xml-c14n-
20010315"/>
                </dsig:Transforms>
```

Figure 7–19   Result of Validating Key Information From an XKMS Client—*continued.*

```
            <dsig:DigestMethod
Algorithm="http://www.w3.org/2000/09/xmldsig#sha1"/>

<dsig:DigestValue>pVfm0jRqqP3FvSj48EK5arE5l8I=</dsig:D
igestValue>
        </dsig:Reference>
      </dsig:SignedInfo>

<dsig:SignatureValue>I9Hs2/DgUuRXpoKWH213b0PPn23BqgkwH
xIykXntptwL7LjgdmqruEqivbsUqLROemqA418z6GFccqWe709A+4Q
Y5WKndzpXZCO4HSkwUYXwBlNpKRKY3xWFZvlDpMxj/EKjW
S/b1kWopk73yGEy8jmKktogollVfBSGEZD+4qs=</dsig:Signatur
eValue>
        <dsig:KeyInfo>
          <d:KeyValue
xmlns:d="http://www.w3.org/2000/09/xmldsig#">
            <d:RSAKeyValue>

<d:Modulus>ANjD0DM0mcCOoEhYC4X551U6q/78RHwF+cZHmMSYTa3
HJKLcmpQ/Xa
    WpPDH7JQ9VIq8QyAT3x1+4Me/LY9Mt/V4KBb+
gEHx9DRpWMY3T85JYIGfvHB1d4k35RBoFBAK8Dg5kvEpaBL2hqsxPx
Jeln0KxDeHu/8bKtO7zd9E9Vn3H</d:Modulus>
                <d:Exponent>AQAB</d:Exponent>
            </d:RSAKeyValue>
          </d:KeyValue>
        </dsig:KeyInfo>
      </dsig:Signature>
    </xkms:ValidateResult>
```

Figure 7–19   Result of Validating Key Information From an XKMS Client—*continued*.

Implication

Many existing key management and PKI implications deployed in the last two years do not support X-KRSS and X-KISS. Most of them use PKI vendor's Java technology implementation. Unless customers change their business model or Trust Domains, it is difficult to envision migration to XKMS just for standards compliance reasons, at least in the near future.

One of the criticisms of XKMS is the complexity of the implementation. This includes awareness and understanding of the PKI and XML technology required to implement XKMS Web Services applications. Besides, the migration from the first-generation PKI implementation (that is, non-XKMS) to XKMS has not yet been well realized.

As key management and digital signatures are the essential elements for implementing secure Web Services applications, XKMS is attractive to customers who have not yet implemented PKI technology. Customers can choose between the business model of implementing an in-house Certificate Authority (which requires lengthy documentations such as Certificate Policies and Certification Practice Statement) or outsourcing to an external Certificate Authority using XKMS standards (which appears to have lower cost of ownership and is easier for interoperability with external business partners).

The original XKMS specification has identified a few security risk areas, including replay attacks and Denial of Service. In essence, developers should include a design that does not allow reusing previous XKMS responses (for example, use of message serial number for identification, timestamps, and processing XKMS requests only with authenticated sources). The quality and reliability of XKMS depends on the design and implementation, not on the specification or toolkit.

Benefits

X-KRSS addresses the issue of vendor-specific PKI implementation and provides an alternative to managed PKI service. X-KISS decouples the dependency of the client support of PKI. It also provides PKI support for mobile devices.

7.5.3   SAML

Background

Security Assertion Markup Language (SAML) is designed to enable the secure exchange of authentication, authorization (entitlement), and profile information between trading partners across heterogeneous platforms. This includes Single Sign-on within the internal organization or across enterprises and is independent of the underlying security infrastructure. SAML is derived from two previous security initiatives: Security Services Markup Language (S2ML) and Authorization Markup Language (AuthXML).

Before SAML emerged, customers used proprietary interfaces, proprietary Single Sign-on vendor products, or directory-based products to address Single Sign-on within an enterprise. Cross-enterprise Single Sign-on has been a challenge for B2B integration.

SAML is a key element in a Network Identity solution because it can collaborate and integrate with Federated Identity services (different authentication and authorization infrastructures). The SAML Issuing Authority may be a third-party security Service Provider (such as Microsoft PASSPORT, XNSORG, or DotGNU) or Project Liberty alliance (a list of the founding members can be found at *http://www.project liberty.org/membership/members.asp*). It is also a core part of Web Services security, if we put SAML, XKMS, and WS-Security into a bigger picture.

Design Features

SAML has a good architectural model that depicts a domain of *Credential Collector, Authentication Authority, Session Authority, Attribute Authority,* and *Policy Decision Point.* Figure 7–20 depicts a scenario where a system entity (client) wants to send an application request to access a system resource. The system entity presents its user credentials to the Credentials Collector, who will authenticate with the associated Authentication Authority (authentication assertion), the Attribute Authority (attribute assertion), and Policy Decision Point (authorization decision assertion) before the system entity can be granted access (Policy). The Policy Enforcement Point will process the application request based on the access rights granted in the Policy. All assertion requests are represented in SAML.

Client requests for access (for example, credential or authentication assertion) come from a *System Entry Point* (refer to the System Entity in Figure 7–20), routed to different Authorities where authenticated and authorized requests will be routed to the relevant *Policy Enforcement Point* for execution.

These architectural entities resemble different instances of Certificate Authority, Registration Authority, and Directory Server in real life, within an enterprise, external trust service, or trading partners. For example, the *Credential Collector* is like a RADIUS protocol that front-ends the authentication process and passes to the Directory Server (or Authentication Authority) relevant user credentials for authenticating the login.

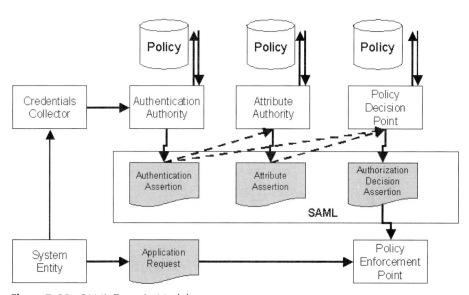

Figure 7–20 SAML Domain Model

SAML differentiates *Attribute Assertion* and *Decision Assertion* within Authentication Assertion. Architecturally, SAML assertions are encoded in an XML package and consist of *Basic Information* (such as unique identifier of the assertion and issue date and time), *Claims* (document describing how the assertion makes claims for Authorization and Key Delegation applications), *Conditions* (dependency or rule for the assertion), and Advice (specification of the assertion for policy decision).

SAML messages bind to SOAP as the underlying transport. SAML uses SOAP-RPC for invoking different assertions. During the login process, SAML allows credentials to be collected from different types of devices, such as mobile phone (for example, Systinet supports this mobile device implementation using a WASP Card [a virtual smart card that stores user credentials] as depicted in *http://www.theserverside.com/resources/article.jsp?l=Systinet-web-services-part-6*). SAML assumes the use of session management for authentication and authorization (entitlement).

Figure 7–21 shows a SAML request sent from a relying party and requesting password authentication by the issuing party.

The Issuing Authority (Service Provider) asserts that the client request has been authenticated and thus returns with a SAML response (see Figure 7–22).

```
<samlp:Request MajorVersion="1" MinorVersion="0"
RequestID="1fgtTGzMXSqpN++/LcFpBmZWrQg=">
<samlp:RespondWith>AuthenticationStatement</samlp:
RespondWith>
<samlp:AuthenticationQuery>
<saml:Subject>
<saml:NameIdentifier Name="test"/>
<saml:SubjectConfirmation>
<saml:ConfirmationMethod>
http://www.oasis-open.org/committies/security/docs/
draft-sstc-core-25/password
</saml:ConfirmationMethod>
<saml:SubjectConfirmationData>
cGFzc3dvcmQ=
</saml:SubjectConfirmationData>
</saml:SubjectConfirmation>
</saml:Subject>
</samlp:AuthenticationQuery>
</samlp:Request>
```

Figure 7–21   Sample SAML Message to Request Password Authentication

```
  <samlp:Response InResponseTo="1fgtTGzMXSpqN++/
LcFpBmZWrQg="
    MajorVersion="1" MinorVersion="0"
  ResponseID="upuSGdmqx7ov01mExYlt+6bDCWE=">
  <samlp:Status>
  <samlp:StatusCode Value="samlp:Success"/>
  </samlp:Status>
  <saml:Assertion
AssertionID="+1UyxJDBUza+ao+LqMrE98wmhAI="
  IssueInstant="2002-03-03T14:33:58.456"
Issuer="WASPCard"
  MajorVersion="1" MinorVersion="0">
  <saml:Conditions NotBefore="2002-03-03T14:33:58.466"
  NotOnOrAfter="2002-03-03T15:03:58.466"/>
  <saml:AuthenticationStatement
  AuthenticationInstant="2002-03-03T14:33:55.201"
  AuthenticationMethod="http://www.oasis-
open.org/committies/security/docs/draft-sstc-core-25/
password">
  <saml:Subject>
  <saml:NameIdentifier Name="test"
SecurityDomain="card:SQLDatabase"/>
  <saml:SubjectConfirmation>
  <saml:ConfirmationMethod>
  http://www.oasis-
open.org/committies/security/docs/draft-sstc-core-25/
password
  </saml:ConfirmationMethod>
  </saml:SubjectConfirmation>
  </saml:Subject>
  </saml:AuthenticationStatement>
  </saml:Assertion>
  </samlp:Response>
```

Figure 7–22 Sample SAML Response—Password Authenticated

Examples of vendors supporting SAML implementation include Sun Microsystems' Sun ONE Identity Server, Entrust's getAccess Portal, Systinet's WASP Secure Identity, Securant's RSA Cleartrust, Entegrity's AssureAccess, and Netegrity's jSAML Toolkit.

Implication

One concern of SAML is related to how it ensures trust between client and SAML entities and perhaps how to register SAML entities. According to the SAML-SOAP binding specification, SAML assumes that some system components will perform authentication for the SAML requester. Thus, it does not enforce any authentication between the SAML requester and responder or mandatory encryption to protect the SAML message contents. Thus, the quality and the robustness of the security implementation will vary by each customer's implementation. If a customer chooses to use strong authentication options (such as smart card with X.509v3 certificate for authentication) and data encryption, then the quality of the security implementation will be higher.

Another area of concern is threat profiling, which was not articulated in early draft specifications. A very good discussion on the threat models for SAML messages and their countermeasures can now be found in Mishra's SAML binding specification paper and McLaren's SAML security consideration paper in *http://www.oasis-open.org/committees/security/docs.*

The integration of an existing security infrastructure with SAML is not clearly articulated in the current SAML specifications. Existing customers who want to implement SAML will be interested in the migration roadmap (for example, what SAML components to buy versus build or what SAML plug-ins are available for Web servers and Directory Server) and implication (for example, upgrade effort for Policy Server and the development impact to existing applications in order to support SAML). Such impact may be much clearer after the final SAML specifications are fully implemented by major security vendors. Baltimore has a good paper on SelectAccess (*http://www.baltimore.com/resources/whitepapers.asp*) to depict how its SAML implementation integrates with its existing security infrastructure using a SAML plug-in. This may give us some ideas of the potential impact.

Benefits

The immediate benefit is the capability for Single Sign-on within the enterprise and across enterprises (B2B integration).

7.5.4   Project Liberty

Background

Project Liberty (*www.projectliberty.org*) is a multi-industry business alliance established to define and promote security standards for network identity, network authentication, and network authorization (entitlement). There is large industry clout behind the supporting community, including AOL and Sun Microsystems. The premise of these security specifications is to provide a federated identity across enterprises that are connected on the Internet. This enables distributed data to be accessible by the "rightful" owner (entitlement) and allows multiple authenticators where merchants can retain control of transaction requirements. More importantly, Project Liberty supports multiple device and platform infrastructures for easier integration and interoperability.

Please note that there are recent discussions (for instance, *http://idevnews.com/Case Studies.asp?ID=36, http://www.eweek.com/article2/0,3959,425843,00.asp*) about the convergence of Project Liberty and other Web Services security specifications under OA-SIS. It is anticipated that OASIS would work closely to bridge the gaps between different security specifications in the next few months, which can benefit the user community.

Design Features

The initial proposal of Project Liberty includes the following stages: *Single Sign-on* for e-Wallet applications (which involves use of context-sensitive cookies and multi-authenticator systems), *Federated Data Exchange* (which uses extensive schema with mappings between partners, and strong cryptographic mechanisms between trading partners), *B2B Transaction Support* (which provides asynchronous communication and non-repudiation), and *Web Services* as end-points (distributed redundant data for identity theft protection).

Figure 7–23 summarizes the Liberty concept in the use of cross-domain Single Sign-on. There are three key actors: User Agent (aka User, security agent), Service Provider (provider of services to users), and Identity Provider (provider for identifying user identity). User Agent sends an HTTP request to Service Provider for Single Sign-on (step 1). Service Provider responds by redirecting to Identity Provider (step 2). User Agent sends a request to Identity Provider (step 3). Identity Provider responds by redirecting to Service Provider (step 4). User Agent sends an authentication request to Service Provider with URI (step 5).

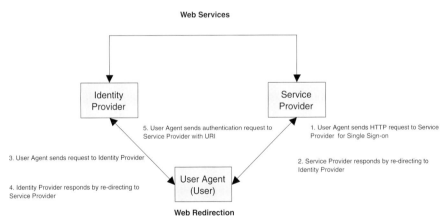

Figure 7–23 Liberty Concept

Implication

Java continues to be the underlying framework and tool for implementing Project Liberty. J2SE version 1.4 Platform Security now incorporates many key elements to support the development of these security features, including Java Authentication and Authorization Service (JAAS), Java Secure Socket Extension (JSSE), Java GSS, Certification

Path (CertPath), and Java Cryptographic Architecture (JCA)/Java Cryptographic Extension (JCE). JAAS provides a Kerberos login module, and Java GSS-API provides functionality to support Kerberos-based authentication. JSSE provides an API to support SSL and TLS, which is a crucial transport layer for SOAP messaging and for mobile commerce. CertPath provides certificate chain validation and LDAP-based certificate validation. JAAS provides Single Sign-on support for Kerberos and digital certificate-based authentication and authorization.

Early discussions of Project Liberty have involved SAML, XML Encryption, and XML Signature elements. Some vendors have announced the availability of their commercial implementation, such as the Sun ONE Identity Server. Microsoft PASSPORT appears to be at the other end of the camp, and there are discussions about incorporating Liberty support by PASSPORT in Liberty 1.1 specification. With the publication of IBM and Microsoft's WS-Security roadmap in April of 2002, it remains to be seen whether the proposed WS-Security roadmap will leverage, converge, or diverge with Project Liberty.

Difference Between Liberty and SAML

Liberty extends the SAML schema for authentication assertion. It adds mobile client support and digital certificates (Public Key Infrastructure) for identity assertion. However, the initial phase of Liberty does not include Authorization Assertion. SAML has included both authorization and attribute assertions. Both Liberty and SAML support Single Sign-on requirements, but each has a different focus. And they are not identical. Please refer to the Liberty specifications for details.

Benefits

The benefits of Project Liberty come from vendor- and technology-platform neutrality. This will also expedite an industry-wide implementation of national identity and federated identity between trading partners for B2B integration.

7.5.5   Other Initiatives

The OASIS (*http://www.oasis-open.org/committees/security/index.shtml*) and XML Trust Center (*http://www.xmltrustcenter.org/index.htm*) Web sites identify some other initiatives. Among these initiatives, XML Access Control Markup Language (XACML), under OASIS, defines policies of using and accessing different parts of XML messages. IBM is driving this using its product, XML Security Suite.

Some early initiatives have either been superseded by the current Web Services security specifications or slowed down. For example, XML Authorization Markup Language (XAML) was proposed in 2000 to support transaction authority, but SAML has emerged to provide a broader functionality.

7.5.6   Some Web Services Security Tools

The following are some examples of useful Web Services security tools that are publicly available. These are not exhaustive, but they are fairly handy for understanding the new technology, evaluation, and Proof of Concept.

Titan (Security Hardening Tool).   Titan is a fairly comprehensive platform-security assessment and hardening tool. You can download it from *http://www.fish.com/titan/.* To install it, uncompress the tar files, and run the installation script. The script "Titan" will scan the target host, and the script "TitanReport" will render the scanning analysis and recommendation.

VeriSign's Trust Services Integration Kit (XKMS).   You can download TSIK version 1.1 from *http://www.xmltrustcenter.org/developer/verisign/ tsik/download.htm.* There is a concise installation document. You need to add a few jar files (tsik.jar, xml_pilot_key.jar, xml_prod_key.jar, and xerces. jar) into the CLASSPATH in order to execute the sample programs or any home-grown programs.

IBM's XML Security Suite (XML-ENC, XML-DSIG, XACML).   You can download the XML Security Suite (XSS4J) from *http://alphaworks. ibm.com/tech/xmlsecuritysuite.* You'll need to add some new jar files (xercesImpl.jar and xmlParserAPIs.jar from Xerces2 and xalan.jar and xml-apis.jar from Xalan2) to the CLASSPATH. The user interface for managing access rights control can be invoked by `java com.ibm.xml.policy. tool.VisualTool.`

7.5.7   Design Considerations

Digital Signature and Signing Server

Some customers implement a Signing Server to generate a digital signature for the client, instead of generating from the client browser. Figure 7–24 depicts a scenario where a service request (client) uses a Signing Server to digitally sign a SOAP message. The Signing Server will authenticate the credentials (usually user id and password, as in step 1) against the client access profile. The client has just made a business transaction from the online shopping Web site. The business data is encapsulated in a SOAP message using JAX (step 2). Upon successful authentication, the signing applet will retrieve the key pairs from a secure database to generate a digital signature for the transaction (step 3) and transmit the transaction with the digital signature (say, in SOAP messages with a digital signature, as in step 4) to the application Service Provider.

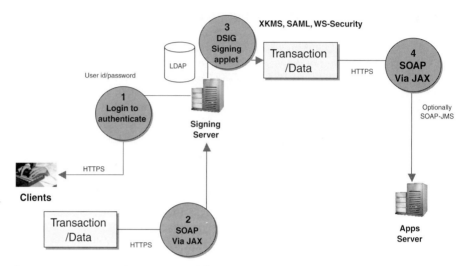

Figure 7–24   Server-Side Signing Model

This design addresses the challenge of a massive PKI security implementation and the associated implementation cost. For example, Internet banking for retail banking services would require tens of thousands of digital certificates to be deployed first. This is a considerable implementation effort with complicated digital certificate management processes and operations. Without the PKI infrastructure, consumers cannot pay their online shopping with their digital signature (generated from their digital certificate). For small and medium-sized financial institutions, PKI implementation would not be pragmatic, in the context of financial risks, implementation risks, and total cost of ownership.

Many online payments via wireless devices utilized the Signing Server design in the early days. For example, most phone handsets do not support a smart card device or cannot store a digital certificate. The Signing Server stores the unique identifier of the phone handset (which is unique for each phone set) and authenticates the user with a valid user id and password. Thus, the Signing Server design would be a good alternative.

Another consideration is that client-side digital-signature generation requires the client browser to install Java Virtual Machine (JVM) version 1.3 or higher. Today's client browsers are configured with JVM version 1.2.x. Users need to install JVM 1.3 or higher manually from Sun's Web site (file size is about 5MB for JRE 1.3 and 12MB for JRE 1.4). If the client browser does not support JVM 1.3 or higher, the client browser session needs to download Java classes (which are jar files of at least 800KB size) in order to sign the transactions at run time. This may take two minutes on a Pentium II 300MHz PC. Alternatively, developers can use some digital signature tools (such as Baltimore's Keytools) that have a lightweight browser plug-in for generating signatures (the Java classes are about 300MB size, which can reduce the signing time to less than a minute).

In summary, client-side generation of digital signatures is conceptually the ideal approach to implementing end-to-end Web Services security. This requires the local client to install a digital certificate and to download a signing applet (JCE/JAAS). The approach is good for customers with PKI infrastructure implemented and for high-value financial transactions. The implementation issue is that most browsers support JVM 1.2.2 or lower, and thus clients either upgrade to JVM 1.3 manually or download a signing applet at run time. The signing applet may have 700KB Java class size. Thus, it has longer response time for the signing. There are also cost and implementation considerations of distributing and administering digital certificates.

Server-side generation of digital signatures denotes an intermediary server generating signatures on behalf of the end users. Certificates will be stored centrally on behalf of customers. A user id and password are used to authenticate the right user before retrieving the corresponding digital certificate for signature generation. This approach is good for mass-market implementation with low-value or zero-value financial transactions. This Signing Server approach does not require each end-user to own and install a digital certificate on its desktop. This raises another security issue—there is a security and liability concern and potentially a legal implication for the intermediary Signing Server. The intermediate server may be vulnerable to hacker or virus attack.

XML Encryption and XML Signature

The current J2SE version 1.4 has provided some building blocks (*http://java. sun.com/security/*) that provide encryption and digital signing functionality—for instance, Java Authentication and Authorization Service (JAAS), Java Cryptography Extension (JCE), and Java Secure Socket Extension (JSSE). On top of that, JSR 183 Web Services message security API (*http://jcp.org/en/jsr/detail?id=183*) is a proposed Java Specification Request to incorporate Java APIs to support WS-Security, including XML Encryption and XML Signature.

Before JSR 183 is accepted and implemented in J2SE, several vendor products have now provided a vendor-specific reference implementation (such as Apache Axis and IBM XML Security Suite) for encrypting and signing SOAP messages. For instance, IBM's XML Security Suite (*http://www.alphaworks.ibm.com/aw.nsf/download/ xmlsecuritysuite*) has some sample source codes found in its binary distribution under /xss4j/samples/enc and /xss4j/samples/dsig.

Buy Versus Build

Most Web Services security tools are publicly available as a download or integrated with application servers. These tools are targeted for the developer audience. Thus, it is much easier to "buy" the tools versus write them from scratch.

Although the security specifications evolve quickly, it is often beneficial and strategic to build some small prototypes yourself to get up to date with the technology so that you can understand more about the design and implementation considerations.

7.6   Web Services Security Patterns

Most of the security technologies depicted in this chapter may not provide a complete solution to many complex business problems. They need to be combined and implemented together in order to be contextual to different business issues. Here are some Web Services security design patterns. For each, we describe a scenario where the design pattern may be applied, followed by some discussion of how different Web Services security technologies can be implemented to provide complete business solutions.

7.6.1   Single Sign-on Pattern

Context

Single Sign-on has been a requirement for many enterprises. Cross-domain Single Sign-on is one of the major challenges of Web Services security. Under a B2B cross-enterprise integration scenario (such as automated dispute management and exceptions management), a trading partner's server may need to access different servers from multiple trading partners' infrastructure. Architects and developers need a vendor-independent framework to perform cross-domain Single Sign-on with login once for each application.

Each of the current security specifications and initiatives, such as Liberty and Security Assertion Markup Language (SAML), can only address certain aspects of cross-domain Single Sign-on. Liberty specification version 1.1 defines an authentication mechanism using a federated identity service model. It extends existing SAML schema for authentication entities, but does not address authorization, access control, or policies. On the other hand, SAML does not validate the identity or credentials presented during the authentication process.

This security design pattern will address the requirement of cross-domain Single Sign-on. SAML assertions can be encapsulated in the XML message payload just like a security token. Upon successful authentication using the Liberty solution, the client will establish a trust with different servers. The system can then pass SAML assertions across trading partners' servers using the existing SAML specification. This will provide a trusted environment to support cross-domain Single Sign-on from authentication and authorization to policies.

Problem

Users who have access to two or more different Service Providers have different login ids and passwords. As the Service Providers are using different platforms and technologies for the applications, users usually need to log in once for each Service Provider's application. If users need to switch from one application to another across different Service Providers (that is, cross-domain), they have to log in twice.

There are security products that support cross-domain Single Sign-on, but most of them require an affiliate agent (proprietary plug-in to the Web Server and/or Application Server that stores session cookies to enable Single Sign-on). Most Service Providers do not accept "foreign" (not their own domain or application systems) security modules or plug-ins from their trading partners to be installed in their application infrastructure because this may expose them to unknown security risks.

Forces

The level of security trust (the environment and level of security protection where the Service Requester may be operating) between the Service Requester and Service Providers varies, and it is difficult to agree on a common security standard.

It may be not viable to install an affiliate agent to all trading partners' production environments to achieve Single Sign-on, as each trading partner may have different security requirements.

There may be considerable security integration costs, if a vendor-specific Single Sign-on product is used.

Solution

It is recommended to adopt the Open Standards security standards SAML and Liberty to meet Single Sign-on requirements. They do not require installing any proprietary affiliate agent on the trading partner's site.

Figure 7–25 depicts what service components need to be built in order to implement cross-domain Single Sign-on. A Service Requester is a subscriber to the user community who provides online shopping and business services in a portal service. There are two different Service Providers supplying the online shopping and business services, each of which has a different system infrastructure (or different domains).

In Figure 7–25, a common security domain needs to be defined to enclose the Service Requester and all the associated Service Providers (trading partners). This requires the use of Identity Server (Identity Provider that centrally authenticates for the Service Requester and redirects to the Service Providers and/or Identity Providers). The physical Identity Server may reside in an external Service Provider that provides identity management services, or in the Service Requester's system environment.

Each of the system resources (for example, Application Server, Messaging Hub) will make use of User Agents (security agents that can intercept and respond to Liberty or SAML assertion requests). User Agents that are compliant with Liberty and SAML specifications can be implemented using Liberty-enabled or SAML-enabled development toolkits (such as Sun ONE Identity Server *http://www.sun.com/software/products/identity_srvr/home_identity.html*). The Service Requester needs to only log in once using a Single Sign-on User Agent. An authentication assertion request will be redirected to the Identity Server. Upon successful authentication, session information will be stored as server cookies in the Common Domain. If the Service Requester needs to access any applications or resources, whether in the Business Tier or in the Resource Tier, the User Agents will create Attribute Assertion or Authorization Assertion requests. It is also recommended to use the XML Access Control Markup Language (XACML) to express policies for information access (refer to *http://www. oasis-open.org/committees/xacml/* for details). Upon the successful processing of these assertions, the Service Requester can access and retrieve information according to the policies set for the entitled access rights and roles.

The Common Domain processes different assertion requests that are processed in each domain. Thus, it doesn't matter if the two domains are using different system architecture; the Identity Server can support Single Sign-on, provided that the User Agents deployed in each resource and in each tier are Liberty- and/or SAML-compliant. Refer to Figure 7–25 for more details.

There are some differences between the Liberty and the SAML approach in implementing Single Sign-on. You can use the SAML approach to implement cross-domain Single Sign-on without using Liberty. However, this will not address identity management issues, such as the authenticity of the Service Requester, or mobile/wireless support for SAML clients. On the other hand, the current Liberty specification version 1.1 does not support Authorization Assertion yet. Thus, it would be a good combina-

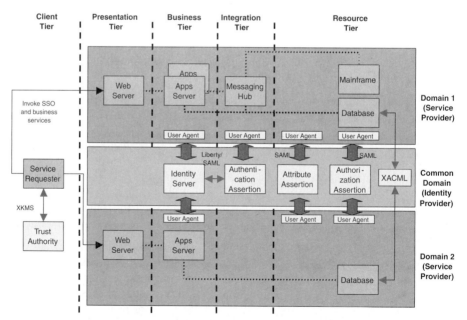

Figure 7–25 Single Sign-on Pattern

tion to use Liberty for identity management and Authentication Assertion while using SAML for Authorization Assertion and XACML for Policy Management. The Service Requester can also make use of an external Trust Authority to provide and administer user credentials (for example, digital certificates or key management), instead of implementing PKI or certificate management solutions within its operating environment. Please also refer to the sections in this chapter on Liberty, SAML, and XML Key Management Specification (XKMS) for details.

Figure 7–26 elaborates the details of the cross-domain Single Sign-on process. Under the hybrid security environment, after the Service Requester provides user credentials for Single Sign-on, the Identity Server will redirect authentication to the Identity Provider or Service Provider in Liberty protocol. Upon the successful processing of the Authentication Assertion request, the Service Requester will be granted sign-on to the common security domain. If the Service Requester makes an application request to access or update a system resource, an Authorization Assertion request will be created. The Policy Management module (for example, Policy Server) will forward the user access rights information to the Policy Decision Point (PDP), which will relate the user access rights information with the Authorization Assertion request. The application request will be also forwarded to Policy Enforcement Point (PEP). The PEP, once it has user access rights and policies from the Policy Management module, will process the Authorization Assertion request.

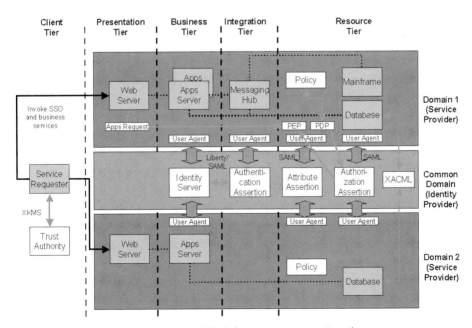

Figure 7–26 Single Sign-on Pattern With Policy Management Details

Liberty specification version 1.1 has depicted the interaction and process between the User Agent, Service Provider, and Identity Provider in detail. The following sequence diagrams recapitulate the detailed processes from "Liberty Bindings and Profiles Specification." (*http://www.projectliberty.org/specs/liberty-architecture- bindings-profiles-v1.1.pdf*).

Figure 7–27 depicts the details of Single Sign-on activities in a sequence diagram. When the Service Requester logs in, the Single Sign-on User Agent will issue an HTTP request for authentication to the Service Provider (in this example, Domain 1). The Service Provider obtains the Identity Provider Id, which is the Identity Server in the Common Domain. The Service Provider will then respond to the User Agent's authentication request with the Identity Provider Id. The User Agent will then redirect the authentication request to the Identity Provider, which is the Identity Server of the Common Domain.

Upon receiving the authentication request from the User Agent, the Identity Provider processes the request and returns with an authentication request response and an artifact. The User Agent now can send an Authentication Assertion request with the artifact to the Service Provider, which will send an HTTP request with the artifact to the Identity Provider. The Identity Provider will then return with an Authentication Assertion request response to the Service Provider. The Service Provider will process the response and return the result (for example, authentication completed and grant access) to the User Agent. A Common Domain cookie may be created (refer to Figure 7–28 for details).

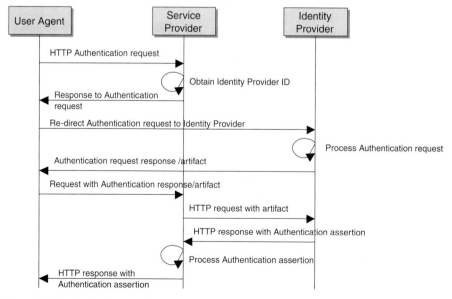

Figure 7–27   Single Sign-on Sequence Diagram

You can create Common Domain cookies to track the Identity Provider ids allowed in the Common Domain. Figure 7–28 elaborates the details of how to create a Common Domain cookie in a sequence diagram. Upon the successful processing of the Authentication Assertion requests, the Identity Provider redirects the User Agent to the cookie-writing service. The User Agent then accesses the cookie-writing service URL. The Common Domain cookie-writing service (implemented in the Identity Server) processes the request to write cookies and redirects to the Identity Provider Return URL upon completion of the cookie-writing service. Then the User Agent can access the Identity Provider Return URL. For details, please refer to "Liberty Bindings and Profiles Specification." (*http://www.projectliberty.org/specs/liberty-architecture-bindings-profiles-v1.1.pdf*).

Benefits

This pattern is intended for cross-domain Single Sign-on. It also works for Single Sign-on within the same domain because the Identity Server for the cross-domain scenario manages the Authentication Assertion the same way as in the cross-domain scenario. Achieving Single Sign-on can improve the user experience and customer expectations, as well as reduce the internal system or B2B integration cost.

The proposed solution does not require a proprietary affiliate agent and is compliant with Liberty, SAML, and XACML where architects and developers can select a wider choice of vendor products for implementation.

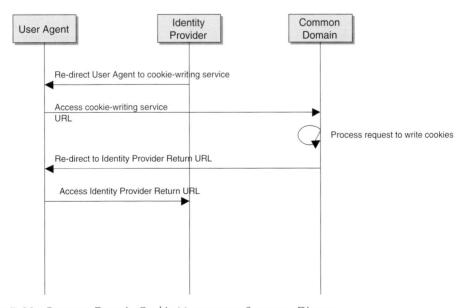

Figure 7–28   Common Domain Cookie Management Sequence Diagram

Risks

Many security specifications and standards are still quickly evolving to add more functionality and features. Liberty specification version 1.1 does not cover authorization, but it may cover authorization and policies in the future releases. If it incorporates SAML Authorization Assertion and XACML Policy Management in the future, architects and developers will be able to use Liberty alone to address the previously mentioned Single Sign-on requirements. The new WS-Security roadmap proposed by IBM, Microsoft, and VeriSign includes similar federation and Policy Management specifications. The existence of similar and competing Web Services security standards and specifications may create industry confusion.

Example

Membership Award Service

The credit card business units of commercial banks that need to provide online membership award services to corporate card customers may require providing Single Sign-on to bank account services (such as credit card account balance and online statements) or membership award redemption from airlines, hotels, and car rental companies. Different trading partners of the commercial bank run different application architectures and do not want to install a proprietary affiliate agent to enable Single Sign-on. Using Liberty-based Identity Server, the commercial bank can enable online corporate customers to sign on once to all membership award service providers. Please also refer to the sample business case in Chapter 2, The Web Services Phenomenon and Emerging Trends.

7.6.2   Messaging Transport Pattern

Context

Early pilots of Web Services applications usually focus on the technology Proof of Concept. Very often, architects and developers do not incorporate any security design in the SOAP message or in the data transport layer. This is because Web Services security for SOAP messaging is still evolving, and there is no reference implementation available yet. In some cases, architects and developers have incorporated the security processing logic in the business logic to provide application security.

Most architects and developers understand that Web Services applications need to secure both the messaging transport and the message contents. The current Web Services security specifications (such as WS-Security *http://www.oasis-open.org/committees/wss/documents/WSS-SOAPMessageSecurity-11-0303.pdf*) describe how the message transport can be secured. Since OASIS has begun to take over the work of Web Services security, there are a few vendor tools that support message-level and data transport layer security for Web Services applications. It is important for architects and developers to be aware of the use of appropriate vendor tools to add message-level and data transport layer security to Web Services applications.

Problem

Many architects and developers embed security business logic into application programs. Thus, when architects and developers need to upgrade the security business logic to a new version or to migrate to a new security standard, they have to modify and retest the application programs.

Tightly coupling the security and application program business logic requires developers to have an in-depth understanding of the security protocols and implementation knowledge.

Force

Many financial services applications require data and message encryption. Developers usually incorporate security-processing logic into the application business logic. Once they make changes to the security-processing standards, considerable effort and impact is required to retrofit changes to all application changes.

The provision of message transport via encryption and digital signature adds performance overhead.

Solution

Web Services security specifications such as WS-Security, XML Encryption, and XML Signature provide guidelines on how to protect the messaging transport layer. Developers can choose to embed the security processing logic (for example, encrypting and decrypting) into the application business logic or decouple the messaging transport from the application business logic.

Figure 7–29 depicts a security pattern where architects and developers decouple the security processing logic (that is, messaging transport security) from the application business logic. Both the consumer (SOAP client) and the Service Provider (SOAP server) should encrypt the business transactions in SOAP messages with XML Encryption and sign them with a digital signature (messaging security). There are SOAP appliances or WS-Security plug-ins for SOAP servers that provide the messaging security without adding the security processing logic in the business logic. The SOAP messages should also be sent over secure data transport such as HTTPS (data transport layer security). Both XML Encryption and XML Signature are used by the WS-Security specification. This allows application business logic to focus on the application processing flow and enables more options to secure the messaging transport based on different costs (for example, operating overheads of encryption and decryption by the application) and benefits (for example, ease of scaling the Web

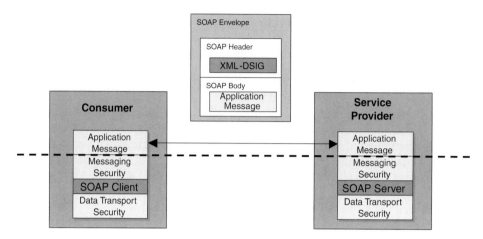

Figure 7–29   Decoupling Messaging Transport From Application Business Logic

Services appliances that handle the XML message encryption). Architects and developers can also easily migrate to a more cost-effective messaging transport solution over time without impacting the application business logic.

Here are some examples of technology options to decouple messaging transport security from the applications:

Web Services Appliances.   There are appliance products that provide XML encryption and decryption, such as Westbridge Technology's (*http://www.westbridgetech.com*). These appliance products, which are usually configured with higher CPU clock speed and encryption hardware devices, are able to use a previously assigned digital certificate (key pairs) to encrypt and decrypt SOAP messages, and thus off-load the performance overhead of the Application Server.

Secure Messaging Provider Class.   There are message provider classes, such as VeriSign's Trust Service Integration Kit, that are designed to provide secure messaging using XML Encryption and XML Signature. They are designed to be the message provider (for example, JAXM message provider) so that the application business logic does not need to cater for the details of message encryption, message decryption, and digital signature.

Risk

The performance overhead of encrypting and decrypting data contents may become a considerable operating cost to the applications. There are different options to address the requirements, such as the use of Web Services appliances to off-load the processing overhead from the applications in a Trust Domain.

Example

Apache Axis provides an example of this Message Transport pattern by implementing a client-signing handler for SOAP messaging security with a digital signature. Refer to the sample code under `%Axis%\samples\security`.

On the accompanying CD-ROM, the `/opt/provider-tsik` subdirectory contains some more examples of the demo code of Secure Messaging Provider Class. Refer to Chapter 8, Web Services in Action Case Study, for more design details.

7.7   Perspectives

7.7.1   Highlights

- XML Encryption and XML Signature are the basic technologies for application- and message-level protection for Web Services applications.
- WS-Security, XKMS, SAML, and XACML are emerging standards and specifications to provide a framework for end-to-end Web Services security. They are complementary in the current stage to cover different aspects. Many of these technologies are implemented as developer toolkits and will be embedded with security infrastructure products.
- Platform security and end-to-end application architecture design are not currently emphasized in Web Services security design. Security hardening tools can be of great help here.

7.7.2   Best Practices and Pitfalls

A checklist for protecting Web Services hosts:

- Run security-hardening tools before development starts and after development completes.
- Always turn off unused network services and ports on the platform operating system.
- Always use encryption and digital signatures for sensitive and confidential transactions.
- Always ensure file protection for configuration files of UDDI registry and WSDL files.

For example, under the Java Web Services Developer Pack development environment (which uses Apache Tomcat as the Web Container), the Web Services objects that may be of interest for security protection and checking are listed in Table 7–3. On the development and production environment (whether Solaris OE™ or Windows), it is always a good practice to protect these objects or files from being a target for attack or exploitation with appropriate access rights.

Table 7–3   Examples of Web Services Objects That Need Security Protection

Web Services Objects	Location	Remarks
Web Container		In this example, this is Apache Tomcat 4.x.
User access control list	D:\Dev\WSDP\conf\tomcat-users.xml	This file contains the user names, user passwords, and roles that are allowed to access and execute resources under the Web Container.
Server configuration file	D:\Dev\WSDP\conf\server.xml	This file contains the server configuration (for example, port number) for running the Tomcat server.
Log Files		
Web Container log files	D:\Dev\WSDP\logs	In this example, Tomcat log files are used. This directory contains log files for Tomcat server (Catalina.out), server administration log (localhost_admin_log°.logand access_log°.log and services_log°.log), as well as Service Registry log (xindice.log).
Developer tool log files	D:\Dev\WSDP\logs\jwsdp_log°.log	In this example, Java Web Services Developer Pack's log files are shown.
Service Registry update activity log file	D:\Dev\WSDP\tools\xindice\logs\xindice.log	In this example, the Xindice database activity log file is used.
Message Provider		
ebXML message provider administration logs	D:\Dev\WSDP\work\Services Engines\jaxm-provider\ebxml	There are four subdirectories that contain the messages received, sent, to be dispatched, and to be sent. This denotes the physical location where the JAXM message provider will send or receive the messages with the reliable message delivery capability.

Table 7–3 Examples of Web Services Objects That Need Security Protection—*continued.*

Web Services Objects	Location	Remarks
SOAP Remote Provider message provider administration logs	D:\Dev\WSDP\work\ Services Engines\ jaxm-provider\soaprp	There are four subdirectories that contain the messages received, sent, to be dispatched, and to be sent. This denotes the physical location where the SOAP remote message provider will send or receive the messages with the reliable message delivery capability
Service Registry		In Java Web Services Developer Pack, UDDI Service Registry is implemented using Xindice object database.
Service Registry files	D:\Dev\WSDP\tools\ xindice\db	This file location contains the subdirectory 'system' for the object database system files and security information, and the subdirectory 'uddi' for the actual UDDI data store.
WSDL documents	N/A	In this demo environment, the WSDL documents are generated dynamically and do not store in the Service Registry.

Here are some considerations:

- Use of HTTPS and encryption has a direct impact on system performance and response time.
- Profile each Web Services call for the benchmarking, and check the log files during the first few months of deployment. The performance statistics can be used as a baseline metric for future comparison and troubleshooting purposes. If there is any abnormal performance or unusual data traffic pattern (for example, a sudden outburst of data traffic may be due to Denial of Service), then security administrators can check the previous Web Services profiling metrics.

7.8   Paper and Pencil

7.8.1   Single Sign-on

Objective

To illustrate how to add a new Service Provider in a SAML-based Single Sign-on environment.

Exercise

Netegrity's jSAML Toolkit (*http://www.netegrity.com/products/index.cfm? leveltwo=JSAML&levelthree=download*) provides a simple Single Sign-on demo environment. This exercise will demonstrate how to add a Foreign Exchange currency exchange service URL (refer to the "Paper and Pencil" exercise in Chapter 3, Web Services Technology Overview, and the demo in Chapter 8, Web Services in Action: Case Study) to the Single Sign-on content provider. It will also be used and referenced in Chapter 8, Web Services in Action: Case Study, as a case study with more details.

Step 1: Set up jSAML Toolkit Demo

Follow the instructions in Appendix C of this book to download and set up a copy of Netegrity's jSAML Toolkit. Extract and install the demo code (`JSAML-toolkit.zip`) under Java the `%JWSDP_HOME%\webapps` of the Web Services Developer Pack's Tomcat server. The following subdirectories should be expected (see Figure 7–30).

Step 2: Verify Set-up

It is recommended to verify the configuration by checking the procedures defined in the jSAML Toolkit documentation "Netegrity JSAML Toolkit In-

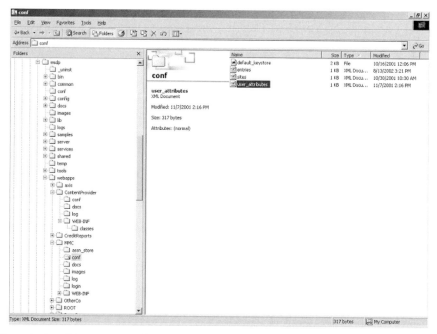

Figure 7–30   jSAML Demo Files Installed under Web Container

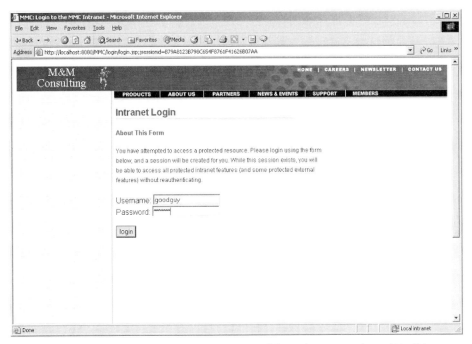

Figure 7–31   Sign-on Screen Shown upon Successful Configuration of Jsaml Toolkit Demo

stallation Guide" version 1.0 from the above URL. Upon successful set-up, developers should see the sign-on screen shown in Figure 7–31 by issuing the URL *http://localhost:8080/MMC/ docs/index.html.*

Step 3: Add New Service URL

Assuming that a new service URL is ready for deploying under a SAML-based Single Sign-on environment, developers can add this new entry in the XML configuration file containing the trading partner URL or service end-point URLs. It is also assumed that the new service URL can be accessed by the same demo id (in this case, goodguy) with full access rights. In some implementations, this may be added as an LDAP entry or an entry in the Policy Server with an administration front-end. In this demo, this entry is added in the configuration file %JWSDP_HOME%\webapps\ MMC\conf\ entries.xml under Java Web Services Developer Pack's Tomcat server. Refer to Figure 7–32 for an example.

```
<ContentsConfiguration>
    <EntryList>
        <Entry>
            <Name>Stock Services</Name>
            <URL>http://www.nasdaq.com</URL>
            <Description>Stock
Services</Description>
            <SiteID>0001</SiteID>
        </Entry>
        <Entry>
            <Name>Techie News</Name>
            <URL>http://www.news.com</URL>
            <Description>Techie News
Service</Description>
            <SiteID>0001</SiteID>
        </Entry>
        <Entry>
            <Name>Financial News</Name>
            <URL>http://www.bloomberg.com</URL>
            <Description>News about finance and
stock</Description>
            <SiteID>0001</SiteID>
        </Entry>
        <Entry>
            <Name>FX Spot Rate Quote</Name>

<URL>http://localhost:8080/ContentProvider/docs/default
Content.htm</URL>
            <Description>Online indicative Foreign
Exchange Spot Rate quote service to meet your traveling
and online shopping needs</Description>
            <SiteID>0001</SiteID>
        </Entry>
    </EntryList>
</ContentsConfiguration>
```

Figure 7–32   Sample Entry in the Service URL Configuration File

In this sample configuration file, it relates the service URL *http://localhost:8080/ContentProvider/docs/defaultContent.htm* to the SiteID 0001 (which is the Service Provider MMC providing Single Sign-on).

Step 4: Modify the Redirect Page to New Service URL

Modify the defaultContent.htm file (see Figure 7–33) to include a URL link to the new service end-point URL *http://localhost:8080/myFX/getFXQuote*. Refer to the HTML file and the sample screen in Figure 7–34.

```
<HTML>
<title>FX Spot Rate Quote Web Service</title>
<body>
<h1>FX Spot Rate Quote Partner Service</h1>
Please click <a
href="http://localhost:8080/myFX/getFXQuote">here
</a>to enter FX Spot Rate Quote Web Service.

</body>
</HTML>
```

Figure 7–33 Modified defaultContent.htm to Redirect to New Service URL

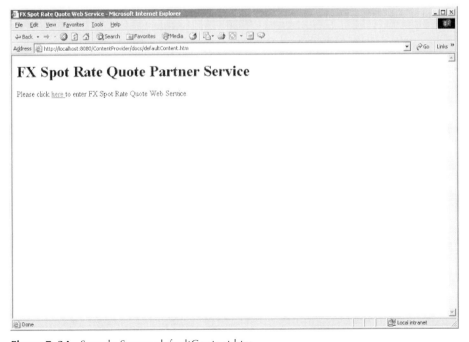

Figure 7–34 Sample Screen defaultContent.htm

7.8.2   Messaging Transport

Objective

To illustrate how to implement a secure messaging provider class for the Messaging Transport pattern.

Exercise

This exercise reuses the JAXM messaging provider class from Chapter 8, Web Services in Action: Case Study, to illustrate the Messaging Transport. Can you find out what transaction information is embedded in the SOAP message with digital signature? (Answers highlighted in bold in the following excerpt).

The SOAP message generated from the JAXM messaging provider class can be found in the file soap_client.out (refer to Figure 7–35) under the directory /opt/myFX/requester.

```
Request message #1
================================
<?xml version="1.0" encoding="UTF-8"?>

<s:Envelope
xmlns:s="http://schemas.xmlsoap.org/soap/envelope/">
    <s:Header>
        <wsse:Security s:mustUnderstand="1"

xmlns:wsse="http://schemas.xmlsoap.org/ws/2002/04/sece
xt/">
            <ds:Signature
xmlns:ds="http://www.w3.org/2000/09/xmldsig#">
                <ds:SignedInfo>
                    <ds:CanonicalizationMethod
Algorithm="http://www.w3.org/2001/10/xml-exc-c14n#"/>
                    <ds:SignatureMethod
Algorithm="http://www.w3.org/2000/09/xmldsig#rsa-
sha1"/>
                    <ds:Reference
URI="#xpointer(/s:Envelope/s:Body)">
                        <ds:Transforms>
                            <ds:Transform
Algorithm="http://www.w3.org/2001/10/xml-exc-c14n#"/>
                        </ds:Transforms>
```

Figure 7–35 Sample JAXM Message for the Service Request

```
                        <ds:DigestMethod
Algorithm="http://www.w3.org/2000/09/xmldsig#sha1"/>

<ds:DigestValue>2nEFD9/gnWcRrjRk0vHJtqfXqqU=</ds:Diges
tValue>
                        </ds:Reference>
                    </ds:SignedInfo>

<ds:SignatureValue>qKOD2oJUzjmk19vKc+pZ4jEVBeseYB1zZPw
ENI032XzEQEgSZCbqeVUsD0uDCPu9R2fIPBQs&#13;
+uw7++lSQNOjHvWVD1nUTPIOp38fNU6XMWfpqF+ww2tBdwkUDiM8no
YtB8CnNx9Tv5ejlzd5&#13;
dxh3NJYblZ21WDLUC2MTzF7STMU=</ds:SignatureValue>
                    <ds:KeyInfo>
                        <ds:KeyName>Public key of
certificate</ds:KeyName>
                        <ds:KeyValue>
                            <ds:RSAKeyValue>

<ds:Modulus>tgpcm093Tjvxi/jVulUMvC5gov+8iamjVxkrwELUQq
kFV+lwZcYrJwaXZvHlJLUw6vFCOl9m&#13;
vhbIGW3t1RKo8sygCqtqe/DBR+XMGYTy6SkP24TDDI43mBgkdVauHC
TgV4JYNLcIlTlPIQEm&#13;
U+f8ftYPLVGFGiHGuYG/SfCnEUE=</ds:Modulus>

<ds:Exponent>AQAB</ds:Exponent>
                            </ds:RSAKeyValue>
                        </ds:KeyValue>
                        <ds:X509Data>

<ds:X509Certificate>MIIDmTCCA0OgAwIBAgIQN7Dt8b73agsj5f
5CW8v+jDANBgkqhkiG9w0BAQQFADCBmTERMA8G&#13;
...
RzuboyCGHqCUMKrFTHr9NdWNxqYigSDIjBvoJeyA1sVXR4tbitco4Z
57+mqUSak53HBOK1iW&#13;
UR9EDaR70A==</ds:X509Certificate>
                        </ds:X509Data>
                    </ds:KeyInfo>
                </ds:Signature>
            </wsse:Security>
        </s:Header>
```

Figure 7–35 Sample JAXM Message for the Service Request—*continued.*

```
    <s:Body>
        <request>
<currency>hkd</currency>
</request>
    </s:Body>
</s:Envelope>

Reply message #1
==============================
<?xml version="1.0" encoding="UTF-8"?>

<s:Envelope
xmlns:s="http://schemas.xmlsoap.org/soap/envelope/">
    <s:Header>
        <wsse:Security s:mustUnderstand="1"

xmlns:wsse="http://schemas.xmlsoap.org/ws/2002/04/sece
xt/">
            <ds:Signature
xmlns:ds="http://www.w3.org/2000/09/xmldsig#">
                <ds:SignedInfo>
                    <ds:CanonicalizationMethod
Algorithm="http://www.w3.org/2001/10/xml-exc-c14n#"/>
                    <ds:SignatureMethod
Algorithm="http://www.w3.org/2000/09/xmldsig#rsa-
sha1"/>
                    <ds:Reference
URI="#xpointer(/s:Envelope/s:Body)">
                        <ds:Transforms>
                            <ds:Transform
Algorithm="http://www.w3.org/2001/10/xml-exc-c14n#"/>
                        </ds:Transforms>
                        <ds:DigestMethod
Algorithm="http://www.w3.org/2000/09/xmldsig#sha1"/>

<ds:DigestValue>NoJLjBHXQG5U3aBBhGYqvOleAf4=</ds:Diges
tValue>
                    </ds:Reference>
                </ds:SignedInfo>
```

Figure 7–35   Sample JAXM Message for the Service Request—*continued.*

```
                <ds:SignatureValue>UThG2f96M7ban5M
TeeBgVkg8bSG482+pH2CImMdKs9saTNpJGDsBBKayhixs1jt+RUvsM
lpT&#13;
eHTL2RipdT3bVNaBi2UZYxuJcGFHFwuW7BDQcPrEI/F6T4qTkzZSNo
aAb27XeGbWbHd5BUTo&#13;
5YEXBxOfY3WGBn/gBYh9qpSFM8E=</ds:SignatureValue>
                <ds:KeyInfo>
                    <ds:KeyName>Public key of
certificate</ds:KeyName>
                    <ds:KeyValue>
                        <ds:RSAKeyValue>

<ds:Modulus>ovig7pVPyrVlhp3BS/TsO/+Fvoa3I8mtzr0aPXVJEg
lBrMuP8HUF+1F41EerIwTkoJS7cJX9&#13;
KqrzYokmLS/NA09Y/Jw3LNwO74tzQRNQ71V7Ifi7DBQWKuJKGBPRvS
SIgYBA9KA5xRLBhXPr&#13;
92YrjgUcJKZ2dM6TNxBzE7JGj0U=</ds:Modulus>

<ds:Exponent>AQAB</ds:Exponent>
                        </ds:RSAKeyValue>
                    </ds:KeyValue>
                    <ds:X509Data>

<ds:X509Certificate>MIICITCCAcsCEDCzpHpOuizSJRp/MNyjeN
kwDQYJKoZIhvcNAQEEBQAwXzELMAkGA1UEBhMC&#13;
...
GHLCmXN5kBU8</ds:X509Certificate>
                    </ds:X509Data>
                </ds:KeyInfo>
            </ds:Signature>
        </wsse:Security>
    </s:Header>
    <s:Body>
        <YourRequestWasAccepted>
            <request>
<currency>hkd</currency>
</request>
            <profile> Hong Kong dollar </profile>
        </YourRequestWasAccepted>
    </s:Body>
</s:Envelope>
```

Figure 7–35 Sample JAXM Message for the Service Request—*continued.*

The Figure 7–35 SOAP message is created by the program `Profile-Servlet.java` (refer to Figure 7–36), which is used by the case study as a secure messaging provider class using WS-Security. The SOAP request message contains a request to look up the currency code "HKD" for the full description. The SOAP reply message returns with the description "Hong Kong Dollars."

This program (refer to Figure 7–36) signs the SOAP messages with a preassigned digital certificate (but it does not encrypt the message in the demo) before sending the contents to the recipient. It is intended to be the underlying JAXM message provider class for other programs.

```
public class ProfileServlet extends HttpServlet
{
    private static final String DEFAULT_KEYSTORE_FILE =
"/opt/myFX/requester/sample_soap_keystore";
    private static final String DEFAULT_KEYSTORE_PASSWORD
= "changeit";
    private static final String DEFAULT_SERVICE_ALIAS =
"service";
    private static final String DEFAULT_CLIENT_ALIAS =
"client";

    private PrivateKey serviceKey;
    private X509Certificate serviceCert;
    private X509Certificate clientCert;
    private SimpleTrustVerifier trustVerifier;
    private Key encryptingKey;
    private static XMLResource xml;

  ...

    public void doPost(HttpServletRequest req, HttpServle-
tResponse res)
    throws ServletException, IOException
    {
        try {
                // Generate the data encrypting key
                //
                //encryptingKey = createTripleDESKey();
```

Figure 7–36 Program Excerpt Showing JAXM Secure Message Provider Class

```
              // parse the xml request
              Document doc = parseRequest(req);

              // reject if not a SOAP message
              if (!SOAPMessage.isSOAPMessage(doc)) {
                    publishFault(null, "s:Client",
                          "This service only accepts SOAP
messages", res);
                    return;
                    }

              // interpret request as a SOAP message
              SOAPMessage msg = new SOAPMessage(doc);

               // verify request signature; the trust verifier
will check that the
              // signing cert is the client's cert (a cert that
we trust)
              try {
                  msg.verify(trustVerifier);
              } catch (Throwable e) {
                    publishFault(e, "wsse:FailedCheck",
                        "Unable to verify signature or signing
key is untrusted",
                        res);
                  return;
              }

              // decrypt body of request
              try {
                  msg.decrypt(serviceKey);
              } catch (Throwable e) {
                  publishFault(e, "wsse:FailedCheck",
                     "Unable to decrypt body of request", res);
                   return;
                  }
```

Figure 7–36 Program Excerpt Showing JAXM Secure Message Provider Class—*continued.*

```
            // create the response body from the request body
            doc = makeResponse(msg.extractBody());

            // create SOAP message from response body
            msg = new SOAPMessage(doc);

            // encrypt the response body
            // msg.encrypt(encryptingKey, null,
              //clientCert.getPublicKey(), null, null);

            // sign the response
            msg.sign(serviceKey, serviceCert);

            // write the response
            publishResponse(doc, res);

    } catch (IOException e) {
        throw e;
    } catch (Exception e) {
        throw new ServletException(e);
        }
    }
```

Figure 7–36   Program Excerpt Showing JAXM Secure Message Provider Class—*continued.*

The technical design details of digital signatures and WS-Security can be referenced in the relevant sections previously in this chapter, as well as in Chapter 8, Web Services in Action: Case Study.

7.8.3   References

General Web Services Security

Web Services Security. *http://www.xwss.org/index.jsp*

Andrew Yang. *"XML Web Services Security Issues."*
    http://www.xwss.org/articlesThread.jsp?forum=34&thread=648

XKMS

Brett Mandel. *"XKMS Headlines XML Security, Takes a Hard Line on Complexity."* March 19, 2002.

http://dcb.sun.com/practices/webservices/overviews/overview_xkms.jsp

SAML

Baltimore Technologies. *"Building Online Partnerships with SAML—A SelectAccess Technical White Paper."* 2002.
http://www.baltimore.com/resources/whitepapers.asp

Chris McLaren, ed. *"Security and Privacy Considerations for the OASIS Security Assertion Markup Language."* OASIS. April 19, 2002. *http://www.oasis-open. org/committees/security/docs*

Mark Glaser. *"SAML Looks to Allay XML Security Concerns."* February 8, 2002. *http://dcb.sun.com/practices/webservices/overviews/overview_saml.jsp*

Prateek Mishra, ed. *"Bindings and Profiles for the OASIS Security Assertion Markup Language."* OASIS. April 19, 2002. *http://www.oasis-open.org/ committees/security/docs*

Zdenek Svoboda. *"Securing Web Services with Single Sign-on." http://www. theserverside.com/resources/article.jsp?l=Systinet-web-services-part-6*

XACML

OASIS eXtensible Access Control Markup Language Technical Committee. *http://www.oasis-open.org/committees/xacml/docs/docs.shtml#link*

Satoshi Hada and Michiharu Kudo. *"XML Access Control Language: Provisional Authorization for XML Documents."*
http://www.trl.ibm.com/projects/xml/xacl/xacl-spec.html

Satoshi Hada and Michiharu Kudo. *"XML Access Control."*
http://www.trl.ibm.com/projects/xml/xacl/xmlac-proposal.html

Project Liberty

Public Liberty version 1.1 specifications. *http://www.projectliberty.org/specs/ liberty-specifications-v1.1.zip*

Liberty Alliance. *"Liberty Architecture Overview."* Version 1.1. Liberty Alliance Project (January 15, 2003). *http://www.projectliberty.org/specs/ liberty-architecture-overview-v1.1.pdf*

Liberty Alliance. *"Liberty Protocols and Schema Specification."* Version 1.1. Liberty Alliance Project (January 15, 2003). *http://www.projectliberty.org/specs/ liberty-architecture-protocols-schema-v1.1.pdf*

Liberty Alliance. *"Liberty Bindings and Profiles Specification."* Version 1.1. Liberty Alliance Project (January 15, 2003). *http://www.projectliberty.org/specs/ liberty-architecture-bindings-profiles-v1.1.pdf*

Liberty Alliance. *"Liberty Authentication Context Specification."* Version 1.1. Liberty Alliance Project (January 15, 2003). *http://www.projectliberty.org/specs/ liberty- architecture-authentication-context-v1.1.pdf*

Liberty Alliance. *"Liberty Architecture Implementation Guidelines."* Version 1.1. Liberty Alliance Project (January 15, 2003). *http://www.projectliberty.org /specs/liberty-architecture-implementation-guidelines-v1.1.pdf*

Security Threats

Denis Piliptchouk and Vince Dovydaitis. *"Securing .NET and Java: Side by Side."* RSA Conference 2002.

http://www.rsaconference.net/RSApresentations/pdfs/devwed1115_piliptchouk.pdf

Saumil Shah and Shreeraj Shah. *"Architectural Threats and Countermeasures for Java Application Servers."* RSA Conference 2002.

http://www.rsaconference.net/RSApresentations/pdfs/devthu1015_shah.pdf

Security Tools

Titan. *http://www.fish.com/titan/*

NMAP. *http://www.insecure.org/nmap/nmap_download.html.*

WS-Security Roadmap

Web Services Security (WS-Security) 1.0 specification (April 5, 2002). *http:// www-106.ibm.com/developerworks/webservices/library/ws-secure/*

Web Services Security 1.0 Addendum (August 18, 2002). *http://msdn.microsoft.com/webservices/default.aspx?pull=/library/ en-us/dnglobspec/html/ws-security-addendum.asp*

Web Services Security Profile for XML-based Tokens (August 28, 2002). *http://msdn.microsoft.com/webservices/default.aspx?pull=/library/ en-us/dnglobspec/html/ws-security-xml-tokens.asp*

Web Services Security Policy Language (WS-SecurityPolicy, or previously WS-Policy) version 1.0 specification (December 18, 2002). *http://msdn.microsoft.com/webservices/default.aspx?pull=/library/ en-us/dnglobspec/html/ws-securitypolicy.asp*

Web Services Secure Conversation Language (WS-SecureConversation) version 1.0 specification (December 18, 2002). *http://msdn.microsoft.com/webservices/default.aspx?pull=/library/ en-us/dnglobspec/html/ws-secureconversation.asp*

Web Services Trust Language (WS-Trust) version 1.0 *http://msdn.microsoft.com/webservices/default.aspx?pull=/library/ en-us/dnglobspec/html/ws-trust.asp*

http://msdn.microsoft.com/webservices/default.aspx?pull=/library/ en-us/dnglobspec/html/ws-trust.asp

Chapter 8

WEB SERVICES IN ACTION: CASE STUDY

8.1 Objective

The objective is to use a simplified Foreign Exchange (FX) Spot Rate Quote Service to illustrate how to wrap a remote FX Quote Service using a mixture of XML messaging (XML document using JAXM) and Remote Procedure Call (JAX-RPC) with secure SOAP Message Service (WS-Security) and Security Assertion Markup Language (SAML) protocol for Single Sign-on purpose. How it works is that given a Sell/Buy currency pair (for example, Sell US Dollars and Buy Euro Dollars), the FX Quote Service will provide a quote based on the average daily exchange rate.

8.2   Assumptions

The business requirements, as depicted in Use Case diagrams and Sequence Diagrams, have been simplified for instructional purposes. The sample physical architecture and future deployment architecture diagrams are for illustration purposes, and they do not trace back to business requirements.

For the definition and technology details of JAXM (asynchronous XML messaging) and JAX-RPC (synchronous Web Services), please refer to Chapter 3, Web Services Technology Overview. For the definition and technology details of WS-Security (XML encryption and digital signature for SOAP Messaging) and SAML protocol (a Single Sign-on security protocol), please refer to Chapter 7, Web Services Security.

A sample "key store" (`sample_soap_keystore`) is placed in the secure message services (aka server key store) and requester (aka client key store) directories. The sample key store is an asymmetric key pair generated for the purpose of demonstrating the use of XML Encryption and digital signature for secure messaging. It comes with VeriSign's Trust Service Integration Kit (TSIK) and stores user credentials (in this case, a valid digital certificate for the MMC entity). For details, please refer to the TSIK documentation. (VeriSign's TSIK is a security toolkit for developing XML Key Management and WS-Security. Refer to Chapter 7, Web Services Security, for more details.)

Netegrity's TSIK is used in this case study to provide secure message services (WS-Security) for SOAP messages in the data transport layer. Refer to Chapter 7, Web Services Security, for details. This denotes that a client request using SOAP messaging will be encrypted and digitally signed with valid security tokens to ensure data integrity, confidentiality, and non-repudiation.

8.3   Use Case Scenario

The business scenarios are based on the existing e-Treasury system of an international Bank. The Investment Banking unit has deployed a Java-based Liquidity Engine for online consumer FX services. It is also private labeling the online FX services for some foreign banks that do not have the infrastructure to support local FX services in some countries.

The Request for FX Spot Rate Quote is chosen to be the demo here because it is relatively simple for instructional purposes. In order for the demo to be generic enough to illustrate the objectives of achieving Single Sign-on and providing FX Spot Rate Quotes via a remote Web Service, we have decided not to include all of the detailed business rules. We also do not include all the necessary exception-handling rules in order to make the demo easier to understand and to modify it for your learning experience.

8.3.1   Business Requirements

Single Sign-on

The demo system should allow users to log in once to access multiple partner services. In other words, users enter login id and password at the front page (for example, user id "goodguy"), and they can access a number of partner Web sites with a list of URLs defined in a profile without hard-coding the URL into the program codes. This should support the use of the SAML protocol as an Open Standard security protocol for Single Sign-on.

The demo system should validate the user credential against the user access list of the Application Server. It should also demonstrate cases where a user id (for example, user id "otherguy") can log in but does not have enough access rights to invoke all partner services.

Request for Quote

The demo system should allow users to enter the Sell and Buy Currency codes to request an indicative FX Spot Rate Quote. This should be an online request for a quote, where the demo system should retrieve the Spot Rate from a local or remote FX Quote Server (aka Market Data Engine or Liquidity Engine).

If the user enters a currency code that is not available in the currency code list or any invalid currency code, then the demo system should simply return a "Do not know" message in the response page.

System Security

Because the demo system is for instructional purposes, we choose not to use HTTPS with SSL for simplicity. However, HTTPS with SSL can be easily turned on by reconfiguring the Web Container's `server.xml file` (in this demo, this is Apache Tomcat's `server.xml`).

The demo system should demonstrate the use of WS-Security, which VeriSign's TSIK provides. This enables the XML message contents to be encrypted using a local sample key store.

Service-Level Requirements

The demo system is designed to be a prototype for instructional purposes. It should support a transaction throughput of at least five Request for FX Quote per minute. The response time requirement for the quote should be less than 15 seconds. As this is a demo system, it does not require $24 \times 7 \times 365$ or 99.999-percent availability. The target service availability for the demo system is 99.0 percent, assuming the development Application Server is running all the time.

8.3.2   Use Cases

Use Case Diagram

Clients need to enter a public or private financial portal that provides a variety of financial services, FX trading, and information services. They need to provide a single user id and password and be able to log in once for all the subscription-based services provided by the financial portal.

In this Use Case scenario (see Figure 8–1), we primarily focus on having a Single Sign-on and Request for FX Quote capability. The Client selects the FX Spot Rate Quote Service to request an indicative spot rate by specifying the Sell and Buy Currency. It will be using 3-letter ISO currency codes. Upon submitting the request, the remote FX Spot Rate Quote Service Provider will return an indicative rate.

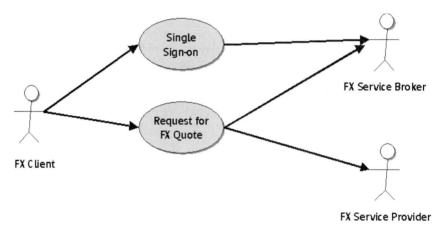

Figure 8–1   Use Cases for FX Spot Rate Quote Service

Actors

FX Client   Corporate users who need to get an indicative Spot Rate Quote for a specific Foreign Currency pair of the current day.

FX Service Broker   Investment Banks, financial institutions, or FX Portals who provide a broker service to provide an indicative FX Spot Rate Quote Service to an FX Client, where a remote FX Service Provider operates the actual FX quote service.

FX Service Provider FX Service Providers are financial institutions who provide either a delayed FX quote or a real-time FX quote to an FX Client. They may be another Investment Bank or financial institution, and can be the Service Broker themselves.

Single Sign-on Use Case

Use Case Name	MyFX-UC-01
Description	Client enters a user id and password in order to access FX Spot Rate Quote and multiple partner Web sites, based on prior trading partner agreements, without having to log in once for each Web site. There may be different access rights for each partner Web site, and thus the Client may not be able to access all partner Web sites without sufficient access rights granted.
Actors	FX Client
	FX Service Broker
Assumptions	Client has an asymmetric key store (X.509v3 certificate) installed in local directory.
Main Flow of Events	1. Client invokes the Single Sign-on screen. The Single Sign-on process will generate a one-time session key and forward the user to a login page.
	2. Client enters user id and password.
	3. The Single Sign-on process will authenticate the user credentials against the Access Control List (in this demo, this will check the user id in the Web Container's Access Control List `tomcat-users.xml` under Tomcat version 4.x).
	4. The Single Sign-on process will check for authorization (in this demo, it will check for the user access rights for different partner URLs in `user_attributes.xml` maintained by Netegrity's jSAML sample program) and forward the user to main menu page.
Alternative Flows	4. The Single Sign-on process cannot find the user id or sufficient access rights. It displays an error page to the user.
	5. A login screen will be redisplayed for the Client to re-log in.
Special Requirements	There should be regular backups of the Client key store.
	The Application Server running the Single Sign-on process should be available online 24 hours every day to provide Single Sign-on.
Precondition	The Client key store must be stored in a local directory before Single Sign-on screen is invoked.
Post-condition	Upon successful login, the demo system will forward the Client to the Request for FX Quote Use Case.
Constraints	For simpler environment set-up, HTTPS with SSL is not used.
Risks/Issues	Without HTTPS, there is a security risk for eavesdropping of the data sent between the Client and the Application Server. Because this is a demo, the risk is manageable.

Request for Quote Use Case

Use Case Name   MyFX-UC-02

Description   Client selects FX Spot Rate Quote Service to request an indicative spot rate by specifying the Sell and Buy Currency. It will use 3-letter ISO currency codes. The quote service will forward the request to a remote FX Quote Service Provider.

Actors   FX Client

    FX Service Broker

    FX Service Provider

Assumptions   Client has done the sign-on with appropriate security verification.

Main Flow of Events

1. Client enters Sell and Buy Currency codes to request an indicative FX Spot Rate for today.

2. Control Servlet looks up the remote FX Quote Service URL from the Service Registry.

3. Control Servlet invokes the FX Price engine to fetch the latest FX Spot Rate based on the given cross currency pair and returns the rate from the remote FX Quote Service.

4. Control Servlet invokes the request for the Buy Currency name from the back-end Reference Data via the Profile Servlet.

5. If there is a Spot Rate available, then the Control Servlet displays the FX Spot Rate Quote on the screen.

Alternative Flows

6. If there is no Spot Rate available, then the Control Servlet will not display the rate on the screen.

7. If the currency code is invalid, then the Control Servlet will display a "Do Not Know" message in the currency description, and there will not be any rate displayed on the screen.

Special Requirements   Active Internet connectivity (with appropriate firewall setting to allow access to the Internet) is available.

SOAP RPC Router (SOAP Server) is running with the Application Server.

FX Spot Rate Quote Web Service is deployed to the Web Container (which is a run-time Web Services engine. In this demo, this refers to JWSDP Tomcat Web Server).

Precondition   Single Sign-on process is complete.

Post-condition   Inquiry completed.

Constraints   If the remote FX Quote Service is unavailable, there is no error message captured. Thus, the quote result will be blank.

Risks/Issues   Insufficient exception handling for invalid currency code or having the remote FX Quote Service out of service will not indicate the error conditions in the demo. It is not easy to troubleshoot from the existing log files.

The debugging design and existing debugging log files are not sufficient for troubleshooting.

8.4   Case Study Design

8.4.1   High-Level Design

A Web Services architecture (please also refer to Chapter 4, Web Services Architecture and Best Practices) typically consists of a *Web Services Consumer* (who uses and invokes the services), *Web Services Service Registry* (which provides a directory of business services available and points to their service end-point URLs) and *Web Services Service Provider* (the business functionality provided to serve the consumers).

The Web Services Consumer finds or discovers different business services from the Web Services Service Registry. In this case, the Web Services Consumer wants to find a Request for FX Spot Rate Quote Service. The Web Services Service Registry hosts all business services information, such as organization name and service end-point URLs where these services can be found. Web Services Service Providers previously publish or register with the Service Registry. Once the Web Services Consumers finds the required business service, the system will bind the service end-point and invoke the business service.

In this demo, we have chosen Sun Microsystems's Java Web Services Developer Pack. It comes with Tomcat 4.0, Xindice database, and UDDI Service Registry. We have also used Netegrity's TSIK as the secure message provider. Please refer to Figure 8–2 for the high-level design. The Web Services Consumer uses JWSDP and TSIK on top of the Tomcat Web server to find/discover business services from the Web Services Service Registry. The Service Registry is implemented using JWSDP with a Xindice server on top of the Tomcat Web server. The Web Services Service Provider registers with the Service Registry and publishes business services to the Service Registry, which can be invoked by the Web Services Consumer.

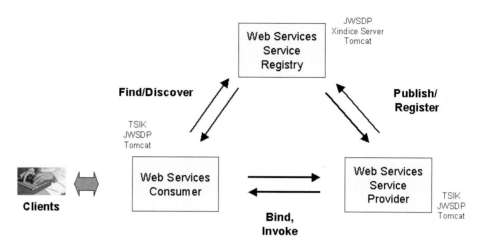

Figure 8–2   FX Spot Rate Quote Web Services Relationship

We need to identify the Open Standards messaging protocols used for the interaction between different components. From a high-level perspective, we have five major entities: Clients, Control Servlet (aka Front Controller to handle Presentation-Tier requests; The concept of Front Controller is discussed in Alur, Crupi, and Malks ([2001], *Core J2EE Patterns*, p. 172), Currency Profile (or Reference Data), FX Price Provider (Service Provider for the FX Spot Rate Quote Service), and the Registry Server. The interaction between these components is depicted in Figure 8–3. The Service Requester (client) accesses the Web Services from the Front Controller via HTTP. The Front Controller acts as a SOAP client to look up the business services dynamically using JAXR, retrieves reference data (currency profile) using JAXM, and invokes remote business service (FX currency rate quote) using JAX-RPC.

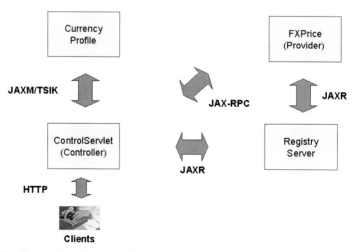

Figure 8–3   Interaction Between Components

We have chosen to use HTTP instead of HTTPS between the Client and the Control Servlet, because it is easier to configure for instructional purposes. From the Control Servlet, requests and messages are sent in secure SOAP messaging using the TSIK message provider. This denotes that Reference Data such as currency code will be transmitted securely over HTTP. Any service lookup, publish, or removal from the registry request to the Registry Server will be using JAXR so that it can shield off from registry-specific APIs or codes. This will ease migration to ebXML Service Registry or switch to another UDDI Service Registry in the future. Between the Control Servlet and the FX Price Provider, we decide to use JAX-RPC as we assume we need a synchronous connectivity to the remote Service Provider.

8.4.2   Logical Architecture

Based on the Use Case scenarios (as in Figure 8–1), we have come up with the following logical components using the Tomcat Application Server platform (also refer to Figure 8–4).

Controller	User interface for Clients to perform Single Sign-on, and specify the Sell and Buy Currency codes to request an FX Spot Rate Quote. This is similar to the Front Controller pattern described in Alur, Crupi, and Malks ([2001], *Core J2EE Patterns*, p. 172).
Single Sign-On Components	These Single Sign-on components are derived from Netegrity's jSAML Toolkit. They include Login Servlet, Contents Servlet, Forward Servlet, Ticket Desk, Article Servlet, and the SAML engine on the Service Provider's side.
Service Registry	This resembles the UDDI Service Registry that comes with the Java Web Services Developer Pack. It is UDDI 2.0–compliant.
Web Container	In this demo, the run-time Web Services engine is Apache Tomcat Application Server 4.1.2. It supports JSP and servlets.
Remote Web Services	These remote Web Services resemble different back-end systems, including Liquidity Engine (aka FX deal system that handles request for quote, deal order management, and so forth), Market Data server (which takes in FX feeds from the Stock Exchange), and Reference Data (such as a currency code description). These systems may reside on a legacy mainframe or be remotely hosted by another Service Provider. The Control Servlet takes in a client request and invokes a remote Web Service (via Server Tie or Skeleton) using the Client Stub.
Article Servlet	This is a module that handles forwarding the partner service Web page to the Client upon successful Single Sign-on.

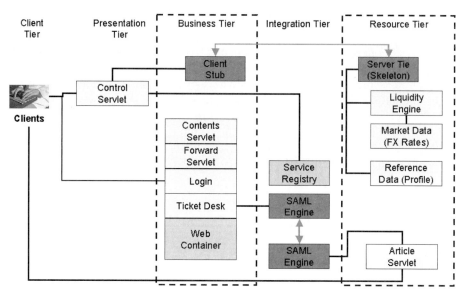

Figure 8–4   Logical Architecture for FX Spot Rate Quote Service

The Quality of Service matrix in Table 8–1 denotes an analysis of different logical components, how they provide scalability, reliability, and availability today, and how they can be extended in the future. Chapter 4, Web Services Architecture and Best Practices, also discusses how to perform a Quality of Services analysis for a Web Services architecture. Although this is a small-scale demo sample, it is educational to illustrate the "ilities" aspects of the Case Study architecture.

The different platform layers refer to different layers of the software stack, from Hardware Platform Layer (for example, hardware and storage), Lower Platform Layer (for example, Operating System), Upper Platform Layer (for example, Application Server), Virtual Platform Layer (for example, middleware) to Application Platform Layer (for example, business applications). The different tiers refer to different components that can be categorized by the physical boundaries of hardware and software products, from Client Tier (for example, Web browser), Presentation Tier (for example, Web Server), Business Tier (for example, EJBs), Integration Tier (for example, messaging services) to Resource Tier (for example, database). Details of these architecture classifications can be found in Unified Process (e.g., *http://www.omg.org*) or SunTone Architecture Methodology (refer to Sun Professional Services (2001) *Dotcom and Beyond,* pp. 67–98.)

Table 8–1 Quality of Services Analysis

			Tiers		
	Client	Presentation	Business	Integration	Resource
Application Platform Layer	User id and password are used for authentication.	Control Servlet uses HTML and JSP for presentation and inquiry. JSPs can be cached to enhance performance.	Java beans are used to implement some of the business logic. The remote FX Quote Service is a black box, accessible via JAX-RPC.	N/A	N/A
Virtual Platform Layer	HTTP HTTPS with SSL can be used for better security.	HTTP HTTPS with SSL can be used for better security.	JAXM-TSIK Message Provider provides secure messaging transport for SOAP messages over HTTP.	JAX-RPC, JAXM are used to integrate different remote services.	JAXR is used to access the Service Registry.
Upper Platform Layer	In the future, 128-bit SSL can be used for better security.	HTTP load balancing can be used for better scalability.	N/A	In the future, server clustering can be used for availability.	In the future, server clustering can be used for availability.
Lower Platform Layer	Basic Operating System security is provided with id and password.	N/A	N/A	N/A	N/A
Hardware Platform Layer	SSL accelerator can be added in the future for faster performance when using HTTPS.	Reliability and securability can be enhanced in the future with server hardening, firewall configuration, and hardware clustering.	Reliability and securability can be enhanced in the future with server hardening, firewall configuration, and hardware clustering.	N/A	Reliability and securability can be enhanced in the future with server hardening, firewall configuration, and hardware clustering.

8.4.3   Major Design Items

There are some major design items that need to be addressed in the technical design. We may not have answers to these questions for this case study yet. But they are good for consideration. These design items are also applicable to any major Web Services development.

Security.   Should we use HTTPS with SSL only, or a mixture of HTTPS and WS-Security? Do we use hardware SSL Accelerator to enhance encryption and decryption performance?

It is more desirable to use HTTPS and WS-Security together. However, we use HTTP and WS-Security instead for instructional purposes. In this demo, we use VeriSign's TSIK to provide XML encryption and XML digital signatures over SOAP messages. For details, please refer to chapter 7 Web Services Security. In production, it would be better to use hardware SSL accelerator to enhance encryption and decryption performance.

Single Sign-on Approach.   Assuming we adopt SAML (or Liberty's Single Sign-on specification using extended SAML) to implement Single Sign-on, should we use the approach of Federated Directory Server with Liberty-compliant agents (off-the-shelf components) or use Netegrity's jSAML-like toolkit to build home-grown components? Liberty is a security specification defined by multiple technology vendors and industry communities to enable federated identity management and cross-domain Single Sign-on. It extends the existing SAML specification for Single Sign-on integration with Directory Servers. Sun ONE Identity Server 6.0 is currently the first commercial implementation that supports both SAML and Liberty functionality. Refer to *http://www.projectliberty.org/* and Chapter 7, Web Services Security, for details.

There is no best answer to this question. However, for instructional purposes we choose to use Netegrity's jSAML toolkit to illustrate how to implement Single Sign-on with home-grown components.

Application Tooling.   What kind of application tooling is necessary for successful Web Services development? When do we use any Application Server Analyzer, Java Unit Testing tool, Web Services Stress Testing tool, or TCP/IP monitor for Web Services?

Web Services application tools are very useful. Owing to resource constraints, we do not cover these tools in this Case Study.

XML Messaging Standards.   Should we adopt industry-specific XML messages such as fpML, even though the remote Web Services engine may be using a proprietary XML message structure? Should we use XSLT (XML stylesheet processor) to transcode from a proprietary XML message structure to an industry-specific XML message structure?

As we do not require FX deal-order processing, we do not need to use any industry-specific XML messages such as fpML. If both industry-specific and proprietary XML messages are used, it would be useful to customize XSLT to handle the transcoding.

Private Label Customization.   Where should we design and implement the customization components, especially for implementing Private Label customers? Should we duplicate different Control Servlets for each Private Label customer or use XML stylesheets?

We do not have any Private Label customization requirements in this Case Study. If we have, then we may need to consider a different technology approach. There is no best approach for every customization requirement.

Use of DOM/SAX Versus JAXP.   For simple programs, should we use DOM or SAX directly, or should we use JAXP all through for consistency and portability purposes?

JAXP is better for portability.

Interoperability With External Systems.   What Web Services functionality should we expose? This is a matter of coarse-grained versus fine-grained Web Services design. The design considerations for coarse-grained or fine-grained Web Services design include the number of APIs to be maintained and the extensibility and flexibility when developers need to modify the data structure or interfaces.

This Case Study only covers two Web Services (remote FX Spot Rate Quote and reference data retrieval), and it is out of its scope to elaborate on whether developers should adopt coarse-grained or fine-grained Web Services design.

8.4.4   Technology and Patterns Applied

Technology Applied

Open Standards technology JAX-RPC, JAXR, and WS-Security using Java Web Services Developer Pack and TSIK are illustrated in this demo. These technologies are also supplemented by a Single Sign-on technology built on top of jSAML Toolkit.

Design Patterns Applied

Two Design Patterns are applied: Model-View-Controller Pattern (J2EE Design Pattern) and Service Consolidation–Broker Integration Pattern (B2Bi Pattern). The former denotes that the Control Servlet acts as a Controller (Presentation Tier) for the Model (business logic) and different Views (data sources or remote Web Services). It provides a cleaner approach to decouple the business logic and data from the presentation. The latter denotes a typical Web Services deployment scenario where a Service Broker needs to consolidate and aggregate information from multiple data sources (or remote Web Services).

Single Sign-on Design

The following components work together to provide Single Sign-on capability (see Figure 8–5):

Login	The Login.jsp accepts the Client's user id and password for performing Single Sign-on. The Single Sign-on Servlet will generate a one-time session id and display in the URL (functioning as the parameter for the next servlet), as in `http://localhost:8080/MMC/login/login.jsp;` `jsessionid=85881E55BC4467368B94B2EF0508DC02`
Contents Servlet	The Contents Servlet generates a list of contents URLs (partner Web sites) as the menu page where the Client can choose to access.
Forward Servlet	The Forward Servlet forwards the Client to the target partner Web site URL once the SAML Assertion request is processed successfully and sufficient access rights are validated.
Ticket Desk	The Ticket Desk handles each SAML Assertion as a request ticket for each partner Web site access. It sends the SAML Assertion request to the Article Servlet of the target Web site for processing.
SAML Engine	The SAML APIs that handle SAML Assertion requests and respond to the Client requester.
Article Servlet	This is a module that handles forwarding the partner service Web site page to the Client upon successful Single Sign-on.

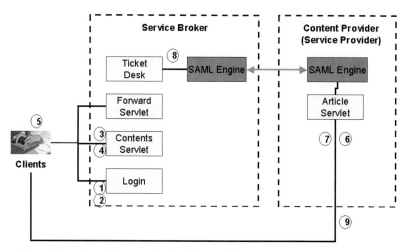

Figure 8–5 Interaction Between Single Sign-on Components

The sequence diagram in Figure 8–6 further depicts the detailed process between the Client and different components of the Single Sign-on process in Figure 8–5. This includes:

1. The Client enters user id and password to sign on.
2. The Login process will create a one-time session id and cookie. It will redirect the Client to a login page and pass control to the Contents Servlet.
3. The Contents Servlet generates a contents page (aka menu page) with a list of partner Web site URLs.
4. The Contents Servlet will return the newly generated contents page to the Client.
5. The Client clicks on the contents page links and submits request.
6. The Forward Servlet will create a SAML Assertion request and send it to the Article Servlet.
7. The Article Servlet makes a call-back to the Ticket Desk with the SAML Assertion request. This ensures the appropriate trading partner has received and acknowledged the request.
8. The Ticket Desk provides the associated SAML Assertion request again to the Article Servlet.
9. The Article Servlet processes the SAML Assertion request and redirects the target partner Web site page to the Client if access is granted.

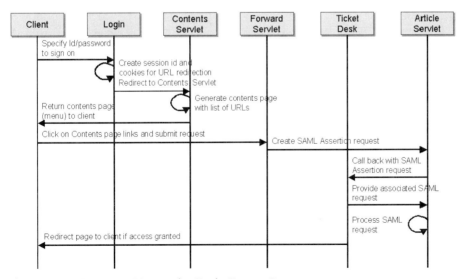

Figure 8–6   Sequence Diagram for Single Sign-on Process

8.4.5   FX Quote Service Design

The following components work together to provide FX Quote Service capability. They help to explain the service components in Figures 8–7 and 8–8.

Control Servlet	The Control Servlet acts as the Presentation Tier for user interaction to request an FX Spot Rate Quote.
Price Fetcher	The Price Fetcher sets the properties of the remote service endpoint and operation name, and gets ready to invoke the remote FX Spot Rate Quote Service.
FXPrice	The FXPrice will find or discover existing Request for FX Spot Rate Quote Services from the UDDI Service Registry.
JAXRQueryByName	A function to query the UDDI Service Registry by name.
ProfileRequest	The ProfileRequest implements how to retrieve the currency name with a given currency code.
CurrencyProfile	This is the service call to ProfileRequest.
FXProviderIF	This is the interface file to FXProviderImpl.
FXProviderImpl	This is the implementation for the FXProvider, which creates a Web Services call to a remote Service Provider for a FX Spot Rate Quote.
OrgPublisher	This is a utility to publish the organization information into the UDDI Service Registry.
OrgRemover	This is a utility to remove the organization information from the UDDI Service Registry.
JAXRPublisher	This is the utility to invoke a JAXR publish API.
JAXRRemover	This is the utility to invoke a JAXR remove API.
ProfileServlet	The ProfileServlet parses the SOAP request (stored in the file `request.xml`) using the JAXM/TSIK Message Provider.
SOAP_KeyStore	This is the key store (storing user credentials) used by TSIK Message Provider for secure SOAP messaging (for example, XML Encryption and XML digital signature).
JAX-RPC Run time	This is the stub or tie (skeleton) to support JAX-RPC.
JAXM/TSIK Run time	This is the TSIK API (stub or tie/skeleton) to support JAXM/TSIK secure SOAP messaging.

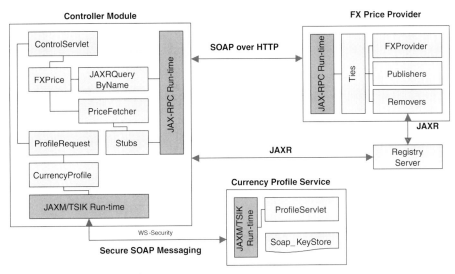

Figure 8–7   FX Quote Web Services Components

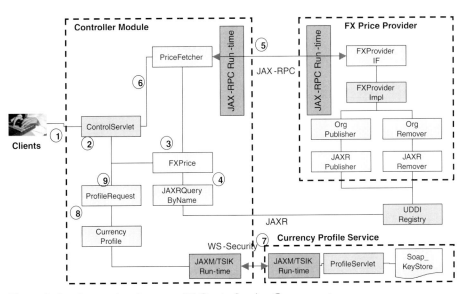

Figure 8–8   Interaction Between FX Quote Service Components

Figures 8–7, 8–8, and 8–9 further depict the detailed process between the Client and different components of the Request for FX Spot Rate Quote process. This includes:

1. The Client specifies the Sell and Buy Currency using 3-letter ISO currency codes.
2. The Control Servlet creates a proxy to get an FX price based on the cross-currency pair.
3. The FX Price looks up the UDDI registry to locate the remote FX Spot Rate Quote Web Services Service Provider.
4. Once the remote Web Service is found, the FX Price will bind the service with the service end-point URL.
5. The FX Price will then invoke the remote Web Service via FXProviderIF.
6. The FXProviderIF will use FXProviderImpl to invoke the remote FX Spot Rate Quote Service. FXProviderImpl will fetch the spot rate from the remote Service Provider and return it to the FXPrice via JAX-RPC. The FXPrice returns the Spot Rate Quote to the Control Servlet.
7. The Control Servlet creates a proxy to look up the Buy Currency name from CurrencyProfile via ProfileRequest.
8. The Profile Request looks up the currency name using Profile Servlet via JAXM with TSIK secure message provider.
9. The ProfileServlet returns the currency name in a text to Profile Request, then to the Control Servlet. The Control Servlet displays the FX quote and the currency name to the Client.

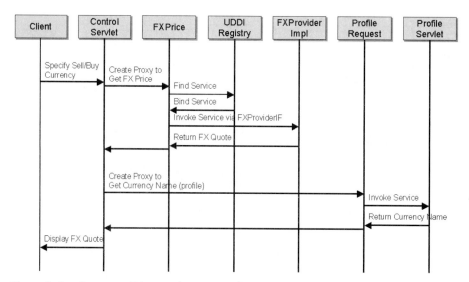

Figure 8–9 Sequence Diagram for Request for FX Spot Rate Quote Process

8.4.6 Physical Architecture

Based on the logical architecture depicted in Figures 8–4 and 8–7, we may derive a physical architecture that is ready for deployment based on the Service-Level Requirements. Assuming the transaction processing requirements of handling 300,000 Request for Quotes per day and the need to support 24 × 7 × 365 high-availability requirements, we may recommend the following physical architecture:

- Two load balancers for handling HTTP traffic
- Three Web Services (FX Spot Rate Quote Service, reference data or profile retrieval, and UDDI discovery service) to handle HTTP requests from client browsers
- Two instances of Application Servers to host the business logic to support High Availability
- Two instances of Reference Data servers to host the common trade reference data to support High Availability
- Two instances of Database Servers using Sun Cluster to host all FX trade transactions to support High Availability
- Two optional servers in the future to host the Directory Servers and Service Registry

The physical architecture diagram in Figure 8–10 is a sample for instructional purposes. It does not trace back to the Service Level Requirements.

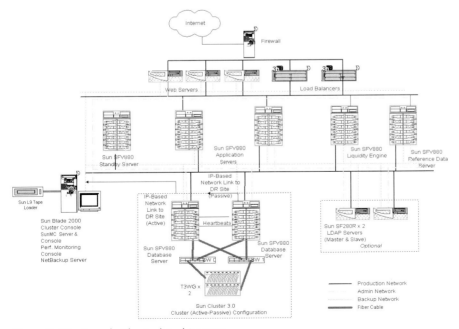

Figure 8–10 Sample Physical Architecture

In reality, we need to conduct a hardware sizing exercise to analyze the data requirements, transaction volumes, and application resource requirements before we derive the physical architecture. Besides, the hardware sizing needs to trace back to the Special Requirements (which is Service-Level Requirements) in the Use Cases.

8.4.7   Future Deployment Architecture

The logical and physical architecture diagrams depicted in Figures 8–4, 8–7, and 8–10 refer to the Use Case based on a simplified demo scenario. Once the demo system is ready to extend to a full-scale production scenario, we may need to include other enterprise components so that they can be operational to support 24 × 7 × 365 non-stop services.

The sample deployment architecture in Figure 8–11 shows a possible deployment when the demo system is extended and integrated in a typical financial institution's Enterprise Architecture, where there may be different delivery channels supporting SMS, WAP phone, Fax and email, and interfaces with the external parties, such as the Stock Exchange and Market Data feed providers. Figures 4–4 and 4–5 have some discussion of this sample future deployment architecture. The integration of the Web Services components will be handled either by a public or private Service Registry and a SOAP RPC Router. It is beyond the scope of this Case Study to cover all aspects of integration.

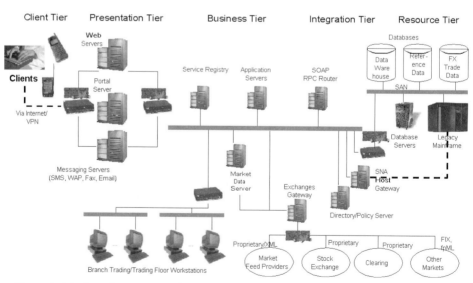

Figure 8–11   Sample Future Deployment Architecture

8.5   User Experience

After the demo code is installed and deployed (refer to Appendix C, Demo Environment Set-Up), you should see the Single Sign-on page upon invoking the URL *http://localhost:8080/MMC/docs/index.html* (see Figure 8–12). If the software prerequisites (such as jSAML toolkit) are not properly installed and configured, users should not be able to see the "Intranet Login" screen in Figure 8–12. The Single Sign-on process will generate a one-time session id, prompt you for security sign-on, and validate your security credentials that are stored in your local PC or workstation.

Next, the demo system will bring you to a main menu (see Figure 8–13), which displays two major sets of functionality: SSO to Content Provider and Corporate Partners Picklist. The demo system has been customized to collaborate with the first option only. Click the "SSO to Content Provider" in the left-hand column.

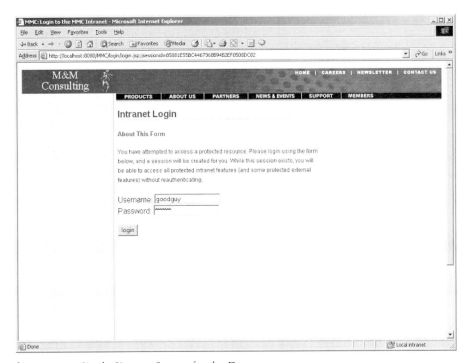

Figure 8–12   Single Sign-on Screen for the Demo

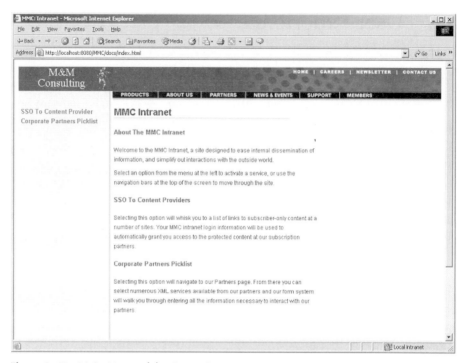

Figure 8–13   Main Menu of the Demo System

The demo system should bring you to another menu page (see Figure 8–14) that displays all existing content providers that are integrated using Single Sign-on. The first three options require active Internet connectivity. Click the last option, "FX Spot Rate Quote."

The demo system will retrieve your security credentials and company profile and compose a security access assertion request using SAML Assertion messaging protocol. For instructional purposes, the demo system will display the actual SAML message on the screen for five seconds (see Figure 8–15) and validate whether you have sufficient access rights to access the FX Spot Rate Quote Service.

Upon successful validation of your access rights with the target Service Provider (that is, FX Spot Rate Quote Service), the demo system will display a default Web page (see Figure 8–16), which prompts you to enter into the remote partner service (that is, FX Spot Rate Quote Service).

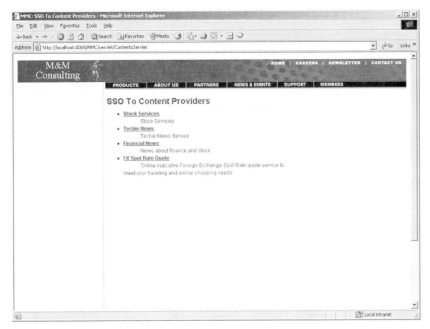

Figure 8–14 Single Sign-on to a List of Partner Services

Figure 8–15 SAML Assertion Request to the Remote FX Quote Web Service

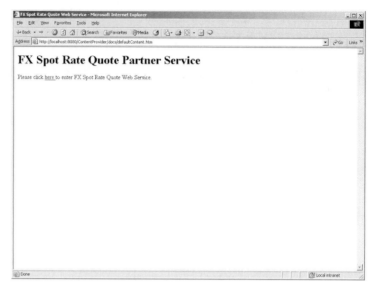

Figure 8–16   Front Page to Accessing Remote FX Quote Web Service

The Content Provider Servlet (aka Service Broker) of the demo system should be able to forward the FX Spot Rate Quote Service main page (see Figure 8–17) to the client. The FX Spot Rate Quote Service prompts the user to enter the Sell Currency and Buy Currency in 3-letter ISO currency codes. Once completed, the user can press the "Submit" button to request for an indicative FX quote. This is a current Spot Rate Quote, where the expected trade date is assumed to be today.

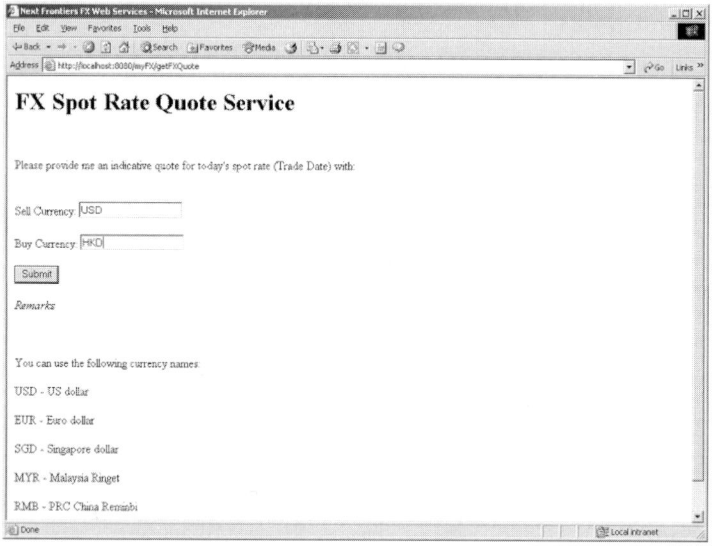

Figure 8–17   FX Spot Rate Quote Web Service Page

The FX Spot Rate Quote Service will look up the indicative price from the remote FX Quote Service, which is currently set to be a delay FX quote provided by `xmethods.org`. It will also look up its internal Reference Data (called "Profile" in this demo) in order to display the name of the Buy Currency code. The Request for FX Spot Rate Quote is then complete (see Figure 8–18).

Figure 8–18 FX Spot Rate Quote Response

8.6   Sample Code Analysis

8.6.1   Single Sign-on Component

In this demo, the ContentsServlet reads in the URL header that contains the unique identifier for the identity (also called the company identifier, a short name that denotes the company identity used in demonstrating Single Sign-on.). The unique identifier consists of _URL, _Name, _Description, and _SiteID. These are configurable in the "mmc.properties" (contents.property.forwardservletlocation section). In real life, you may have a different set of schema to implement the user identity. This can be also linked up with your credentials stored in the Directory Server.

Two major SAML assertion Java classes provide methods to create SAML requests and support the data transport (see Figure 8–19):

```
import com.netegrity.jsaml.assertion.*;
import com.netegrity.jsaml.protocol.*;
```

Figure 8–19 Two Major Java Classes Used to Support SAML

The ForwardServlet manages the process of creating a SAML Assertion request. It requires the user name, category, and the given access level and looks up whether the requester has sufficient access rights for the target partner Web site. Then the `gen-erateAssertion` method of the ForwardServlet will create the conditions (such as AbstractCondition), subject (such as Security Domain, user name), authentication statement (such as authentication locality with IP address and DNS address), and the associated attributes (for example, attribute name="Partner Block").

8.6.2   FX Spot Rate Quote

The FX Spot Rate Quote requester that invokes the remote FX Spot Rate Quote engine needs to set the parameters of the service end-point or URL and the operation name. This is usually found in the WSDL published by the remote Service Provider. In this demo, the remote FX Spot Rate Quote Service is provided by xmethods.org, and the WSDL can be downloaded from *http://www.xmethods.net/sd/2001/CurrencyExchangeService.wsdl.*

By reading the WSDL, we can identify the service end-point to be *http://services. xmethods.net:80/soap* (<soap:address location />), the namespace is ("urn: xmethods-CurrencyExchange"), and the operation name is "getRate" (<operation />). We need to examine the input and output data type as defined in the WSDL. Complex data types may need special handling or data type conversion.

The program in Figure 8–20 is extracted to highlight how a SOAP client is used to invoke a remote FX Spot Rate Quote Service. Apache Axis (the next generation of Apache SOAP engine; refer to *http://xml.apache.org/axis*) is used to illustrate that it is ready for the next-generation SOAP engine. The same FX Spot Rate Quote Web Service can also be invoked by an Apache SOAP client or a Perl client (using SOAP-Lite; refer to *http://www.soaplite.com*).

```
package com.sun.webservicedemo;

import java.math.BigDecimal;
import java.util.*;

import org.apache.axis.client.Call;
import org.apache.axis.client.Service;

import org.apache.axis.AxisFault;
import org.apache.axis.encoding.XMLType;
import org.apache.axis.utils.Options;
```

Figure 8–20   Sample Client Invoking FX Spot Rate Quote Service

```
import javax.xml.namespace.QName;


public class FXProviderImpl implements FXProviderIF {

//  FX conversion rate
    public String getPrice(String sellCurrency, String
buyCurrency) {

    String sell = "";
    String buy  = "";
    String myQuote = "";

//  Mapping input parameter for the remote FX quote
engine
        if (sellCurrency.equalsIgnoreCase("HKD"))
            sell = "hong kong";
        if (sellCurrency.equalsIgnoreCase("USD"))
            sell = "us";
        if (sellCurrency.equalsIgnoreCase("EUR"))
            sell = "euro";
        if (sellCurrency.equalsIgnoreCase("RMB"))
            sell = "china";
        if (sellCurrency.equalsIgnoreCase("SGD"))
            sell = "singapore";
        if (sellCurrency.equalsIgnoreCase("MYR"))
            sell = "malaysia";

        if (buyCurrency.equalsIgnoreCase("HKD"))
            buy = "hong kong";
        if (buyCurrency.equalsIgnoreCase("USD"))
            buy = "us";
        if (buyCurrency.equalsIgnoreCase("EUR"))
            buy = "euro";
        if (buyCurrency.equalsIgnoreCase("RMB"))
            buy = "china";
        if (buyCurrency.equalsIgnoreCase("SGD"))
            buy = "singapore";
        if (buyCurrency.equalsIgnoreCase("MYR"))
            buy = "malaysia";
```

Figure 8–20 Sample Client Invoking FX Spot Rate Quote Service—*continued.*

```
        try {
            String endpoint =

            "http://services.xmethods.net:80/soap";

            Service  service = new Service();
            Call     call    = (Call)
service.createCall();

            call.setTargetEndpointAddress( new
java.net.URL(endpoint) );
            call.setOperationName(new
QName("urn:xmethods-CurrencyExchange", "getRate") );

            Object resp = call.invoke( new Object[] {
sell, buy } );
            Float ret = (Float)resp;
            myQuote = (String)ret.toString();
            // System.out.println("We offer you a spot
rate of " + ret + " for " + sellCurrency + "-" +
buyCurrency + " if you confirm acceptance in 3 seconds
today.");

        } catch (Exception e) {
            System.err.println(e.toString());
        }
        return myQuote;
    }  // getPrice
} // class
```

Figure 8–20 Sample Client Invoking FX Spot Rate Quote Service—*continued.*

8.6.3   Secure Message Service

We choose WS-Security implementation to provide secure message service. VeriSign's Trust Service Integration Kit (TSIK) is one of the early WS-Security implementations (another is XML Key Management Service). WS-Security can work with multiple security token implementations, ranging from Kerberos ticket to digital certificate, and provide XML encryption and XML digital signature. Refer to Chapter 7, Web Services Security, for details. The advantage is that developers can rely on the secure message service provided by WS-Security to perform data transport and message security and focus on application business logic in the server codes. This enables decoupling the security-related logic from the application business logic, instead of tightly coupling security processing logic into the application codes. WS-Security also integrates with SSL over HTTPS to ensure the client-server connection is secure.

To create a TSIK Client, you need to create a message (Document), get the client's private key and certificate, get the service's certificate, create a "trust verifier" using the X.509v3 certificate (see method below), and generate the data encryption key (for example, Triple DES key with SHA-1). Then you need to create the transport with the client's private key and certificate, send the message over the transport, and retrieve the contents from a response message. Finally, you can create and retrieve a SOAP fault element (see Figure 8–21).

```
import
org.xmltrustcenter.verifier.SimpleTrustVerifier;

...
trustVerifier = new SimpleTrustVerifier(

Collections.singleton(clientCert.getPublicKey()));
```

Figure 8–21   Sample XKMS Trust Verifiers

In this demo, the ProfileServlet (which retrieves the currency name with a given currency code) reads in a predefined key store, which is an X.509v3 certificate, and creates a "trust verifier" as follows: It receives a message and converts to SOAPMessage. It verifies the requester's signature, decrypts the SOAP request body, creates a response message, and then encrypts the response body. The ProfileServlet will not proceed to retrieve the currency description if the certificate cannot be verified.

8.6.4   Integration of Different Components

There are two files that need to be replaced in order to integrate the FX Spot Rate Quote Service with jSAML Single Sign-on demo program. First, we simply modify the file "defaultContent.htm" (the page that originally shows local contents) under the %JWSDP_HOME%\webapps\ContentProvider\docs. This is the HTML page that the ArticleServlet redirects to upon successful SAML Assertion processing and access approval. Next, you also need to modify the entry in the entries.xml under the directory %JWSDP_HOME%\webapps\MMC\conf to display the FX Spot Rate Quote Service (see Figure 8–22):

```
<Entry>
    <Name>FX Spot Rate Quote</Name>

<URL>http://localhost:8080/ContentProvider/docs/defaul
tContent.htm</URL>
    <Description>Online indicative Foreign Exchange
Spot Rate quote service to meet your traveling and
online shopping needs</Description>
    <SiteID>0001</SiteID>
</Entry>
```

Figure 8–22   Sample Configuration File for jSAML Demo

8.7   Code Customization and Deployment

8.7.1   Environment Set-up

The demo system assumes the installation and configuration of J2SE, JWSDP, TSIK, and jSAML. The environment set-up of these components is recapitulated in Appendix C, Demo Environment Set-up of this book. The demo program files should be installed under C:\opt\myFX, and the jSAML demo program files should be installed under %JWSDP_ HOME%\webapps (something similar to the following figure).

You should have the following directories set up for the demo system (see Figure 8–23):

```
C:\opt\myFX
D:\Dev\jSAML
D:\Dev\TSIK
D:\Dev\WSDP
D:\Dev\WSDP with the sub-directories ContentProvider,
CreditReports, MMC, OtherCo, SomeCo
```

Figure 8–23   Environment Set-up for Directories

After these components are installed, you may want to verify the set-up to ensure all components are working before you install the demo codes (see Figure 8–24).

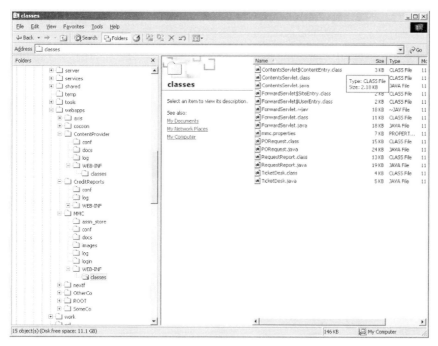

Figure 8–24 Demo Program Files Installed under `%JWSDP_HOME%\webapps`

The demo code files are zipped under the file name "myFX.zip" in the CD-ROM accompanying this book under /labs/ch8. Extract the files under `/opt/myFX` of your local drive (or `/opt/myFX` on your Unix machine). If you choose to install under a different directory, then you need to modify all the file locations in the properties files and some program codes (with program comments).

To make use of the ANT scripts, it is essential to understand that these scripts assume a specific directory structure (with the subdirectories build, dist, src, web) for the program files (also refer to Appendix C, Demo Environment Set-up).

8.7.2   Customizing ANT Scripts

If we need to modify the file location or change the build directory, we do not need to modify the ANT scripts. We can modify the property file "**build.properties**" in each subdirectory. The ANT script will read in the "**build.properties**" and substitute the macro or variables into the "`build.xml`" of the same directory.

For instance, the "`build.properties`" (see Figure 8–25) for the FX Price Provider specifies the source file location ("src"), class library ("clib" and "elib"), and the service end-point ("endpoint"). Most of these variables can be reusable for similar Web Services development. This also does not require developers to modify these parameters for software migration and deployment.

```
build=build
src=src/com/sun/webservicedemo
url=http://localhost:8080/manager
docs.path=c:
example.path=${docs.path}/myFX/provider

endpoint=http://localhost:8080/jaxrpc-fx-
provider/provider/FXProviderIF

web.inf.config=FXProvider_Config.properties
context.path=jaxrpc-fx-provider
war.file=${context.path}.war
build.path=${docs.path}/myFX/provider/${build}
client.jar=provider-client.jar
jaxr.org.jar=jaxr-org.jar
clib=${jwsdp.home}/common/lib
elib=${jwsdp.home}/common/endorsed

clib-jars=${clib}/activation.jar:${clib}/castor-
0.9.3.9-xml.jar:${clib}/commons-JXPath-0.1-
dev.jar:${clib}/commons-
collections.jar:${clib}/commons-
dbcp.jar:${clib}/commons-logging.jar:${clib}/commons-
pool.jar:${clib}/dom4j.jar:${clib}/fscontext.jar:${cli
b}/jaas.jar:${clib}/jasper-compiler.jar:${clib}/
jasper-runtime.jar:${clib}/jaxm-api.jar:${clib}/jaxm-
runtime.jar:${clib}/jaxp-api.jar:${clib}/jaxr-
api.jar:${clib}/jaxr-ri.jar:${clib}/jaxrpc-
api.jar:${clib}/jaxrpc-
ri.jar:${clib}/jcert.jar:${clib}/jdbc2_0-
stdext.jar:${clib}/jnet.jar:${clib}/jsse.jar:${clib}/j
ta-spec1_0_1.jar:${clib}/mail.jar:${clib}/naming-
common.jar:${clib}/naming-factory.jar:${clib}/naming-
resources.jar:${clib}/openorb.jar:${clib}/providerutil
.jar:${clib}/saaj-api.jar:${clib}/saaj-
ri.jar:${clib}/servlet.jar:${clib}/soap.jar:${clib}/xi
ndice.jar:${clib}/xmldb-xupdate.jar:${clib}/xmldb.jar

elib-
jars=${elib}/dom.jar:${elib}/sax.jar:${elib}/xalan.jar
:${elib}/xercesImpl.jar:${elib}/xsltc.jar

jwsdp-jars=${elib-jars}:${clib-jars}
```

Figure 8–25   Sample build.properties File

8.7.3 Running ANT Scripts

Step 1: Compile FX Quote Provider

Go to `/opt.myFX/provider` and run the command "`ant build.`" You should see the compilation result as follows. This process will compile all Java code into classes and generates stubs and ties for the Web Services (see Figure 8–26).

```
C:\opt\myFX\provider>ant build
Buildfile: build.xml

clean:
   [delete] Deleting directory
C:\opt\myFX\provider\build
   [delete] Deleting directory
C:\opt\myFX\provider\dist

prepare:
     [echo] Creating the required directories....
    [mkdir] Created dir:
C:\opt\myFX\provider\build\client
    [mkdir] Created dir:
C:\opt\myFX\provider\build\server
    [mkdir] Created dir:
C:\opt\myFX\provider\build\service-class
    [mkdir] Created dir:
C:\opt\myFX\provider\build\registry
    [mkdir] Created dir: C:\opt\myFX\provider\dist

compile-jaxr:
     [echo] Compiling the JAXR source code....
    [javac] Compiling 4 source files to
C:\opt\myFX\provider\build\registry

jar-jaxr:
     [echo] Building the jaxr-org.jar  file....
     [copy] Copying 1 file to
C:\opt\myFX\provider\build\registry\com\sun\webservice
demo
      [jar] Building jar:
C:\opt\myFX\provider\dist\jaxr-org.jar

set-xrpcc:
```

Figure 8–26 Step 1—Compile FX Quote Provider

```
compile-server:
     [echo] Compiling the server-side source code....
    [javac] Compiling 2 source files to
C:\opt\myFX\provider\build\service-class

xrpcc-server:
     [echo] Running xrpcc for the server:

xrpcc-client:
     [echo] Running xrpcc for the client:

compile-client:
     [echo] Compiling the client source code....

jar-client:
     [echo] Building the provider-client.jar file....
      [jar] Building jar:
C:\opt\myFX\provider\dist\provider-client.jar

copy-to-web-inf:
     [echo] Setting up build/WEB-INF....
    [mkdir] Created dir:
C:\opt\myFX\provider\build\WEB-INF\classes
     [copy] Copying 14 files to
C:\opt\myFX\provider\build\WEB-INF\classes
     [copy] Copying 1 file to
C:\opt\myFX\provider\build\WEB-INF
     [copy] Copying 1 file to
C:\opt\myFX\provider\build\WEB-INF

build:

BUILD SUCCESSFUL

Total time: 23 seconds
```

Figure 8–26 Step 1—Compile FX Quote Provider—*continued.*

Please note that the ANT script has used `xrpcc` to generate the appropriate stubs and ties with a given `config.xml` for the client and the server modules respectively.

Step 2: Set up FX Quote Service

Go to /opt/myFX/provider and issue the command "ant set-up-service." You should see the compilation result as in Figure 8–27. This process will publish the FX Quote Service to the UDDI Service Registry.

```
C:\opt\myFX\provider>ant set-up-service
Buildfile: build.xml

install:
     [echo] Installing the application....
  [install] OK - Installed application at context path
/jaxrpc-fx-provider
  [install]

run-jaxr-publish:
     [echo] Running OrgPublisher.
     [echo] Note: Remember to start the registry
server before running this prog
ram.
     [java]
uname,pwd,endpoint:testuser:testuser:http://localhost:
8080/jaxrpc-fx
-provider/provider/FXProviderIF
     [java] Created connection to registry
     [java] Got registry service, query manager, and
life cycle manager
     [java] Established security credentials
     [java] Before binding, endpoint is:
http://localhost:8080/jaxrpc-fx-provide
r/provider/FXProviderIF
     [java] Organization saved
     [java] Organization key is efa5c6ac-a7ef-a5c6-
48d8-563b22d11005

set-up-service:

BUILD SUCCESSFUL

Total time: 16 seconds
```

Figure 8–27 Step 2—Set Up FX Quote Service

Please note that the set-up service step will check security credentials, publish the provider to the UDDI Service Registry, and render an organization key efa5c6ac-a7ef-a5c6-48d8-563b22d11005.

Step 3: Compile the Message Provider

Go to /opt/myFX/provider-tsik, and issue the command "ant build." You should see the compilation result as in Figure 8–28.

```
C:\opt\myFX\provider-tsik>ant build
Buildfile: build.xml

clean:
    [delete] Deleting directory C:\opt\myFX\provider-
tsik\build
    [delete] Deleting directory C:\opt\myFX\provider-
tsik\dist

prepare:
     [echo] Creating the required directories....
    [mkdir] Created dir: C:\opt\myFX\provider-
tsik\build\client
    [mkdir] Created dir: C:\opt\myFX\provider-
tsik\build\server
    [mkdir] Created dir: C:\opt\myFX\provider-
tsik\dist

compile-server:
     [echo] Compiling the server-side source code....
    [javac] Compiling 1 source file to
C:\opt\myFX\provider-tsik\build\server

compile-client:
     [echo] Compiling the client source code....

jar-client:
     [echo] Building the jaxm-client.jar file....
      [jar] Building jar: C:\opt\myFX\provider-
tsik\dist\jaxm-client.jar
```

Figure 8–28 Compile the Message Provider

```
setup-web-inf:
     [echo] Setting up build/WEB-INF....
     [mkdir] Created dir: C:\opt\myFX\provider-
tsik\build\WEB-INF\classes
      [copy] Copying 1 file to C:\opt\myFX\provider-
tsik\build\WEB-INF\classes
      [copy] Copying 1 file to C:\opt\myFX\provider-
tsik\build\WEB-INF

build:

BUILD SUCCESSFUL

Total time: 44 seconds
```

Figure 8–28 Compile the Message Provider—*continued.*

Step 4: Install the Message Provider

Go to /opt/myFX/provider-tsik, and issue the command "ant install."
You should see the compilation result as in Figure 8–29.

```
C:\opt\myFX\provider-tsik>ant install
Buildfile: build.xml

clean:
    [delete] Deleting directory C:\opt\myFX\provider-
tsik\build
    [delete] Deleting directory C:\opt\myFX\provider-
tsik\dist

prepare:
     [echo] Creating the required directories....
     [mkdir] Created dir: C:\opt\myFX\provider-
tsik\build\client
     [mkdir] Created dir: C:\opt\myFX\provider-
tsik\build\server
     [mkdir] Created dir: C:\opt\myFX\provider-
tsik\dist
```

Figure 8–29 Install the Message Provider

```
compile-server:
     [echo] Compiling the server-side source code....
    [javac] Compiling 1 source file to
C:\opt\myFX\provider-tsik\build\server

compile-client:
     [echo] Compiling the client source code....

jar-client:
     [echo] Building the jaxm-client.jar file....
      [jar] Building jar: C:\opt\myFX\provider-
tsik\dist\jaxm-client.jar

setup-web-inf:
     [echo] Setting up build/WEB-INF....
    [mkdir] Created dir: C:\opt\myFX\provider-
tsik\build\WEB-INF\classes
     [copy] Copying 1 file to C:\opt\myFX\provider-
tsik\build\WEB-INF\classes
     [copy] Copying 1 file to C:\opt\myFX\provider-
tsik\build\WEB-INF

build:

install:
     [echo] Installing the application....
  [install] OK - Installed application at context path
/jaxm-profile-provider
  [install]

BUILD SUCCESSFUL
```

Figure 8–29 Install the Message Provider—*continued.*

Please note that this process will make the message provider available under the context /jaxm-profile-provider.

Step 5: Compile the Client Requester

Go to /opt/myFX/requester, and issue the command "ant build." You should see the compilation result as in Figure 8–30. This process simply compiles all Java classes into the build directory.

```
C:\opt\myFX\requester>ant build
Buildfile: build.xml

init:

prepare:

build:
    [javac] Compiling 6 source files to
C:\opt\myFX\requester\build\WEB-INF\classes
    [echo] finish compile....

BUILD SUCCESSFUL

Total time: 6 seconds
```

Figure 8–30 Compile the Client Requester

Step 6: Install the Client Requester

Go to /opt/myFX/requester, and issue the command "ant install." You should see the compilation result as in Figure 8–31.

```
C:\opt\myFX\requester>ant install
Buildfile: build.xml

init:

prepare:

build:
    [echo] finish compile....

install:
    [echo] Installing the application....
  [install] OK - Installed application at context path/
myFX
  [install]

BUILD SUCCESSFUL

Total time: 5 seconds
```

Figure 8–31 Install the Client Requester

Please note that this process will make the FX Spot Rate Quote Service available under the context /myFX.

Step 7: Verify the Deployed Services

Go to a browser, and issue the URL *http://localhost:8080/manager.list*. You should see the compilation result as in Figure 8–32. You will be prompted for login as the admin id during the first-time login. Alternatively, you can issue the command "ant list" from any one of the previous ANT script. Please also refer to the next section "Verifying Set-up and Remote Services."

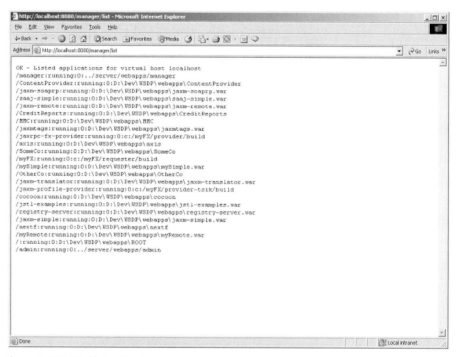

Figure 8–32 Verifying Deployment

Step 8: Invoke the Client

Go to a browser, and issue the URL *http://localhost:8080/MMC/docs/index.html*. You should see the same screens as in the "User Experience" section. If you just want to invoke the FX Spot Rate Quote screen, you may choose to issue the URL *http://localhost:8080/myFX/getFXQuote*.

8.7.4 Modifying the Remote FX Quote Engine

If you would like to build a local FX Spot Rate Quote engine, you may wish to replace the `FXPriceImpl.java` file under the subdirectory `C:\opt\myFX\provider`. The program in Figure 8–33 shows a sample implementation of the local engine.

```
package com.sun.webservicedemo;

import java.math.BigDecimal;
import java.util.*;

public class FXProviderImpl implements FXProviderIF {

// FX conversion rate
    public String getPrice(String sellCurrency, String buyCurrency) {

            if (sellCurrency.equalsIgnoreCase("HKD")) {
                if
(buyCurrency.equalsIgnoreCase("USD")) {
                    return "0.128";
                } else
                if (buyCurrency.equalsIgnoreCase("EUR"))
{
                        return "0.123";
                } else
                if (buyCurrency.equalsIgnoreCase("RMB")) {
                    return "1.25";
                } else
                if
(buyCurrency.equalsIgnoreCase("SGD")) {
                    return "0.22";
                } else
                if
(buyCurrency.equalsIgnoreCase("MYR")) {
                        return "2.85";
                } else return "0.00";
```

Figure 8–33 Modifying the Remote FX Quote Engine

```
        } else
        if (sellCurrency.equalsIgnoreCase("USD")) {
             if
(buyCurrency.equalsIgnoreCase("HKD")) {
                 return "7.78";
             } else
             if (buyCurrency.equalsIgnoreCase("EUR"))
{
                   return "0.92";
             } else
             if (buyCurrency.equalsIgnoreCase("RMB"))
{
                 return "8.20";
             } else
             if
(buyCurrency.equalsIgnoreCase("SGD")) {
                 return "2.5";
             } else
             if
(buyCurrency.equalsIgnoreCase("MYR")) {
                 return "3.45";
             } else return "0.00";
        } else return "0.00";
        // end-if
    } // getPrice
} // class
```

Figure 8–33 Modifying the Remote FX Quote Engine—*continued.*

There may be times when you want to provide a more personalized service instead of using the remote Web Services or to enhance the performance. Then you can replace your own codes under the method "getPrice." You simply rerun the ANT script to compile and install the services again. There will be no change in the user experience.

8.7.5   Verifying Set-up and Remote Services

Before invoking the remote Web Services, you may wish to verify whether your Internet (or VPN) connectivity is active and that the remote Service Provider is alive.

Next, you can verify the list of services deployed on your Application Server. Do this by issuing the URL *http://localhost:8080/manager/list* in your browser. Alternatively, you can issue the command `ant list` in a Command Prompt (depending upon whether there is a "list" target defined in your `build.xml` script). Either action will list all deployed Web Services in your Application Server. You should see `/myFX` and `/jaxm-profile-provider` services deployed at run time (see Figure 8–34).

```
C:\opt\myFX\provider-tsik>ant list
Buildfile: build.xml

list:
     [echo] Listing the application....
     [list] OK - Listed applications for virtual host
localhost
     [list]
     [list]
/manager:running:0:../server/webapps/manager
     [list]
     [list]
/ContentProvider:running:0:D:\Dev\WSDP\webapps\Content
Provider
     [list]
     [list] /jaxm-
soaprp:running:0:D:\Dev\WSDP\webapps\jaxm-soaprp.war
     [list]
     [list] /saaj-
simple:running:0:D:\Dev\WSDP\webapps\saaj-simple.war
     [list]
     [list] /jaxm-
remote:running:0:D:\Dev\WSDP\webapps\jaxm-remote.war
     [list]
     [list]
/CreditReports:running:0:D:\Dev\WSDP\webapps\
CreditReports
     [list]
     [list] /MMC:running:0:D:\Dev\WSDP\webapps\MMC
     [list]
     [list]
/jaxmtags:running:0:D:\Dev\WSDP\webapps\jaxmtags.war
     [list]
     [list] /axis:running:0:D:\Dev\WSDP\webapps\axis
     [list]
     [list]
/SomeCo:running:0:D:\Dev\WSDP\webapps\SomeCo
```

Figure 8–34 Verify Set-up and Remote Services

```
      [list]
      [list]  /myFX:running:0:c:/myFX/requester/build
      [list]
      [list]
/OtherCo:running:0:D:\Dev\WSDP\webapps\OtherCo
      [list]
      [list] /jaxm-
translator:running:0:D:\Dev\WSDP\webapps\jaxm-
translator.war
      [list]
      [list]  /jaxm-profile-
provider:running:0:c:/myFX/provider-tsik/build
      [list]
      [list]
/cocoon:running:0:D:\Dev\WSDP\webapps\cocoon
      [list]
      [list] /jstl-
examples:running:0:D:\Dev\WSDP\webapps\jstl-
examples.war
      [list]
      [list] /registry-
server:running:0:D:\Dev\WSDP\webapps\registry-
server.war
      [list]
      [list] /jaxm-
simple:running:0:D:\Dev\WSDP\webapps\jaxm-simple.war
      [list]
      [list] /:running:0:D:\Dev\WSDP\webapps\ROOT
      [list]
      [list] /admin:running:0:../server/webapps/admin
      [list]

BUILD SUCCESSFUL

Total time: 3 seconds
```

Figure 8–34 Verify Set-up and Remote Services—*continued.*

8.7.6 Managing Program Changes

To recompile the program codes, you need to undeploy the Web Services from the Application Server with the ANT script shown in Figure 8–35.

```
C:\opt\myFX\provider>ant remove
Buildfile: build.xml

remove:
     [echo] Removing the application....
   [remove] OK - Removed application at context path
/jaxrpc-fx-provider
   [remove]

BUILD SUCCESSFUL

Total time: 2 seconds
```

Figure 8–35   Managing Program Changes

8.7.7 Unit Testing

Currently, the unit testing is manual. For future extension, it is possible to make use of the JUnit testing tool to write unit testing scripts.

8.7.8 Integration Testing

The integration testing is done manually. Typically, test engineers need to write Use Cases for integration testing to cover both positive and negative test cases. It is also a good time to consider using Web Services stress-testing tools that can randomly generate test cases and benchmark the performance.

8.7.9 Deploying Codes

Running the ANT scripts from the previous sections will not permanently deploy the code. In other words, after the Application Server restarts, you need to rerun all of the ANT scripts again to make the services available. To deploy the Web Services permanently, you need to remove the services (by running "ant remove" under each subdirectory) and to deploy them once and for all (by running "ant deploy"). The deploy script will generate a myFX.war file and place it in the webapps directory.

Many developer tools (such as IDE, Studio) embed ANT and automate the application code seamlessly. Yet in a real-life deployment situation, these deployment scripts need to be customized for the local operating environment and integrated with the existing software version control and/or software migration tools.

If you use a Windows NT or Linux platform to compile and test code, and deploy on a separate platform, you may need to deploy the war files. You also need to ensure the UDDI Service Registry is being updated on the target deployment platform. Achieve this by replicating the UDDI Service Registry from the development platform to the production platform (for example, using some automated scripts or UDDI Service Registry replication features) or manually enter the business service information (manual data re-entry is undesirable for production owing to potential data entry errors).

8.8   Lessons Learned

We have learned how to expose existing business functionality as Web Services using JAXM and JAX-RPC. Using JAXR, we can publish or unpublish business services in a public or private Service Registry. These new Open Standards technologies provide a vendor-independent API to develop Web Services.

The demo shows a script-based process of how to deploy the demo program in Tomcat Application Server. However, you may consider using developer tools (such as Sun ONE Studio) to simplify and manage the entire application life cycle.

TSIK is one initiative to provide a secure and seamless message service without requiring the developers to put security verification and encryption/decryption logic into the business logic. With the availability of Apache Axis, there will be a built-in message service that can provide TSIK-like secure SOAP messaging over HTTP/S transport. Developers do not need to customize their secure messaging handlers in their business logic.

Although the Case Study is a trivial business requirement, we attempt to highlight that a systemic architecture design and analysis is essential to a good Web Services implementation.

8.8.1   References

Web Services Implementation Case Studies

Bumiputra Commerce Bank. Implementation of portal services using Web Services.
   http://www.sun.com/finance/docs/bumiputra.pdf

Hewitt Associates. Exposing mainframe applications as Web Services.

Tim Hilgenberg and John A. Hansen. *"Building a Highly Robust, Secure Web Services Architecture to Process Four Million Transactions per Day."* IBM developerWorks Live! 2002 conference.

Rima Patel Sriganesh. *"Implementing Single Sign-on in Java Technology-based Web Services."* Java One conference 2002. (this includes a case study that illustrates Single Sign-on with Hewitt.com using SAML)

Iron Mountain. Implementation of records and information management using Web Services.
http://wwws.sun.com/success-servers/pdfs/iron_mountain.pdf
(There will be a case study available soon at *http://www.sun.com*)

People's Insurance Company of China Group. Integration of insurance portal with call center using Web Services.
http://www.sun.com/software/cluster/peoplesinsuranceofchina.pdf

Sabre. Implementation of collaborative Web Services using ebXML.
Paul Milo, Dan Malks, and John MacDonald. *"Architecting and Delivering ebXML-based Collaborative Web Services"* SunNetwork Conference 2002.

Standard and Poor. Implementation of UDDI Service Registry.
http://techupdate.zdnet.com/techupdate/stories/main/0,14179,2855469,00.html
(There will be a case study available soon at *http://www.sun.com*)

Trans-Canada Pipeline. Development of a Web Services conceptual framework.
http://wwws.sun.com/software/sunone/wp-spine/spine.pdf
http://wwws.sun.com/software/sunone/success/SunTCPL.pdf

Web Services Technologies Illustrated in This Chapter

Netegrity's jSAML Toolkit. jSAML toolkit supports implementing Single Sign-on using SAML.*http://www.netegrity.com/products/index.cfm?leveltwo=JSAML&levelthree=download*

Sun's Java Web Services Developer Pack (JWSDP). JWSDP provides development tool kit for Web Services. *http://java.sun.com/webservices/downloads/webservicespack.html*

VeriSign's Trust Services Integration Kit (TSIK). TSIK provides support for XKMS and WS-Security.*http://www.xmltrustcenter.org/developer/verisign/tsik/download.htm*

Chapter 9

THE NEXT
FRONTIERS

9.1 So Many Changes

The year 2002 saw many innovations and changes in the Web Services space. Technology vendors rolled out several major releases of Web Services toolkits or reference implementations. For example, we have seen several releases of Java Web Services Developer Pack since March of 2002 (Early Access 1, Early Access 2, Version 1.0, and recently Version 1.0_1). IBM's Web Services Toolkit has also drastically upgraded from Release 2.0, 3.0, 3.1 and 3.3.2 with considerable architectural changes, to support new Web Services specifications.

The Web Services user marketplace is also responding to Web Services technology. We have seen faster adoption of ebXML in the industry, such as Open Applications Group (*http://www.openapplications.org/projects/projects.htm*) and Open Travel Alliance (*http://www.opentravel.org/opentravel/spec.cfm*). The Google search engine has added Web Services support by providing a Web API developer's kit (*http://www.google.com/apis/*). This enables a remote client to perform extensible information or product search from one of the largest search engines on the Web and get the search result returned in XML.

Another interesting example is that Amazon now provides Web Services integration to its potential business partners who want it (refer to Chapter 2, The Web Services Phenomenon and Emerging Trends). In other words, online stores who want to cross-sell Amazon's books, electronics, video products, or even auction services can now provide these services using their own branding. This allows Amazon's potential business partners to search Amazon's products online and even add items to an Amazon.com Shopping Cart, Wish List, or Wedding Registry directly from their applications. The search result will be returned as XML documents (see Figure 9–1). Developers can download a sample toolkit from the URL *http://www.amazon. com/ webservices.*

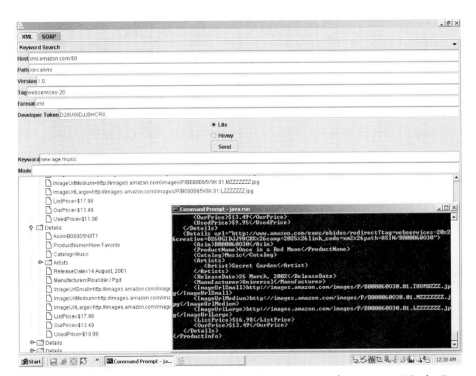

Figure 9–1   Amazon Web Services Toolkit Enabling Partners to be an Agent ("Broker") for Amazon Services

9.2   Are There Any Next Frontiers?

So far, we have seen many new technology innovations emerge. The technology trends and Open Standards are evolving speedily. Honestly speaking, it would be extremely difficult to predict what comes after the current Web Services technology. Nevertheless, we can better manage these changes by understanding the rapid "delta" of these specifications and the new APIs that are published under standards bodies such as W3C and OASIS. Based on these new specifications, we can identify three major technology areas, which may be called the "Next Frontiers" of Web Services technology: convergence of Web Services standards, wireless Web Services, and open source software and standards. The last section will conclude the discussion by identifying some emerging Web Services technologies that may influence the technology directions of Web Services for the next three years.

9.2.1   Convergence of Web Services Standards

There were many interesting evolutionary changes among leading vendors and Web Services standards bodies in 2002. These changes have dramatically affected the landscape of the Web Services standards. The timeline in Table 9–1 offers some examples:

Table 9–1 Tracking Recent Web Services Standards and Specifications

February 6, 2002	IBM, BEA, Microsoft, and Intel formed the Web Services Interoperability Organization to promote Web Services technology. *http://www.ws-i.org/*
April 5, 2002	IBM, VeriSign, and Microsoft announced a new WS-Security specification to supersede IBM and Microsoft's SOAP-SEC, Microsoft's WS-Security and WS-License, and IBM's security tokens and encryption documents. Sun and other leading vendors also later announced WS-Security support.
June 14, 2002	Sun, SAP, BEA, and Intalio jointly propose a specification Web Services Choreography Interface (WSCI) on using XML messages to describe the flow of messages exchanged by a Web Service in the context of high-level business process.
July 15, 2002	Liberty Alliance releases Liberty specification 1.0. This is found and backed up by technology vendors (such as Sun, RSA, and HP) and industry members (such as Sony and American Express).
July 30, 2002	UDDI.org is transitioned to OASIS Standards Consortium

Table 9–1 Tracking Recent Web Services Standards and Specifications—
continued.

August 9, 2002	IBM, BEA, and Microsoft announced the new specifications WS-Transaction, WS-Coordination, and Business Process Execution Language for Web Services (BPEL4WS or BPEL). The latter will supersede IBM's Web Services Flow Language (WSFL) and Microsoft's XLANG.
August 30, 2002	Sun continues to contribute to the second major iteration of Universal Business Language (UBL), which consists of over 500 reusable business information entities. UBL is intended to be the XML contents that can fill the "payload" slot in Business-to-Business framework such as ebXML. In this way, the XML contents (instead of having different XML standards for different industry domains) can be converged into a common semantics.
September 16, 2002	Oracle, together with other supporting vendors, including Sun, proposes a W3C Working Group to form a new industry-wide working group to find consensus on the several variant specifications of Web Services choreographing Business-to-Business transactions.
September 18, 2002	Sun announces the first Liberty Alliance tool, Sun ONE Identity Server version 6.0, since the Liberty specification went public on July 15, 2002.
December 19, 2002	W3C's XML Protocol Working Group publishes SOAP 1.2 as a candidate recommendation.
January 13, 2003	Liberty Alliance announces version 1.1 of the Liberty specification, which supports cross-domain Single Sign-on.
January 14, 2003	W3C creates a Web Services Choreography Working Group to address the ability to compose and design the relationships between Web Services. This is a step toward convergence from similar business process orchestration specifications.
February 12, 2003	The Web Services Basic Profile specification version 1.0 is approved. Sun is now part of the WS-I community. An interoperability test (WS-I test) has been demonstrated by various vendors in Web Services Edge 2002. Better understanding has been gained in achieving Web Services interoperability between their existing vendor products. *http://www.ws-i.org/Profiles/Basic/2003-01/BasicProfile-1.0-WGAD.html*
March 3, 2003	OASIS Web Services Technical Committee releases a public draft of the new Web Services specification, since OASIS has taken up the work to converge different Web Services specifications. *http://www.oasis-open.org/committees/wss/*
May 28, 2003	OASIS's New Web Services Security Technical Committee announces the establishment of classification standards for Web Services vulnerabilities.

We shall continue to see more convergence of different technologies and standards. The new WS-Security core specification and the related profile specification issued in March of 2003 by OASIS (*http://www.oasis-open.org/committees/wss/*) is an early success of the convergence. The positive side is that convergence helps the business community to stay focused on a common standard. This bridges the gap between different Web Services technology alternatives and variants. Unfortunately, there is the negative side where the "standards" are predominantly steered by a few technology vendors without extensive community involvement (similar to Java Community Process). We do not yet see a clear technology transition plan outlined for architects and developers who have developed solutions using the obsolete technology specifications (for example, transitioning from existing programs using SOAP-SEC or Microsoft-specific WS-Security to the new WS-Security specification). Architects and developers may need to re-engineer their code to accommodate the new Web Services specifications, and thus resources previously spent on implementing the obsolete technology specifications will be wasted because the program code cannot be reused.

One interesting progress is from the interoperability testing (WS-I test) demonstrated by several Web Services vendors at the recent Web Services Edge Conference 2002 (*http://www.infoworld.com/article/02/10/03/021003hncheng_1.html*). It was found that some vendors were using XML encoding in the SOAP messaging that may not interoperate with other vendor implementations. Thus, WS-I has published a Web Services Basic Profile specification that provides some guidelines in interoperability between Web Services (*http://www.ws-i.org/Profiles/Basic/2003-01/BasicProfile-1.0-WGAD.html*). The new J2EE 1.4 release in the summer of 2003 will also reflect any relevant updates. These are good signs for the convergence of Web Services specifications and reference implementations.

9.2.2   Wireless Web Services

With the availability of J2ME technology and Java phones, wireless access to Web Services is another big emerging trend. The coming of 3G will be another accelerator for wireless Web Services. SOAP is now available to mobile devices such as the Palm PDA, Pocket PC, and Java phones using J2ME. Developers can implement a thin Web Services client using J2ME Wireless Toolkit (*http://java.sun.com/products/j2mewtoolkit/*) and the kSOAP reference implementation (*http://ksoap.enhydra.org/*). Coding a mobile device using kSOAP is similar to coding a normal SOAP Client. Sun ONE Studio 4 (*http://wwws.sun.com/software/sundev/jde/buy/index.html*) has a sample "Vineyard Demo" that illustrates the use of kSOAP and MIDP technology, as in Figure 9–2.

```
import org.ksoap.*;
import org.ksoap.transport.*;
...
   public VClientkSOAPProxy() {
      this.serviceURL =
"http://localhost:8000/VApp/servlet/rpcrouter";
      initMappingRegistry();
   }
...
   public java.lang.String
getPriceForWine(java.lang.String winename,
java.lang.String wineyear) throws java.io.IOException
{
      HttpTransport call =
getNewCall("getBottlesInStock");
      lastResponse = call;
//     This invokes the Web Services call based on the
WSDL
//              end-point URL=serviceURN
//              operation name=getBottlesInStock
      SoapObject so = new SoapObject(serviceURN,
"getBottlesInStock");
      so.addProperty("winename", winename);
      so.addProperty("wineyear", wineyear);

      Object result = call.call(so);
      if (result instanceof java.lang.String)
         return (java.lang.String)result;
      return result.toString();
   }
```

Figure 9–2   Sample Wireless Web Services Client Code

This sample wireless Web Service can be accessed by any MIDP-compliant mobile device such as a WAP phone or a Palm PDA. Figure 9–3 shows a simulated Motorola WAP phone accessing the sample wireless Web Service.

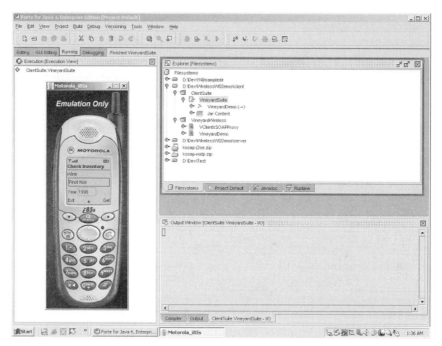

Figure 9–3 Wireless Web Services Client Using Sun ONE Studio 4

9.2.3   Open Source Software and Standards

New Web Services-Related Java Specifications

More new Java Specification Requests (JSRs) are coming out to support Web Services implementations. They not only converge different home-grown or vendor-specific implementations into a single Open Standard, but they also prompt developers and architects to get ready for the migration when the JSRs are finalized. At the time of writing, the list of recent Java Specifications shown in Table 9–2 would be essential to Web Services implementations, as found at *http://www.jcp.org/jsr/all/index.en.jsp.*

Table 9–2 List of Web Services-Related JSRs

JSR #	JSR Description	JCP Version	Release Date	Status
5	XML Parsing Specification—Java API for Parsing (JAXP)	1.0	Mar 21, 2002	Final Release
16	J2EE Connector Architecture (JCA)	2.0	Sep 24, 2001	Final Release

Table 9–2　List of Web Services-Related JSRs—*continued.*

JSR #	JSR Description	JCP Version	Release Date	Status
31	XML Data Binding Specification—Java API for Binding (JAXB); binding for XML Schema-to-Java class	2.1	Mar 4, 2003	Final Release
63	Java API for Processing 1.1 (JAXP)	2.1	Sep 10, 2002	Final Release 2
67	Java API for Messaging 1.0 (JAXM)	2.1	Jun 12, 2002	Final Release 2
93	Java API for XML Registries 1.0 (JAXR)	2.1	Jun 11, 2002	Final Release
101	Java APIs for XML-based RPC	2.1	Jun 11, 2002	Final Release
104	XML Trust Service APIs	2.1	Mar 13, 2001	Expert Group Formation
105	XML Digital Signature APIs	2.1	Apr 7, 2003	Community Draft Ballot
109	Implementing Enterprise Web Services—programming model for developing Web Services, analogous to EJB	2.1	Nov 15, 2002	Final Release
110	Java APIs for WSDL	2.1	Sep 29, 2002	Public Review
112	J2EE Connector Architecture 1.5—asynchronous integration with EIS and JMS provider pluggability	2.1	Nov 6, 2002	Proposed Final Draft 2
155	Web Services Security Assertion	2.1	Oct 30, 2001	Expert Group Formation
156	XML Transactioning API for Java (JAXTX)	2.1	Nov 6, 2001	Expert Group Formation
157	ebXML CPP/A APIs for Java	2.1	Nov 6, 2001	Expert Group Formation
172	J2ME Web Services Specification	2.1	Mar 22, 2003	Public Review
181	Web Services Metadata for the Java Platform	2.1	Apr 16, 2002	Expert Group Formation
183	Web Services Message Security API	2.1	Apr 23, 2002	Expert Group Formation

JAXM, JAXP, JAX-RPC, and JAXR specifications are accepted and implemented in Java Web Services Developer Pack. Not all of these JSRs, especially those in Expert Group Formation status, may be approved and implemented in the J2SE or J2EE reference implementation. Among these JSRs, JSR 31 (JAXB), JSR 109 (Web Services Programming Model), and JSR 110 (WSDL), are fairly interesting and promising.

Similarly, you can look at *http://www.w3.org/2002/ws/* for a list of Worldwide Web Consortium upcoming standards for Web Services technology.

New W3C Specifications

W3C has a different process to manage Internet and Web Services standards specifications. Members can submit Notes (dated public records about some technology ideas, comments, or documents, with no W3C commitment to pursue), which may evolve into Working Drafts (technology papers with W3C commitment to pursue), Candidate Recommendations, Proposed Recommendations, or Recommendations.

Table 9–3 presents a list of Working Drafts and Notes extracted from *http://www.w3.org/TR*. The highlighted W3C Notes denote some forthcoming specifications that may impact Web Services technologies and implementations in 2003 and early 2004.

Table 9–3   List of W3C Web Services Specifications

Description	Release Date	Status
Web Services Description Language specification Version 1.2	Mar 3, 2003	Working Draft
SOAP Version 1.2 Specification Assertions and Test Collection	Dec 19, 2002	Candidate recommendation
SOAP Version 1.2 Part 0: Primer	Dec 19, 2002	Candidate recommendation
SOAP Version 1.2 Part 1: Messaging Framework	Dec 19, 2002	Candidate recommendation
SOAP Version 1.2 Part 2: Adjuncts	Dec 19, 2002	Candidate recommendation
XML Key Management (2.0) Requirements	Mar 18, 2002	Working Draft (Last Call)
Web Services Architecture Requirements	Nov 14, 2002	Working Draft (Development)
SOAP 1.2 Attachment Feature	Aug 14, 2002	Working Draft (Development)

Table 9–3 List of W3C Web Services Specifications–*continued.*

Description	Release Date	Status
Web Service Description Usage Scenarios	Jun 4, 2002	Working Draft (Development)
Web Service Description Requirements	Apr 29, 2002	Working Draft (Development)
XML Key Management Specification (XKMS 2.0)	Mar 18, 2002	Working Draft (Development)
XML Key Management Specification Bulk Operation (X-BULK)	Mar 18, 2002	Working Draft (Development)
XML-Signature Requirements	Oct 14, 1999	Working Draft (Development)
Web Service Choreography Interface (WSCI) 1.0	Aug 8, 2002	W3C Notes
Web Services Conversation Language (WSCL) 1.0	Mar 14, 2002	W3C Notes
XML Key Management Specification (XKMS)	Mar 30, 2001	W3C Notes
Web Services Description Language (WSDL) 1.1	Mar 15, 2001	W3C Notes
SOAP Security Extensions: Digital Signature	Feb 6, 2001	W3C Notes
SOAP Messages with Attachments	Dec 11, 2000	W3C Notes
Simple Object Access Protocol (SOAP) 1.1	May 8, 2000	W3C Notes

Some Recent OASIS Initiatives

OASIS is another Web Services standards body that endorses Open Standards. It has the support of a large community. Many of the community members are also UN/CEFACT members who are actively involved in the EDI implementation. OASIS and the United Nations jointly sponsor ebXML. That is another reason that it draws such worldwide community support. In addition to the ongoing ebXML initiatives, the list in Table 9–4 identifies some recent OASIS initiatives (*http://www.oasis-open.org/committees/committees.shtml*) that are related to Web Services and may have an impact on the next frontiers of Web Services technology.

Table 9–4   List of OASIS Web Services Specifications

Technical Committee	Description	Status
eXtensible Access Control Markup Language (XACML)	XML specification for expressing policies for information access over the Internet. *http://www.oasis-open.org/committees/xacml/index.shtml*	Working draft 16 (Aug 22, 2002)
Business Transactions (BTP)	XML protocol for managing complex B2B transactions over the Internet. *http://www.oasis-open.org/committees/business-transactions/index.shtml*	Version 1.0 specification approved in May 2002
Directory Services (DSML)	XML specification for marking up directory services information. *http://www.oasis-open.org/committees/dsml/index.shtml*	Version 2.0 specification approved in Nov 2002
XML-based Security Services (SSTC)	Advancing SAML, an XML-based security standard for exchanging authentication and authorization information. This technical committee will also coordinate with other similar security initiatives (for example, XML Key Management Specification, XML Signature, XML Encryption, BEEP, Shibboleth, DSML, and XACML) to avoid duplicate effort. *http://www.oasis-open.org/committees/security/index.shtml*	SAML version 1.0 specification is at maturity level in Nov 2002
Web Services Security (WSS)	Continuation of the WS-Security security foundation published by IBM, Microsoft, and VeriSign's WS-Security in Apr 2002. *http://www.oasis-open.org/committees/wss/index.shtml*	Draft 11 specification issued on Mar 3, 2003
Web Services for Interactive Applications	Creation of an XML- and Web Services-centric component model for interactive Web Services applications. *http://www.oasis-open.org/committees/wsia/index.shtml* *http://www.oasis-open.org/committees/wsia/documents/WSRP-Specification-v0.90-1.html*	Early draft available for review

Table 9–4 List of OASIS Web Services Specifications—*continued.*

Technical Committee	Description	Status
Web Services for Remote Portals (WSRP)	Definition of an XML and Web Services standard that will allow plug-and-play, user-facing Web Services with portals and other intermediary Web applications. *http://www.oasis-open.org/committees/ wsrp/index.shtml http://www.oasis-open.org/committees/ wsrp/documents/version1/*	Initial draft issued in Feb 2003 for review
UDDI Specifications	Continuation of the development of UDDI specification from UDDI.org for publication and discovery of Web Services both within and between enterprises. *http://www.oasis-open.org/committees/uddi-spec/index.shtml*	UDDI version 3.0 specification
Universal Business Language (UBL)	Development of a standard library of XML business documents by modifying an already existing library of XML Schema to incorporate the best features of other existing XML business libraries. *http://www.oasis-open.org/committees/ ubl/index.shtml http://www.oasis-open.org/committees/ubl/*	First draft of public release made on Jan 27, 2003.

Open Source Web Services Software

We have seen many new Web Services software and tools coming from Open Source and freeware. There is also an emerging trend of using Linux for business applications. Many IT management and enterprise architects are concerned about the stability, reliability, and support services of Open Source software, especially in developing and implementing Web Services for mission-critical applications. This is a valid concern from a risk-management perspective.

The new Apache Axis (the next generation SOAP engine) allows developers to wrap business functionality without writing additional code. All you need to do is rename the Java file to `.jws` (e.g. StockQuoteService.java to `StockQuote-Service.jws`) and drop it in your `%JWSDP_HOME%\webapps\ axis` directory. You should be able to publish the system functionality as Web Services without writing additional server-side code (see Figure 9–4.). This appears to be fast and convenient, yet developers still need to configure the application settings for better performance and scalability, modify the code to accommodate any additional validation or exceptions handling, and deploy the services. There are also design and deployment considerations for transaction management, trading partner agreement (for example, service level), transactional reliability, and security aspects. Refer to Chapter 4, Web Services Architecture and Best Practices, for details.

You can also turn on the secure message services, which provide encryption and decryption of SOAP messages automatically using security tokens such as X.509v3 certificates (also refer to the sample "security" under the directory samples/security of the Axis distribution.) These new programming paradigms have changed the way we think of Web Services.

Figure 9–4 shows the default screen output if the StockQuoteService.jws Web Service is being invoked. Developers have placed a default Java program under the `%JWSDP_HOME%\webapps\axis` subdirectory, and Apache Axis will automatically expose it as a Web Service. If there is no custom-built code to handle the SOAP message reply, Apache Axis will return the message "Hi there, this is an Axis service!" by default.

Figure 9–4   Deploying a Java Source File as Web Services Using Axis Instantly

The availability of Apache SOAP (and its descendant Apache Axis), Java Web Services Developer Pack, and various reference implementations for Web Services security standards have made Open Source software more visible. Many Web Services software vendors have embedded Web Services APIs (practically in jar file formats) into their Application Server and Developer Studio products. Thus, developers can purchase software support services of Open Source Web Services software.

9.2.4   The Frontiers of Web Services Technologies

Between 2002 and 2003, there were some interesting technologies announced by leading Web Services vendors. These emerging technologies may have a major role in influencing the technology direction of Web Services development and implementation (aka the new frontiers of Web Services technology). The following section briefly discusses what these technologies are (in layman's terms, instead of technical details), their benefits, and how they may influence the future development of Web Services solutions in the next two to three years.

Disruptive Technologies

Disruptive technologies are new technologies that create a "paradigm shift" in the way we use technologies in solving business problems. They are likely to create cultural changes (or disruption of the current culture) and will have a great impact on the current technologies. For instance, an Internet browser is a disruptive technology to the traditional rich client. It has drastically changed the perspective we have for the client front-end. The term *disruptive* may not appeal to many people because it implies a negative connotation of business changes.

Further details of the emerging technologies discussed in the following sections can be found in the references at the end of the chapter.

Sun's N1

Sun's N1 is a "long-term vision and architectural blueprint that coincides with Sun's core values of aligning with the needs of enterprises everywhere" (*http://wwws.sun. com/software/solutions/n1/*). Sun announced the N1 technology at the Worldwide Analyst Conferences in 2002 and 2003. N1 consists of service components from stateless computer domains, which include environment elements (such as racks and power), storage elements (such as intelligent storage and SAN servers), network elements (such as switches), appliances (such as dedicated function nodes), computer elements (such as partitioned hardware SMPs/nodes), and N1 control fabrics (such as hardware management, work load balancing, and network-side billing).

N1 is a virtualization server that can provision network, computation power, and storage capabilities dynamically. It supports "service on demand" by adding or decreasing capacity on-the-fly, without impacting the service-level requirements. It also supports utility computing by billing on the actual use of computing resources (instead of the hardware and software licenses). Computing resources, which are Web Services, can be dynamically adjusted and reallocated to other locations when there is an unanticipated increase of business transactions.

For instance, if a customer needs huge computing capacity to meet large Christmas online shopping transaction volume, he/she can reprovision the N1 components from one machine (say, a low-end machine) to another larger computing platform (say, a mid-range machine) using the "flare" utility (in layman's terminology, it is like the Norton Ghost utility on a PC machine). The flare utility will transfer the entire machine disk image, data storage, and all configuration settings to another machine (or another network platform), and the new machine can start up without reconfiguring or retesting the application services.

Such flexible network computing power is a key technology enabler for Web Services because infrastructure and application services are no longer limited to one particular machine. Web Services (back-end business applications wrapped as Web Services) running in the remote data center can be scaled up or down easily using N1. It is anticipated that there will be more coverage on N1 for Web Services.

JXTA

Project JXTA (*http://www.jxta.org*) is an Open Source initiative for designing and implementing peer-to-peer solutions. JXTA technology runs on Linux and J2SE platforms (*http://www.jxta.org/servlets/ReadMsg?msgId565924&listName5announce*). There are many similarities between JXTA and Web Services, both of which have evangelized service-oriented architecture, reusable components, and distributed computing. For instance, JXTA technology can be used to connect to a range of network resources to support auctioning or to provide business information sharing.

JXTA technology has its own implementation of service discovery and service invocation. It is a complementing technology to Web Services technology. Besides, it can also initiate a SOAP call using a JXTA bridge (*http://relativity.yi.org/jxta-bridge/*). Both of these technologies provide different low-cost options to implement service-oriented architecture and reusable components, and they can interoperate using a JXTA bridge. Examples of peer-to-peer applications are the sharing and aggregation of business information (such as aggregating research data) from multiple enterprises and peer-to-peer payment. It is anticipated that there will be more examples of collaboration between JXTA and Web Services in mid- to late 2003.

Grid Computing

Grid computing technology allows reusing available computing resources to perform business services collectively. This is a cost-effective architecture approach to leverage existing computing resources. Grid computing requires a grid computing agent installed on each machine. The grid computing master will manage the scheduling and policies for different computing applications. If there is any conflict or any exception, the policies should handle them according to the predefined processing rules. Each grid computing agent can be programmed to invoke remote business applications (that is, Web Services). Besides, each machine running the grid computing agent can become a Web Service (Service Provider for the Web Services).

One example of how grid computing might be used: a grid of risk-management applications can be set up to calculate the market risk using tens of low-cost Linux and Unix machines. Each of the risk-management applications is exposed as Web Services. This risk-management solution could be an extremely expensive and time-consuming task if it is performed on a monolithic mainframe system.

In Chapter 2, Web Services Phenomenon and Emerging Trends, we discussed some trends in developing grid computing applications. We are beginning to see grid computing technology used with Web Services in the industry (such as grid computing for the capital market, *http://www.simc-inc.org/archive0203/Grid/agenda19nov2002.htm*). It is anticipated that with Web Services available there will be more examples of grid computing in the near future.

Web Services Management and Appliances

The Era of Web Services Management

As Web Services technologies and tools mature, the demand for managing Web Services applications is increasing. There are an increasing number of Web Services management vendors in the market. Chapter 3, Web Services Technology Overview, identified some examples of Web Services management tools and vendors.

Web Services management tools can provide black box-style infrastructure to manage message encryption/decryption (for message-level and data transport layer security), message compression (for faster performance and throughput), service versioning (for managing different versions of remote applications), Web Services testing (for stress testing and regression testing a service end-point URL), and service-level management (such as monitoring service-level targets and analyzing bottlenecks for remote SOAP calls). There is no single vendor today that provides all these functionalities. Some of the existing infrastructure or application server vendor products can provide partial Web Services management functionality. For example, J2EE application analyzer tools can enable tracing and tracking some of the performance bottlenecks if the remote Web Service is implemented using an EJB. If the remote Web Services are not EJBs, then the J2EE application analyzer will not help, even though the SOAP client is written in Java.

Several Web Services management tools can be consolidated into one machine to provide an integrated management platform. These management tools can be embedded in low-cost Unix or Linux machines for massive deployment. These are sometimes called Web Services appliances. We are beginning to see some of these Web Services appliances, such as Westbridge's XML Message Server *(http://www. westbridgetech.com/architecture.html)*, Westbridge's SOAP monitor *(http://www. westbridgetech.com/soapmonitor.html)*, and IBM's Web Services Gateway *(http:// alphaworks.ibm.com/tech/wsgw)* in the market.

It is anticipated that more technology vendors will enter the Web Services management space by extending their existing infrastructure products, systems management tools, middleware products, application developer tools, or application server products. Another technology trend is the emergence of Web Services appliances from new startups and niche vendors.

These Web Services management tools address two important technology problems: the monitoring, analysis, metering, and billing of Web Services for service-level management and using a black box-style Web Services appliance approach to simplify development and deployment. Currently, there is no standard and structured way to monitor, analyze, and troubleshoot Web Services applications. The black box-style appliance approach denotes that developers do not need to modify their existing application code or infrastructure to add monitoring or troubleshooting Web Services capability. For example, a Web Services appliance (black box) can encrypt/decrypt and compress/decompress the SOAP messages speedily using dedicated hardware or firmware components. It can then forward the SOAP messages to the target SOAP proxy without adding new Web Services security and compression logic in the existing applications. These Web Services management tools would be a major boost to productivity and manageability.

Web Services Technologies Continue to Evolve

Next-Generation SOAP Engine

Apache Axis is designed to be the next-generation SOAP engine with high performance and throughput. It not only provides better tools to generate SOAP client stubs and server skeletons (or tiers), but also provides new infrastructure features to support Web Services security (such as encryption and digital signatures). Before Apache Axis was available, developers needed to use a separate Web Services development tool to generate SOAP client stubs and server skeletons (or tiers). Then they needed to wrap the remote business applications in a SOAP proxy, and deploy the program code. Now Apache Axis provides a simple way to wrap remote business applications. The "Paper and Pencil" exercise in this chapter illustrates how this can be done.

Apache Axis can also be embedded in a Web Container to become a SOAP appliance. Apache SOAP is an important milestone in Web Services technology because many application servers have incorporated it. It is anticipated that the Web Services development area will be very receptive to Apache Axis (and it will have stronger traction) in the next few months.

SOAP on CICS

IBM announced a CICS SOAP technology preview on March 5, 2003 (*http://www.infoworld.com/article/03/03/05/HNcicssoap_1.html?web*). This enables developers to invoke a COBOL application in the remote CICS region through SOAP requests over HTTP request or WebSphere MQ messages. The software can be downloaded from (*http://alphaworks.ibm.com/tech/soap4cics.*)

In Chapter 5, Mainframe Integration and Interoperability, we reviewed some of the mainframe integration and interoperability options. This new capability of CICS SOAP will make mainframe integration and interoperability even easier. However, it is not clear whether this new technology will foster more Web Services implementation on IBM's mainframe platform or not.

9.3   Managing the Next Wave

How should we manage the next wave of Web Services technology? One key lesson learned from the Web Services technology evolution is that we need to believe in the value proposition and benefits of Web Services technology (such as easier integration and interoperability with legacy systems). Chasing after each wave of technology evolution will not help us manage our business and technology challenges. By learning how to apply the appropriate technology to the relevant business challenge, in the right business context, we can reap the benefits within months.

There are ample opportunities for technology training, including Webcasts (seminars or technical talks on the Web) and conferences, that can help us to understand the latest developments in Web Services. Most resources from the Web are also available free (refer to Appendix A). From my own personal experience, I would strongly recommend Web Services architects and developers to keep track of major industry events via email news alerts if they plan to implement Web Services initiatives soon. Look ahead at what new standards are coming (as in the example of JSRs identified previously) and what impact they may have on the existing development. Focus on one technology area (such as Java Web Services Developer Pack) to start with. Stay in tune with one or two major Web Services portals at a time. And more excitingly, keep your hands dirty with product demos and prototypes. Get a reputable Web Services technology vendor who has Web Services implementation experience to act as your Web

Services mentor or technology trusted advisor. This can help you to identify the business scenarios and build a quick Proof of Concept. Some technology vendors, such as Sun Services (*http://www.sun.com/service/sunps/sunpsovw.html*), also provide these services.

There will always be the next wave coming. And it will never end.

9.4   Paper and Pencil

9.4.1   Objective

Apache Axis is a next-generation SOAP engine. This exercise is meant to have you practice using Apache Axis to expose an existing interface as a Web Service.

Apache Axis has a different architecture design from previous versions of Apache SOAP. It can generate SOAP client and server components directly, without using a third-party developer IDE/workbench tool.

9.4.2   Exercise

Using the Foreign Exchange Spot Rate Quote example in Chapter 8, Web Services in Action Case Study, you are to expose the interface as a Web Service using Apache Axis's utilities java2wsdl and wsdl2java.

The source code files FXProviderIF.java and FXProviderImpl.java can be found on the CD-ROM accompanying this book under /labs/ch9. They are also listed here for reference (refer to the following excerpts in Figures 9–6 through 9–16).

Procedures to Create a Web Service Using Apache Axis

Step 1: Define Web Services Interfaces

First, define the interfaces (that is, methods or APIs) you want to expose as Web Services. Refer to the excerpt FXProviderIF.java in Figure 9–5. A new procedure, getPrice, is added under the public interface FXProviderIF. The getPrice procedure takes in two input parameters sellCurrency and buyCurrency and returns the price in a string format.

```
package myAxis;

import java.rmi.Remote;
import java.rmi.RemoteException;

public interface FXProviderIF extends Remote {
    public String getPrice(String sellCurrency, String
buyCurrency) throws RemoteException;
}
```

Figure 9–5   Start by Defining the Interface First (FXProviderIF.java)

Step 2: Define Web Services Implementation

Then, define the business logic for the interface to be exposed as Web Services. This may be implemented by developing custom-built code or invoking remote procedure calls from back-office systems (such as a mainframe). Figure 9–6 shows an example of how to implement the Web Services business logic in the program FXProviderImpl. java. The getPrice procedure is now expanded to incorporate the price quote for the currency pairs HKD-USD, HKD-EUR, HKD-RMB, HKD-SGD, HKD-MYR, and so forth. In this example, the same business logic used in the exercise in Chapter 3, Web Services Technology Overview, is reused for instructional purposes.

```
package myAxis;

import java.math.BigDecimal;
import java.util.*;

public class FXProviderImpl implements FXProviderIF {

//   FX conversion rate
    public String getPrice(String sellCurrency, String
buyCurrency) {

        if (sellCurrency.equalsIgnoreCase("HKD")) {
                if
(buyCurrency.equalsIgnoreCase("USD")) {
                    return "0.128";
```

Figure 9–6   Defining the Business Logic to Implement the Web Service
(FXProviderImpl.java)

```
                    } else
                    if (buyCurrency.equalsIgnoreCase("EUR"))
{
                            return "0.123";
                } else
                if (buyCurrency.equalsIgnoreCase("RMB")) {
                    return "1.25";
                    } else
                    if
(buyCurrency.equalsIgnoreCase("SGD")) {
                    return "0.22";
                } else
                    if
(buyCurrency.equalsIgnoreCase("MYR")) {
                        return "2.85";
                    } else return "0.00";
            } else
            if (sellCurrency.equalsIgnoreCase("USD")) {
                    if
(buyCurrency.equalsIgnoreCase("HKD")) {
                    return "7.78";
                } else
                if (buyCurrency.equalsIgnoreCase("EUR"))
{
                            return "0.92";
                } else
                if (buyCurrency.equalsIgnoreCase("RMB"))
{
                    return "8.20";
                    } else
                    if
(buyCurrency.equalsIgnoreCase("SGD")) {
                    return "2.5";
                } else
                    if
(buyCurrency.equalsIgnoreCase("MYR")) {
                        return "3.45";
                    } else return "0.00";
            } else return "0.00";
            // end-if
    } // getPrice
} // class
```

Figure 9–6   Defining the Business Logic to Implement the Web Service
(FXProviderImpl.java)—*continued.*

Step 3: Prepare for Stub/Skeleton Generation

Compile the source code to Java classes to prepare stub (client module) and skeleton (server module) generation. Figure 9–7 shows the command javac to compile the Java code.

```
D:\Dev\mydemo\myAxis>javac FX*.java

D:\Dev\mydemo\myAxis>dir
 Volume in drive D is WIN2K
 Volume Serial Number is 3D2F-1863

 Directory of D:\Dev\mydemo\myAxis

09/22/2002  03:16p       <DIR>             .
09/22/2002  03:16p       <DIR>             ..
09/22/2002  03:19p                1,761
FXProviderImpl.java
09/22/2002  03:18p                  394
FXProviderIF.java
09/24/2002  12:13a                  266
FXProviderIF.class
09/24/2002  12:13a                  827
FXProviderImpl.class
              10 File(s)         12,736 bytes
               3 Dir(s)    9,780,002,816 bytes free
```

Figure 9–7   Prepare for Stub/Skeleton Generation

Step 4: Create WSDL

Generate a Web Services Description Language (WSDL) from the interface files (Java classes are required) created in the previous steps. The utility org.apache. axis.wsdl.Java2WSDL will generate the WSDL called FXProvider.wsdl in the same directory, with the Universal Resource Name (URN, or namespace) FXProvider and the service end-point http://localhost: 8080/axis/ FXProvider, provided with the implementation file FXProviderImpl.class. In Figure 9–8, the utility Java2WSDL will generate a WSDL FXProvider.wsdl that specifies the service end-point URL *http://localhost:8080/ axis/FXProvider,* the URN FX-Provider based on the interface file FXProviderImpl. java. The Java2WSDL utility requires the implementation file to be precompiled first.

```
D:\Dev\mydemo\myAxis>java
org.apache.axis.wsdl.Java2WSDL -o FXProvider.wsdl  -l"
http://localhost:8080/axis/FXProvider" -n
"urn:FXProvider" -p"myAxis" "urn:FXProvider"
myAxis.FXProviderImpl
```

Figure 9–8   Creating WSDL

In the WSDL generated (shown in Figure 9–9), the business service ("operation name" or the method exposed), service end-point ("address location"), input parameters ("in0" and "in1" of the incoming message name "getPriceRequest"), and output parameter ("getPriceReturn") are highlighted for easy reference. These are the key elements to be specified in writing a Web Services client. Refer to the exercise in Chapter 3, Web Services Technology Overview, for more details.

```
<?xml version="1.0" encoding="UTF-8"?>
<wsdl:definitions targetNamespace="urn:FXProvider"
xmlns="http://schemas.xmlsoap.org/wsdl/"
xmlns:apachesoap="http://xml.apache.org/xml-soap"
xmlns:impl="urn:FXProvider"
xmlns:intf="urn:FXProvider"
xmlns:soapenc="http://schemas.xmlsoap.org/soap/encodin
g/" xmlns:wsdl="http://schemas.xmlsoap.org/wsdl/"
xmlns:wsdlsoap="http://schemas.xmlsoap.org/wsdl/soap/"
xmlns:xsd="http://www.w3.org/2001/XMLSchema">

   <wsdl:message name="getPriceResponse">
      <wsdl:part name="getPriceReturn"
type="xsd:string"/>
   </wsdl:message>
   <wsdl:message name="getPriceRequest">
      <wsdl:part name="in0" type="xsd:string"/>
      <wsdl:part name="in1" type="xsd:string"/>
   </wsdl:message>
   <wsdl:portType name="FXProviderImpl">
      <wsdl:operation name="getPrice"
parameterOrder="in0 in1">
         <wsdl:input message="impl:getPriceRequest"
name="getPriceRequest"/>
```

Figure 9–9   Generating WSDL Using Apache Axis Utility

```
              <wsdl:output message="impl:getPriceResponse"
name="getPriceResponse"/>
        </wsdl:operation>
    </wsdl:portType>
    <wsdl:binding name="FXProviderSoapBinding"
type="impl:FXProviderImpl">
        <wsdlsoap:binding style="rpc"
transport="http://schemas.xmlsoap.org/soap/http"/>
        <wsdl:operation name="getPrice">
            <wsdlsoap:operation soapAction=""/>
            <wsdl:input name="getPriceRequest">
                <wsdlsoap:body
encodingStyle="http://schemas.xmlsoap.org/soap/encodin
g/" namespace="urn:FXProvider" use="encoded"/>
            </wsdl:input>
            <wsdl:output name="getPriceResponse">
                <wsdlsoap:body
encodingStyle="http://schemas.xmlsoap.org/soap/encodin
g/" namespace="urn:FXProvider" use="encoded"/>
            </wsdl:output>
        </wsdl:operation>
    </wsdl:binding>
    <wsdl:service name="FXProviderImplService">
        <wsdl:port binding="impl:FXProviderSoapBinding"
name="FXProvider">
            <wsdlsoap:address
location="http://localhost:8080/axis/FXProvider"/>
        </wsdl:port>
    </wsdl:service>
</wsdl:definitions>
```

Figure 9–9   Generating WSDL Using Apache Axis Utility—*continued.*

Step 5: Generate Stub/Skeleton

The next step is to generate the club stubs and the server skeletons in order to expose the implementation Java classes as Web Services. Figure 9–10 shows the command WSDL2Java that generates both the SOAP stub (client-side component) and skeleton (server-side component). Both the stubs and the skeletons will provide a proxy for the Web Services using SOAP messaging. The following command WSDL2Java in Figure 9–10 will generate the client stubs and the server skeletons under a subdirectory "myAxis" based on the specified WSDL (FXProvider.wsdl) and the namespace ("urn:FXProvider"). This step will also generate the Web Services Deployment Descriptors (WSDD) for deployment and undeployment. These descriptors are similar to J2EE deployment descriptors and contain deployment-related information (such as service end-points and input and output parameters). Refer to Figure 9–11 for an example.

```
D:\Dev\mydemo\myAxis>java
org.apache.axis.wsdl.WSDL2Java -s -d Session -
Nurn:FXProvider myAxis FXProvider.wsdl

D:\Dev\mydemo\myAxis>dir myAxis
 Volume in drive D is WIN2K
 Volume Serial Number is 3D2F-1863

 Directory of D:\Dev\mydemo\myAxis\myAxis

09/24/2002  12:34a        <DIR>           .
09/24/2002  12:34a        <DIR>           ..
09/24/2002  12:34a                  485
FXProviderImplService.java
09/24/2002  12:34a                3,640
FXProviderImplServiceLocator.java
09/24/2002  12:34a                  321
FXProviderImpl.java
09/24/2002  12:34a                6,607
FXProviderSoapBindingStub.java
09/24/2002  12:34a                  379
FXProviderSoapBindingImpl.java
09/24/2002  12:34a                1,644 deploy.wsdd
09/24/2002  12:34a                  689 undeploy.wsdd
               7 File(s)         13,765 bytes
               2 Dir(s)    9,779,838,976 bytes free
```

Figure 9–10   Generating Client Stubs and Server Skeletons

Figure 9–11 shows a Web Services Deployment Descriptor (WSDD). In the WSDD file, it contains some deployment information, including the namespace, port name, and class name. This is slightly different from a normal deployment descriptor and includes some WSL information. It is proprietary and cannot be used by other SOAP engines.

```
<deployment
    xmlns="http://xml.apache.org/axis/wsdd/"
xmlns:java="http://xml.apache.org/axis/wsdd/providers/
java">

  <!- Services from FXProviderImplService WSDL service
->

  <service name="FXProvider" provider="java:RPC">
      <parameter name="wsdlTargetNamespace"
value="urn:FXProvider"/>
      <parameter name="wsdlServiceElement"
value="FXProviderImplService"/>
      <parameter name="wsdlServicePort"
value="FXProvider"/>
      <parameter name="className"
value="myAxis.FXProviderSoapBindingImpl"/>
      <parameter name="wsdlPortType"
value="FXProviderImpl"/>
      <operation name="getPrice"
qname="operNS:getPrice" xmlns:operNS="urn:FXProvider"
returnQName="getPriceReturn" returnType="rtns:string"
xmlns:rtns="http://www.w3.org/2001/XMLSchema" >
        <parameter name="in0" type="tns:string"
xmlns:tns="http://www.w3.org/2001/XMLSchema"/>
        <parameter name="in1" type="tns:string"
xmlns:tns="http://www.w3.org/2001/XMLSchema"/>
      </operation>
      <parameter name="allowedMethods"
value="getPrice"/>
      <parameter name="scope" value="Session"/>

  </service>
</deployment>
```

Figure 9–11 Web Services Deployment Descriptor Will Be Created During Stubs/Skeletons Generation

Step 6: Compile Stub/Skeleton into Java Classes

The client stubs and the server skeletons need to be compiled into Java classes, as shown in Figure 9–12.

```
D:\Dev\mydemo\myAxis>cd myAxis

D:\Dev\mydemo\myAxis\myAxis>javac *.java
```

Figure 9–12   Compiling the Client Stubs and the Server Skeletons

Step 7: Prepare for Deployment

To prepare for Web Services deployment, copy the compiled classes into the Web Container's Axis class directory (see Figure 9–13). In this demo environment, Apache Axis can be found under the subdirectory **myAxis** of the Apache Axis class directory `%JWSDP_HOME%\axis\web-inf\classes`.

```
D:\Dev\mydemo\myAxis\myAxis>copy *.class
d:\dev\wsdp\webapps\axis\web-inf\classes\myAxis\
```

Figure 9–13   Preparing for Deployment by Copying the Classes to Web Container

Step 8: Deploy Web Services

To start the implementation, deploy the Web Services Deployment Descriptor (WSDD) generated earlier, as shown in Figure 9–14. The AdminClient will deploy the Web Services and the associated proxy and Java classes to the SOAP server run-time environment.

```
D:\Dev\mydemo\myAxis\myAxis>java
org.apache.axis.client.AdminClient deploy.wsdd
- Processing file deploy.wsdd
- <Admin>Done processing</Admin>
```

Figure 9–14   Deploying Web Services With WSDD

Step 9: Verify Web Services Deployed

Upon successful deployment, you can verify the Web Services deployment by entering either one of the following URLs. The first URL *http://localhost:8080/axis/services/FX-Provider* should confirm the service is deployed using the Axis engine (see Figure 9–15). The second URL *http://localhost:8080/axis/services/FXProvider?WSDL* should return a WSDL that is identical to the WSDL generated in earlier steps (see Figure 9–16). This also confirms that the Web Service FX Provider is deployed and appropriate Java classes are deployed under the Axis class directory.

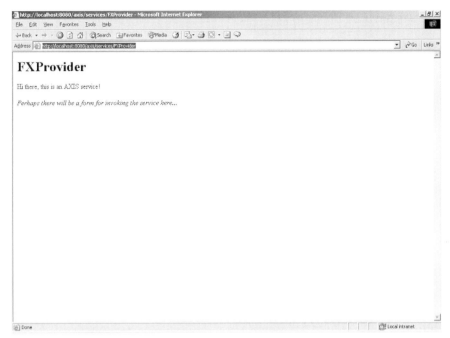

Figure 9–15   Verifying Web Services by Checking the Service End-Point URL

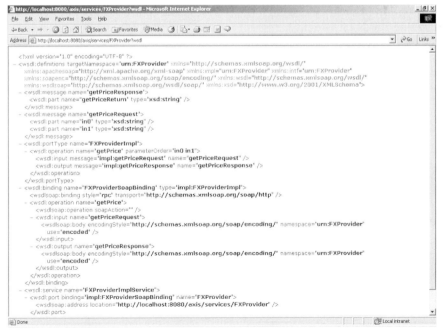

Figure 9–16   Verifying Web Services Deployment by Checking the WSDL

Concluding Remarks

Apache Axis has the capability to generate stubs (client modules) and skeletons (server modules) that is comparable to Java Web Service Developer Pack (JWSDP)'s wscompile. It does, however, have different design objectives and usage than JWSDP. It has a wider range of functionality to be the next generation of SOAP engines. Thus, both products complement each other in developing and implementing Web Services solutions.

It is amazing to see how these Open Sources and publicly available tools evolve speedily to support the next frontiers of Web Services technology.

9.4.3   References

Apache Axis

Apache Axis official Web site. *http://ws.apache.org/axis/index.html*

Grid Computing

Global Grid Forum. *http://www.gridforum.org/ogsi-wg/drafts/draft-ggf-ogsi-gridservice-23_2003-02-17.pdf*

The Globus Project. *http://www.globus.org/research/papers.html#Overview Papers*

The Securities Industry Middleware Council. *"The Future of Middleware: Grid Computing and Web Services."* November 19, 2002, General Meeting. *http://www.simc-inc.org/archive0203/Grid/agenda19nov2002.htm*

Tom Sullivan. *"Sun Combines Grid Computing, Web services."* *http://www.infoworld.com/article/02/02/15/020215hnsunonegrid_1.html*

Liang-Jie Zhang, Jen-Yao Chung, and Qun Zhou. *"Developing Grid Computing Applications, Part 1."* *http://www-106.ibm.com/developerworks/webservices/library/ws-grid1/*

Liang-Jie Zhang, Jen-Yao Chung, and Qun Zhou. *"Developing Grid Computing Applications, Part 2."* *http://www-106.ibm.com/developerworks/webservices/library/ws-grid2/*

JXTA

Max Goff. *"Jini, JXTA and Web Services: a Comparison of Network/Distributed Computing Approaches."* *http://developer.java.sun.com/developer/onlineTraining/webcasts/20plus/pdf/mgoff.pdf*

JXTA Bridge (a tool to allow SOAP messaging over a JXTA peer-to-peer network. *http://relativity.yi.org/jxta-bridge/*

Articles that discuss and compare JXTA with Web Services.
  http://www.openp2p.com/pub/a/p2p/2001/07/20/convergence.html
  http://www.croftsoft.com/library/tutorials/jxta/

N1

Yousef A. Khalidi. *"N1 Architecture."* SunNetwork Conference 2002.
  Paul Strong. *"N1 System."* SunNetwork Conference 2002.
  Sun's N1 official website. *http://wwws.sun.com/software/solutions/n1/*

Web Services Management Tools

Actional. *http://www.actional.com/*
Adjoin. *http://www.adjoin.com/*
Amberpoint. *http://www.amberpoint.com/*
Confluent. *http://www.confluentsoftware.com/*
Empirix. *http://www.empirix.com/*
Flamenco Network. *http://www.flamenconetwork.com/*
IBM alphaWorks has several niche technologies that can be used as Web Services management tools.
  http://alphaworks.ibm.com or *http://alphaworks.ibm.com/tech/wsgw*
Iopsis. *http://www.iopsis.com/*
Systinet. *http://www.systinet.com/*
Talking Blocks. *http://www.talkingblocks.com/*
WestBridge Technology. *http://www.westbridgetech.com*

Appendix A

RESOURCES AND REFERENCES

The following URLs are online resources and references for different aspects of Web Services. Some URLs, such as information and news articles, may be updated or changed from time to time. Specific resources and references can be found at the end of each chapter.

A.1 Web Services Portals

The following portals contain a variety of Web Services sites with news, technical articles, and white papers. They not only provide some technical resources, but also references to other Web Services links. They are good starters.

ebXML.org. *http://www.ebxml.org/*

LearnXMLWS. *http://www.vbws.com/*

O'Reilly XML.com. *http://www.xml.com/*

SOAPRPC. *http://www.soaprpc.com/*

Value-added Web Service Suppliers. *http://www.vawss.org/*

Web Services Architect. *http://www.webservicesarchitect.com/resources.asp*

WebServices.org. *http://www.webservices.org/*

Xmethods. *http://www.xmethods.net/*

XML.org. *http://www.xml.org/xml/news_market.shtml*

A.2   Web Services News

The following Web sites contain many news and product updates related to Web Services. Some of them provide email alerts for subscription.

CBDiForm. *http://www.cbdiforum.com/report.php3?topic_id=9*

CFOInfo. http://team.cfoinfo.com/ (Original website is *www.cfoinfo.com*, Now has moved. Login user id=s2b, password=shaston)

ecademy. *http://www.theecademy.com/node.php?id=318*

I.T. Director. *http://www.it-director.com/ts-section.php?section=17* (or select Web Services column)

I.T. Works. *http://www.itworks.be/webservices/*

OASIS. *http://www.oasis-open.org/cover/sgmlnew.html*

SearchWebServices. *http://searchwebservices.techtarget.com/*

TheServerSide. *http://www.theserverside.com/home/index.jsp*

The Stencil Group. *http://www.stencilgroup.com/ideas_scope_wsindex.html*

TopXML. *http://www.topxml.com/*

W3C. *http://www.w3.org/2001/03/WSWS-popa/*

XML Web Services Magazine. *http://www.fawcette.com/xmlmag/*

XMLHack. *http://www.xmlhack.com/*

A.3   Development Platforms and Tools, Including Tutorials and Articles

These Web sites contain good online tutorials and technical articles, from technology overview to specific technical details. Some of them have sample codes for download.

Advisor. *http://advisor.com/Articles.nsf/vTechLookup!OpenView&Restrict ToCategory=Web%20Services*

Eclipse. *http://www.eclipse.org/*

IBM Web Services (developerWorks). *http://www-106.ibm.com/ developerworks/webservices/*

Microsoft Web Services. *http://msdn.microsoft.com/library/default.asp?url=/ nhp/Default.asp?contentid=28000442*

Sun Microsystems's Java™ Technology and Web Services. *http://java.sun. com/webservices/*

Sun ONE Studio™ (Forte). *http://wwws.sun.com/software/sundev/index.html*

A.4   Vendor-Specific Web Services Sites

These are vendor-specific Web Services Web sites that provide technical white papers and product evaluation copies for download.

Avinon. *http://www.avinon.com/products/overview.html*

BEA. *http://www.bea.com/products/index.shtml*

bindsystems. *http://www.bindsystems.com/products.htm*

bowstreet. *http://www.bowstreet.com/products/businesswebfactory/index.html*

CapeClear. *http://capescience.capeclear.com/index.php* and *http://www.capeclear.com/products/index.shtml*

C# Station. *http://www.csharp-station.com/*

IBM. *http://www-3.ibm.com/software/info1/websphere/index.jsp?tab=high lights* and *http://alphaworks.ibm.com/webservices*

IONA. *http://www.xmlbus.com/*

Killdara. *http://www.killdara.com/products/vitiris/vitirisIntroduction.pdf*, *http://www.killdara.com/products/vitiris/index.htm* and *http://www.killdara.com/products/products.htm*

Microsoft. *http://www.microsoft.com/net*

Mind Electric. *http://www.themindelectric.com/*

Novell (Silverstream). *http://www.silverstream.com/Website/app/en_US/ProductsLanding*

Progress eXcelon. *http://www.exln.com/products/*

Sun Microsystems. *http://wwws.sun.com/software/* and *http://dcb.sun.com/practices/webservices/*

Systinet. *http://www.systinet.com/products/index.html*

WestBridge. *http://www.westbridgetech.com/resources.html*

XML Global. *http://www.xmlglobal.com/prod/index.jsp*

A.5   Web Services Standards Bodies and Communities

Here are some Web Services standards bodies and communities that support Web Services implementation.

ebPML. *http://www.ebpml.org/*

OASIS. *http://www.oasis-open.org/*

W3C. *http://www.w3.org/2002/ws/*
WS-I. *http://www.ws-i.org/*

A.6 SOAP-Specific

Here is a list of SOAP-specific resources.

Apach SOAP. *http://xml.apache.org*
DevelopMentor. *http://www.develop.com/soap/*
SOAPClient. *http://www.soapclient.com/*
SOAPLite. *http://www.soaplite.com/*
SOAPWeblog. *http://soap.weblogs.com/*

A.7 UDDI-Specific

Some UDDI-specific resources. UDDI has some good technical white papers on best practices.

UDDI.org. *http://www.uddi.org/* (Now under OASIS. Refer to *http://www.oasis-open.org/committees/uddi-spec/*)
jUDDI.org. *http://www.juddi.org/*

A.8 Web Services Security

There are an increasing number of Web Services security resources. More references can be found in the Web Services security chapter.

OASIS Web Services Security TC. *http://www.oasis-open.org/committees/wss/*
RSA. *http://www.rsasecurity.com/*
Web Services Security Forum. RSA. *http://www.rsasecurity.com/*
XML Trust Center. *http://www.xmltrustcenter.org/index.htm*

A.9 Web Services Conferences

There are a few Web Services-focused conferences that are held regularly in different regions and countries. The following URLs are likely to change, as they are timely. They are listed here as examples.

IBM developerWorks LIVE! Conference (previously IBM Solutions Conference). *http://www-3.ibm.com/events/solutionsevent/*

RSA Conference. *http://www.rsaconference.com/*

SunNetwork Conference. *http://sunnetwork.sun.com/sf2002/topcoder/index.jsp*

Web Services Conference. *http://www.idg.co.jp/expo/wsc/english/index.html*

Web Services DevCon. *http://www.sellsbrothers.com/conference/*

Web Services Edge. *http://www.sys-con.com/WebServicesEdge2002East/*

XML Web Services One. *http://www.xmlconference.com/boston/*

A.10 Miscellaneous

These URLs contain some other categories, including security (such as XML Trust Center) and Web Services developer tools (such as Eclipse).

BPEL4WS. *http://www.ebpml.org/bpel4ws.htm*

SOAP-WRC/James Snell. *http://www.soap-wrc.com/webservices/*

TechMetrix.
http://www.techmetrix.com/trendmarkers/topics/tmktopic.php?topic=asp

Web Services Security Forum. *http://www.xwss.org/index.jsp*

XML Trust Center. *http://www.xmltrustcenter.org/index.htm*

Appendix B

SOME WEB SERVICES VENDORS

B.1   Objectives

This summary identifies major Web Services vendors and their products and discusses what market space they penetrate into. It is not intended to be exhaustive, as there are many niche companies locally and globally. The product architecture, if available, is depicted along with the products. Company background and product information can be found on their official URLs. Some of the information here may be outdated by the time this book is published.

Apart from the following vendors, there are many niche Web Services products not listed here. Examples are Web Services Quality of Services products (such as Flamenco Networks *http://www.flamenconetworks.com/solutions/solutions.html* and Talking Blocks *http://www.talkingblocks.com/*), Web Services edge devices, such as XML Firewall products (for example, *http://daxfi.sourceforge.net/ and http://www.quadrasis.com/solutions/products/easi_product_packages/easi_soap.htm*), and SOAP Cache (for example, *http://www.exln.com/products/XIS, http://www2002.org/ CDROM/ poster/126/,* and *http://www.javaworld.com/javaworld/jw-03-2002/jw-0308- soap_p .html*). As these products are still maturing, it may be useful to start keeping them on the technology watch list.

B.2   Avinon

Avinon provides development tools to Web Services developers through its Business Service Management software—the NetScenario software. NetScenario business templates can be created for future reuse when building codes and objects. Its product architecture can be found in Figure B–1.

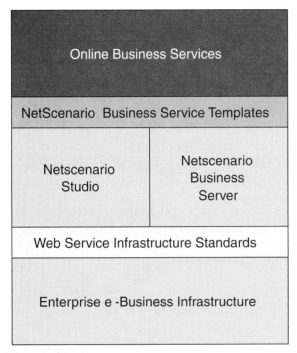

Figure B–1   Avinon Architecture

Web Services Tools
- NetScenario Studio
- NetScenario Business Server
- NetScenario Business Service Templates

Reference
http://www.avinon.com/products/overview.html

B.3   BEA

BEA Web Services architecture is based on J2EE. It has a comprehensive programming model with Weblogic features, such as IDE (developer workbench), UDDI registry, and UDDI browser. They support SOAP 1.2 and SOAP 1.2 with attachment. BEA has a new product, Java Adapter for Mainframe (J2EE Connector), for mainframe integration (for example, CICS and IMS).

All Weblogic Web Services automatically generate a home page (useful for testing) and user-defined data type components (using the ANT extension). *http://www.bea. com/products/weblogic/server/paper_webservices.pdf* is a brief white paper describing BEA's Web Services capability.

BEA has contributed to Web Services Choreography Interface (WSCI) with Sun Microsystems recently, WS-Coordination, WS-Transaction, and Business Process Execution Language for Web Services (BPEL4WS).

Application Servers

*   Weblogic Server 7.0

Middleware

*   JMS Messaging Bridge (part of Weblogic Server 7.0)

Specialized Tools

*   Weblogic Workshop (IDE) version 8.1
*   Weblogic Integration (on top of Weblogic Server)

Reference

http://www.bea.com/products/index.shtml

B.4   bindsystems

bindsystems is one of the ebXML technology vendors and supporters. It also supports a variety of B2B standards, such as RosettaNet PIPs, xCBL, and so forth. Its flagship product is bindStudio version 2.0, which provides process modeling and XML orchestration. It has a Web Services orchestration edition that handles WSDL import, WSDL generation, and BPEL4WS functionality.

Web Services Tools

*   bindStudio Collaborative Process Modeling—for building process models with support for RosettaNet PIPs, xCBL, and OAG BODs

- bindStudio Model-to-WSDL Generation—generating WSDL from process models, with support for synchronous and asynchronous processes
- bindStudio Model-to-ebXML Generation—generating ebXML BPS, CPP, and CPA from process models

Reference

http://www.bindsystems.com/products.htm

B.5   bowstreet

bowstreet is one of the portal and B2B Integration solution providers. Figure B–2 shows its flagship product, Factory 5's, product architecture. Factory 5 can be used to build portals, business partner integration (via portal), and contents syndication. Its Service Call Builder can generate Web Services with a given WSDL (by integrating with the portal framework) and facilitate testing of Web Services (using "Test Service" base model). Details can be found at *http://www.bowstreet.com/resources/whitepapers/factory_technical.html.*

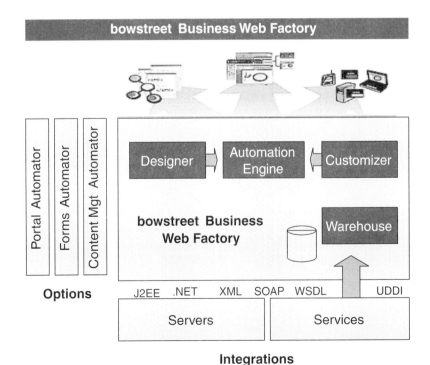

Figure B–2   bowstreet Architecture

Web Services Tools

- Business Web Factory 5—this is a software automation toolset to build and automate Web Services (aka developer workbench). It has components of Business Web Browser (aka UDDI browser), Business Web Automation Engine, Business Web Customizer (for example, manage application profile set), and Business Web Warehouse (aka Service Registry and repository).

- Factory Options—these are additional models and libraries for Business Web Factory. They have components of Portal Automator, Forms Automator, and Content Management Automator.

- Factory Integrations—these components provide integration with BEA and IBM servers.

Reference

http://www.bowstreet.com/products/businesswebfactory

B.6 CapeClear

Cape Clear is a niche developer tools company. It supplies an integrated developer environment that can run on multiple platforms. Figure B–3 depicts its product architecture. Cape Clear version 4.0 has three key components: Cape Clear 4 Studio, Cape Clear 4 Server, and Cape Clear 4 Manager.

Web Services Platform

- Cape Clear 4 Server—runs on top of J2EE applications, supports SOAP 1.2, and generates WSDL. It is bundled with WSDL repository and UDDI registry. It can support both MQ/message-based Web Services and CORBA-based Web Services.

Developer Tools

- Cape Clear 4 Studio—provides an integrated development environment and Web Services generation tools for developers. It has data transformation capabilities supporting both XML and non-XML (such as SWIFT and SAP).

- Cape Clear 4 Manager—provides a security and management platform for deployment, configuration, service management, authentication, routing and protocol translation, performance diagnosis, clustering, and firewall proxy.

Reference

http://www.capeclear.com/products/index.shtml

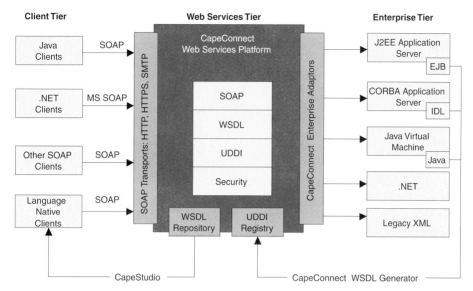

Figure B–3   CapeClear Architecture

B.7   IBM

IBM is a highly diversified technology vendor of Web Services developer tools, application server, and infrastructure platform. It has a Research and Development unit called alphaWorks that provides new Web Services tools. "Graduated" (mature) tools will be incorporated into the WebSphere product line or other commercial products. Figure B–4 shows the current WebSphere product architecture.

Application Server
- WebSphere Application Server 5.0 (Enterprise, Advanced)

Web Services Supporting Products
- DB2 (UDB) with XML Extender
- WebSphere MQ (including MQ Series with JMS)
- UDDI registry

Developer Tools
- WebSphere Studio
- WebSphere Studio Application Developer
- Web Services Toolkit 3.3.2

- Web Services Gateway
- Web Services Invocation Framework
- UDDI Explorer
- Lotus Domino

Web Services Technology
- UDDI4J
- SOAP4J
- XML Security Suite (XSS)
- BPWS4J (for Business Process Execution Language for Web Services)

References

http://www-3.ibm.com/software/info1/websphere/index.jsp?tab=highlights
http://alphaworks.ibm.com/webservices

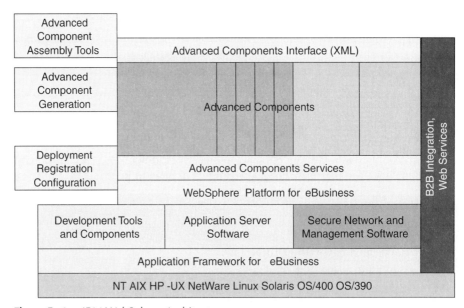

Figure B–4   IBM WebSphere Architecture

B.8 IONA's XMLBus

IONA has been a technology innovator in CORBA-based architecture and middleware products. It has extended the coverage to Web Services. XMLBus is its flagship product (refer to its product architecture in Figure B–5). It has an integrated developer environment. It can expose CORBA objects as Web Services.

Orbix2A XMLBus

- XMLBus automatically wraps and deploys applications as Web Services (URLs to WSDLs). It has a new Web Services container and XMLBus Archive (XAR). XMLBus comes with a developer IDE platform called Web Service Builder. There is a specialized UDDI browser available.

Reference

http://www.xmlbus.com/

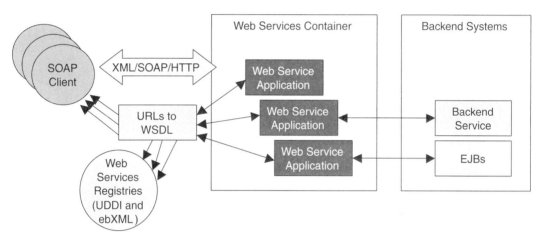

Figure B–5 IONA XMLBus Architecture

B.9 Kildara

Kildara's flagship product, Vitrius, is positioned to be an add-on to existing software packages. Figure B–6 shows the product architecture. Vitrius supports a lightweight J2ME. It claims compatibility (interoperability) with other Web Services frameworks, such as Biztalk and e-Speak. It specializes in supporting vertical industry XML standards (for example, HL7, OAGIS, RosettaNet, ACORD, HR-XML, and VICS). It has the following core components: Message Sources (create XML/SOAP messages), Message Sinks (deliver messages to applications), Syntax Processors (translator), and Semantic Processors (interpreter).

Web Services Tools

- Vitrius Web Services Engine—is a grid computing with Web Services tool
- IBX (interbind products)

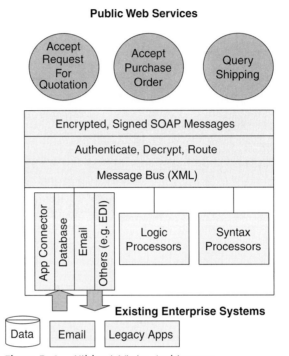

Figure B–6   Kildara's Vitrius Architecture

Web Services Solutions

- HDCourier—health care integration device
- DMSConnect—Dealer Management System for automotive retailers
- Previous Products under interbind (IBX)
- interbindIPX 1.2—Web Services container
- interbindXIO 1.0—Java package to map Java to XML
- interbindAUTHOR 1.0—WSDL generation from different languages
- interbindMANAGE 1.0—management of Web Services nodes
- interbindDATA 1.0—data capture and integration

References

http://www.kildara.com/products/vitiris/vitirisIntroduction.pdf

http://www.kildara.com/products/vitiris/index.htm

http://www.kildara.com/products/products.htm

B.10 Microsoft

Microsoft is a technology innovator in Web Services using its Visual Studio .NET product suite. Visual Studio .NET products have a considerable number of developers in the market for Web Services. Figure B–7 shows its global Web Services architecture. With IBM and VeriSign, it has jointly published Web Services roadmap specifications.

Application Server

- ASP.NET server
  (*http://msdn.microsoft.com/library/default.asp?url=/nhp/Default.asp?contentid=28000440*)
- BizTalk server
  (*http://msdn.microsoft.com/library/default.asp?url=/nhp/Default.asp?contentid=28000399&frame=true*)

Web Services Supporting Tools

- SQL Server
- Web Services Tools—for example, Web Services Development Kit
  (*http://msdn.microsoft.com/downloads/default.asp?url=/downloads/topic.asp?URL=/MSDN-FILES/028/000/123/topic.xml*)
- Microsoft SOAP Toolkit
- Web Services Enhancements (WSE) 1.0
- Visual.NET studio
- C#

Web Services Technology

- Security—WS-Security, CAPICOM (PKI integration toolkit, refer to
  http://msdn.microsoft.com/library/default.asp?url=/library/en-us/security/Security/cryptography_cryptoapi_and_capicom.asp)
- WS-Routing
- WS-Referral
- WS-Addressing—refer to
  http://msdn.microsoft.com/webservices/default.aspx?pull=/library/en-us/dnglobspec/html/ws-addressing.asp for details

References

http://www.microsoft.com/net

http://msdn.microsoft.com/webservices/

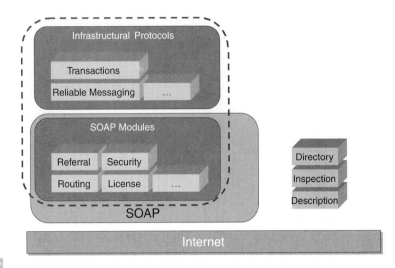

Figure B–7   Microsoft Architecture

B.11 mindElectric

mindElectric is one of the early evangelists for Web Services. It has a developer environment product, SOAP run time, and UDDI Service Registry. Figure B–8 shows its product architecture.

Web Services Tools

- GLUE 3.2/4.0
- Supports SOAP 1.1 and SOAP 1.2
- UDDI server and browser
- Electric Server Page
- GAIA—grid computing platform for Web Services
- Superset of GLUE with clustering, load balancing, fault tolerance
- Adopts a P2P architecture
- Electric XML 4.0—a fast XML parser and Java-to-XML serializer

Reference

http://www.themindelectric.com/

1. GLUE servlet is hosted in web server and routes inbound SOAP/HTTP messages to the GLUE SOAP processor

2. The GLUE SOAP processor routes the message to the Java object which was previously published as a Web Service from GLUE

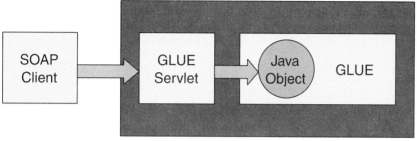

Web Server with Servlet Engine

Figure B–8   The mindElectric Architecture

B.12 Novell (Silverstream)

Novell acquired Silverstream and rebranded the Web Services products as Novell eteNd. Silverstream's flagship product exteNd includes an application server, developer environment, and messaging tools.

Application Server
- Novell exteNd Application Server—bundled with a messaging tool jBroker

Web Services Tools
- Novell exteNd Workbench—wizard and deployment tool
- Novell exteNd Director—content management, work flow, user profiling, portal, and so forth
- eXtend Composer—visual design, data transformation, back-end integration, action model processing, and UDDI registry. This is the integration server
- jBroker—messaging tools supporting CORBA, XML-RPC, MQ, and so forth. It is bundled with Novell extend Application Server

Reference
http://www.silverstream.com/Website/app/en_US/ProductsLanding

B.13 Sun Microsystems

Sun is the inventor of Java technology. Apart from Java and Web Services technologies, Sun also supplies diversified technologies and software products, including an application server, middleware, a directory server, and an identity management product. Sun has recently rebranded iPlanet™ and Forte™ products as Sun ONE™.

Figure B–9 shows the Sun ONE™ architecture framework for building Web Services. It is a meta-architecture framework. In addition, there are supporting software products (branded under Sun ONE™) that provide each of the architecture components. Recently, N1 is the vision and new technology strategy.

Application Server

- Sun ONE™ Application Server 7.0 (previously iPlanet™ Application Server)—SOAP is bundled in Sun ONE™ Application Server 6.5. SOAP 1.2, WSDL generation; JAX Pack is bundled in version 7.0

Middleware

- Sun ONE™ Integration Server (previously iPlanet™ Integration Server) 3.0—B2B and EAI editions. It is SOAP enabled and integrated well with UDS, XML Adapter, and Sun ONE™ Studio. The new release supports ebXML
- Sun ONE™ XML Adapter 1.0
- Sun ONE™ Message Queue 3.0—a flagship JMS 1.1 compliant product. It supports JAXM

Developer Tools

- Sun ONE™ Studio (previously Forte™ for Java) 3.0/4.0—developer IDE with plug-in modules for SOAP and WSDL generation
- Sun ONE™ Unified Development Server 5.0—building block and developer platform for Sun ONE™ Integration Server and Sun ONE™ Application Server, together with Sun ONE™ Studio (previously Forte™ for Java)
- Web Services Developer Pack 1.1—an all-in-one JAX-SOAP-UDDI-ebXML development kit

Web Services Security

- Sun ONE™ Identity Server 6.0—a Liberty solution for managing federated identity and cross-domain Single Sign-on using SAML and Liberty
  http://wwws.sun.com/software/products/identity_srvr/home_identity.html

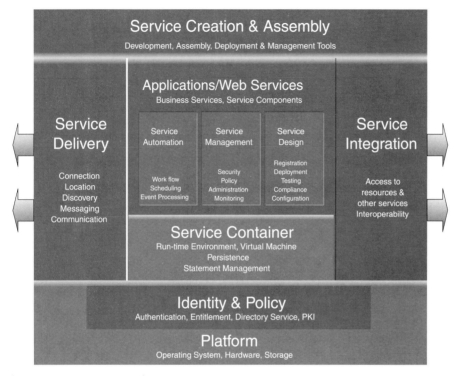

Figure B–9 Sun ONE Architecture

- Sun ONE™ Directory Server—enterprise and federated directory solutions to support identity management

References

http://wwws.sun.com/software/

http://dcb.sun.com/practices/webservices/

B.14 Systinet

Systinet is another evangelist of Web Services technology. It is a developer environment company. Systinet's flagship product WASP 4.5 Product Suite has been released. It has claimed some interesting benchmarking figures of average round-trip response time compared to Apache Axis. Besides, it has a high-performance and reputable UDDI Service Registry. It has some good Web Services management and monitoring capabilities.

Web Services Tools

- WASP Developer
- WASP Server (Lite, Advanced)
- WASP UDDI

Features

- WASP tools are targeted to enhance major vendors' developer environment (for example, Sun ONE Studio)
- SOAP add-on—for example, EJB, JMS, and JDBC
- Security add-on—for example, GSS-API/SPKM, SSL, and JAAS

References

http://www.systinet.com/products/index.html

http://www.systinet.com/index.php?nav=/products/overview

B.15 XML Global

XML Global is another leading ebXML technology vendor and supporter. Figure B–10 shows the product architecture of its flagship product GoXML. It contains a data transformation tool, messaging product, ebXML Service Registry, and an XML object database.

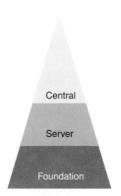

*ebXMLRegistry, Message Service and
    Component Dictionary
* Web Services Support

* Routing and workflow
* Back-end connectors
* Links to MQSeries, SOAP, HTTP
  and more

* Patented transformation engine
* Design studio
* EDI dictionaries for X12, EDIFACT,
  HIPAA, SWIFT

Central

Server

Foundation

* Dynamic transformation
* Consistent use of business terms
* Adopt different formats of trading
  partners

* Enterprise connectivity
* Complex business transactions

* Content management
* Data aggregation

Figure B–10   XML Global Architecture

Web Services Tools

- XML Business Integrator—business process collaboration and orchestration tool for complex business environments (such as Straight-through Processing)
- GoXML Transform and GoXML Transform XTE—flexible data transformation engine to support numerous electronic data standards such as EDI, X12, SWIFT, and so forth
- GoXML Registry—an ebXML Service Registry
- GoXML Messaging—provides ebXML Message Service 2.0 functionality
- GoXML Integration Workbench—an integrated development environment, bundled with XMLSpy 5.0
- GoXML Repository—an XML data repository

Reference

http://www.xmlglobal.com/prod/index.jsp

Appendix C

DEMO ENVIRONMENT SET-UP

C.1   Platform Requirements

For reasons of mobility and convenience, I chose to develop the samples on Open Source software and publicly available software on a notebook PC to illustrate the concepts and technology in this book. I have also verified and tested it on Solaris OE ™ version 8 on an Ultra-10 ™ system. Conceptually, these examples should be executable on any Unix operating system with minor modification of the class paths. Obviously, there are small platform differences in Unix when specifying the file name and path notation; for example, the Windows platform uses a backslash "\" while Unix uses a forward slash "/". The details should be referred to in the individual software product.

C.1.1 Hardware Requirements

The minimal hardware platform is recommended to be a Pentium 3 processor with a 400MHz CPU, 128MB RAM and at least 400MB additional hard disk space. You will require another 200MB or more to install the optional components. The sample programs in this book are tested on a Pentium 3 notebook PC with 700MHz CPU, 256MB RAM, and a 30GB hard disk, as well as on an Ultra-10™ with 128MB RAM and a 20GB hard disk running on Solaris OE™ version 8.

C.1.2 Software Requirements

The sample programs are tested on Windows 2000 and Solaris OE™ version 8, respectively. The software products listed in Tables C–1 and C–2 are used to support the sample programs and the Case Study in this book. The software used here will likely have newer versions by the time the book is published. Conceptually, the installation procedures should be similar, and the set-up files will have slightly different file names. Please note that you may need to check the compatibility in the release notes, revalidate the set-up, and retest all sample programs if you use a newer software release. If you are using the Unix platform, you also need to verify the file locations in the `build.` `properties` (such as the environment variable `docs.path`), `build.xml`, and in the source program files (such as the file location for the "`sample_soap_keystore`" in the file `ProfileServlet.java`).

Netegrity's jSAML Toolkit version 1.0, which comes with an existing Single Sign-on sample program, is used here to illustrate Single Sign-on integration using Security Assertion Markup Language (SAML). Liberty specification (for cross-domain Single Sign-on and federated identity management) is already available online at *http://www.projectliberty.org*. There have been recent updates to SAML since then. Netegrity's jSAML Toolkit does not have any new updates to support these new changes yet. Thus, the software toolkit is used, for instruction purposes, as it is, and there are likely some architectural or software changes required in order to be compliant with the latest SAML or Liberty specifications. Sun ONE Identity Server 6.0 (*http://wwws.sun.com/software/products/identity_srvr/home_identity.html*) now provides a similar SAML toolkit and supports the latest SAML and Liberty specifications.

VeriSign's Trust Service Integration Kit is an up-to-date toolkit to support XML Key Management Specification and WS-Security.

Core Software Components

Table C–1 Core System Components Used in This Book

Software	Version Used	Description	Download From
J2SE SDK	1.4.1.02	Software Development Kit to enable compiling and customizing sample codes.	*http://java.sun.com/j2se/1.4.1/download.html*
Java Web Services Developer Pack	1.0_01	Also known as JWSDP. All-in-one development toolkit with Tomcat 4.1.2, Apache SOAP 2.2, and JAX Packs. This is the core component for this book.	*http://java.sun.com/webservices/downloads/webservicespack.html* (JWSDP and JWSDP Tutorial)
Axis	1.0	New generation Apache SOAP engine. This is a good complementary product with JWSDP and is essential to run many samples in this book.	*http://xml.apache.org/axis/index.html* *http://ws.apache.org/axis/releases.html*
Xalan	2.4D1	Latest Apache Xalan stylesheet processor used by Axis.	*http://xml.apache.org/xalanj/index.html*
ANT	1.5	A prerequisite for installing Axis version 1.0.	*http://jakarta.apache.org/ant/index.html* *http://ant.apache.org/bindownload.cgi*
Xerces	2.3.0	Latest Apache XML parser used by Axis.	*http://xml.apache.org/xerces2-j/index.html*
XML Security	1.05D2	Optional security support used by Axis.	*http://xml.apache.org/security/index.html*
JUnit	3.7	Required component for unit testing within Axis if you want to run all examples in Axis.	*http://www.junit.org/index.htm*
Trust Services Integration Kit	1.3	Also known as TSIK. XKMS and WS-Security support. This component is essential to run the Case Study sample programs.	*http://www.xmltrustcenter.org/developer/verisign/tsik/download.htm*
BouncyCastle JCE Provider	1.14	Required JCE provider component for TSIK.	*http://www.bouncycastle.org/latest_releases.html*

Table C–1   Core System Components Used in This Book—*continued.*

Software	Version Used	Description	Download From
jSAML Toolkit	1.0	A SAML-based toolkit for implementing Single Sign-on. (Currently, this version does not support Liberty specification.) You'll need to register for download. Select download from the "Product Downloads" in the left-hand column. This component is essential to run the Case Study sample programs.	*http://www.netegrity.com/products/ index.cfm?leveltwo= JSAML&levelthree= download*
Acrobat Reader	5.0	Acrobat reader to access PDF documentation of different software products.	*http://www.adobe.com/support/ downloads/main.html*
Winzip	8.1	Zip utilities to compress and uncompress sample codes or documentation from different software products.	*http://www.winzip.com/ddchomea.htm*

Optional Software Components

Table C–2   Optional System Components Used in This Book

Software	Version Used	Description	Download From
Textpad	4.5	Simple coding IDE.	*http://www.textpad.com/download/ index.html*
Sun ONE Studio	4.0	Powerful IDE to build Java Web Services. A good sample is available to illustrate how to build wireless Web Services. Free try-and-buy Enterprise Edition is available for download. Community version is free for the public. User registration required.	*http://wwws.sun.com/software/sundev/ jde/buy/* Also select "Update Center" to download wireless module.

Table C–2   Optional System Components Used in This Book—*continued.*

Software	Version Used	Description	Download From
SOAP-Lite	0.55	Accessing SOAP from a Perl client. Requires Perl version 5.0 or later. This is instrumental to illustrate we do not require a Java client to invoke Web Services.	*http://www.soaplite.com/*
Perl	5.0	Perl script binaries required to support SOAP-Lite client that invokes Web Services.	*http://www.cpan.org/ports/index.html* or *http://perl.apache.org/download/*

C.2   Installation and Configuration

For software installation, please refer to the individual installation instructions and procedures that come with each software product. The following summarizes some additional installation procedures when integrating these software products together. Unix Platform refers to Solaris OE™ but it also applies to Linux. The installation procedures for these platforms are similar.

C.3   Java 2 Standard Edition (J2SE)

C.3.1 Windows Platform

Download `j2sdk-1_4_1_02-windows-i586.exe` from the site *http://java. sun.com/j2se/1.4.1/download.html.* Simply invoke the program, and it will set up the SDK. Remember to add `JAVA_HOME` in your environment variable to point to the J2SE installation location (for example, `D:\J2SE`).

C.3.2 Unix Platform

Download `j2sdk-1_4_1_02-solaris-sparc.sh` from the site *http://java. sun.com/j2se/1.4.1/download.html.* Simply execute the installation script. Remember to add `JAVA_HOME` in your environment variable to point to the J2SE installation location (for example, `/usr/j2se`). You may want to link your `/usr/java` to your J2SE installation location (for example, `ln -s /usr/j2se /usr/java`). Refer to the installation guide for details.

C.4   Java Web Services Developer Pack (JWSDP)

C.4.1 Windows Platform

Download `jwsdp-1_0_01-windows-i586.exe` from the site *http://java.sun. com/webservices/downloads/webservicespack.html.* Simply invoke the program, and it will set up the `JWSDP`. Remember to add the following environment variables to point to the JWSDP installation location in Figure C–1, for example.

```
JAVA_HOME=D:\j2se
JWSDP_HOME=D:\Dev\WSDP
PATH=%PATH%;D:\Dev\WSDP
```

Figure C–1   Environment Variables Settings for JWSDP

The default TCP port for the embedded TOMCAT server is 8080. If you also need to change to another port (for example, port 8000), you need to modify the `server.xml` in the `%JWSDP_HOME%\conf` directory. If you need to use HTTPS, you will also need to make configuration changes in the same `file server.xml`. In the demo configuration, we use the default port 8080 and do not use HTTPS.

During the installation, you will be prompted to provide an administrator user id and password (that is, with admin, manager, and provider roles). If you need to add a new test user or administrator, you may wish to modify the `tomcat-users.xml` in the `%JWSDP%\conf` directory. You should have something like Figure C–2.

```
<?xml version='1.0'?>
<tomcat-users>
  <role rolename="admin"/>
  <role rolename="manager"/>
  <role rolename="user"/>
  <role rolename="provider"/>
  <user username="goodguy" password="goodguy"
roles="user"/>
  <user username="otherguy" password="otherguy"
roles="user"/>
  <user username="ray" password="x792y1z0"
roles="admin,manager,provider"/>
</tomcat-users>
```

Figure C–2   Sample tomcat-users.xml Setting

This sample `tomcat-users.xml` file shows three newly added ids, where "ray" is the administrator id (added during installation); "goodguy" and "otherguy" are user ids required by the jSAML demo.

To experience more examples, you may install the JWSDP tutorial examples.

Do not forget to create a "`build.properties`" file under your home directory (usually c:\Documents and Settings\yourProfile), that contains your username and password. The ANT build tool will authenticate the username and password against the entries in the `tomcat-users.xml` file. If they do not match the entries in the `tomcat-users.xml` file, ANT will not compile and execute the scripts successfully.

C.4.2 Unix Platform

The installation procedure is similar to that of the Windows version. Download `jwsdp-1_0_01-unix.sh` from the site *http://java.sun.com/webservices/downloads/web servicespack.html.* Simply execute the installation script and specify the target installation location (for example, `/opt/jwsdp`) from the installation wizard. Please also add the additional users in the `tomcat-users.xml` file as in the procedures in the previous section (the procedures are similar to the Windows platform installation).

Upon successful installation, JWSDP will update the Solaris Product Registry under Unclassified Software called "product1." You can verify the set-up by issuing the command "`pkginfo`" as shown in Figure C–3.

```
# pkginfo -i | grep product1
application IS9419995      product1
```

Figure C–3 Verifying the Unix Set-Up Using pkginfo

To validate successful set-up, you can invoke the Tomcat server (that is, Web Container) and Xindice database (that is, XML object database supporting UDDI Service Registry) using root access (that is, user id=root). Refer to Figure C–4.

```
#cd /opt/jwsdp/bin
#./startup.sh
#./xindice-start.sh
```

Figure C–4 Start up JWSDP Processes

You can also verify that the server processes are running by "`ps -ef | grep java`" and the system will report two processes running in the background, as shown in Figure C–5. The first process with parameter "`-Dcom.sun.launcher.`

displayMinimized" refers to Xindice database start-up, and the second process with parameter "-Dcatalina" refers to the Tomcat Web Container start-up process.

```
# ps -ef | grep java
   root   999     1  0 12:31:46 ?          0:13
/usr/j2sdk141/jre/bin/java -Xms16m -Xmx168m -
Dcom.sun.launcher.displayMinimized
   root   996     1  0 12:31:35 ? 1:36
/usr/j2sdk141/jre/bin/java-
Dcom.sun.launcher.displayMinimizedFrame= -Dcatalina
   root  1305  1301  0 16:07:25 pts/5    0:00 grep java
```

Figure C–5   Verify JWSDP Set-up

C.4.3 Remarks

JWSDP 1.01 was released in August of 2002. One key change from version 1.0 is the use of wscompile and wsdeploy instead of xrpcc to generate client and server stubs. wscompile requires using a new XML configuration file jaxrpc-ri.xml for JAX-RPC. Version 1.01 can also generate WSDL "on-the-fly" by specifying the suffix "?WSDL" for the service end-point.

There is an installation note (under the file location %JWSDP_HOME%\docs\jwsdponj2ee.html) for JWSDP 1.01 on J2EE 1.3.x SDK. JWSDP 1.1 can be configured under a J2EE application server such as the Sun ONE application server. There is a customized installation note jwsdpons1as7.html under JWSDP 1.1. The Sun ONE application server version 7.0 uses a customized version of Apache ANT 1.4.1 called Asant to perform the build processing. Basically, Asant adds Sun ONE application server-specific extension, including sun-appserv-deploy, sun-appserv-undeploy, sun-appserv-instance, sun-appserv-component, sun-appserv-admin, and sun-appserv-jspc.

C.5   AXIS

Axis assumes the installation of the Apache Axis distribution, latest Xalan, Xerces, XML Security, and JUnit binaries.

C.5.1 Windows Platform

Download xml-axis-10.zip from the Axis distribution site *http://xml.apache.org/axis/*. Simply extract the zipped files into your target Axis installation location.

Please also refer to the installation page `axis-1_0\docs\install.html` for details.

Copy the subdirectory `axis` and all files inside from the Axis distribution to the `%JWSDP_HOME%\webapps` directory. Copy `axis.jar`, `axis-ant.jar`, `commons-discovery.jar`, `wsdl4j.jar`, and `log4j-1.2.4.jar` from the `%JWSDP_HOME%\webapps\axis\lib` to `%JWSDP_HOME%\common\lib`. You also need to add the latest `xercesImpl.jar` and `xalan.jar` from the Apache distribution, `Xerces-J-bin.2.0.2.zip` and `xalan-j_2_4_D1-bin.zip`, respectively, to `%JWSDP_HOME%\common\lib`.

XML Security is an optional component for Axis. Download xml-security-bin-1_0_4.zip and extract `xmlsec.jar`. Copy the file into `%JWSDP_HOME%\common\lib` and `%JWSDP_HOME%\webapps\axis\lib`. Also, you may want to add it to the `CLASSPATH`.

Copy the junit.jar from Junit binary distribution to the directory `%JWSDP_HOME%\common\lib`.

Because Axis requires some updated files for J2SE SDK's `javac` compiler, you need to add `tools.jar` in your `CLASSPATH` as well. In addition, add these newly added jar files to your `CLASSPATH`.

To be able to run the sample programs from Axis, you need to add your Axis installation location (for example, D:\dev\axis-1_0) into your `CLASSPATH` as well.

C.5.2 Unix Platform

The installation procedure is similar to that of the Windows version. Download `xml-axis-10.tar.gz` from the Axis distribution site *http://xml.apache.org/axis/* and extract to your target location. Similar to the Windows version installation, you can extract the Axis distribution to your target location and move the `webapps` subdirectory to JWSDP's `webapps` (for example, `/opt/jwsdp/webapps/axis`).

C.5.3 Remarks

Apache Axis was released as version 1.0 on October 7, 2002. Since Beta 3, Axis has added some new jar files (for example, `commons-discovery.jar`, `axis-ant.jar`) and updated some existing files (for example, `saaj.jar`). `tt-bytecode.jar`, which is provided by Apache Axis Beta 3, is not available in RC1. It is still documented as a mandatory file in the installation section of the User Guide. There is no major change indicated in the Axis Architecture Guide documentation.

C.6   ANT

C.6.1 Windows Platform

Download `jakarta-ant-1.5-bin.zip` from *http://ant.apache.org/old-releases/ v1.5/bin/*. Extract the file into a temporary directory, copy the files `ant.jar` and `optional.jar`, and replace the existing files under `%JWSDP_HOME%\lib`. Axis files require ANT 1.5 to execute.

C.6.2 Unix Platform

Download `jakarta-ant-1.5-bin.tar.gz` from *http://ant.apache.org/old-releases/v1.5/bin/*. Extract the file into a temporary directory, copy the files `ant.jar` and `optional.jar`, and replace the existing files under $JWSDP_HOME/lib. Axis files require ANT 1.5 to execute.

C.7   Trust Service Integration Kit (TSIK)

VeriSign's TSIK assumes the installation of a JCE provider, which in this case is Bouncy Castle JCE.

C.7.1 Windows Platform

Download the jar file, `tsik1_3.jar` from the site *http://www.xmltrustcenter.org/ developer/verisign/tsik/download.htm* into a temporary directory. Verify the signature using Sun's `jarsigner` tool, as shown in Figure C–6. You may need to specify the full path of "tsik1_3.jar" if necessary.

The output should display "`jar verified.`"

Uncompress the `tsik1_3.jar` into a temporary directory and extract all files. Copy the files `jce.jar`, `tsik.jar`, `xml_pilot_key.jar` and `xml_prod_key.jar` from your `%tsik%\jars` into `%JWSDP%\common\lib`.

```
D:\>jarsigner -verify -keystore
D:\J2SE\jre\lib\security\cacerts tsik1_3.jar
```

Figure C–6   Verify TSIK Binary Distribution

```
security.provider.1=sun.security.provider.Sun
security.provider.2=org.bouncycastle.jce.provider.Boun
cyCastleProvider
#security.provider.2=com.sun.net.ssl.internal.ssl.
Provider
security.provider.3=com.sun.rsajca.Provider
security.provider.4=com.sun.crypto.provider.SunJCE
security.provider.5=sun.security.jgss.SunProvider
```

Figure C–7 J2SE Security Provider Class Set-up

Download the JCE provider bcprov-jdk14-113.jar from the BouncyCastle provider located at *http://www.bouncycastle.org/latest_releases.html.* Copy the provider jar file to your J2SE directory `%JAVA_HOME%\jre\lib\ext`. Then modify your `%JAVA_HOME%\jre\lib\security\java.security` file to insert the `org.bouncycastle.jce.provider.BouncyCastleProvider` class as the number 2 security provider. It should look like Figure C–7:

Remember to add these newly added jar files to your `CLASSPATH`.

C.7.2 Unix Platform

The installation procedure is similar to that of the Windows version. Download the `tsik1_3.jar` TSIK distribution and extract to your target location. Similar to the Windows version installation, you can extract the TSIK distribution to your target location and move the TSIK jar files subdirectory to JWSDP's common/lib sub-directory (for example, `/opt/jwsdp/webapps/common/lib`). You need to modify the JRE security library settings and add the Bouncy Castle JCE Provider as well.

C.8   jSAML

Netegrity's jSAML is a developer toolkit to illustrate Single Sign-on with business partners using Security Access Markup Language (SAML). It has not been updated with the recent Liberty specification.

C.8.1 Windows Platform

`jSAML-toolkit-1.0.zip` can be downloaded from *http://www.netegrity.com/ products/index.cfm?leveltwo=JSAML&levelthree=download.* Extract all files into a temporary directory.

Copy the files jSAML.jar (from jSAML toolkit) and the `xss4j.jar` file (from XSS4J) into `%JWSDP_HOME%\common\lib`.

To install the demo program for the Case Study in this book, you need to unzip and copy all files into `%JWSDP_HOME%\webapps`.

C.8.2 Unix Platform

The installation procedure is similar to that of the Windows version. Download the Axis distribution and extract to your target location. Similar to the Windows version installation, you can extract the Axis distribution to your target location and move the webapps subdirectory to JWSDP's webapps (for example, `/opt/jwsdp/webapps/axis`).

C.9   SOAP-Lite

C.9.1 Windows Platform

SOAP-Lite requires Perl 5 (`perl-5.8-win32-bin.tar` from *http://perl.apache. org/download/*) to be installed. The SOAP-Lite executable `SOAP-Lite-latest. zip` can be downloaded from *http://www.soaplite.com/*.

You need to add the Perl installation location to the `PATH`.

C.10 Directory Structure

When developing and deploying Web Services clients and server modules using JWSDP, you may wish to adopt the following project directory to reuse the ANT build.xml templates as in Figure C–8:

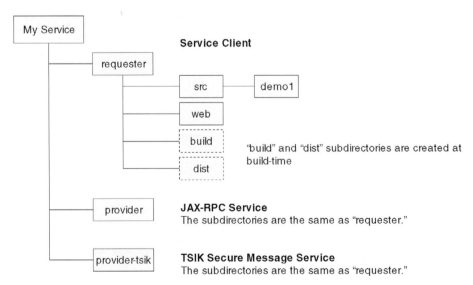

Figure C–8   Recommended Directory Structure for Web Services Programs Using JWSDP

When ANT executes the `build.xml` script, it will compile and generate Java classes and necessary files under the "build" subdirectory (if "`ANT build`" is invoked) or deploy all necessary Java classes and files in a single war file (if "`ANT deploy`" is invoked). The "build" subdirectory stores all compiled Java classes, and the "dist" stores the war file for deployment in the application server.

C.11 Software Environment Configuration

C.11.1 Environment Variables Setting

Table C–3 lists all major environment variables used to support the sample programs and Case Study in this book. The directory locations may vary, and they denote the J2SE (`JAVA_HOME` and `CLASSPATH`), and JWSDP (`JWSDP_HOME` and `CATALINA_OPTS`). The following settings are examples of Windows platform settings for reference only. For the Unix platform, there are minor variations in the file location naming convention (for example, `D:\J2SE` on Windows corresponds to `/opt/j2se` on Unix).

Table C–3   Summary of Environment Variables Used in This Book

Variable	Settings

PATH	`D:\Dev\WSDP\bin;D:\J2EE\bin;`
	`%SystemRoot%\system32;%SystemRoot%;`
	`%SystemRoot%\System32\Wbem;d:\j2se\`
	`bin;d:\dev\perl\bin;`

JAVA_HOME	`D:\J2SE`
JWSDP_HOME	`D:\Dev\WSDP`

CATALINA_OPTS	`-Dhttp.proxyHost=myproxy.`
	`nextfrontiers.com -Dhttp.proxyPort=80`
	`-Dhttp.nonProxyHosts="localhost" -`
	`Djava.awt.headless=true`

CLASSPATH	`.;D:\dev\wsdp\common\lib\xerces.jar;`
	`D:\dev\wsdp\common\lib\jce.jar;`
	`D:\dev\wsdp\common\lib\tsik.jar;`
	`D:\dev\wsdp\common\lib\xml_pilot_key.`
	`jar;D:\dev\wsdp\common\lib\`
	`xml_prod_key.jar;D:\Dev\wsdp\`
	`common\lib\JSAML.jar;D:\Dev\wsdp\`
	`common\lib\soap.jar;D:\dev\wsdp\`

Table C–3   Summary of Environment Variables Used in This Book—*continued.*

Variable	Settings

	`common\lib\xalan.jar;D:\dev\wsdp\`
	`common\lib\junit.jar;D:\dev\wsdp\`
	`common\lib\xmlsec.jar;D:\dev\wsdp\`
	`common\lib\xss4j.jar; D:\dev\wsdp\`
	`common\lib\servlet.jar;D:\Dev\wsdp\`
	`common\lib\axis.jar;D:\dev\`
	`wsdp\common\lib\axis-ant.jar;`
	`D:\dev\wsdp\common\lib\commons-`
	`discovery.jar;D:\Dev\wsdp\common\lib`
	`\commons-logging.jar;D:\Dev\wsdp\`
	`common\lib\jaxrpc-api.jar;D:\Dev\wsdp\`
	`common\lib\log4j-1.2.4.jar;`
	`D:\Dev\wsdp\common\lib\saaj-api.jar;`
	`D:\Dev\wsdp\common\lib\wsdl4j.jar;`

C.12 CLASSPATH Set-up

The CLASSPATH variable should include the jar files from Axis, Xerces, Xalan, TSIK, and XML Security. An example of the CLASSPATH variable is given in Figure C–9 (line feeds are added to make the CLASSPATH more readable).

```
.;
D:\dev\wsdp\common\lib\xerces.jar;
D:\dev\wsdp\common\lib\jce.jar;
D:\dev\wsdp\common\lib\tsik.jar;
D:\dev\wsdp\common\lib\xml_pilot_key.jar;
D:\dev\wsdp\common\lib\xml_prod_key.jar;

D:\Dev\wsdp\common\lib\JSAML.jar;
D:\Dev\wsdp\common\lib\soap.jar;
D:\dev\wsdp\common\lib\xalan.jar;

D:\dev\wsdp\common\lib\junit.jar;
D:\dev\wsdp\common\lib\xmlsec.jar;
D:\dev\wsdp\common\lib\xss4j.jar;

D:\Dev\wsdp\common\lib\axis.jar;
D:\dev\wsdp\common\lib\axis-ant.jar;
```

Figure C–9   List of Class Paths Defined in the CLASSPATH Variable Used in This Book

```
D:\dev\wsdp\common\lib\commons-discovery.jar;
D:\Dev\wsdp\common\lib\commons-logging.jar;
D:\Dev\wsdp\common\lib\jaxrpc-api.jar;
D:\Dev\wsdp\common\lib\log4j-1.2.4.jar;
D:\Dev\wsdp\common\lib\saaj-api.jar;
D:\Dev\wsdp\common\lib\wsdl4j.jar;
D:\Dev\wsdp\common\lib\tt-bytecode.jar;

D:\dev\wsdp\common\lib\xml-apis.jar;
D:\Dev\wsdp\common\lib\mail.jar;
D:\Dev\wsdp\common\lib\activation.jar;
D:\Dev\wsdp\common\lib\servlet.jar;

D:\Dev\xml-axis-10\tools;
D:\Dev\xml-axis-10;
D:\Dev\xml-axis-10\test;
D:\opt;
```

Figure C–9   List of Class Paths Defined in the CLASSPATH Variable Used in This Book—*continued.*

C.13 Verifying Set-up

C.13.1 Java 2 Standard Edition (J2SE)

Windows Platform

Verify the CLASSPATH and CP variables, as shown in Figure C–10.

```
D:\>Set | more
```

Figure C–10 Verify CLASSPATH Variables

This should show the same environment variables as in your previous definition.

Verify the JRE installation by checking the version of the run time (see Figure C–11).

```
D:\>java -version
java version "1.4.0_01"
Java(TM) 2 Runtime Environment, Standard Edition
(build 1.4.0_01-b03)
Java HotSpot(TM) Client VM (build 1.4.0_01-b03, mixed mode)
```

Figure C–11 Verify the J2SE Version Number

This verifies the same software version of the J2SE run-time library.

Verify the SDK installation, as shown in Figure C–12.

This denotes the Java compiler is available for compiling Java classes now.

```
D:\>javac -help
Usage: javac <options> <source files>
where possible options include:
  -g                          Generate all debugging
info
  -g:none                   Generate no debugging info
  -g:{lines,vars,source}  Generate only some debugging
info
  -O                        Optimize; may hinder
debugging or enlarge class file

  -nowarn                   Generate no warnings
  -verbose                  Output messages about what
the compiler is doing
  -deprecation              Output source locations
where deprecated APIs are used
  -classpath <path>         Specify where to find user
class files
  -sourcepath <path>        Specify where to find input
source files
  -bootclasspath <path>     Override location of
bootstrap class files
  -extdirs <dirs>           Override location of
installed extensions
  -d <directory>            Specify where to place
generated class files
  -encoding <encoding>      Specify character encoding
used by source files
  -source <release>         Provide source compatibility
with specified release
  -target <release>         Generate class files for
specific VM version
  -help                     Print a synopsis of standard
options
```

Figure C–12 Verify the J2SE SDK Installation

C.14 Java Web Services Developer Pack (JWSDP)

C.14.1 Windows and Unix Platforms

Upon successful installation, start Tomcat and Xindice from the program menu (`Start | Program | Java ™ Web Services Developer Pack 1.0`). Enter *http://localhost:8080* from a client browser. You should see the start-up screen, as shown in Figure C–13.

You should also be able to run all examples from the start-up screen. For example, you may wish to start the Tomcat Server Administration (see Figure C–14) with your administrator user id and password (during installation).

This administration tool allows configuration of different system parameters (for example, log files) or review of systems settings.

Alternatively, you may want to verify the Web Application Manager by issuing the URL *http://localhost:8080/manager/list* from a browser. This will list all services published by your JWSDP installation.

Upon successful installation of JWSDP, you may want to start the Tomcat Web Server and the Xindice database (for UDDI Service Registry). On Windows, you can

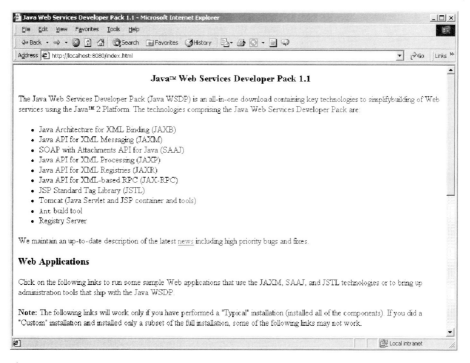

Figure C–13 JWSDP Start-up Screen

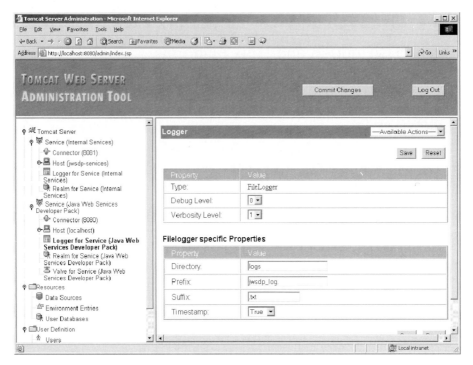

Figure C–14   JWSDP Server Administration

start by selecting `Start | Program | Java`™ `Web Services Developer Pack 1_0_01 | Start Tomcat` and `Start Xindice` respectively. After invoking these two processes, there should be two icons of Command prompt-like background processes running in the tool bar of your Windows desktop (showing Tomcat and Xindice, respectively).

On Unix, you may wish to issue the following commands with root access (that is, user=root) as in Figure C–15.

```
#cd /opt/jwsdp/bin
#./startup.sh
#./xindice-start.sh
```

Figure C–15   Start up JWSDP in Unix

You can check whether the two processes are running by issuing the command "`ps -ef | grep java.`" You should expect to see two Java processes (one with the parameter Catalina for Tomcat, and another for Xindice).

C.15 AXIS

Upon successful installation, you should be able to invoke Apache Axis by issuing the URL *http://localhost:8080/axis/index.html,* as in Figure C–16.

Verify your Axis installation by issuing the URL *http://localhost:8080/axis/index.html* from a browser. This should display a start-up screen for Axis (see Figure C–16).

By selecting the "Validate" option of the start-up screen, you should be able to see whether your Axis installation is complete and ready to go. If your configuration is complete, you should be able to see all needed components required for installing Apache Axis, as in Figure C–17.

You can also select "Administer Axis" to bring up or down ("bounce") the Axis server. This is useful if you want to deploy a new Web Service.

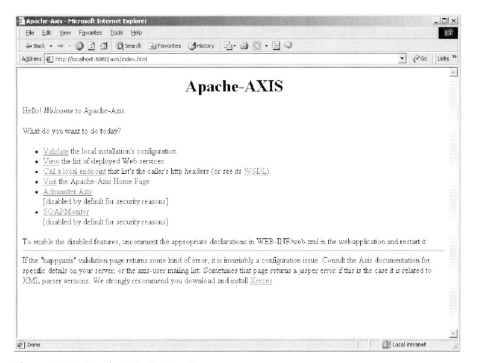

Figure C–16 Apache Axis Start-up Screen

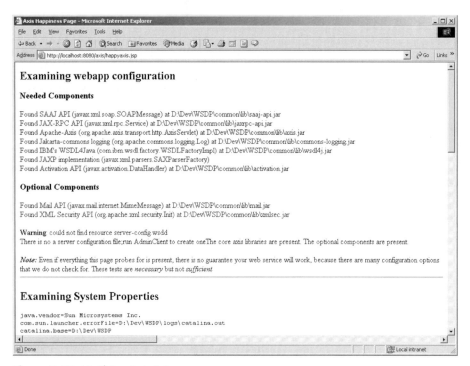

Figure C–17   Verifying Axis Set-up

C.16 Trust Service Integration Kit (TSIK)

C.16.1 Windows Platform

From the TSIK installation samples directory (for example, D:\Dev\TSIK\ samples\xkms), issue the following command as shown in Figure C–18. This will verify the XKMS installation. Please ensure you get an Internet connection with appropriate proxy settings.

```
D:\Dev\Test\tsik1_0\samples\xkms>java SampleXKMSClient
http://interop-xkms.verisign.com/xkms/Acceptor.nano
locate http://xkms.verisign.com/key?jurisdiction=
d7ea68c518b2602ca4bbca895826a7dd&mail_email=valid@
xkms.org
```

Figure C–18   Verify the TSIK Installation

It denotes TSIK's XML Key Management Specification (XKMS) is properly installed, configured, and you can locate a key stored at the VeriSign Web site.

This should return the result with key information, as shown in Figure C–19.

```
sending debug output to D:\Temp\xkmsclient.out
Response status is true
KeyInfos is
[com.verisign.xkms.client.XKMSKeyInfoImpl@bd7848]
```

Figure C–19 Verification Result of TSIK

C.17 jSAML

C.17.1 Windows Platform

Before you invoke any demo program from the jSAML Toolkit, you may wish to check your file location in the %JWSDP_HOME%\webapps, as in Figure C–20.

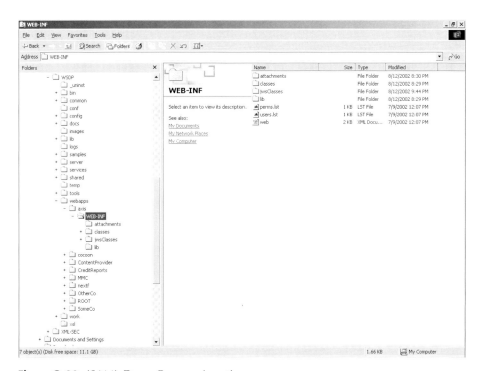

Figure C–20 jSAML Demo Program Location

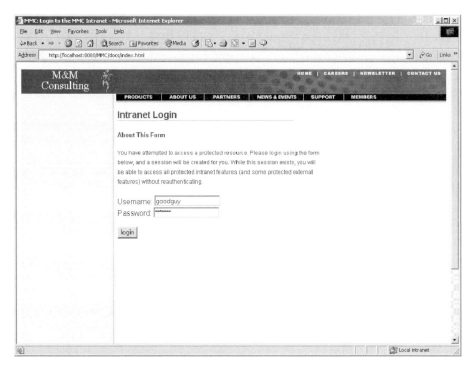

Figure C–21 jSAML Demo Program Log-in Screen

Invoke the demo program by issuing the URL *http://localhost:8080/MMC/docs/ index.html* from a browser. You should see the log-in screen as shown in Figure C–21.

Upon successful login, you should be able to see the user menu as shown in Figure C–22.

You should be able to select any option from the "SSO To Content Provider" (left-hand column) and login seamlessly to these Service Providers. Please ensure you have the appropriate proxy and firewall settings configured. Then you should be able to see a SAML Assertion Request displayed, which will be sent to the Service Provider for Single Sign-on if the access rights permit.

The expected result should display "Access rights validated" (see Figure C–23). This denotes all SAML configurations are complete and ready for testing.

Within the next five seconds, the jSAML Toolkit Forward Servlet should forward the user screen to the target Service Provider, upon successful validation of user credentials.

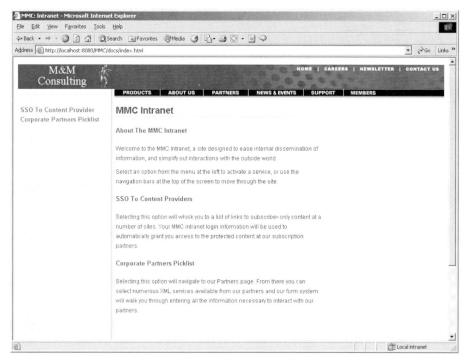

Figure C–22 User Menu for jSAML Demo Program

Figure C–23 SAML Assertion Request Sent to Service Provider

C.17.2 Remarks

Netegrity has recently removed the jSAML Toolkit from its public Web site. The accompanying CD-ROM includes a copy of the jSAML Toolkit for instructional purposes under /src/jSAML. Please bear in mind this software product is no longer supported by Netegrity.

C.18 SOAP-Lite

C.18.1 Windows Platform

To verify the set-up, issue the following command from a Command Prompt, as shown in Figure C–24.

The StockQuoteService.jws is a sample Web Service application that comes with the Axis installation. Instead of writing your client, you can invoke the service by calling the exposed functionality, getQuote, based on the WSDL.

Press Control-Z to exit from the Perl session.

Alternatively, you can run any sample program from the SOAP-Lite distribution (for example, %SOAP-Lite%\examples\XMLRPC\simple1.pl), as shown in Figure C–25.

```
D:\Dev\SOAP-Lite\bin>perl soapsh.pl
http://localhost:8080/axis/StockQuoteService.jws
Usage: method[(parameters)]
> getQuote("SUNW")
-- SOAP RESULT --
'35.84'

> getQuote("MFST")
-- SOAP RESULT ---/---
'0.0'

> getQuote("AOL")
-- SOAP RESULT ---/---
'11.0'
```

Figure C–24   Verifying Set-up With a SOAP-Lite Client

```
D:\Dev\SOAP-Lite\examples\XMLRPC>perl simple1.pl
Missouri
D:\Dev\SOAP-Lite\examples\XMLRPC>
```

Figure C–25   Invoking Web Services From a SOAP-Lite Client

C.19 Troubleshooting

It requires good skills to troubleshoot any anomaly or incident that may be caused by system configuration problems or an incomplete configuration. For example, a tested program deployed in war files that runs very well on a Windows platform may not run on a Unix platform. This may be due to incorrect configuration on the Unix platform—for example, a misspelled file name, missing CLASSPATH entries, or empty UDDI Service Registry entries.

It is always a good habit to look at the log files under %JWSDP_HOME%\logs. Many of the debug messages about the run-time errors are informative and can help track down the errors. For example, if the file location for the `sample_soap_keystore` is misplaced, the JWSDP log file jwsdp_log.YYYY-MM-DD will indicate the error message "java.io.FileNotFoundException: \opt\myFX\requester\ sample_soap_keystore (The system cannot find the path specified)." Then you can verify the file locations in your source programs. If a SOAP client does not return any result from invoking a remote Web Service, you may wish to check the Web Container log file `catalina.out`. If the remote connection is down or the remote Web Service is offline, the `catalina.out` file will show "AxisFault faultCode: *[http://xml.apache.org/axis/Server.NoService.*"* Then you can verify whether the remote Web Service is online.

It is outside the scope of this book to cover troubleshooting guidelines for developing and deploying Web Services. However, it is recommended that developers verify each installation step and validate the system configuration before development starts and keep a baseline configuration record of all system parameters (for example, CLASSPATH entries) used for future troubleshooting purposes.

Index